Triathlon Success

MARIO SCHMIDT-WENDLING

Foreword by Dennis Sandig

TRIATHLON
SUCCESS

The Ultimate Training Guide to
Winning the Long-Distance Triathlon

MEYER & MEYER SPORT

British Library of Cataloguing in Publication Data
A catalogue record for this book is available from the British Library
Originally published as *Triathlon – Erfolg auf der Langdistanz,* © 2022 by Meyer & Meyer Verlag

Triathlon Success
Maidenhead: Meyer & Meyer Sport (UK) Ltd., 2024
ISBN: 978-1-78255-262-8

© 2024 by Meyer & Meyer Sport (UK) Ltd.
Aachen, Auckland, Beirut, Cairo, Cape Town, Dubai, Hägendorf, Hong Kong, Indianapolis, Maidenhead, Manila, New Delhi, Singapore, Sydney, Tehran, Vienna
Member of the World Sport Publishers' Association (WSPA), www.w-s-p-a.org

Printed by Versa Press, East Peoria, IL
Printed in the United States of America

ISBN: 978-1-78255-262-8
Email: info@m-m-sports.com
www.thesportspublisher.com

CONTENTS

FOREWORD

Triathlon is so much more than swimming plus cycling plus running. During coach's training, we try to teach primarily one thing based on this credo: there is no simple training recipe.

The challenges coaches face is quite apparent, particularly in light of the findings regarding the complexity of human performance on a physical and psychological level. They are experts in sports biology and training theory. They must be as familiar with the 101 of sports psychology as the didactic methodological components of training. Here good coaches distinguish themselves primarily by one thing: an independent training philosophy that allows them to undogmatically search for answers to the many daily questions about training that are right for their athlete.

I first became aware of Mario Schmidt-Wendling early in his coaching career because he had this ability. Close observation of his athletes and the ability to define achievable goals have helped him develop his own training philosophy. He also challenged that philosophy and refined it during his coach's training at the German Triathlon Union during many open and critical discussions.

To this effect, I hope this book will be a starting dive for our readers with an interest in triathlon into developing an independent training philosophy that fits their personal needs.

Next to the many components of training, one thing should not fall by the wayside: the person, the social being, is so much more than the sum of his parts.

Have fun reading and training!

Dennis Sandig

Science Coordinator and Education Contributor for the German Triathlon Federation

1 INTRODUCTION

Really? Another book about triathlon?

I asked myself that question as well when the publisher approached me with this book project. But, it has always been my dream to put down on paper my knowledge and experience from more than 30 years of endurance sports—almost 20 of those years as a full-time professional coach.

Dreams do come true, and so I sat down and wrote what I know. The theoretical principles of training, physiology, and sport already fascinated me as a teenager, and back then I devoured a few books on these topics. I remember carrying around one book in particular, *Alles unter Kontrolle* (Everything Is Under Control) by Neumann, Pfützner, and Hottenrott, in my gym bag for a long time.

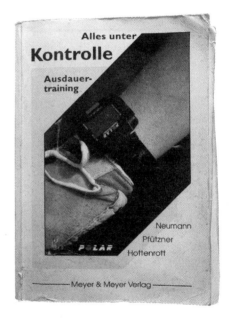

The fact that I am now able to publish my ideas, approaches, and principles regarding long-distance triathlons with the same publisher nearly 30 years later fills me with pride, and I feel like I am coming full circle.

A few years ago, I wrote short stories about all things pertaining to long-distance triathlon in the form of a blog for magazines, or rather for the athletes in my care. To me, sharing knowledge was and is a labor of love because

Figure 1: Alles unter Kontrolle (Everything Is Under Control).

as an athlete and coach I, like many other people in everyday life, made some mistakes. But in my view, it is precisely those mistakes that ensure the survival of mankind, because anyone with the ability to self-reflect, recognize mistakes, and use them to make changes will emerge stronger and more knowledgeable.

I would like to help as many athletes with the long-distance goal as possible to avoid making my mistakes, develop avoidance strategies, and embark on a less rocky path towards long-distance success.

This book reflects my current body of knowledge and my approaches, which over the years have been put to the test time and again. I don't like using the term *philosophy* as I feel it is used excessively in this context, and I cannot and do not want to claim that I know everything and thus assume to be the keeper of the triathlon grail.

I understand there are completely different ideas, principles, and approaches for how a long-distance race can be prepared and structured. But I am also quite sure that I have found one of these completely different paths that helped a large number of athletes on their way to fulfilling their competition dreams. In doing so, I can point to a wealth of experience from more than 1,200 successful, individually coached long-distance races with countless world, European, and national titles.

As a husband, father, and freelancer, I am aware of the everyday pitfalls and can relate to the fact that next to the sport there is a life outside the triathlon microcosm. With this book I would like to encourage athletes to not take the assertions posted on the internet at face value without thinking. In recent years, I have observed allegedly new trends in training and nutrition, that have been around for years, being marketed as innovations.

I am not trying to lay claim to a scientific work but in the appendix, I will cite several sources on which I based my training principle. Maybe some coaches will also find ideas and tips that can help them in their daily work. I understand some things may rub some people the wrong way and that I will not meet everyone's expectations regarding long-distance triathlon.

Speaking of everyone, in this book I will limit myself to the male form of address, so the text doesn't get too voluminous. As a happy father of four daughters, I will gladly face the accusations of chauvinism, lack of equality, and a lack of respect for the female gender, and hope for understanding from the female readers.

In my opinion there should be no blanket training programs because I see each athlete as an individual, way beyond the sport. Rather it is my wish to teach the principles and basics so athletes can make their own decisions about planning their training. For the sake of completeness, in the book's appendix, I nevertheless included a sample training plan framework for a fictitious athlete to use in the final sixteen weeks leading up to a long-distance event to provide a possible path to success.

I do assume that readers have a certain amount of background experience in the practical and theoretical aspects of the sport, as this book is not intended for triathlon beginners.

I would be very happy if this book inspired reflection and discussion, because that would mean I fulfilled my vision and mission.

My sincere wish is that some athletes will carry this book along in their gym bags as a reference much as I used to do in the past, and in a few years from now, another author writes that I was able to inspire him with this book. In sports there is no real right or wrong. One can and should have differing opinions and experience some friction.

Friction is good and important because, as is well known, friction also produces warmth.

Train hard AND smart!

2   QUO VADIS TRIATHLON?

Triathlon is still considered a young sport. Most triathletes know the story of the three young American marines who, while slightly intoxicated, came up with the idea of the Ironman triathlon in Hawaii just over 40 years ago. Since its rough beginnings, the professionalization of the triathlon has gained incredible momentum, and there is probably no other sport that underwent such rapid development.

When I first saw the images from the Hawaii triathlon in the 1980s, triathletes seemed exotic, their clothing far too flashy and skimpy. The sport quickly shed its reputation as a fringe sport, and with its inclusion in the Olympic program, sports associations worldwide received financial backing from their government. The German Triathlon Union (DTU) is a permanent part of the German Olympic Sports Confederation (DOSB) and is the umbrella organization with the largest membership worldwide.

I have always been fascinated by an openness to new things and the irrepressible drive for innovations in triathlon. But not every innovation was and is permanently successful. Some disappeared after just a short period of time.

Things like, for instance, the seat shifter, that allowed the rider to shift the seat horizontally and made it possible to adjust the sitting position while riding based on the respective topography, or the bike frame without a seat tube and instead a springy top tube, to date have been unable to gain traction, much like 26-inch wheel size.

But triathletes have been and are not just very innovative when it comes to equipment and finding ways to improve performance. In recent years, sport science in endurance sports, particularly in triathlon, has made enormous progress. New and increasingly less expensive measuring devices and methods and significantly bigger research budgets bring more power to sport science.

Especially in the past 5-8 years, social media made these findings more accessible to more people, and of those some even created a business model for services in training planning, performance diagnostics, or bike fitting. Some of them have even achieved a kind of guru status, even without having a real education in the area of sports.

The fact is that being an active and successful coach or being able to look back on a successful career does not make one a good trainer or coach. Watching YouTube tutorials and reading various print magazines don't and shouldn't replace such an education. I simply don't understand why still today a coach's professional profile is not protected. Anyone can use that title without having to provide any proof of qualification.

Other occupations that deal with people or their health require professional training or a state exam, but that has yet to happen in sports. Often financial interests take priority, and shockingly, any responsibility for the athletes' health quickly becomes a secondary concern. The result is that scientific findings are in some cases misinterpreted and promoted on the internet.

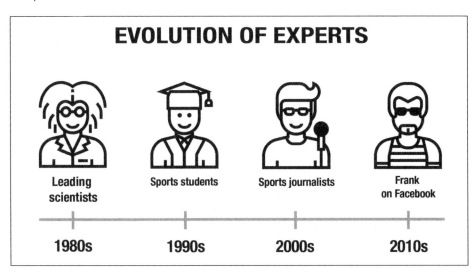

Figure 2: Frank on Facebook.

In 2020, the German Triathlon Union (DTU) launched an initiative that issues a digital logo to coaches who are licensed by the organization so they can be easily identified as qualified coaches and trainers on their websites and in other marketing materials, enabling them to set themselves apart from coaches without a valid education.

Figure 3: License badge issued by the German Triathlon Union (DTU).

Moreover, some print magazines, blogs, and YouTube channels also pick up the allegedly latest findings without always checking for meaningfulness and proof, and findings are publicized prematurely only to suddenly disappear 1–2 years later.

I can certainly understand that a publisher of a magazine or an administrator of a social media platform has to continuously provide content to capture viewers' attention and increase the number of clicks. But unfortunately, this is increasingly causing confusion among athletes.

Time and again athletes reach out to me because they have trouble navigating that jungle of information and are no longer able to differentiate which information is right, wrong, important, unimportant, or simply unsuitable.

As I already mentioned in the introduction, a coach should not claim that his way is the only way. As we all know, many roads lead to Rome; however, some are rocky and studded with obstacles, while others lead to success without complications.

A coach can choose to work old school, or be considered innovative, jumping on every new trend and using new principles with athletes without thinking or testing them first. I tend to be more restrained.

In the following chapters, I will try to explain what that means and why a conservative approach that is limited to the essentials is not a disadvantage.

3 ATHLETE TYPES

Looking back, I can say what a great privilege and fortune it is to work with so many athletes since 2004. This pool of athletes consists of beginners, overweight people, people with diabetes, youth athletes, and people over sixty, all the way to para-triathletes, Ironman Hawaii participants, amateur world champions, and world-class athletes. Each of these athletes has a highly individual history with unique problems, skills, and abilities.

This large spread alone should demonstrate how different athletes can be. It quickly becomes apparent that universal recommendations or even frameworks that don't take into consideration individual strengths and weaknesses don't necessarily lead to success. The athlete should be seen as an individual. Here we do not only consider physiological and training-relevant markers. The athlete's personality and character play an equally important role.

Over the years, some structures and behavior patterns have repeated themselves in my work as a coach, allowing me to at some point bundle and catalog these characteristics, which have evolved into eight different athlete types. Although these groups include athletes of both genders, I did also put women in a separate group because, as you will see later on, they possess some special attributes. Classification into these different groups should not be viewed as blanket compartmentalization. Rather there are consistently occurring behavior patterns which I would like to share below.

Occupational groups play an important role here as well. Since I am impartial on principle, I hope no reader feels personally offended because they belong to a certain profession or might even feel exposed in some way. Finding yourself in one of these eight groups does not suggest prejudgment or that you have fallen in disfavor with me. I deliberately included these categories in the book to inspire in the reader contemplation of and reflection on their own behavior patterns in the sport.

Here, too, exceptions confirm the rule, particularly because as Karl Heinrich Waggerl once said, "prejudgment is the snooty receptionist in the outer office of rationality." The following are merely my observations that should be referred to in coaching where applicable.

Working together with completely different personalities makes my job as a coach so interesting. Being classified as belonging to one of these groups does not mean that an athlete won't succeed, because when one knows, recognizes, and considers the peculiarities of each group, they can be used to achieve top performances and wins. My categorization is intended to show the strengths and weaknesses of the different groups.

3.1   The Alpha Leader

The Alpha Leader is almost exclusively male and between the ages of 35 and 55, most often works in banking, law, or from home in an executive position. The alpha leader generally knows only one speed and that's full throttle. Rest periods, relaxed training, and unloading weeks are not part of his outlook on life. The number of physicians in this group is also alarming. They are largely nonreflective and tend to have only rudimentary ideas regarding performance physiology and training per se.

The Alpha tends to turn every training session into a kind of competition or to draw comparisons to the male genitalia, because if a training session wasn't painful enough it was, in the eyes of the Alpha, not training but a waste of time.

In group cycling training, the Alpha can always be found in the very front. He can barely tolerate it when an adjacent rider's front wheel is at a level with his own. The Alpha is the classic front wheel extender who always has to position his front wheel a few centimeters in front of his neighbor's.

The Alpha generally completes his training too quickly based on the motto *No pain, no gain.* Due to the overly fast training, the fat metabolism often does not develop optimally, and the maximum lactate production rate (Vlamax) is therefore generally elevated in these athletes, which is in part compensated by a large amount of carbohydrates during training and competition.

This undesirable development of the metabolism results in competitive long-distance results generally being worse than those for mid or Ironman 70.3 distances. These bad results tend to be mistakenly viewed as resulting from training that was too lax in the run-up.

Communication by the Alpha and training documentation in the journal often leave much to be desired. Criticism from the coach is rarely embraced. Listening is not one of the Alpha's strong suits because he does not like to be told what to do. Fulfillment of the training plan, while almost always too intensive, is nearly 100%.

As a coach, in order to achieve a halfway reasonable training speed, I deliberately set lower speed specifications because I know that the Alpha leader will always have the need to overachieve.

3.2   The Counter

The Counter is part of a group that only originated in recent years with the spread of training science topics on social media. The Counter is also almost exclusively male and largely in the age group 18–45. His tendency to evaluate numbers is also reflected in his occupation. Engineers, controllers, and IT specialists make up the bulk of occupations.

The Counter has a very technocratic vision of training. He thinks that training is exclusively subject to certain algorithms and that everything can be planned down to the very last detail based on the numbers. To do so, the Counter has access to nearly all of the measuring devices the market has produced. He collects data and gets entirely lost in the depths of his data sets, but without applying then to the actual practice.

At times, training analysis takes up more time than the training itself. The Counter rarely participated in club sports as a child. He is the classic late bloomer and therefore lacks a certain amount of body awareness. He struggles to assess his training loads without a watch, speedometer, power meter, etc. If a measuring device fails, he quicky loses control and discontinues the training session or competition.

Communication is limited primarily to the exchange and analysis of metrics. For instance, if the side-by-side left/right ground contact time while running is 47.6–52.4, he starts to ruminate. Training specifications are completed meticulously, but in doing so the subjective feeling is ignored, which can definitely lead to *non-functional overreaching*.

3.3   The Social Media Athlete

The Social Media Athlete can be found in both genders and is rarely older than 45. He is not part of a specific occupational group. He is the hipster among the athletes, wears matching outfits from head to toe and in doing so copies the look of many pros. The optics are very important to him and he self-defines by the likes and number of followers on social media. Nearly every training session is documented there and all training is accompanied by a camera.

As up to date as he is in all things fashion and equipment, as unfortunately erratic is his approach to training. Whenever he reads about a new training approach in a magazine, he immediately integrates it into his own training. When he comes across something new a few weeks later, he again immediately seizes on it.

The Social Media Athlete allows himself to be excessively influenced by the things he sees on social media and from other athletes, and quickly jumps on the band wagon of training challenges (Everesting, Zwift-races, streak running, etc.).

There is an above average number of vegans among Social Media Athletes. The Social Media Athlete has trouble developing a good foundation and confidence in his training, which in turn often results in worse competition results. Before a competition, he is often more engaged in posting photos than focusing on himself and his strengths.

When the competition goes badly, he tends to falsely blame external factors such as diet, the weather, etc. With respect to weather, he generally dreads bad weather and rarely possesses training attire for adverse weather conditions.

Unfortunately, his communication is largely limited to social media rather than entrusting himself to his coach.

3.4   The Impatient One

Approximately two-thirds of Impatient Ones are male and can be found across all age groups. He does not fall into a specific occupational group.

The term *endurance sport* includes the word *endurance*. But while the Impatient One possesses this ability in a physical sense, he rather lacks it mentally. He considers his performance development too slow, and rest periods and unloading weeks cause him to practically lose his mind, particularly if he is also a Social Media Athlete and can see those other athletes that train significantly more than he does.

The Impatient One struggles with admitting to weaknesses and tends to extend training volume by 10–15%. Much like the Alpha Leader, his training plan has to be slightly mitigated so the desired training goal can ultimately be achieved. If that does not happen, the Impatient One has a tendency to get injured.

He abhors mobility and athletic training as he does not recognize the necessity and wants to spend his training time swimming, cycling, or running which, combined with the excessive mileage, results in a higher injury risk.

Once the Impatient One is injured, he very quickly loses his motivation and asks himself whether he wants to continue with the sport. His loss of motivation then tends to vanish pretty quickly, and he resumes training too soon, too fast and too intensely, throwing him into another downward spiral.

The Impatient One must be fed much knowledge and background information to pull him out of his impatience. He communicates often and eagerly.

3.5   The Brooder

The Brooder is largely male and tends to be in the age group 25–40. He is also not part of a specific occupational group.

He is quickly and easily knocked off his training plan. As soon as he reads about the training units of other athletes, he doubts himself and his path. He struggles to draw self-confidence from his own training, is at odds with himself, is subsequently dissatisfied with his training units, and can be quite fatalistic.

He suffers from so-called *Stravanoia*, meaning he allows himself to be negatively influenced by other athletes on the platform Strava. For instance, when he hears from other athletes during competition week that they completed six 30-km runs and he did none, he already sees the race as being over before it even happened.

The Brooder unfortunately tends to evaluate his performance too early in the competition instead of waiting for the analysis of the post-race list of results. This results in his giving up early in the race and becoming a DNF (Did Not Finish).

He, too, requires many theoretical arguments so he can develop confidence in his own strength. His communications are regular, if rather negative, both in choice of words and content. Next to the Social Media Athlete, the Brooder has the lowest values in the target-performance comparison between planned training and actual plan fulfillment.

3.6   Women

As I mentioned at the beginning of this chapter, female athletes can also be found in other groups. But I do want to mention a few special characteristics when coaching women. Women are often easier to coach than men. They are somehow significantly more relaxed, don't feel the need to turn every training session into a testosterone-fueled race, and don't tend to constantly put their training concept to the test. They often follow the guidelines scrupulously but do so without losing touch with their body.

Since they are often not as techy as men and don't really care as much about the various metrics and parameters as men do, they usually develop a better ability to correctly read their training load and themselves.

They are more likely to complete too little of the training rather than too much, but not due to laziness but rather because they are better able to read their body. However, some fret about their body weight because they think they don't meet some alleged beauty ideal. This unfortunately often results in too little energy being absorbed from food, in daily life as well as during training.

When a coach can communicate the advantages and importance of food, women become training soldiers who overall are significantly more resilient than men. Sorry, fellow men, it doesn't look good for us!

3.7   The Woodsman

The Woodsman is primarily male and tends to be in older age groups. He can often be found in executive positions, among law enforcement, firefighters, and craftsmen. I refer to him as very stoic. He is very robust and has a high load capacity. He doesn't care which training units are on the training plan; he completes them regardless of weather, time of day and how he feels on that particular day.

He is not really concerned about what he looks like, doesn't care if his cycling jersey matches his cycling pants, and whether his legs are shaved. His bicycle is often an older model, which does not prevent him from bringing very strong performances on it. His equipment is often in poor condition, his bike chain completely dirty, which does not particularly bother him.

The Woodsman is predestined for long distances and has very good endurance numbers. One could call him—and this is not meant disrespectfully—a diesel engine. He prefers to avoid higher intensity sessions and would rather train longer at a more relaxed pace. His maximum lactate production rate tends to be quite low. He doesn't need a particular diet, but just eats what's put in front of him.

The Woodsmen group has a greater than average number of athletes that have been doing triathlons since the 1990s. The Woodsman tends to minimal communication, but he is reliable, because whatever is on the plan gets done even if it isn't recorded daily and precisely in the training journal.

3.8   The Champion

Of course, there are champions of both genders and in all age groups. They share good body sense and a certain intuition about when to push their training and when to take a day off. They tend to trust their feelings more so than the parameters shown on their watches.

Interestingly their feelings almost always match the measured values. Overall, I would characterize Champions as makers more so than grumblers or brooders. They are not easily dissuaded from their principles by information from the internet or magazines but tend to just digest the information and carefully evaluate whether such a change would make sense. They are patient, understanding that it takes a certain amount of time to develop certain abilities in training. Their patience is underpinned by goal-oriented action and thinking. They are never hasty, do not insert imprudent panic-based training units, but rather trust their own training concept.

Champions are aware of the significance and importance of regeneration and balance. Except for the Woodsman, they are better able than any other group to shift their thinking away from the triathlon. Their communication is very precise, and they can relay their current status in a very nuanced way. They are very forthcoming, stick to their word, and are very punctual and disciplined in their daily activities.

The Champion builds a people network that accompanies him on his path. Here coaches, physical therapists, life partners, etc. form a team.

It isn't always possible to precisely assign a category, which can result in some overlap. The most frequent overlaps can be seen in the following constellations.

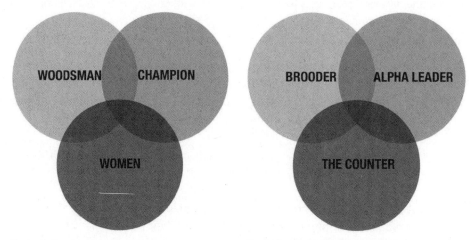

Figure 4: Overlap Woodsman–
Champion–Women

Figure 5: Overlap Brooder–Alpha
Leader–The Counter

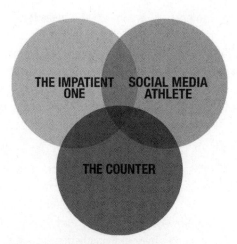

Figure 6: Overlap–The Impatient One–
Social Media Athlete–The Counter

Blanket classification into one of these groups is not forever set in stone. I constantly see athletes shift and evolve. Coaching is highly complex and not just the simple use of formulas. Skillful guidance and communicating the right content allow athletes from all groups to evolve into Champions, and that is precisely the job of a coach.

Adaptive	Nutrition	Respect	Tactics
Basic form	Health	Integrity	Motor skills
Refined form	Fitness	Control	Psychology
Superior form	Height	Passion	Physiology
Commitment	Heat	Energetic	Environment
Self-confidence	Cold	Offensive	Character
Focus	Empathy	Defensive	Emotions

Figure 7: Coaching is highly complex.

4   A COACH'S JOB

"Champions are all around us, all you have to do is to train them properly."

Sir Arthur Lydiard

Along with the rapid changes in the triathlon, the coaching business has also changed a lot. When I started to offer training plans in 2004, there really were no commercial coaches outside of clubs, national associations, and the training centers of the German Triathlon Union (DTU). Moreover, back then, few athletes chose to hire a personal and individual coach.

Here I am deliberately avoiding the term *personal trainer* because people generally associate that term with fitness coaches for the rich and beautiful, like Heidi Klum, Madonna, etc.

But the workplace has changed as well; for example, the permanent reachability by smart phone has significantly affected working hours which makes it not always possible to participate in training offers from triathlon clubs, and it isn't possible to get a response from a qualified coach when one can, must, or chooses to primarily train on one's own.

I don't have any hard numbers, but I suspect that 30–40% of participants in Ironman events employ the services of a processional trainer or coach. Approximately the same percentage of participants trains based on plans in magazines and books or on internet platforms, some of which are completely free.

Training provided at triathlon clubs with DTU-certified coaches is generally very good, but a club coach doesn't have sufficient time to focus on the individual needs of every athlete. As a result, the athlete does not always receive the optimal care according to his strengths and weaknesses.

Whenever I get inquiries about training planning for beginners, I always refer them to clubs because there they will learn the most important basics and could meet other like-minded people. Training together builds social skills and to me is a very important aspect of the sport.

4.1 What does a coach have to offer?

Next to creating training plans and analyzing training and competition results, there are almost certainly a few other aspects that speak for a coach. I would like to list the most important ones here.

4.1.1 Bastard personified

I am frequently told that without me as a coach, even when at times my presence is virtual, some training units would not have been completed. Many athletes feel a kind of obligation to provide and feel bad when they don't complete the planned units.

Training continuity clearly leads to success, but not at all costs. When an athlete's signs of exhaustion are not recognized and the plan fulfillment mode is switched on, it can manifest in negative and contrary performance development.

4.1.2 Lack of time for planning training independently

Most athletes are short on goals. Next to family, job, and training, most have few opportunities to think about the concept of individual training plans.

4.1.3 The feeling of giving up control

Some athletes are incredibly relieved when they hand over their training planning to a professional. The pressure of always putting all the right content in the own training plan is suddenly gone because an external person is taking over. It has been my experience that athletes who consult a coach for primarily this reason and agree to his training concept tend to have above-average success.

4.2   Technological Changes

When I first got started, there were no options for documenting training data in the form of the nowadays numerous online coaching platforms. Back then communication of relevant data was much more difficult than it is today. I started by attaching the training plans I created to emails as Excel files. Athletes were able to enter their completed training units on this form.

With advanced digitalization, totally new opportunities opened for coaching athletes from afar. Preparing files for training analysis and access to training plans and training journals on mobile devices (phone, tablet, etc.) have made the work of coaches in endurance sports significantly easier, more effective, and productive.

The improved communication opportunities have also been a major plus. Sending voice messages to communicate more complex information in my opinion has been a blessing, because the written word can always be interpreted differently and thus contains a certain conflict risk when the recipient misunderstands the message.

The nowadays ubiquitous smart phone can certainly be considered the Swiss army knife of the 21st century. It is permanently in everyone's pocket, allowing the athlete to record videos and send them to the coach. Evaluating movement quality or technical execution is therefore also possible without being on location. Training content can be reviewed on the smart phone on the way to the pool and training documentation as well as uploading files today is clearly easier, more efficient, and immediate, and can be done on the go.

Specifically, the fact that coaches no longer must wait several days for journal entries is a serious improvement in quality because the coach is now permanently informed and can enter changes to the plan. The technical requirements for young coaches are much easier today than they were at the beginning of the millennium. It solely depends on how these opportunities are utilized.

4.3   A Coach's Responsibilities

This point sounds dumb, but conversations with some athletes and other coaches showed me that a coach's responsibilities cannot always be clearly defined. Some athletes think the coach is a person who himself permanently trains, gets to fly to the most beautiful places in the world for competitions, and always has a great tan. There certainly are coaches who fit that description and who make these things part of their coaching (more on that in chapter 4.6).

But reality looks quite different, at least for most full-time coaches. Sixty- to seventy-hour work weeks, 24/7 availability, and no real downtime tell a different story. The danger of burnout cannot be ignored and sadly is still largely made taboo. This to some extent very exhausting effort only works with a large amount of passion, setting aside the own ego and much understanding from one's life partner.

A coach's main responsibility is to develop and support the athlete. To me coaching seems like an easy-to-describe activity, namely the attempt to fundamentally change a person, because in a year that individual will not be the same athlete he is today. This process of change is my highest priority and is in no way limited to a purely physical change, as the adjacent figure shows.

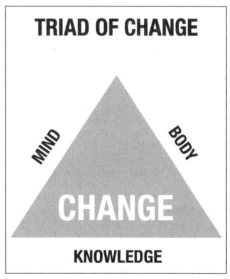

This change begins with a starting point, meaning the beginning of collaboration, and has a specific end point in the form of season highlights or major competitions. The coach's job is to accompany the athlete on this path, to guide him and protect him from the danger of potential mistakes.

Figure 8: Triad of change.

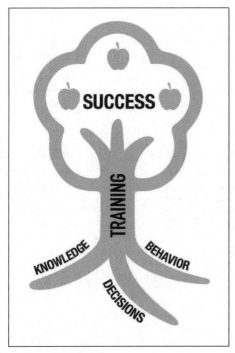

Figure 9: Tree of success.

But in my opinion, when an athlete does make such mistakes, they are not the athlete's mistakes but those of the coach because he failed to call sufficient attention to the various aspects and dangers and did not see the problem early on. The coach should advise the athlete and provide him with the necessary knowledge so the athlete is able to correctly direct his *behavior* and his *decisions*.

To me coaching is about planting these three characteristics. Once these elements take root, the tree of success can grow, and the fruits of success can be harvested. To expand on this image here, one could absolutely refer to the *Tree-Athlon*.

4.4   The Interaction Between Athletes and Coach

To me coaching is not a one-way street but should be seen a teamwork. The athlete should be involved in all decision-making processes. But since every athlete has a unique personality (see chapter 3) there can be no single approach to the daily work. I therefore prefer to put the ball back in the athlete's court and pull him into the boat with me. Meaning, the more the athlete asks of me as a coach the more he gets in return.

Figure 10: TEAM

Here there are very different manifestations. Some athletes are curt, while others write lengthy prose in their journals every day. The manner of working together does not only differ from athlete to athlete but also with the same athlete within a training year.

Phases that require more support alternate with phases with a long leash. All interaction should always take place openly and at eye level; honesty and loyalty from both sides are the basic conditions for developing great performances. Here communication is the most important criterion. If the coach can set aside his own ego, to listen and watch, the athlete will voluntarily tell the coach everything.

As a coach, one is on the athlete's side, in good times and in bad. In doing so, one enters into a kind of relationship or marriage. Particularly in bad times (e.g., illness, injuries, etc.) the athlete needs more encouragement and requires more guidance. In my opinion there is no better training gadget in these situations than a listening, empathetic coach who can convey assurance and show paths out of the crisis.

I frequently come across situations where athletes are given alleged advice from outside, be it by independently studying various internet forums, magazines, Facebook groups, or the like, or via influence from external persons.

To me the below graphic image is of fundamental importance when it comes to the relationship between athlete and coach.

The athlete is at the center and is shielded from the outside by the coach. This does not mean that there should be no contact with other sport-related occupational groups, but it is important to me that information from those with influence in the next-in-size circle should first be brought to the attention of the coach and not blindly transferred to the athlete. In past years, there have been several misunderstandings and false information, particularly when the athlete has attended organized training camps with other training philosophies or visited external performance diagnostics providers.

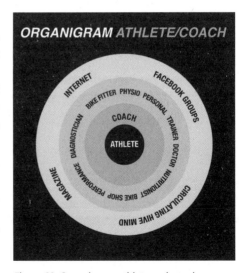

Figure 11: Organigram athlete and coach.

Teamwork between coach and athlete is based on mutual trust, a common foundation that can at times be threatened from the outside. I think, as figure 11 shows, that informational content continues to lose importance and significance from the center of the circle to the outside. That is not to say that the coach should be considered the ultimate source of wisdom, because even a well-trained coach with a large knowledge base cannot know everything.

That's why outside ideas and suggestions should always be discussed with the coach first so he may also understand these ideas and can draw his own conclusions for daily training. That is the only way to ensure that knowledge from external experts will be implemented sensibly.

Teamwork, yes, but only according to plan!

4.5   Things That Annoy a Coach

People regularly ask me what annoys me as a coach. Here are seven things.

4.5.1   Lack of communication

Not every athlete is by nature a chatterbox and that's just fine. However, athletes' communication should include at least the basics such as time availability, physical and mental state, and subjective perception of the training unit. This does not require lengthy prose texts; brief and concise information is totally sufficient.

If an athlete leaves me on my own, gives little to no feedback, and after multiple requests from me still rarely responds, I do feel annoyed because I have the feeling that my work isn't valued.

4.5.2   Pushy emails

When an athlete asks me a question at 10:30 on a Friday night about the rolling resistance of certain tires and I think to myself that a reply can wait until Monday, but I receive four reminder messages from Friday night to Sunday night, I go into stubborn mode.

I am available nearly 24/7 and guarantee a response within three hours to questions relevant to that training day. Some things really aren't that urgent and can wait!

4.5.3   Social media mania

When I read things on Strava, Facebook, or Instagram that are completely different than what's written in the training journal, I must wonder about our mutual trust. Have you ever wondered why the best athletes (except for the Norwegian national team) rarely post content about their training units?

4.5.4   Sharing training plans, texts, and standings

Ultimately an athlete buys the services of a coach and the corresponding know-how. But I think it is not so nice when I see on social media that friends of these athletes post the same training units on the same days or I am asked about articles that are meant exclusively for paying athletes.

I find it particularly aggravating when athletes suddenly build their own coaching business and mercilessly use texts and training units and sometimes make them accessible to the public. Unfortunately training units cannot be protected by patents.

PLEASE NOTE

A reminder: I get immense satisfaction from my job as a coach, but at the end of the day it is a business and I have four kids to feed. However, in sports there still seems to be this attitude of no-holds-barred and we're all friends.

4.5.5   Remonstrations about the training concept

As a responsible coach I constantly question myself or rather the training concept I used, and regularly adjust the parameters. That does not imply that I have the answer to everything and don't make mistakes. I can and should be questioned.

But I don't particularly like it when, after discussing a concept, there are permanent objections because the athlete received different recommendations from training partners, from social media, magazines, etc. In spite of my readiness to discuss and compromise, at the end of the day I am the one who has the final say, because otherwise you would not need to hire a coach.

My experiences in recent years have shown me that performance development only happens when there is mutual trust.

4.5.6 Generous and creative interpretation of the training plan

I give athletes a certain amount of leeway, but when the training plan is interpreted too creatively, I again ask myself why I was hired as a coach.

This also includes generously exceeding the speed during tempo units. Intervals is merely a method used in training and does not mean one should be at the verge of vomiting or see stars every time. A permanent, definite increase of the volume by more than 10% of the planned volume is also not welcome.

With some athletes I build the higher testosterone value into the training plan from the start.

4.5.7 Impatience

Success doesn't happen overnight. Looking for shortcuts to success is a waste of time because they don't exist. Triathlon is an endurance sport, which requires not only physical, but also mental endurance and patience.

CONCLUSION

When, as an athlete, I ask myself what I expect from a coach, these things should really be obvious.

4.6 A Coach's Thumbprint

"Coaching isn't just creating training plans,
analyzing data. Coaching is the ability to listen to
the athlete and to understand him.
There is no license or training for that. It is a mixture
of experience, knowledge, empathy, and a love of detail."

Mario Schmidt-Wendling

As the saying goes, all roads lead to Rome. In sports in particular, there are many such roads to success. Training science, especially in the relatively young sport of triathlon, is a rather new field. In the 1990s, training science for the independent sport of triathlon developed from what was then known about the sports of swimming, cycling, and running, and studies derived from that knowledge.

I always find it difficult to say that a training approach is right or wrong. In medicine it is said that he who heals is right. In sports one could change that to he who has success is right. Some coaches vehemently defend their philosophy (in my view a term that in this context is used too much and incorrectly), referring to the successes they achieved with one athlete. But not every concept or every approach can be used with every athlete simultaneously and lead to success.

Triathlon demands have changed a lot in recent years, and as a coach one must adapt and react. I certainly made some mistakes at the beginning of my work as a coach and trained more than one athlete to the wall. Everyone makes mistakes and mistakes are part of every development process. Only those who recognize their mistakes, remain self-aware, and continuously question their thinking and actions will emerge stronger from their mistakes.

I constantly take notes, writing down the things that worked well in a training year and those that didn't. Here it is important to not react blindly and overly hastily when some things occasionally don't go as might be desired. I tend to be more restrained, wait to see if it might still develop in a positive direction or gets worse.

During the season I frequently get out my notes, have a closed meeting of sorts, and tweak the concept. That's when you need to have the courage to admit to mistakes you may have made.

For example, years ago, I was vehemently opposed to kick training for triathletes in swimming. Since then, I have reevaluated and now have a different opinion, which can be confusing to some athletes. But when they are included in the decision-making process and are given the reasons for the change of mind, the worry lines tend to smooth out.

Learning, adapting, and changing is an important quality in a coach. But we can see time and again, that some go off-course too quickly and have too little patience during the development of their concept. This often happens in response to magazine articles, podcasts, or YouTube videos. Allegedly new approaches are constantly publicized, which in some cases are built into the training concept without thinking, without testing or validating them.

A mixture of proven and thoughtfully incorporated innovations is an important pillar to success.

4.7 Different Types of Coaches

I don't think coaches should be judged wholesale by their actions without pointing to the differences of, to some extent, basic nature. When I look at the market, I see the following groupings. It is the great variety of coaches with different approaches that gives each athlete the opportunity to find one that's the right fit for him. After all, not every lid fits every pot.

4.7.1 Club coaches

The club coach is usually a volunteer. But more and more coaches offer individual training plans to club members. Since he doesn't make a living with coaching, his prices are unfortunately often below those of full-time coaches. Most of them have at least a level C license from the German Triathlon Union.

4.7.2 Recreational or social media coaches

Similar to the club coach, recreational coaches are volunteers because they make a living with a real job. They usually cannot offer the service of a full-time coach because focus and time availability are limited by their primary occupation.

Unfortunately, this group includes a number of coaches without any qualifications. When I surf the websites of these coaches and read that they plan to get coach's training, I can only shake my head.

In my view this group has the largest number of black sheep who think that you can just make a quick buck on the side with coaching and don't need training or experience. Having a blog or a YouTube channel in my opinion does not legitimize training athletes and trifling with people's health. Some even gain the status of an online guru without having any real experience on deck.

"One tends to remember the bitter taste of poor service long after the sweet taste of a low price has been forgotten."

John Ruskin

4.7.3   Current professional athletes

In professional triathlon, it isn't possible to earn big money like athletes in some other sports, and only a few are able to make a living that way. Athletes without large sponsor contracts bolster their income by offering their services to a small number of athletes.

But I often hear that their own training and ego tend to be a priority and the pro athlete as coach does not, cannot, or only conditionally breaks himself down for the requirements of athletes in different age groups.

4.7.4   Former professional athletes

Like the still active pros, there are a number of former athletes who switched to coaching at the end of their career. They often have lots of experience, even if they sometimes lack the scientific foundation. When they can mentally relate to athletes from different age groups, this combination often works very well.

4.7.5   Scientists

The name of the game is program. The scientist is often mentally anchored in theory and studies. But he frequently lacks the ability to apply his sound professional knowledge to the sport practice and is not necessarily able to describe complex facts and situations in a way that people outside of the science microcosm can understand.

This group includes all coaches that practically collect licenses and continued education credits. Knowledge is power, but not effective without the correct application to practice. Unfortunately, some coaches offer a scientific approach on the internet. Data and numbers are deliberately emphasized as an important part of coaching in order to suggest a greater value.

A closer look at the resumes of some coaches unfortunately shows that they have no scientific background in sports.

4.7.6   Empirical scientists

The most successful coaches can be found in this group. They have highly qualified training but also lots of practical experience, personally and from working with athletes every day. They possess the best of both worlds and, depending on the type of athlete, can draw from both camps for their working method.

In contrast to the scientist, the empirical scientist is not led by science but only uses it as information and to undergird his observations and experiences.

"Data = background noise. Data in the right context = information.
Trial and error = experience. Information plus experience = knowledge.
Knowledge plus empathy = wisdom."

Mario Schmidt-Wendling

This breakdown alone shows that not all coaches can have the same entrance requirements and objectives. And not every athlete is a good fit for every coach, for instance, athletes from the Woodsman group often aren't able to work with a coach with a strictly scientific approach.

A coach's thumbprint can certainly change over the years. For example, scientists might ditch their lab rat existence. On the other hand, practitioners and empiricists might delve deeper into theoretical principles and training science.

A coach's ideas and approaches should never be set in stone.

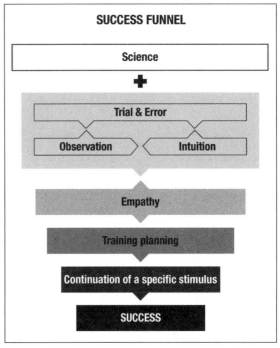

Figure 12: Success funnel.

4.8   What makes a good coach?

"The most dangerous person is the one who listens, thinks, and observes."

Bruce Lee

People often ask me what attributes a good coach should have. The most important ability is listening or communication per se. A coach should be so well-versed in his language, both in speech and writing, that he can explain complex concepts easily and comprehensibly. He should respect the person opposite him, listen to him, and be attentive. He should not differentiate between athletes on principal and should treat them the same, regardless of their performance level.

Not every athlete has what it takes to bring top performances. Treating him badly for that reason in my opinion would be disastrous. Treating all the athletes I work with equally is a very important principle of mine that has caused me to no longer offer different training packages.

At the beginning of my coaching career, I offered three coaching levels, but soon discontinued that because I always felt bad about giving an athlete less attention for a lower price than the athlete who purchased the most expensive package. A coach should see an athlete as a human being, even independently of sport-related matters.

But all the communication in the world is meaningless if a coach has nothing to say. That means he must understand the complexity of the triathlon sport with its three individual disciplines of swimming, cycling, and running.

A coach should be willing to put himself and his actions to the test, recognize mistakes, and own them. When he is willing to accept change, is willing to learn, adapt, and change, he will be successful. He should talk to other coaches, but here, too, listening is important, to reflect on his points of view and opinions.

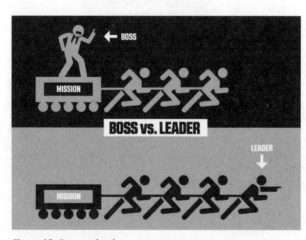

Figure 13: Boss vs. leader.

Ultimately a good coach should be a motivator, providing inspiration and also a little entertainment. He should be less of a boss and more of a leader.

It is a persistent myth that a coach is only successful if he produces champions and world champions (i.e., achieves the successes the media covers). Success is relative and can happen on a completely different level, especially since not every coach works with world-class athletes.

When successes come very quickly, they tend to create tunnel vision and prevent one from seeing the bigger picture. I am a definite opponent of one-way-street coaching. Some coaches are downright dictatorial, don't allow any other opinions, and always impose their will.

I never refer to "my athletes" because that would imply that I oversee them and on a higher hierarchical level. Rather it is about finding a common solution to problems and a joint path to success.

4.9   Suggestions for New Coaches

I always get requests for tips I might have for new coaches. I would like to hereby accommodate that request. Here are my top eight tips.

4.9.1   Work, work, work

It is difficult to become a successful sports coach without the willingness to work. Success is very much tied to the number of working hours.

4.9.2   Education and continuing education are fundamental.

Knowledge is power! Not knowing anything unfortunately matters a lot. For instance, the DTU in cooperation with the IAT (Institute for Applied Training Science in Leipzig, Germany) offers a knowledge newsletter. They send out studies and articles on training topics on a weekly basis.

4.9.3   Mentoring

A beginning coach should look for one or more experienced coaches as mentors and frequently ask them for their opinions. Communication with other coaches is important for finding one's own thumbprint.

4.9.4   Developing an independent methodology.

Patience and time are essential for developing one's own thumbprint. Some self-criticism helps to sharpen the senses.

4.9.5   Evidence of an independent methodology

It is easier to win the trust of athletes when one can explain one's own methodology and can support it with facts.

4.9.6   Respecting traditions and older coaches

When an experienced coach can celebrate successes with his methods, but a younger coach does not consider them up to the current level of knowledge, one should nevertheless never lose respect for the work of an older coach.

4.9.7   Owning mistakes

When we make mistakes, we should own them. When an athlete we coach makes a mistake, we should always ask ourselves if we could have prevented him from making that mistake before being hard on him.

4.9.8   Marking texts or graphic images
with your own name or logo

Texts and ideas are intellectual property. Based on my own painful experiences I can say that this knowledge should be protected so plagiarism doesn't have a chance. Sadly, I have had to learn the hard way.

CONCLUSION

A coach's work is very multi-faceted and exciting. Those who internalize the above points and make them their mission will experience lots of gratification and satisfaction.

Figure 14: Coaching is highly complex.

5 TRAINING THEORY FOR LONG-DISTANCE TRIATHLONS

Before we focus on the practice of the three disciplines in the subsequent chapters, I would like to at this point talk about my ideas and general principles regarding training theory. Here, too, one can find very different approaches and strategies about how to train for a long-distance event.

I would prefer to stick to elementary science because one, this book does not claim to be a scientific dissertation and two, as a coach I am a hands-on man and want to provide the readers with the greatest possible benefit specifically for the daily work of practicing the sport. But before we go into further detail, we should clarify what training really means and how it is defined.

5.1 What Exactly Does This Training Look Like?

The original definition describes training as systematically planned actions with the goal of improving performance in a particular sport. This sounds pretty complicated and describes nothing more than the fact that the goal is a specific end point in the form of a competition.

Starting from the point in time when planning begins, a fixed period of time is created within which to condition all relevant abilities in order to, at the endpoint, meaning the day of competition, be in the best possible physical and mental condition.

5.2 Is Use of the Supercompensation Principle Viable?

The principle of supercompensation has established itself in training theory over roughly the past 50 years. Countless books, lectures, and sports careers have been or still are linked to this schematic diagram and the wishful thinking of having certainty in training planning. Before I disarm this model just a little, I would like to briefly explain it so all readers will have the same level of knowledge.

The idea behind this principle was to explain the link between load and the resulting training effect. Training means deliberately calculated stress that is intended to throw the human organism off balance, out of homeostasis. According to that, the body's response to this stress and its readiness for a comparable future stress is supposed to denote the performance increase.

This model is supposed to indicate the timing of the next training and a systematic performance increase or performance decrease, depending on whether loading and unloading were planned in the correct ratio. But the main problem with this theoretic model lies in the complex relationship between the different adaptive responses during the desired process.

Anticipated responses and adaptations on a muscular level, in neural structures, in the cardiovascular system, and in the athlete's biochemistry, are linked to each other and occur in different phases and spaces of time. Moreover, this model in its structure does not differentiate based on gender, muscle fiber distribution, maximum oxygen uptake, body weight, etc., and thus represents very simplistic wishful thinking with respect to predictability, the use of which should be very limited in a coach's work.

The following figure shows the chronologically different trajectories of the different responses to the previously applied stimulus.

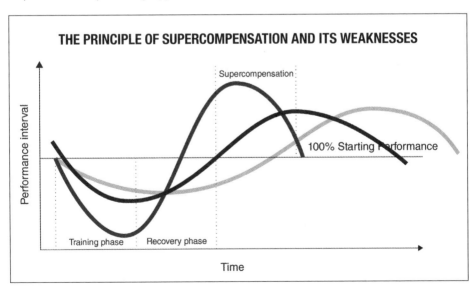

Figure 15: The principle of supercompensation and its weaknesses.

5.3   Periodization

Periodization is a time-based strategy within the training process with the goal of standing at the starting line of an athletic competition in tapered peak form at the end of this process. This period of training is divided into different phases.

These are called base, building, or prep phases in which different training content is used. The time frames of the various phases are determined before the start of training. A season plan that is created beforehand outlines which training content must be completed at what point during the season.

In this context I always get questions from athletes about how such a periodization takes place. Analogous to the faulty thinking about supercompensation that many in sports have, in my opinion, many heads have been filled with a rigid, almost technocratic way of thinking about training. I personally think that a coach should probably forget about what he learned about periodization, because it does not necessarily lead to success. To me a rigid annual plan comes with too many question marks.

- Will the athlete remain injury free?
- Will the weather stay good enough to complete the necessary training volume?
- Will the circumstances surrounding the athlete's life allow continuous training?
- Will the athlete exhibit the desired adaptive responses?

If as a coach I would be able to confidently answer all these questions beforehand, I would buy lottery tickets. Ensuring an athlete's reliable performance development requires feedback in order to adjust the strategy in question, build in rest periods, or to tighten the screws and step up his training.

But this feedback opportunity is missing if, after a 16-week training plan, the athlete trains off the internet or a coach gives him a 4-week training plan. Adaptations of any kind don't happen; during missed training due to illness or lack of time the already drawn-up plan simply continues.

To me planning for a longer period, meaning more than a week, is like gazing into a crystal ball.

We already heard about another argument against classic periodization in my critique of the principle of supercompensation. During a certain training unit, we don't just train one component (e.g., endurance, strength, speed, etc.) but several of these aspects simultaneously. Therefore, dividing the year into specific training contents would not work.

Like supercompensation, classic periodization assumes that performance development is always linear, meaning it can be trained in a straight line until day X. But reality looks much different. This type of wishful thinking doesn't take into consideration life with all its facets. The everyday stressors of family, work, weather, etc., often don't allow linear performance development. Injuries and illnesses cannot be anticipated in the run-up, and they do the rest.

Dividing the triathlon season into different phases should be viewed as a didactic method or rough orientation from which young coaches can benefit at the start of their coaching activity, but only if they are willing to depart from rigid planning when required. One should of course not lose sight of the often-quoted big picture.

When one is familiar with the abilities required for a successful long-distance finish one can extrapolate which contents should be included in training. Later we will learn what those are specifically.

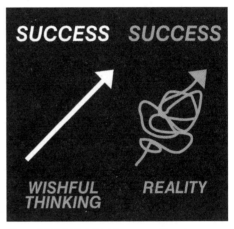

Figure 16: Wishful thinking vs. reality.

When the training year is divided into phases from the get-go, it is not possible to ensure that individual adaptations to the training will take place. In my view an optimal stimulus should always be ensured within the context of the athlete's current physical and mental status.

When that stimulus takes longer than a specified period of one week during a certain training phase, this rigid construct should be broken up. To me training is much more than understanding a dynamic process and pressing it into rigid scheduling. To identify and advance the stimulus, communication between athlete and coach has to be really good, because that is the only way the coach can respond, tweak, and adapt.

Often adaptations also happen during a training unit. For instance, a planned swimming program is frequently modified after the warm-up when I, as coach, notice certain deficiencies while observing the athletes from the pool deck. I have much less opportunity for this type of observation when coaching online or remotely. This makes it even more important to be able to communicate with the athletes from a distance and in close succession, and also to be able to read between the lines.

However, this necessitates that the athlete understand that coaching is not a one-way street but that he is invited to feed the coach all types of information. It is the only way to ensure that the desired stimulus makes sense.

Some coaches or training concepts use a 2:1 or 3:1 training ratio. Training load or volume increases for two or three weeks followed by a resting week with decreased volume and intensity. But I am unaware of any evidence that this rhythm is particularly effective. In my opinion these resting weeks can be eliminated if within a training week there is a sensible balance between loading and unloading.

One of my guiding principles since the beginning of my coaching career is continuity of the specific stimulus. We will learn why this regularity is so important when we get to performance physiology.

I therefore prefer periods of hours per week that the athlete can map reliably and realistically. Rest days as such only happen when the athlete clearly demands it, so he is able to organize his life outside the triathlon sport.

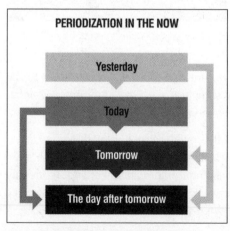

To me periodization takes place on a significantly smaller temporal level. There is no planning of weekly or monthly phases. I tend to work in a planning rhythm of one week and call it coaching and planning in the now. Here the previous day's training determines today's training. And today's unit in turn determines that of tomorrow.

Here it is important to consider the particular complexity of the three disciplines in triathlon and the relationship between loading and resting.

Figure 17: Periodization in the now.

Triathlon should clearly be viewed as an independent sport and not as the detached, in terms of content, stringing together of the sports of swimming, cycling, and running. Planning in such short time periods is more likely to permit a more individual adaptation of the athlete to the chosen stimulus.

I would characterize my form of periodization as a linear-specific progression. This means that there can absolutely be intensive units over a period of 20–30 weeks prior to the long-distance event. The speeds, number of intervals, and the length of the intervals then gradually increase during the weeks prior to the competition date. Hence there is no starting point after the off-season during which training only takes place at the basic endurance level. But to plan and evaluate training performances I must first talk to the athlete and have a clear understanding of his competition goals.

When an athlete plans a race time of 9 h 30 min in the Ironman and needs to divide his overall time into, for instance, 1 h swimming, 5 h cycling and 3 h 30 min running, you have a pretty good idea which training performances need to be achieved to be able to later achieve the desired time.

I like to compare the planned training process to the planning of a meal. The initial weeks are for purchasing ingredients. Abilities such as basic kilometers, strength, and speed are purchased here.

After this phase, the length of which is not predetermined, the cooking phase begins. Here all the ingredients are tossed into a pot and combined into a tasty meal.

During this phase, training of race-specific abilities and skills begins. If this phase is too long or too intense there is the risk of burning the food, meaning the athlete, before it is time to eat, or rather compete. Bon appétit!

5.3.1   The off-season

A phase of complete rest, the off-season, should follow a (hopefully) successful season. This time period is incredibly important to ensure physical and mental unloading. Beginning triathlon athletes in particular are afraid of losing some of their performance capacity during this time without training. The following points are intended to underscore the importance of the off-season.

Training stimuli are processed in the body during subsequent resting phases and the athlete gradually adjusts to a higher level. Here it can be said that training represents deliberately provoked stress. Additional stressors are added to this stress in the form of family, work, finances, etc.

Age-group athletes, but also professionals, must manage all of these factors. There is a permanent weighing of which life aspects currently seem most important. Opportunities for deliberately switching off, doing nothing, and simply tuning out are becoming increasingly rare, especially when we need these resting phases the most, namely during phases with lots of training volume and high intensities.

The athlete's body is experiencing increasing fatigue due to a lack of these rest periods. While loading is decreased prior to competitions, the stress of the competition creates additional fatigue.

Based on this principle, the sensitive hormonal system moves increasingly into negative territory, the stress hormone cortisol takes over and testosterone that is essential to regeneration and adaptations during training, decreases.

When there is no break at the end of the season, this hormonal imbalance will continue to deteriorate, risk of infection increases significantly, and even worse, the passive motor system (ligaments, tendons, joints) does not get a chance to reduce the stress that accumulated during the season. Athletes who vehemently refuse to build in a period of inactivity run the risk of sooner or later getting injured.

Based on empirical evidence, such injuries increase after skipping the season break, between mid-January and mid-February. Thus, he needs a post-season phase of complete regeneration to fully recover if he plans to pursue a new and higher performance level in the following year. Of course, an inactivity phase results in an initial performance decrease and the athlete feels bad and far removed from his performance when he resumes training. But it is nothing to worry about, because competitions generally don't start for months and there is more than enough time to get the seemingly lost performance back on track.

The feedback I always get from athletes is that after the first 2-3 weeks of training after the off-season they feel fresh, rested, and in terms of motor function, much fitter than before.

5.3.1.1 Suggestions for creating an effective off-season

It is recommended to have 2-3 weeks of complete rest from triathlon training, meaning no swimming, cycling, or running. Instead, athletes should practice alternative exercise. Hiking and yoga (for relaxation, NO power yoga) are very good options.

Athletes don't just need physical distance from the sport, but also mental. Many athletes make the mistake of further engaging in the sport mentally, but this does not produce the desired mental relaxation. Instead, athletes should focus on the other aspects of life: go to the movies, sleep in, read a book (NOT a book about sports; if anything, this one), celebrate with friends, and even stay up all night.

I avoid contacting athletes during this time so they can also get some mental distance from their coach.

5.4   Basic Performance Physiology

In this segment, I would like to provide a rough description of the two most important means of energy production. As a hands-on man, I only want to give a brief overview of this topic, especially since I expect athletes who want to compete in long-distance events to have a certain amount of theoretical background training.

With respect to the energy supply, we differentiate between an aerobic and an anaerobic system. The difference lies primarily in the use of oxygen during energy conversion. Energy for muscular activity is produced by burning carbohydrates and fat.

In the aerobic system, oxygen is used for energy production. In this part of the metabolism, the primarily recruited muscles are the slow-twitch endurance-supporting or type-I muscle fibers. Here energy is won from carbohydrates and the faster-working type-II fibers are triggered. Lactate accumulates during this energy production process. In the past, lactate was referred to as an end product of metabolism. Nowadays the science is more advanced.

While lactate is the end product of glycolysis, it is further metabolized in the oxidative metabolism, meaning with the addition of oxygen. Hence the old adage "Fats burn in the carbohydrate fire" makes total sense. The more oxygen that can be absorbed the more the accumulated lactate can also be removed in the oxidative metabolism.

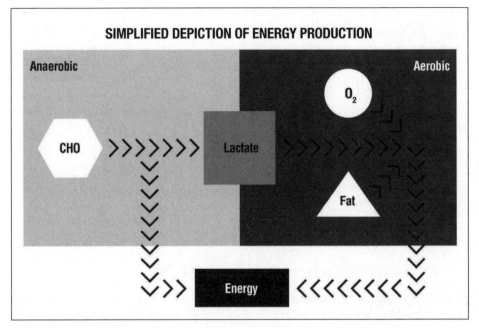

Figure 18: Basic energy production.

A simple formula can be deduced from this. The higher the lactate concentration in the blood, the higher the carbohydrate consumption.

But since carbohydrate stores in the form of glycogen are severely limited in the human body and fats exist in nearly unlimited amounts, it quickly becomes apparent which form of energy production should be prioritized for long-distance.

One of the greatest fallacies in this context is that both systems function independently of each other (i.e., that no carbohydrates are burned at a lower intensity level, and at a certain load no more fats are burned for energy production). Both systems operate simultaneously. Weighting within energy production only changes with different intensities.

> **For the athlete this means adjusting three parameters to increase Ironman performance:**
>
> 1. Increasing maximum oxygen uptake to optimize aerobic capacity via the ability to metabolize accumulating lactate.
> 2. Decreasing lactate production within the long-distance-specific load range, and, linked to that, lower carbohydrate consumption.
> 3. Increasing carbohydrate intake in the form of gels, bars, and fluids.

If we eliminate that last point (more on that in chapters 9 and 11), two parameters clearly come to the fore. One is the maximum oxygen uptake VO_2max and the other is the maximum lactate production rate Vlamax.

5.4.1 VO_2max or aerobic capacity

VO_2max is a frequently used term in endurance sports. This value refers to the maximum oxygen uptake ability, meaning it shows how much oxygen an athlete can utilize during a certain amount of time, and thus is an important indicator in the assessment of aerobic endurance capacity. Colloquially this is also referred to as the size of the engine.

This value is affected by oxygen uptake in the lungs, but also transport capacity in the blood and consumption in organs and muscles. Next to performance capacity, gender, bodyweight, and body composition play a role in the assessment of this value.

The greater the VO_2max the more oxygen the body is able to convert and the sooner can accumulate lactate from the anaerobic metabolism be further metabolized, resulting in more energy production.

Along with the growing knowledge about this value a development has taken place that is moving in the wrong direction. In recent years, training in VO_2max intervals to increase maximum oxygen uptake has become very popular. Suddenly many people think that this method is the single valid means for increasing this value. At some point in recent years, training within the basic endurance range has gone out of fashion, although it continues to be a reliable and less injury-prone training method.

Training to increase VO_2max is geared towards improved oxygen utilization, improved peripheral perfusion, and an improved supply network of the skeletal muscles with the smallest blood vessels, the capillaries. Since fat burning requires a certain amount of oxygen, it is clear that an increase in oxygen increases the amount of energy produced from fat, meaning there is a higher fat oxidation rate.

VO_2max can not only be increased within the basic endurance range, but also by training at very high intensities.

5.4.1.1 Training suggestions to increase VO_2max

- Polarized training approach (see intensity distribution)
- High training volumes at low intensity (i.e., classic basic endurance training)
- Intervals at high intensities (e.g., 40 seconds high intensity/20 seconds active recovery)
- VO_2max intervals of maximally 7–8 minutes

5.4.2 Vlamax or glycolytic power

Unlike the VO_2max, many athletes are still unfamiliar with the maximum lactate production rate. This value was long considered a secret weapon in the toolbox of the world's most successful coaches in endurance sports.

Lactate is produced from carbohydrates during breakdown in the glycolytic metabolism. This form of energy production takes place significantly faster than in the aerobic fat metabolism. The amount of generated anaerobic energy is significantly smaller, especially due to limited carbohydrate storage, and cannot be sustained longer-term.

Due to the very rapid supply of energy from sugar we can deduce that this form is primarily required during very explosive and highly intense loading. But since in the Ironman triathlon we operate in every area except the former, it is apparent that the amount of produced lactate or rather energy production from carbohydrates should take a backseat.

Simply put, one can say that the Vlamax reflects the amount of burned carbohydrates, meaning it should be very low during long-distances in order to protect the body's own carbohydrate stores in the form of glycogen for as long as possible. The goal should be to increase performance via training to the extent that the amount of carbohydrates that needs to be burned for the demand relevant to the Ironman triathlon is as low as possible.

Another point is that a higher lactate production rate diminishes the fat metabolism function, which is something that should clearly be avoided in long-distance sports. Athletes feel a low Vlamax via a slower energy supply. Accelerations and sprint performances get noticeably slower, and they feel increasingly like diesel engines. This effect is absolutely desired in long-distance sports to ensure more effective energy management during a race. But it also shows that it is difficult to achieve personal bests in 5k distances on foot during a long-distance season, because that would require a greater anaerobic capacity in the form of a higher lactate production rate.

5.4.2.1   Training suggestions to lower Vlamax

- Regular training on a nearly daily basis
- Strength endurance training for metabolization by lowering the glycolytic enzyme activity in fast-twitch fibers, and with the conversion into slow-twitch fibers with lower carbohydrate consumption
- Avoiding very high intensities
- Units with low carbohydrate stores, FatMax training

5.4.3   Metabolism summary

The goal should be to stand at the starting line with a high VO_2max, meaning a big engine, and an optimal fat metabolism. At the same time the V8 engine should have low fuel requirements, meaning a low Vlamax.

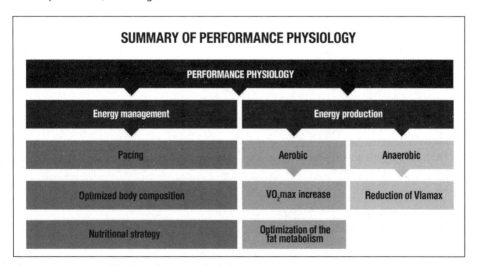

Figure 19: Summary of basic performance physiology.

And if one now makes sure that the fuel quantity is ensured regularly and in sufficient amounts from the outside in the form of carbohydrates from gels, bars, and liquids, nothing should go wrong for a successful long-distance finish, at least from an energy perspective.

5.5   Areas of Training and Intensity Zones

Now that we have learned about the metabolism background information, we will focus on how to safely and reliably control it in everyday training. Training at different intensities and with different intentions is divided into different training ranges or zones. But in recent years, a veritable jungle of numbers, definitions, and concepts has established itself in this area. This means that at the end of the day we have to make absolutely certain that we know what we are talking about.

Figure 20 shows the differences in nomenclature via examples. Here different definitions were created depending on the sport and the country. Some coaches draw on an eight-zone model for control, others use five training zones. I am in the five-zone camp, although it actually amounts to only three training zones when training for long-distance.

The two training zones that don't have an appreciable right to exist in long-distance triathlon are the compensation zone and the top range.

OVERVIEW OF NOMENCLATURE AND DEFINITION OF TRAINING ZONES

Zone	Racing Intensity	Physiology	Training goals	DTU	BDR	Allen/Coggan
1		Active recovery	Active recovery		RK	1. Act Regeneration
2		Aerobic Endurance ext.	Basic aerobic endurance	BE1 CO	G 1	2. Endurance
2		Prim. Aerobic	Basic aerobic endurance			3. Tempo
3	LD MD OD SD	Aerobic-anaerobic transition, lactate threshold	Race-specific endurance	BE2 Dur..	G 2	4. Lactate threshold
3		Aerobic-anaerobic performance capacity VO$_2$max	Race-specific endurance	BE2 Tempo	EB K3	5. VO$_2$max
4		Neuromuscular Training	Anaerobic endurance, Basic speed	Speed, Speed endurance Racespecific fresh Endurance	SB/SN C1/C2	6. Anaerobic Capacity
4		Anaerobic Capacity				7. Neuromuscular Performance

Figure 20: Nomenclature and definition of training zones.

I used to be a fan of regenerative endurance training, but over the years have increasingly moved away from it and now prefer regeneration techniques outside of endurance training.

The top range with its very high intensities brings with it a certain injury risk, particularly when an athlete's motor abilities have not yet been sufficiently developed. Less than optimal movement execution combined with high intensity unfortunately is not always without consequences in terms of overloading and injuries. But since good health should be the highest priority and ensures continuous training, I largely forego units in this speed range. I call it a kind of safety reserve.

There are different types of nomenclature common these days; I would like to keep them as simple as possible, using basic endurance BE 1 and BE 2 and development zone. Some would explain them as zone 2, zone 3, or zone 4.

Hence training tends to be limited to the areas of basic endurance BE 1, BE 2, and the development zone. Blanket quantification of zone limits into attributable percentages of the individual anaerobic threshold, the functional threshold power (FTP), or the maximum heart rate makes little sense to me because, as previously mentioned in the chapter about athlete types, personality aspects must be considered for intensity control, independent of classic physiology.

But for the sake of completeness, I would nevertheless like to list a rough and never-etched-in-stone overview regarding training zones, whereby they should always be adjusted situationally for the aforementioned reasons.

TRAINING ZONES RELEVANT TO LONG-DISTANCE AND THEIR CHARACTERISTICS

	Basic endurance (BE) 1	Basic endurance (BE) 2	Development zone (DZ)
Goal/ Characteristics	Improvement of aerobic long-term endurance, fat metabolism, improvement of movement economy	LD-specific endurance, increasing glycolysis, tempo stamina	Speed development Improved VO_2max
Type of training	Continuous method Low intensity FatMax units Fasting training (Cave!!)	Continuous method or intervals medium/higher intensity, strength endurance bike (C3 or SE), tempo run, LD-specific intervals, sweet-spot training	Intervals VO_2max intervals
Energy production	Aerobic dominant	Aerobic-anaerobic transition	Anaerobic dominant
Lactate concentration	1.5–2.5 mmol/l	2,8-4,0 mmol/l	4,0-6,5 mmol/l
Percent of FTP	57-75 %	76-93 %	93-111 %
Percent of max. HR	62-79 %	79-87 %	> 87 %
Percent of threshold HR	68-86 %	86-98 %	> 98 %
Length of interval	None	8-40 min	2-8 min
RPE 1-10	3 to 4.5	4.5 to 6.5	6.5 to 8

Figure 21: Training zones relevant to long-distance and their characteristics according to MSW.

I prefer the simple style principle and try to avoid any preventable complexity in training. A zone model that is too differentiated, particularly when training age group athletes, to me isn't really practicable. When an athlete, as has happened, asks me while clinging to the edge of the pool if the interval should be completed in upper BE or in low DZ, I just have to shake my head. In chapter 6, I will explain in more detail why dividing intensity into specific zones works only conditionally.

Instead of implementing my instruction fast tempo, the athlete was busy messing with his GPS watch and thinking about the required tempo zone. Sometimes a well-aimed throw with a pull buoy as a wake-up call would be very helpful. Simply dividing into slow, medium, and fast is often much more effective because it is easier to implement.

It is advisable to occasionally train completely without numbers (i.e., water clock, watch or GPS signal) to promote development of improved subjective perceived exertion. I have been using the following classification for more than a decade to bring the respective training zones in line with individual perception.

SCALE FOR THE EVALUATION OF SUBJECTIVE PERCEIVED EXERTION

	Perception	
1	Sitting on the couch eating junk food	NE
2	I feel good, could do this pace all day	NE
3	Still feeling good, but breathing a little heavier	BE 1
4	Sweating a little, but can talk without a problem	BE 1
5	Sweating more, but can still talk easily	BE 2
6	Can still talk, but more breathless	BE 2
7	Can barely talk, sweating profusely	DZ
8	Can no longer respond adequately, tempo is too high	DZ
9	I see a white light at the end of the tunnel	VHE
10	Dead	VHE

Figure 22: Subjective evaluation of exertion (RPE).

When taking a closer look at a long-distance demand profile one notices that the required intensity, irrespective of the athlete's level, lies in the transition area between BE 1 and BE 2. To me that means training primarily in the previously mentioned three load ranges to achieve a preferably major bearing on the racing intensity.

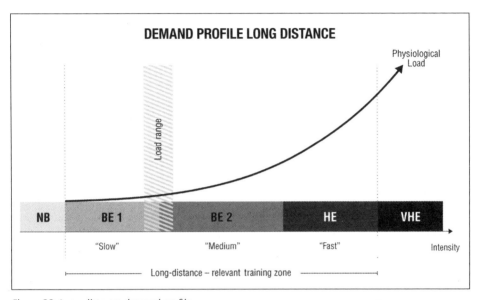

Figure 23: Long-distance demand profile.

5.5.1 A critical look at high-intensity interval training (HIIT), or speed with intensity interval training (IIT)

A term about which I felt skeptical from the start began to increasingly float around the triathlon gazettes a few years ago, namely training with the HIT method, Tabata, or the like, meaning training in the highest intensity zone. The goal was to improve speed performance, improve movement economy, shift the testosterone/cortisol hormone balance towards testosterone, and do so with a paradoxically also elevated basic endurance. At least that was the science.

But I experimented on myself and with a few athletes in my care and came to the conclusion that this should be used little or not at all in the area of long-distance training. I am happy to tell you why.

5.5.1.1   Risk of injury

Most triathletes have sedentary day jobs and thereby permanently diminish their body static. Mobility decreases and consequently the risk of sub-optimal movement execution in sports increases. When such an athlete is supposed to complete intervals at the highest intensity after sitting for a 10-hour workday, I can guarantee that he will be injured sooner or later.

5.5.1.2   Non-specific

For years, I have been preaching about continuity of a specific stimulus. To me it isn't necessary to kill oneself with such hard sessions only to be totally exhausted or even injured. While extremely intense units are good for likes on social media, I think they are less effective for building form than the previously mentioned continuity, meaning training in the Ironman-relevant training zone.

While this requires a certain polarity in terms of intensity, one should proceed carefully. To me training in the top range has no relationship to the demand profile in the Ironman, namely the BE 1/BE 2 transition zone.

5.5.1.3   Mental abilities

HIIT is marketed as time-saving training. You can often read that it can achieve similar effects as hours of BE 1 training. Even if this were possible on a physiological level, to me it is still not a pro-HIT argument.

I think a successful Ironman finish still requires hours. Hours of orthopedic adaptation, hours of training of mental abilities, and hours of just toughening up.

5.5.1.4   Worsening Vlamax

I have seen tons of results from performance diagnostics of athletes who trained to the high-intensity principle for extended periods of time. I saw in nearly all of the tests that the promised basic endurance was almost non-existent. Despite training very hard these athletes had disastrous values with respect to their fat metabolism and the Vlamax was definitely too high.

Developing the fat metabolism is still a guarantee for success in the area of long-distance endurance. When an athlete burns too little fat but too many carbohydrates during low intensity, he will have a giant energy problem during a race, because he will hardly be able to absorb the necessary amount of carbohydrates during exertion without terribly stressing his GI tract.

Athletes who spend a lot of time training in the HIT zone are often the ones that report stomach problems after the race or who crept along the running course completely desolate. Unfortunately, they often don't make the connection between this failure and the improperly weighted training sessions. They tend to blame an intolerance to the energy gel they consumed.

5.6   Breaking Down Training Zones

Athletes should pay particular attention to the weighting of individual training sessions during the training process. Here it is recommended to follow a thoroughly polarized approach. Polarized means predominantly spending time in the lower and upper intensity zones.

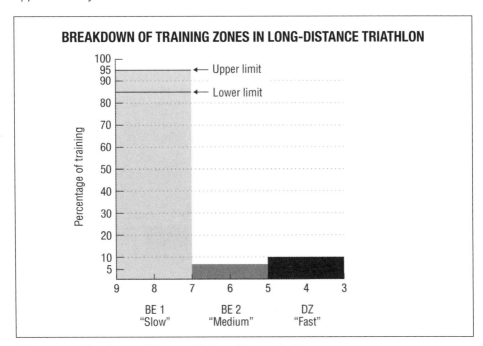

Figure 24: Breaking down training zones in long-distance triathlon.

Due to the reasons of injury prevention, I would not structure the upper zone with unlimited intensity. Most endurance sports show evidence that a distribution of approximately 80% in the basic zone and 20% of higher intensity is the best option for increasing maximum oxygen uptake. In our specific case of long-distance triathlon, I would even modify the ratio further.

In my view, developing the necessary fat metabolism requires at least 85% of the entire training volume to be competed in the BE 1 zone. Depending on the athlete type, it can even be 90–92%. The remaining 15% are divided between BE 2 and the development zone (DZ).

One of the most common mistakes made when choosing intensity is a training pace that is permanently too high. Number-oriented athletes often tend to turn every basic endurance unit into a kind of tempo run or tempo endurance ride. In their view, training must always be latently painful because as is well known, no pain, no gain.

The 30k average on the bike and faster than 5 min/k on foot are often considered the magic limit that must be exceeded or undercut, because otherwise the workout is worthless.

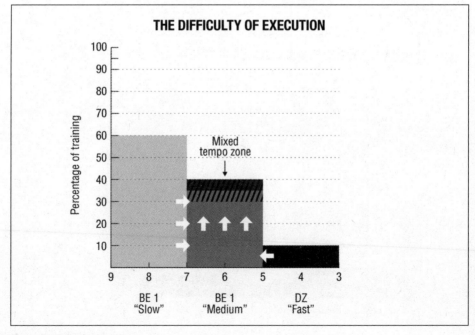

Figure 25: Mixed tempo zone.

Next to inferior development of the VO_2max, athletes who train based on this pyramid-type principle experience a lot of fatigue. They are often so exhausted that they are unable to meet the targets during intensive units. The training pace then moves increasingly into a medium range, a mixed tempo zone.

Next to poorer adaptation to the training stimulus, in this athlete group the risk of overloading and injury increases significantly. The Alpha Leader athlete type can often be found here. If one were to choose an image to explain this incorrectly weighted hunt for specific numbers, an athlete who always needs to see average performances on his watch display could certainly be called an average Joe.

5.7   Interplay of Loading and Unloading

Training creates deliberately generated stress on the human body. This training stimulus leads to increased performance as stated in the theory of supercompensation, when a recovery phase follows a successful stimulus. Only when these two aspects exist in a balanced ratio will a performance increase occur that is permanent and justifiable from a health standpoint. Along with the training-induced stress, the athlete is subject to additional stress factors.

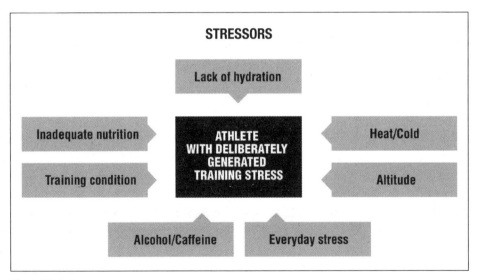

Figure 26: Stressors.

Regeneration processes and repair measures in the body on a muscular and neuronal level already take place towards the end of the training load. Energy stores in the muscles begin to replenish. Regeneration can simply be described as the sum of all restoration processes that take place after exertion.

Unfortunately, the knowledge of sensible regeneration has not manifested in the heads of some athletes. Often the focus is only on the actual training and the necessary recovery falls by the wayside. In athlete circles, regeneration tends to still be considered a sign of weakness. This kind of thinking does not do much to improve self-confidence.

In many triathletes, confidence in their own strength unfortunately only develops after completing epic sessions or when a certain number of weekly training hours have been recorded in the training journal.

Some readers may have seen sentences like: Training stimulus happens during recovery, and are aware of the importance of rest periods. But as an age-group athlete, one must accommodate all aspects of daily life as well as the extensive training with respect to long-distance.

This often results in an imbalance between stress (training) and regeneration. And when everyday stress factors (family, finances, work, time management, social obligations) are added to the training stress, the entire system often tilts towards stress.

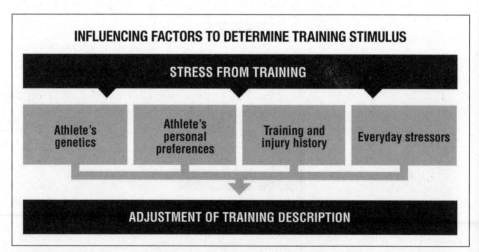

Figure 27: Influencing factors to determine the optimal training stimulus.

5.7.1   Endocrine balance

During stress the body releases large amounts of the hormone cortisol. Cortisol is also referred to as the stress hormone or fight-or-flight hormone. Cortisol diminishes the release of the body's most potent hormone, the growth hormone (HGH).

But this growth hormone is essential to the regeneration processes in the human organism. It regulates cell division and boosts the metabolism and thus fat burning. The male sex hormone testosterone acts as the antagonist to cortisol. This hormone that turns boys into men has an anabolic (i.e., building) effect.

Studies have shown that endurance training units of more than 90 minutes lead to a significant drop in testosterone. Endurance training is also referred to as catabolic. When permanently training in the endurance range and additional stressors come into play due to the athlete's everyday life, the accessible testosterone level drops further.

Athletes with lots of muscle mass need a little more testosterone for regeneration than small-boned men or women. Therefore, training should ideally also match the athlete's body type. A drop in the testosterone level is also one reason why male endurance athletes tend to father more girls than boys.

An additional risk is the fact that adapting to aerobic endurance training is more noticeable than the negative effects of a drop in the testosterone level. The athlete feels good and sees that he is making headway in training, but does not notice that he is gradually moving into an imbalance between testosterone and cortisol. Once the bottom falls out of the amount of accessible testosterone, the same happens to the performance capacity.

By the way, this is where illegal testosterone doping in endurance sports comes into play. Here it is less about building muscles like a bodybuilder, but rather about the relationship between testosterone and cortisol to rebalance the testosterone level. In 99% of cases, an approach along the lines of more is more is doomed to fail.

When athletes can only define themselves via a high testosterone level and thereby engage in comparisons of the male primary reproductive organs, their performance capacity will soon go into a downward spiral.

5.7.2 Functional overreaching, non-functional overreaching, and overtraining

There are phases in the training year, and more frequently in weeks 4-6 prior to a long-distance unit, when an athlete feels tired and flat. He is weighed down by the length of preparation, the training continuity, and the increased training load.

* But what is one to do in such a situation?
* Knuckling down through the next session, quitting and skipping the session, or continuing with a reduced load?

The first step in making a decision is understanding your training plan and knowing the reason why and when you should train what. Once you have understood that you will automatically learn more about yourself as an athlete and you will feel your body adapting to the training.

Here are two fundamental questions to consider.

5.7.2.1 Is it all consciously provoked fatigue?

Fatigue isn't automatically a counterproductive state. Quite the contrary, fatigue is a consciously provoked state that is necessary so the adaptation from stimuli can take place in the body.

This form of fatigue is deliberately calculated and built into training plans, for instance, in a tough or long training block or during training camp. This fatigue is normal and should be expected. It helps the athlete adjust to a new training level.

The athlete worked hard for this type of fatigue and thus earned it. In this case fatigue has a definite function, also referred to as functional overreaching in this context.

5.7.2.2 Which type of fatigue am I currently experiencing?

Normal fatigue is felt primarily in the muscles, the legs feel tight and heavy, the heart rate is elevated, and training feels subjectively harder. Training guidelines take subjectively more effort to meet if at all, meaning more strength is required.

Beyond that there is a type of fatigue or exhaustion that is hormone related, and should be taken far more seriously. When regeneration times are no longer sufficient and testosterone continues to drop through the floor and the stress hormone cortisol is fully in charge, one should call it quits and take a break. In this context we talk about non-functional overreaching or overtraining.

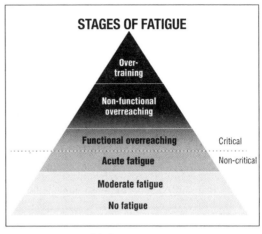

Figure 28: Stages of fatigue.

5.7.2.3   Symptoms of non-functional overreaching and overtraining

Symptoms that should ring the alarm bells include:

* Extreme drop in the heart rate relative to the performance
* Problems raising the heart rate
* Elevated resting heart rate
* Trouble falling asleep
* Restless sleep, night sweats
* Extreme cravings for sweets
* Susceptibility to infections
* Delayed wound repair
* Change in heart rate variability (HRV)
* Depressed basic mood
* Irritability
* Daytime fatigue
* Loss of appetite
* Thick legs right after getting up in the morning
* Burning sensation in legs even with light training
* Weight gain (HGH release is suppressed)
* Canker sores and herpes

If these symptoms appear frequently or for a longer period of time, a break is indicated. In my view the term *overtraining* should be changed to *under-regeneration* because the cause almost always isn't too much training but not observing the regeneration periods.

5.7.2.4   Ways to stop overtraining

Regaining freshness and reestablishing hormonal balance requires a training adjustment. This primarily means that there needs to be a break from training for some period of time to give the body time to repair and regenerate. To this end the mix of more intensive and more relaxed units should be chosen carefully.

In such a phase, age-group athletes who, for time reasons, need to train in the early mornings should skip that training in favor of sleeping longer. Sleep unfortunately often falls victim to a tight schedule when one wishes to combine all everyday life's aspects, but unfortunately doing so is not successful in the long run and sooner or later leads to a performance drop or eventually to adverse health effects.

In general, one should not spend every free minute in training in order to inflate the training journal unnecessarily. External stress factors should be kept to a minimum if possible. The expression *minimum of the necessary* or the minimax principle describes the ideal training effort, meaning achieving the maximum with minimal effort.

Acceleration and deceleration run sessions or strength training can act as the antithesis to an endurance-related drop in the testosterone level, both preventatively and therapeutically. To avoid this condition athletes should really refrain from inflating the training journal. Quite a large number of athletes define themselves primarily by a certain number of training hours per week.

Training in the BE 1 zone, as we have already learned and hopefully understood, is the most important factor in long-distance triathlon. But it is both a blessing and a curse. Adaptations from basic aerobic training are initially immense and the athlete often feels encouraged to increase the training volume.

So, when the aforementioned hormonal imbalance establishes itself in the background and the athlete notices that his performance gets increasingly worse, he often responds in the wrong direction. Instead of taking a few days off from training, he trains even more in order to make up for the perceived performance loss.

In the end it is not the athlete with the highest training volume or the most training hours who is successful, but the athlete who is able to adequately regenerate the highest training volume and can generate performance increases from this combination. Here a mix of basic kilometers, strength, speed, motor function/technique, and mobility beats purely collecting as many weekly hours as possible in the basic zone.

But the previously mentioned mix may require longer regeneration times so that the number of total weekly hours can be lower. Therefore, athletes should really refrain from evaluating their training strictly by time categories. To that end, here is a short formula: **Content beats volume!**

In order to prevent a drop in testosterone due to too much endurance training early on in the winter, it helps to deal honestly with training priorities and content. The following graphic is intended to show which content individual athletes should focus on during the winter.

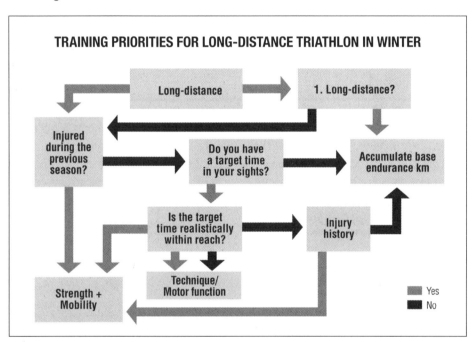

Figure 29: Training priorities in winter.

5.8　Load Management

In recent years, several metrics were created for accurately classifying training-generated stresses, whose use is of some value in sports. How a coach or a self-coaching athlete uses these values depends on the individual's working method.

Values such as the training stress score (TSS), acute training load (ATL), chronic training load (CTL), or training stress balance (TSB) are intended to help objectively measure the stress to which an athlete is exposed.

But when taking a closer look at the various formulas to calculate these metrics it becomes apparent that all these values depend on the functional threshold power (FTP).

Later, in chapter 7, I will explain in more detail why FTP cannot be used as an indicator for training assessment. In my own coaching world, I do not use these values and only look at them within the context of other, in my view, more sensible options for load assessment.

5.8.1   Subjective assessment of an athlete

I am not a big fan of relying blindly on measured numbers and the metrics derived therefrom. Athletes who immerse themselves too deeply in the world of data often tend to cut off the connection to their own physical awareness. In my training approach, a certain amount of self-awareness regarding their own status and to assess a particular performance is much more helpful in evaluating the training-related stress.

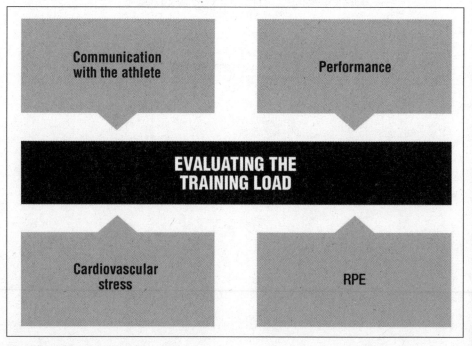

Figure 30: Evaluating the training load.

The above metrics reflect the physiology, but cannot subjectively capture the athlete's mental state. I therefore created a chart a few years ago, that can assist athletes with assessing their own emotional state.

With this list the athlete can subjectively document various general markers regarding his daily state. Here the status is rated numerically with 1 being very good and 6 being insufficient. In addition, notes about perceived stress, the session rate of perceived exertion (session RPE) during the training units, can be made on the chart. Here I work with a range of 1–10 based on the Borg scale to allow for a slightly more precise differentiation, with 1 being very good and 10 being very bad.

Modern online platforms like, for instance, Today's Plan, offer a myriad of such subjective evaluation parameters under their training journal tab.

Evaluating training load should thereby not simply be performed by analyzing data and files.

To further finetune subjective assessment it is also recommended that the athlete ask himself prior to a session how he is feeling before training. The below graphic is intended to help make a decision that is in line with one's own mental state. But this also necessitates being honest with oneself.

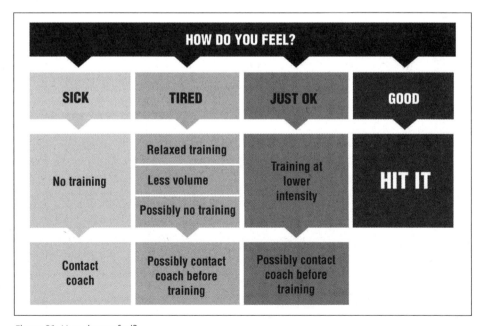

Figure 31: How do you feel?

ADDITIONAL INFORMATION

An often-used method for assessing the status of athletes is the breakfast test. Athletes are observed as they walk to the *breakfast buffet* in the morning at training camp. Recommendations for that training day can be made based on the way they walk, their body language, and facial expression.

5.8.2   Measuring stress via heart rate variability (HRV)

Even in ancient China, people knew that heartbeats are not always regular, meaning the time lag between two heartbeats can vary. The human organism regulates this lag autonomously based on current needs. Physical exertion or stress result in a rising heart rate which generally returns to the starting level when at rest.

The fresher an athlete is the more apparent is his ability to adapt to the stress factors of training and everyday life with greater variability in the time lags between two heartbeats. But when the athlete is permanently very stressed, be it due to training, other factors, or a combination of both, this adaptability decreases, resulting in less heartbeat variability.

5.8.2.1   Physiology

A brief outline of the relevant nexuses for better comprehension.

Heart contractions are triggered subconsciously and not intentionally by an impulse of the sinus node in the heart.

The autonomous nervous system is responsible for this process. It in turn is divided into the sympathetic nervous system which is the activating or fight-or-flight part. This sympathetic nervous system is responsible for the heart's rhythm. It generates a rise in blood pressure and heart rate, mydriasis of the eyes, etc.

Its antagonist is the parasympathetic nervous system which is controlled by the vagus nerve. This parasympathetic part of the nervous system controls the function of the internal organs, is considered a rest nerve or recovery nerve, and promotes recovery,

Build-up of the body's own reserves, digestion, lowering blood pressure, and a number of other functions.

When looking at these two antagonists, it is easy to imagine which part might be advantageous to performance development. But one should also be strong and resistant in the sympathetic part. These two systems work together every millisecond to keep the organism alive.

The balance between the sympathetic and parasympathetic nervous system is a perfectly natural, healthy, and permanent process.

5.8.2.2 Sympathetic nervous system dominance

This branch of the vegetative nervous system causes the blood sugar level to rise as well as blood pressure and heart rate (i.e., all things we need as triathletes for performance development during competitions and in training).

But when the athlete spends too much time in the sympathetic part it becomes problematic because this results in long-term disruption of basic regeneration and performance development. When this state persists over a long period of time it is considered chronic stress.

This status then leads to accelerated aging and loss of bone density and muscle as well as a diminished memory. This status can be triggered by inadequate training loads (epic monster units), lack of sleep, everyday stress factors (see above), inflammation-causing foods, etc.

5.8.2.3 Parasympathetic nervous system dominance

Developing excellent health and performance requires both parts of the vegetative nervous system to be well-developed. In sports this means that we must switch on our sympathetic nervous system when we need it for sport-related loads, but we also need to be able to immediately switch it off again afterwards to be back in the parasympathetic part that helps us to regenerate.

Like the dominance of the fight-and-flight part, it is also possible to achieve a surplus of parasympathetic activity. For this to happen the athlete must be in a state of overtraining for a long period of time so the organism switches off the sympathetic nervous system to avoid major damage. Other possibilities are that the athlete is harboring an infection or is recovering from illness.

5.8.2.4   Troubleshooting

When the two parts are significantly out of balance the athlete should almost always rest, meaning reducing the training volume or intensity or, in the worst case, taking a break.

5.8.2.5   The importance of breathing and its effect on HRV

The human breath is closely linked to the cardiovascular system, the nervous system, and the brain. The heart rate increases slightly when inhaling and drops slightly when exhaling. This cyclical process creates a balance between performance delivery and regeneration.

This results in another benefit of HRV measurement because really deep belly breaths or diaphragmatic breathing dramatically improves the autonomous nervous system.

This form of breathing improves brain capacity, promotes better circulation, reduces muscle tightness, etc. But in today's society we can see that diaphragm function is restricted due to daily sitting, no longer contracts properly, and its cross-section gradually decreases.

But the diaphragm is the most important muscle in breathing and is particularly important in swimming, because here we must exhale into the water against added resistance.

Another aspect to watch out for is that the stomach is often pulled in for esthetic reasons, to look as slim as possible. Pulling the stomach in results in thoracic breathing which does not permit the benefits of diaphragmatic breathing.

Yoga classes can be very beneficial for athletes with inefficient breathing to develop awareness of correct deep diaphragmatic breathing.

5.8.2.6   Measuring

With respect to HRV we differentiate between long-term and short-term measurements. The latter is more practical for everyday use. To do so, a measurement is taken for one to five minutes in the morning while resting in a reclined position. To be completely relaxed the measurement should be taken after using the restroom but before breakfast and coffee.

For valid results regarding the stress level this brief measurement should be taken every day, because the correct conclusions can only be drawn over a period of weeks and months. Nowadays, several apps are on the market; the modern EKG breast straps are completely sufficient for measuring HRV.

5.8.2.7   Valuation and transfer to athletic practice

HRV can be used as an objective marker for global assessment of the training load. However, I would never blindly rely exclusively on this assessment score but would see it as one puzzle piece in the overall assessment. There are always fluctuations within this score, especially in women where the HRV changes within the menstrual cycle. To me HRV shows merely a trend.

I would therefore not adjust my planned training after a single bad score but would keep a close eye on the change over a period of 2-4 days. Like so many things in life, the mix seems to be the right approach. A combination of objectively measured values along with the athlete's own subjective assessment to me is the gold standard for assessing the training load.

5.9   Regeneration Measures

Regeneration in endurance sports is immensely important. The necessary large training volume in preparation for long-distance events requires adequate recovery time. In recent years, a lot of effort was put into developing tools and measures to accelerate regeneration.

The broad study with the nice name *Regman* (short for regeneration management) done by the German Federal Institute for Sports Science examined different possibilities. A general recommendation cannot be made as to which measure safely functions in what amount. The response to such a regeneration measure is very different from athlete to athlete.

I would therefore like to mention the most popular methods and encourage the reader to try them and figure out which measures are beneficial and which might be counterproductive:

- Cool-down
- Static stretching
- Fasciae training
- Sauna
- Cold-water immersion or ice bath
- Massage
- Electric muscle stimulation (EMS)
- Compression garments
- Compression from *recovery boots*
- Power naps

But before looking into these options for regeneration acceleration, an athlete should focus on the arguably most important parameter for accelerated regeneration. I'm talking about nocturnal sleep.

When athletes ask me how they can improve their triathlon performance outside of training, I always tell them to please optimize the amount and quality of their sleep. Sleep duration certainly differs from one athlete to the next, but my experiences in recent years have shown me that when it comes to sleep, a lot really helps.

To improve sleep quality, the room should be aired out, the room temperature should be 18 degrees C (64 F), and athletes should forgo stimulants (coffee, alcohol, etc.) and too much screen time (smart phone, tablet, etc.) right before bedtime.

But enough beating around the bush. Let's get down to business, namely swimming, cycling, and running.

6 SWIMMING

After all the small talk of the previous chapters, let's focus on the practice. Like a triathlon, we will begin with the discipline of swimming. There is a certain ambivalence attached to the swimming component because on the one hand, an improved swimming performance doesn't win much time, but on the other hand, a worse swimming performance can lose several minutes or even hours.

An old wise triathlon saying claims that long-distance triathlons are never, or at least rarely, won with the swimming part, but can often be lost in the water. This is true for the pros as well as age-group athletes. This ambivalence often leads to a kind of love–hate relationship with the wet discipline.

Some athletes have a regular aversion to the first sport. Particularly lateral entrants or late starters struggle to acquire the necessary basic movement patterns and beyond that the endurance, strength, and speed. Other athletes, who learned to swim as children and have mastered an economically efficient technique, love this discipline. But it is true for both groups that swimming is a fundamental part of the overall triathlon performance.

At this point, I would like to repeat one of my favorite maxims to be committed to memory: Triathlon is triathlon, and not swimming, cycling, and running. Despite its small portion timewise of approximately 10% of the overall time, it has a major effect on the overall result when crossing the finish line. Swimming is also an important part of training. I will explain the why and how on the following pages.

What I cannot and don't want to do in this book, or what would be difficult to explain in a book, is the correct swimming technique. First of all, one should question if there even is such a technical model that can be applied to all swimmers, and secondly it is difficult to learn movement patterns strictly verbally from written form. There are definitely different learning types who can learn from text, but in my opinion, such a complex movement as swimming cannot be taught nor learned in this form.

Taking the time to look at scientific papers on the technique of the crawl stroke, one finds some pretty contrasting results even there. I basically do see myself as a science nerd, but when it comes to swimming, I must latently refuse because to me it seems too detached from the practice. Even on YouTube one can find countless tutorials on the subject, in some cases with completely opposite views.

That is also why I am not a big fan of learning or improving the crawl stroke from such videos by imitating what was shown in the video. I will therefore only address some bigger blunders that are definitely wrong, definitely impede propulsion, and thus can be called mistakes.

6.1   Swimming vs. Swimming in a Triathlon

Let's take a look at some of the differences between swimming as an individual sport and swimming in triathlon to understand swimming's specific features and demands.

6.1.1   Amount of training

An easy-to-spot difference is the amount of available training time. Next to his time in the water and general athletic and mobility training, a swimmer has no additional items on his training schedule, while a triathlete must still hop on his bike and lace up his running shoes. Hence the swimmer has more time to complete the different intensities and technical work.

A triathlete's time in the water, particularly age-group athletes, is limited so that this time must be used as effectively and productively as possible. For this reason, triathlon swim training represents more of a compromise or a definite weighing of effort and reward.

I find it problematic when in group training for triathletes a coach, who either has a background as a swimmer or has not understood the particularities and complexity of the triathlon sport, stands at the edge of the pool and doesn't recognize the differences between the sport of indoor swimming and triathlon.

6.1.2   Competition requirements

While the pool swimmer is alone in his lane, which is separated from neighboring lanes by wave breakers, the triathlete is in a completely different environment. The water is rarely as calm as in a pool, he must deal with hundreds or thousands of competitors, and must use buoys for orientation.

Wearing a neoprene suit for heat insulation changes or improves the body's position in the water and the suit's material in the shoulder region reduces mobility in that area, even if today's suits are much improved over those from the 1990s or 2000s, particularly when it comes to flexibility.

6.1.3   Physical requirements

Competitive swimmers often have a different physical appearance than triathletes. The triathlete is more muscular, especially his thighs and gluteal muscles. Elite swimmers have very long arms with a wide spread, often have short legs, and have very good mobility in shoulders, hip flexors, and ankles that they have been training since childhood.

These areas of the body are often significantly less flexible in triathletes and particularly working athletes. The ankles also require a certain amount of stiffness for cycling and even more so for running. Swimmers who at some point decide to compete in triathlon, often have ankle problems because due to their hypermobility they lack the necessary stiffness and are less able to compensate for the impact forces while running.

Shoulder and chest muscles, for instance, are permanently oriented forward (protracted) due to hours of sitting at a desk and are tight and rigid. When adding a certain number of hours spent on the aero bars in this position, it exacerbates this unfavorable posture for swimming. The same is true for the hip flexor muscles used in cycling and running.

Not without reason is everyday sitting now called the new smoking, because the negative effects on health are certainly comparable. In this context I cannot understand why age-group athletes in spring training camp with high cycling volumes want to also complete high volumes in the water during these camps and are surprised when their swim splits are slower than at home.

When the volume on the bike is drastically increased, shoulders and hip flexors complain and no longer allow fast swimming times. In my view, swim training at training camp for age-group athletes should have more of a regenerative character. Athletes who don't have the opportunity for feedback at home from a coach standing at the edge of the pool can nevertheless seize the opportunity for correction by a coach at an organized training camp.

Such units should be completed with a focus on technical training and capped at 1,500–2,500 min, depending on performance level.

6.1.4   Motion perception or a feel for the water

A swimmer with years of training and big volumes under his belt is most likely to possess a mysterious quality that probably doesn't even exist, namely the dubious water sense. Lateral entrants in triathlon with less available training time will likely struggle to develop this feeling or even just the perception of their motions, especially since, unlike in cycling and running, the ability to control movements through visualization is almost nonexistent.

In swimming we only see one small segment of the total movement, which inevitably leads to more proprioception, the awareness of the own body, to direct and control. I therefore have been asking myself this question for many years:

* Why then should a latecomer swim highly complex technical exercises he read about in magazines, books, and on internet platforms or was taught by various swim coaches?

6.2   Swimmer Types

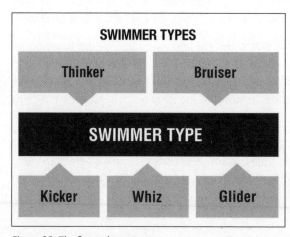

Figure 32: The five swimmer types.

Similar to the athlete types we already learned about in my personal world of triathlon coaching, there are also different triathlete types in the water. I was able to identify five different swimmer types during more than 7,000 individual hours and at least 5,000 more hours of group training on the pool deck. Classification into specific groups is in no way intended to embarrass certain athletes, but here, too, is meant to inspire self-reflection.

6.2.1　The Thinker

The Thinker tries to constantly put himself and his technique to the test. The execution of every movement is deliberate. Unfortunately, the essential idea, namely swimming fast, gets completely lost here. The Thinker is so preoccupied with swimming pretty that he is only able to swim at one pace, which unfortunately often isn't very fast.

The supposedly clean swimming techinque leads to such uptightness that his movements feel downright mechanical or robotic. The Thinker can be found predominantly, not surprisingly, in the Brooder athlete group.

MAIN MISTAKES

Stroke rate is too slow, lowering of arms above the water is too controlled, overcrossing.

6.2.2　The Bruiser

The Bruiser loves swimming with paddles and pull buoys, because that's when he can display his strength. His position in the water worsens significantly without the pull buoy because he tends to be muscular. In classic fashion, his head is high above the water, there is no rotation around the long axis of the body; he is more like a surfboard.

Many athletes in the Woodsman group swim like a Bruiser. They struggle with the alternating tension and relaxation within the arm cycle; he is permanently in the tension phase. The Bruiser greatly benefits from the neoprene suit.

MAIN MISTAKES

The head is too far out of the water, little to no arm extension after immersion, no rotation around the body's long axis.

6.2.3   The Kicker

The Kicker swims with a high kick rate. This group consists almost entirely of women.

When asked why they swim with such a high kick rate most of the female athletes say that they think they lack arm strength and try to generate propulsion with a strong kick to compensate for the allegedly missing arm strength.

MAIN MISTAKES

Extremely high kick rate (in some cases with large amplitude). The arm rate is lower than 35-38 strokes per minute. The head is too far above the water. The arm stroke is too short, often missing a push phase at the end.

6.2.4   The Glider

The Glider tries to glide through the water with as few strokes as possible and envisions an inaccurate technical model. He very often wears a watch and checks various metrics after each interval.

The Glider is primarily a member of the Counter group. He has trouble swimming at varying speeds; his pace tends to be nearly always the same.

MAIN MISTAKES

Stroke rate is much too low, too much rotation around the body's long axis, heavily emphasized and unfortunately incorrect water throwing.

6.2.5   The Whiz

Even among triathletes there are athletes who are swimmers, meaning they can perform very close to the optimal technique (whatever that looks like). This level of skill is difficult to learn as an adult. Nearly all the Whiz athletes stood out as competitive swimmers during their childhood or adolescence. For lateral entrants this ability and the corresponding skills are difficult to learn, if at all.

In my opinion, swim times faster than 51.30 minutes for men and 53.30 minutes for women in the Ironman triathlon are hardly achievable for late starters. However, as always in life, there are also exceptions. But I really do think this marker is as good as it gets for non-swimmers.

6.3   An Attempt at a Technical Definition of Swimming

Sports science attempts to create a model for the crawl stroke by including physical regularities. But the main problem is that there are no constant conditions when swimming in water, and even less so in open water.

Currents, vortexes caused by competitors, or differences in water temperature in lakes, rivers, and the ocean make these conditions even more difficult. But many theoretical approaches to swimming forget that all physical forces act continuously and simultaneously and that not just one of the acting forces alone is relevant.

The feeling of lightness tends to come from the water being a kind of support surface for the body. *Dead man float* is usually the exercise of choice to feel the support surface and promote perception.

For the opposite effect, in order to feel the effects of gravity, which is also prevalent in water, you can stand in water with your arms against your sides. This will result in quickly sinking to the bottom of the pool. Therefore, we cannot switch off this force or think it away.

In my view, in everyday training or dealing with athletes, it isn't important which theoretical construct swimming is based on. It is more about teaching comprehension of the movement that athletes can build into their ability to imagine the movement and effectively and purposefully develop a schematic to that end.

There is much debate about whether we move forward through water based on Newton's law in response to our pushing against it, or that propulsion, according to the Vortex theory, is produced with water vortexes like mini tornadoes. Here we must mentally differentiate whether the hand is pulled from front to back and according to Isaac Newton, the body responds by pushing into the swimming direction, or whether the hand remains fixed or anchored and the body moves.

In my view and in working with athletes, I think it is the latter. Everyone is familiar with the monkey bars on a playground where one moves hand over hand from one end to the other, which nowadays can also be seen in many fitness studios or CrossFit boxes. You hang unsupported by your hands from the bars and move forward hand over hand from one crossbar to the next.

I try to explain swimming as crossing one of these playground structures that rests at the bottom of a body of water. The athlete swims across the crossbars and tries to pull the horizontal body through the water with forearms and hands from crossbar to crossbar.

In my theory, swimming is the alternating anchoring or fixing of the forearms and hands on those crossbars, and the resulting gliding of the body is the propulsion.

Figure 33: Swimming across an imaginary playground structure.

But this requires accurate timing and letting go of the crossbar at just the right moment. On the crossbars at the playground or gym, the user must briefly let go of the crossbar to swing to the next one to hold one. When hanging for an extended period from two crossbars with both hands, the body stops swinging and gravity causes it to simply hang vertically and motionless.

This image brings me to the most common mistake pattern in triathlon, namely the principle and romantic notion of gliding through the water with as few arm strokes as possible. Like not moving the hands or moving them too late on the crossbars, a slow arm stroke also results in a kind of standstill. But more on that later.

Figure 34: Lack of momentum on the monkey bars.

6.4   Technical Mistakes and an Inaccurate Technical Model

I do not have a background as a youth swimmer. While I started doing triathlons relatively early in the 1990s, swim training back then was far from learning the correct technique. My swimming performance in competitions was correspondingly bad, which has always frustrated me.

Only when I analyzed my own swimming and did a cost-benefit analysis was I able to see my mistakes and correct them, if only years later. I have seen those same mistakes, and we'll get back to that in a moment, hundreds of times in the training journals of athletes or heard about them in our conversations. I felt somewhat reassured because clearly, I wasn't the only one to make those mistakes and set the wrong priorities.

This chapter is intended to provoke reflection so my mistakes which, as we already learned, aren't just mine, will not be repeated by the readers of this book.

Some readers will doubt my approaches because in recent years, the approaches to and principles of swimming published in all sorts of magazines and on internet platforms have manifested themselves almost dogmatically in the minds of some or rather many triathletes.

But I consider myself an absolute practician and my working experience with hundreds of athletes offers proof as to which principles work and lead to success, and which approaches and guidelines athletes should maybe stay away from. Of course, here, too, there is no definite right or wrong; as always, exceptions confirm the rule, meaning there are cases where changing the technique wasn't productive or could not bring success.

The reasons are not necessarily strictly physical, because not all athletes can mentally accept such a change. Some may not be intellectually able to fully comprehend the full scope of the things they desire. When an athlete doesn't accept the necessity of learning to optimize a movement technique it becomes difficult to convince him despite in my opinion, very good and plausible arguments.

Humans are just creatures of habit and don't like to relinquish their prior achievements, even when they can anticipate a performance increase. But athletes who are willing to step outside their comfort zone and try something new (i.e., are willing to innovate and adapt) will be more successful. A nice maxim here would be: He who won't diversify will stagnate.

Here are the six biggest mistakes in triathlon swimming:

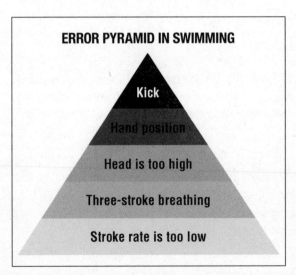

Figure 35: Error pyramid in swimming.

6.4.1 Gliding phase is too long

We'll get right to the biggest mistake. Who remembers Johnny Weissmüller? Sure, he was an actor and played Tarzan back in the 1930s. But some may know that he was a swimmer. And he wasn't just any swimmer but the first human to swim the 100 m freestyle at 58.6 seconds back in 1922, below the magic one-minute mark. A time that remains unachievable for 99% of current triathletes.

When watching video recordings of his swimming style today, four things immediately jump out:

1. He didn't wear goggles because those were only introduced to swimming in around 1970.
2. He swam with his head almost completely out of the water like a water polo player. One reason why some coaches still today call the technical drill called water polo crawl the Tarzan crawl or Tarzan drill.
3. He swam with a very high arm stroke rate.
4. He swam with a vertical forearm, also known as high elbow catch.

Through the introduction of goggles, a revolutionary moment in swimming, training volumes could be drastically increased because until then the chlorine and saltwater in the athletes' eyes had severely limited the training performances of swimmers.

When taking the first two items off the above list, because Weissmüller swam with his head above water since he lacked goggles, only items 3 and 4 remain, which can still be observed in elite swimmers 100 years later. I don't really understand why some people at some point took a wrong turn in swimming and got on the wrong track with respect to technique.

Suddenly more and more concepts were developed that heavily focused on practically gliding through the pool like a fish with as few strokes as possible and with very exaggerated rotation around the body's long axis. More and more authors of reference books and magazines jumped on the bandwagon, so that these concepts very quickly spread to a very large group of people in the triathlon realm.

The ordinary triathlete, ready to innovate, believes the promises propagated by the gliding delirium, and just like me back in the day, falls for it.

* But is it really such an outstanding concept?
* Or how can this approach be unarmed relatively easily?
* What does science say?

When I began to work as a triathlon coach back in 2004 and first immersed myself in the subject of technique, while overlooking the pool I noticed relatively quickly what the biggest difference is between triathletes and swimmers—and I don't mean the fact that swimmers unlike triathletes don't wear a watch during training.

The biggest difference lies in the number of strokes per minute or the stroke rate. I have spent many hours on a pool deck armed with a stopwatch, watching swimmers of all stripes. I have made the same observations as a spectator at triathlons while comparing the strokes of top athletes to those further behind.

I noticed that some of the slower swimmers had a stroke rate of only 36-40 strokes per minute. Top athletes have a long-distance stroke rate of 56-65 strokes per minute.

I would like to use a calculation as the first argument against excessive gliding. Let's take two fictitious swimmers. Swimmer A swims 25 m with 20 strokes and in a time of 1.6 seconds for one left and one right arm stroke. He will need 16 seconds to complete this distance. Swimmer B swims with 12 strokes, but requires 3.4 seconds, which means he will complete the distance in 20.4 seconds.

When watching swimmers with a stroke rate that is too slow, one notices some jerkiness in their forward movements. A stroke is completed, followed by too much gliding, so that the water resistance slows the swimmer down because water is approximately 800 times denser than air. Then comes the next stroke and he accelerates again. It is really a continuous deceleration and acceleration.

The deceleration factor is even more visible in open water. It would be much more effective if deceleration caused by water density could be avoided or at least minimized with a higher stroke rate to ensure uniform forward speed.

Let's use driving a car for comparison. In this example the arm stroke represents stepping on the gas pedal. The swimmer whose stroke rate is too low pushes the pedal to the floor, but then suddenly takes his foot completely off only to push it to the floor again with the next arm stroke.

I think this example illustrates quite well how much energy is wasted. Increasing the stroke rate, meaning increasing the number of strokes, would mean that the gas pedal is continuously only halfway to the floor, ergo less energy is needed.

To achieve a highly efficient gliding phase the swimmer has to get in a streamlined position like a torpedo. Here the goal is to minimize the attack surface, first and foremost the frontally flowing surface of the forehead. Water resistance increases exponentially with increasing speed. Hence an optimized forehead surface becomes increasingly important.

At least that is the theory of the over-glider, because the principle of gliding involves a very exaggerated rotation of

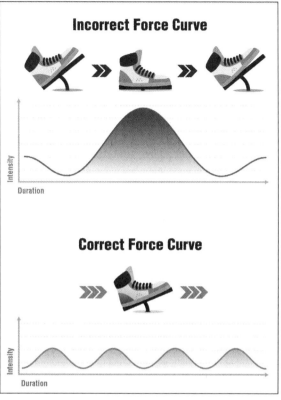

Figure 36: Force progression using the example of a gas pedal.

the body's long axis. The idea is to lever more of the body out of the water to thereby create less attack surface. But implementing this rotation requires a very strong kick to stabilize the body or to initiate or rather terminate the rotation.

As previously mentioned, most triathletes have more muscular legs than swimmers. To generate a certain amount of intensity, amplitude, and frequency, the triathlete requires more energy and oxygen for his muscular legs which within the context of long-distance triathlon, is considered rather more counterproductive because energy management, meaning the conscious budgeting of available energy sources, plays a critical role in a race.

Moreover, the question remains why swimmers have broad shoulders and distinctive latissimus dorsi muscles, much like an upside-down Christmas tree. If decreasing the forehead surface is so important, shouldn't swimmers have narrow shoulders? The increased use of sports watches in triathlete training has created a downright hype with respect to exaggerated gliding. Most manufacturers make watches that provide a value called *SWOLF*.

The term is comprised of the words *swim* and *golf*. This metric is based on the idea that a swimmer's efficiency can be quantified with it. To do so, the user enters the length of

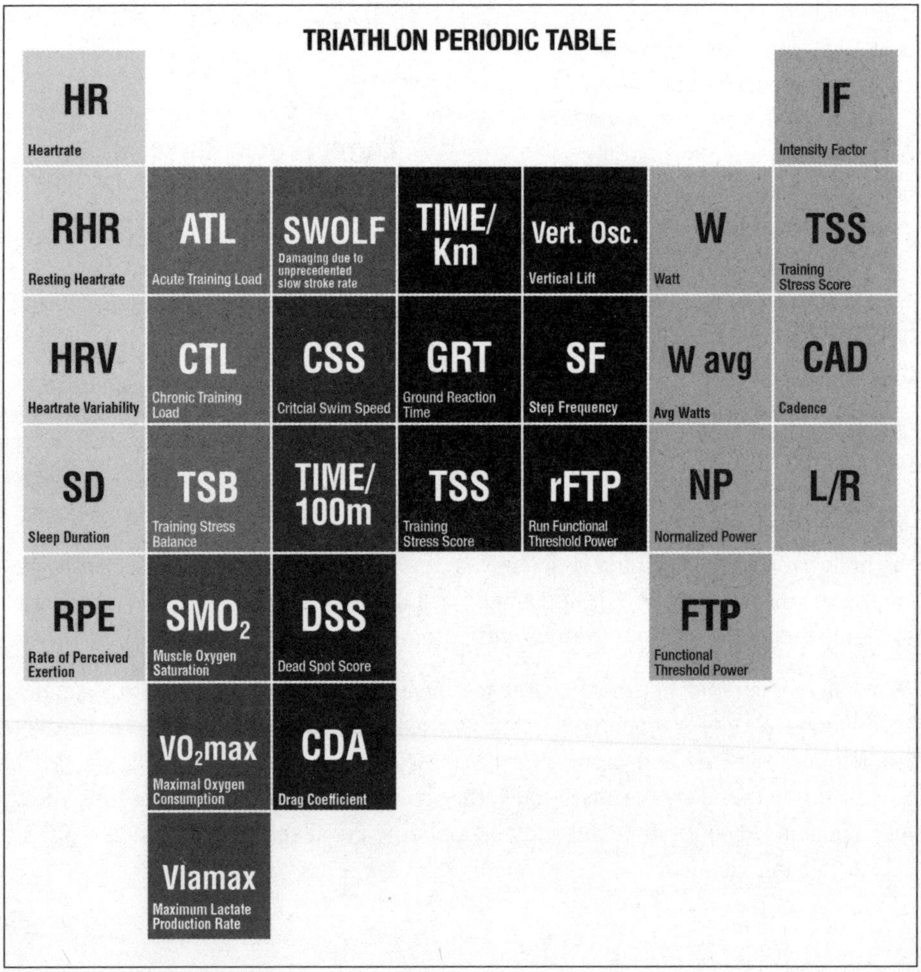

Figure 37: SWOLF.

the pool. Acceleration sensors in the watch measure the number of required arm strokes for the length of a specific lane and combine that measurement with the amount of time needed to swim that lane.

Example: If an athlete swims 25 m in 20 seconds using 20 strokes, the SWOLF score will be 40 (20 + 20).

The lower the number resulting from adding the number of strokes to the swim time, the more efficient the athlete allegedly is in his swim performance. But here is the rub, because what will most athletes take away from that? They decrease the number of strokes to lower the SWOLF score, supposedly making it better. In almost all cases they are initially able to achieve a nearly equal speed with fewer strokes, however, only for a short distance.

Swimming at the same speed with fewer strokes is so exhausting that after 100-200 m at the same stroke rate the speed significant worsens. Instead of focusing on speed these athletes continue to work on a slower stroke rate and gradually SWOLF themselves.

In my more than 30 years in triathlon, I have never seen a SWOLF counter at the water exit of an event. In my recollection, there is only a clock that captures the swimming time.

Speaking of swim time, there are five ways to improve swimming speed. Reducing the stroke rate but with a bigger stroke is one of these options but is not practicable for a 3,800 m Ironman swim because it is simply too strength sapping.

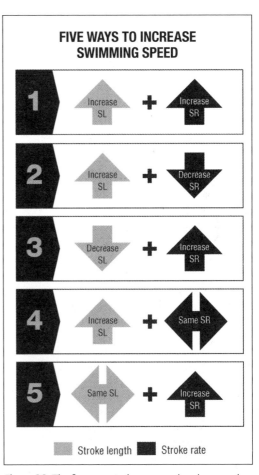

Figure 38: The five ways to increase swimming speed.

- So why should an athlete work on a swimming technique that isn't even practical in a race due to fatigue?

It would be better to train with anticipation, meaning learning the content and technical elements an athlete can expect after approximately 3,000 m of a long-distance race.

It has now been proven that deliberately decreasing the stroke rate causes an increase in oxygen demand as well as the heart rate, while simultaneously decreasing the subjective perceived exertion.

CONCLUSION

Not every measurable metric can be considered useful. To me, SWOLF therefore stands for:

S Stop
W Working
O On
L Low
F Frequency

6.4.2 Incorrect breathing rhythm

Unlike fish, who can breathe through their gills, the human as a mammal needs to get oxygen from the air to adequately supply his muscles while swimming. Therefore, oxygen uptake should be considered very important.

Breathing and especially maintaining a certain rhythm should be consciously practiced when learning to swim and should also be kept in mind later in daily training and during competitions. Here the breathing rate should be linked to the arm stroke rate. When swimming with a very slow arm stroke rate the oxygen delivery rate is also very slow and delivers less fresh oxygen to the lungs.

When the space between the inhalation movements is too long it results in successive oxygen debt and the swimming speed will continue to decrease. A higher arm stroke rate leads to a shorter inhalation interval, and therefore is very beneficial to performance for this reason, too.

One often reads that three-stroke breathing is the only correct breathing pattern. I personally think that such a sweeping statement isn't necessarily correct, because these breathing patterns depend on various factors. Even for swimmers with a high arm stroke rate, three-stroke breathing isn't automatically right.

But what are the actual reasons for the popularity of bilateral breathing?

Alternating sides for breathing surely creates a certain symmetry between the two halves of the body. One-sided breathing inevitably results in an uneven movement. For the open-water swimmer, breathing on both sides means orientation to both sides which, along with the greater symmetry, can cause him to end up away from his competitors and off the course even without deviating from the idea line.

Both arguments are valid, but I would again like to throw the performance aspect in the balance. When a swimmer uses three-stroke breathing he gets fresh oxygen twice during six arm strokes. When he breathes every two strokes, he gets a total of three breaths. Anyone reading the initial lines of the breathing segment again will understand why I am a proponent of two-stroke breathing.

A reliable oxygen supply is more important than the best swimming technique on the planet. Or in other words, what good is the best swim technique if I don't have oxygen?

Oxygen demand increases with increasing speed, which should make it quite obvious that during greater intensities an athlete should switch from three-stroke to two-stroke breathing. I maintain that athletes who swam the entire 3,800 m of a long-distance race with three-stroke breathing almost certainly swam too slow and did not meet their expectations.

This does not mean that the athlete should only be able to breathe primarily on his sweet side. It is essential that he be able to breathe on both sides, so he is able to react to the various situations during a race. This includes the sun standing low over the horizon on race morning, which, due to the very bright light can interfere with orientation. Waves on one side can also be extremely unpleasant when one can only breathe into the wave.

While the rolling start in many races has staggered the often-described washing machine right after the starting signal, some unpleasant physical contact with other participants can still occur. For instance, if an athlete can only breathe to the left, but keeps getting hit in the face or water splashed in his face by a competitor to his left, it is pretty annoying.

One last point in opposition to breathing strictly to one side is the fact that long-distance swimming while wearing a neoprene suit can cause one-side muscular issues in the low back. For instance, when an athlete breathes exclusively to the right while swimming, the area around the m. quadratus lumborum (Latin for square loin muscle) can get painfully tight, which can already become apparent during the swim or while cycling and is a performance-limiting factor.

To put it straight, this means: Someone who wants to swim fast should switch to two-stroke breathing and should be able to breathe to both sides. Three-stroke breathing can certainly be used for slow tempos during training.

It is alarming how many athletes can be seen on underwater video not breathing out through their mouth or only allowing the used-up oxygen to bubble out with very little pressure. The mouth is a bigger opening than the nostrils, and thus is better suited to effective exhalation. When exhaling under water with insufficient pressure some residual air remains in the lungs, which then reduces the amount of oxygen-rich incoming air, causing a cumulative oxygen deficit.

Due to the fact that water is denser than air the most important muscle in breathing, the diaphragm, is being particularly stressed. MRIs of swimmers show a significant increase in this muscle's cross section compared to that of non-swimmers. The better trained the diaphragm, the later it becomes fatigued, which can definitely be felt in long-distance running, because not only is the diaphragm concomitant with the breathing function, but it also has a body-erecting effect and is essential to posture and an effective running technique.

By the way, improving breathing is one reason why more and more professional cyclists use swim training as an alternative training tool. While swimming used to be frowned upon for fear of weight gain in the form of upper body muscle, today the benefits of swimming are better known and are thus valued more than additional weight due to more muscle.

6.4.3   High elbow catch

The high elbow catch refers to the vertical position of the forearm at the beginning of the pull phase. According to my technical theory, placing the forearm in a vertical position creates more surface for moving hand over hand along the monkey bars, or rather fix the arm to be able to pull the body forward more efficiently.

Since there is no real comparable movement in everyday life, many late starters or lateral entrants find learning this essential element difficult. Having trouble imagining movement and limited visual self-monitoring of the movement unfortunately don't make it any easier.

Many athletes are familiar with the term *high elbow catch* but don't really know how to convert it from theory to practice. Here I would like to offer a few tips and some assistance, if that is even possible in writing.

The basic prerequisite for ensuring clean and effective positioning of the forearm is an arm extension after immersion. To facilitate this extension the swimmer needs good to very good shoulder mobility. If mobility is already limited due to sitting at the office all day or riding a bike for hours, it becomes difficult to execute this extension after immersion.

Another factor that can prevent the extension is an above-water movement that is too slow or an active lowering of the arms that is too controlled. Swimming is a sport with cyclical character, meaning with repetitive movement sequences. Hence there is a loading phase and an unloading phase.

Unloading should occur once the arm has left the water and is moving forward in the above-water phase. This includes letting the hand, or the entire arm that is being pulled downward by gravity, splash on the water.

Swimmers from the Thinker group often try to execute immersion as actively and controlled as possible. They think of water splashing as a technical error. But when placing the arm, which was nearly straight just before immersion, above the water surface, it forms a rather long lever; deliberately slow and controlled on top of the water, it takes lots of strength and causes the shoulder muscles to get very tired.

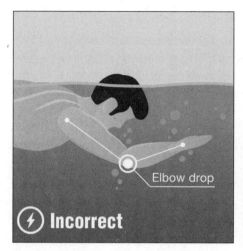

Figure 39: Elbow drop plus correct extension.

Therefore, swimmers who lower their arms actively and too slowly have less recovery time within the arm cycle and thus lack the strength of keeping the arm straight after immersion, which in turn results in the elbow dropping during the extension phase.

If during the phase of the swimming movement the elbow is lower than the hand, it is nearly impossible to move the forearm into a vertical position. Often the coaches at the edge of the pool don't see the link between correct immersion and arm extension.

Instead of initiating the correction while still above water, athletes are emphatically told to straighten the arm along with gliding, which results in the athlete quickly getting frustrated because he doesn't see any progress.

Another mistake in this context is the Moses phenomenon. One can often see triathletes' arms enter the water leading with the thumb as though they, like Moses, are trying to part the waters.

However, this type of immersion means that the water has a significantly smaller contact surface compared to entering it with the palm and the middle finger. The arm sinks more easily and more quickly which also results in a more awkward starting position for the high elbow catch.

But back to the actual forearm position. Here the arm is divided into two levers, one from the shoulder to the elbow, the second from the elbow to the wrist.

Figure 40: Wine barrel.

When the pull is initiated with the extension, the shoulder rotates inward towards the chin, the fingertips of that hand point downward, and the forearm folds down. Here forearm and hand should form one solid unit.

Many triathletes have lots of trouble fixing the wrist, and instead allow the hand to fold downward. But when the wrist remains rigid and the fingertips press downward, the elbow remains in place and the forearm and hand act as a kind of paddle. This allows the swimmer to effectively push against the water, as he is better able to fix his hand to the imaginary monkey bars.

If there is too much bend in the wrist there is a risk of it transferring to the elbow, meaning the elbow would also bend. When elbow and wrist fold, I refer to it as the ironing motion, whereby this ironing has nothing to do with the Ironman.

6.4.4 Head position

Everyone knows that winning and losing happens between the ears. But not only the contents of the head, but the head itself has an important effect on swimming.

The fact that, unlike cyclists and runners, swimmers cannot turn their head in the direction of movement is a particular challenge. Inexperienced swimmers in particular tend to look forward too much which results in the head being held too high. This lifting of the head, also called tonic neck reflex, after a while not only stresses the cervical spine, which later will be negatively affected anyway by the aerodynamic position on the time trial bike, but it also greatly affects the body's position in the water.

When the head position is too high, abdominal tension is suspended. When the head is held in the neutral position in extension of the spine, the athlete can create more tension in the abdominal muscles, which allows hips and butt to be held higher near the water surface. When the head is lifted too high and close to the nape, abdominal tension is significantly lower, and the hips sink.

Again, providing a visual here for better comprehension, one could describe the lack of abdominal tension as the pot-bellied-pig syndrome. To physically feel this mistake, do a classic sit-up or abdominal crunch with your head tilted back and for comparison do another with the head in neutral position. It should be pretty easy to feel the difference in the engagement of the abdominal muscles.

Athletes who make precisely this mistake greatly benefit from swimming with the pull buoy or a neoprene suit, because both generate buoyancy and lift the hips up higher.

Another argument for a lower head position is the fact that when the head is held correctly more of the facial portion of the skull points downward, and as a result the water provides a larger contact surface. When the head is tilted too far back the water offers little buoyancy and the neck muscles must carry the weight of the head.

Breathing also worsens when the head is held too high because the trachea is no longer as open as it should be. This is easy to demonstrate while standing on the pool deck by asking the swimmer to tilt his head far back to raise awareness of mouth breathing. He will notice how difficult it is to suck in the air in this hyperextended position.

6.4.5   Hand position

There are countless scientific studies on the subject of hand position, which I don't want to address in detail. For instance, they examined the correct space between fingers. To date, I have often noticed that many athletes hold their hands like shovels because they apparently believe that it is a better way to shovel the water from front to back. But with respect to propulsion, the hand is the most important part of the body. When the hand is held incorrectly there is no optimal pushing off the imaginary monkey bars or pushing the water back.

This should also make it very clear that the hand must remain open in order to be able to utilize the entire palm. A shovel-like hand position means less palm and contact surface, even if at first glance it looks like a marginal difference.

Athletes with a shovel-like hand position often also tend to execute the above-water phase and immersion with too much control; the hand tends to be very rigid even above water and there is very little unloading. We will come back to this characteristic in chapter 6.6.1.

6.4.6   Kick

Until just a few years ago, I had believed the kick was unimportant for triathletes. I have since then revised that opinion.

Most triathletes hate kick training, and for that reason this aspect of swimming is given little if any consideration in training.

But why is that?

Here are some arguments that are always raised in this context:

* Rigid, immobile ankles often make it impossible for the swimmer to perform an economical kick. I have seen tons of athletes who during kick training were either at a standstill or were swimming backwards!
* The time and effort are not proportional to the improved swim times.
* Heavy, rigid legs from cycling and running training.
* No kick when racing in a neoprene suit, hence practicing in training isn't necessary.
* The necessary time would be better spent developing the arm stroke.

Triathlon is one giant compromise. Rigid ankles are a must have for running in order to convert the existing forces into energy. The hypermobile ankles of swimmers are counterproductive in running. But as long as there is no medical reason for the rigid ankles, mobility can be significantly improved with regular stretching and working on the fasciae. Kick training with flippers can be a helpful tool for athletes with very rigid ankles, because the length of the flipper hyperextends the foot more intensively (caution is recommended in cases of existing foot problems and pain of the plantar fascia or the Achilles tendon).

Improving the kick will not necessarily lead to faster times right away. But when watching videos of athletes and observing their kick, one notices that a high percentage perform unorthodox movements with their legs. These incorrect movements (kick to the side, flexed feet, scissor legs, cycling motion) result in increased resistance because they are not swimming in a truly streamlined or torpedo-like position.

When the kick is optimized, these incorrect movements decrease and subsequently lead to a faster swimming speed. Even if many athletes think they will only require little to no kick in a race when wearing a neoprene suit, they will still perform the incorrect movements with a corresponding higher resistance, even if on a smaller scale.

I also don't believe that muscular legs from cycling and running automatically lead to a lower and worse leg position. It is actually the lack of mobility of the hip flexors caused by the two dry-land sports that cause a worse position of the body in the water and the leg position. Once the mobility and function of the hip flexors have been optimized the kick will improve as well.

Eight-point plan to improve the kick

1. Work on ankle and hip flexor mobility. This will take no more than five minutes a day.
2. Complete 5–10% of the total volume as kick training.
3. Start by using flippers because this will cut down on frustration and facilitate propulsion while also improving ankle mobility.
4. Kick from the hip; knee movement is insufficient.
5. Performing kick training vertically helps to get a feel for an effective kick.
6. Practicing kicks in a supine position teaches hip and whole-body extension. Moreover, you can see if the kick originates more from the knees because they will stick out of the water.
7. To start, complete 25 or 50 leg-kick series with focus on maintaining quality of movement.
8. Pay more attention to learning leg height and minimizing resistance and less on generating speed with your legs.

Beyond that, kick training really speeds up the heart rate because the working muscles of the legs are significantly larger than swimming without leg kick with a pull buoy. Kick training is tough and that is unfortunately one reason why triathletes try to avoid it. I notice time and again that when it comes to swimming, many athletes have a kind of intensity allergy. For a few athletes, being willing to step outside of their comfort zone seems to be more difficult in the water than on land.

6.5 Training

After having thoroughly immersed ourselves in swimming technique, we will now move on to the training as such. We will take a look at training content, use of different tools, and the most popular and most practicable testing methods for determining current performance capacity.

Here, too, many triathletes make some mistakes in their everyday training. They incorporate things into training that require incredible amounts of strength, time, and effort, but in the end don't yield a good return. I am aware that I am to some extent still battling existing myths and that people can certainly have different opinions on the subject.

6.5.1 Technical training

We always hear how important technical training is in swimming. The list of technical exercises to improve the crawl technique alone would probably exceed the content of this book, but hold on a second.

- Does it have to be that way?
- What is this really about?

Despite its complex technique and water being a different medium, at the end of the day swimming is still an aerobic sport. So why the excessive motor and technical training?

In cycling and running, one or two technical training units a week is sufficient, but according to some magazines and coaches, in the water there should be lots of training content with emphasis on improving technique.

I so often see athletes attending group or club training three times a week, where they complete heavily technical training and leave the pool after an hour, but with only 1,800-2,200 m volume. Unfortunately, those are also the athletes that are very dissatisfied with their swimming performance in a competition, in spite of having spent a lot of time on swim training in the run-up.

Those athletes simply swim too few strokes in the run-up and during a competition tend to swim 2,500 pretty well but lose lots of time or many places over the final third of the course. The swim course is approximately 3,800 m long and requires 3,500–3,900 arm strokes. Anyone who hasn't sufficiently trained his cardiovascular system as well as muscles and strength, will experience his personal Waterloo in a race.

When an athlete gets tired, his technique will simply fall apart and he will lose tons of speed. I therefore wonder why so much emphasis is placed on technique when in the end it won't matter if there is a lack of swimming fitness. As previously mentioned, triathletes do not have the same abilities and skills as strictly swimmers, especially if the triathlete only learned the crawl as an adult.

Such an athlete is completely overchallenged by the highly complex technical exercises. He either lacks the physical prerequisites or doesn't understand why which techniques must be practiced. Some athletes also don't know or understand the purpose of some of these technical exercises. But an uninformed athlete will only conditionally achieve the quality of movement essential to the implementation of some of these drills.

And if the athlete's time budget for training or even just for swimming is heavily regimented it is important that he prioritizes specifically how the available training time could be put to optimal use, meaning increasing the return on investment *(ROI)*.

Analogous to athletic training, which includes increasingly more circus-like or artistic content, I tend to be a fan of the basics. I frequently get the impression that working on the basics is rather frowned upon today and is often overcomplicated while losing sight of the essentials. Coaches who want their athletes to know the basics are considered backward looking or less innovative. To me the following technical exercises are totally sufficient when working with long-distance athletes.

6.5.1.1 Single-arm swimming

In my opinion, single-arm swimming, when executed cleanly, is the most important technical exercise because here the swimmer has the opportunity to implement individual technical elements consciously and in a controlled manner. I prefer the version with the extended arm in front of the head to simultaneously work on body extension.

Beyond technical training, single-arm swimming offers another important component. By reducing propulsion to one arm, the underwater pull speed is significantly faster, which will automatically increase propulsion speed later when swimming with both arms. Single-arm swimming can be enhanced with paddles, a pull buoy and strap, a combination of those, or separately.

6.5.1.2 Hand-over-hand swimming

Hand-over-hand swimming, or catch-up, to me is the continuation of single-arm swimming towards swimming in full position. It is alternating single-arm swimming with breathing on alternate sides.

6.5.1.3 Fist swimming

With this technique the palm surface is deliberately reduced to create less contact area on the hand and force the vertical position of the forearm. Here the thumb should be tucked under the fingers, something one should never do in a fight because the thumb would break when throwing a punch.

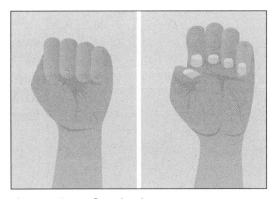

Figure 41: Correct fist swimming

But athletes often only bend the fingers at the second phalange and the palm remains open. In this context I would call that a cheat fist.

6.5.1.4   Breaststroke arms and crawl legs

Combining these two strokes has a positive effect on an even kick. Some athletes swim with a four-beat kick, allowing a pause between several kicks during which the legs sag. A continuous kick is critical to maintaining a good body position in the water so the legs don't sag.

6.5.1.5   Streamline drill

The streamline drill promotes full extension of the body and is performed after every turn. Here the arms should be as straight as possible, one hand resting on top of the other, and the head is an extension of the spine between the shoulders. Hips are extended, gluteal muscles are taut, and the feet are hyperextended.

To me this drill is a kind of bonus yoga class because it works on mobility. By getting into a streamlined position while also vigorously pushing off the wall, the swimming speed is very fast at the start of the lane, and the body is positioned for the high elbow catch.

Figure 42: Streamline drill.

6.5.1.6   Swimming with paddles and pull buoy

You read correctly. Paddles and the pull buoy are also implements that, when used correctly, will have a correcting effect, as we will see in chapter 6.6.

ANECDOTE

In my view, that's all that's needed in terms of technical training. I sometimes must chuckle when I watch triathletes train.

Often, an athlete will dig out a sheet of paper to look up the next technical exercise. Sometimes you can practically see the question mark above his head. After 50 m, the spectacle repeats itself, so that in the end the athlete swam many different drills but has practically overdosed on technique and is completely overwhelmed.

6.5.2   Other strokes

This segment is not intended for the accomplished swimmer. So, anyone who learned to swim as a child can move along because you are probably already able to swim all four strokes. But everyone else should read the following lines.

You often hear that practicing the other strokes (breast, back, and butterfly) promotes coordination and thus would be beneficial to swimming the primary stroke in triathlon, the crawl.

What would be the advantage of swimming medleys when the triathlete has barely mastered the crawl?

In the Ironman triathlon it is not a requirement to swim at the 3,200-m mark with a pretty backstroke or butterfly. From a psychological and motivational perspective, swimming the butterfly, for a late entrant for instance, would be nothing but frustration. He simply cannot do it, feels bad, and increasingly loses interest in swimming if the coach on the pool deck or the training plan regularly calls for this stroke.

To me it's simply a waste of time instead of long-distance training. Exceptions would be warming down or active recovery during tough series. But in all my years, I have never seen a triathlete swim butterfly for active recovery because with a bad technique it is simply too strenuous. I would probably also avoid the breaststroke as the lateral kick stresses the knees.

I would pass, particularly during a phase with lots of running and cycling training, to avoid further stress on the knees. By contrast the backstroke offers two definite advantages that can be beneficial. One, it opens the shoulders with the contrarotating backward arm movement, and two, it promotes better hip and whole-body extension.

6.5.3   Intensities and pause lengths

The subject of training tempo is in some cases unnecessarily overcomplicated. Since swimming is part of the complex interplay of three different sports that impact each other, to me defining certain training intensities in triathlon is only conditionally practicable. Daily form plays an important role here. I will reduce and simplify swim training into four areas of training:

- Slow or easy
- Mid-tempo or Ironman pace
- Fast or brisk
- All-out sprint or full throttle

Example: If an athlete spent five hours on the bike the previous day and is supposed to swim 20 x 100 m in the BE 1 range the next day, and this BE 1 means a tempo of 1:35 min/100 m, the energy expenditure to achieve this speed is potentially completely different than during a training without the previous load from cycling. When chest muscles and hip flexors are strained from the previous day the athlete must add significantly more intensity in this situation to compensate for his inferior daily form.

I therefore prefer division by subjective criteria, as described above. The athlete trains subjectively according to the specification; the times he swam are then secondary. I thereby try to ensure that the athlete loads correctly and doesn't drift into another training zone because he absolutely has to meet the specified time. If the athlete from the above example loaded correctly but ends up swimming a tempo of 1:40 min/100 m, I consider that more important to the long-term training development than achieving 1:35 minutes at any cost, meaning with a different exertion.

On a different day, 1:35 min/100 m might be too slow because the athlete has all the necessary makings for a successful swim (i.e., he would have performed below his potential) and in this case would not have trained hard enough.

Moreover, many triathletes have trouble varying their training tempo. I see it again and again when I stand on the pool deck and the instructions are 100 m slow, 100 m mid-tempo, and 100 m fast. With some age-group athletes the answer is less than three seconds between the slow and the fast 100, but they have no real feel for the tempo in the water and are only conditionally able to meet specified times.

In swimming the principle of interval training with fixed starting times, for instance 40 x 50 m with a start every 60 seconds, has been used for many years now. That means the athlete must swim 50 m in under 60 seconds and then calculates the pause length from the difference between 60 seconds and the time he actually swam. This principle works well with athletes who can precisely define their current performance level, but it rarely works for the vast majority of athletes, especially beginners, because they

- have trouble assessing their current performance level;
- lack a feel for tempo; and
- do not vary their tempo, but tend to swim at a consistent speed.

The above session can also be completed for different reasons. For instance, to improve endurance one should swim at a slow tempo with a short pause. Those who want to swim hard and improve their speed or stamina should take a longer pause.

But as previously mentioned, swimming very much depends on daily form. After a hard day at work, a poor night's sleep, or simply being tired from the day before, swimming with fixed starting times can be a disaster because in order to stick to the starting times one might train completely past the original training goal.

At this point, I would like to come back to our fictitious athlete. He capable of swimming 1:30 min/100 m as his intermediate time in the Ironman triathlon, meaning 57 minutes.

On a normal day, slow for him means 1:35 min/100 m, medium 1:30 min/100 m, fast 1:25 min/100 m, and all out 1:20 min/100 m. On a different day he is so tired that all his times are approximately five seconds slower per 100 m. Some athletes swim 3–5 seconds per 100 m slower in the early morning than they do in the evening because their biorhythms won't allow anything else.

If the plan called for 10 x 100 m all out with starts every 1:40 min/100, he would on a bad day swim 1:30 min/100 instead of the 1:25 min/100 m, but would also have five fewer seconds pause, which doesn't work at all for him in his poor training condition, and he would thereby have missed the training goal.

I therefore think it would be much more beneficial if the starting times were replaced with fixed pauses so the athlete can swim the intervals according to his daily condition, meaning he is able to convert the correct pause length.

When observing triathletes during swim training it is apparent that their breathing often returns to normal very quickly during interval pauses and they rarely swim outside their comfort zone (i.e., swim really hard). Here the mistake lies in the to some extent incorrectly chosen length of the intervals, as is described in the next paragraph.

6.5.4   Length of legs

As I already mentioned, swimming is an aerobic sport, but that doesn't mean that athletes should use the continuous method like in running or cycling (i.e., not swimming x time at a stretch).

ANECDOTE

Here is an anecdote from a coach's workday:

In the past, I was able to watch a triathlete every Monday at 1 pm swim 3,800 m in one stretch, but he never improved over the years.

The reason was almost certainly that he never swam faster than that easy tempo, but also that his technique worsened the farther he swam. Back then I asked him why he didn't swim intervals.

His response was that the pauses destroy the endurance stimulus and that after all he doesn't pause in a race and he needs to practice swimming the entire 3,800 m.

So, I asked him if he also runs a marathon once a week in training, to which he responded no.

But performance development in swimming greatly depends on the intensities an athlete swims and on maintaining the technique. Both are elements that in long-distance swimming get progressively worse over time due to fatigue.

When asking athletes if they prefer swimming 3 x 1000 m with one-minute pauses or 30 x 100 with 15 second pauses, most will opt for the 1000 m intervals. But swimming development requires speed and a correct technique combined with optimal body extension. These elements are more easily realized when swimming shorter distances where speed and technical focus is more likely than on longer legs.

The pause after each 100 m interval ensures that the quality of the subsequent interval can be just as high. The pause between intervals is brief to provide a continuous metabolic stimulus.

Many athletes are downright afraid of swimming shorter legs because they think they will then be unable to swim 3.8 km in one stretch on race day. That fear can be alleviated, because longer legs in open water should be built into the training program at the appropriate time.

When an athlete clearly communicates this concern or has never completed such a distance without a break, I generally have him swim 3,800 m in the pool 5-8 weeks before race day. Here it is less about the training effect and more about self-confidence and inner strength.

My preferred distances are between 25 and 200 m. One set of 80 x 50 m or 15 x 200 m can be part of the plan just as much as a session of 100-200 x 25 m.

6.5.5 Fewer variations

As already mentioned in the segment about technical training, I always see athletes constantly referring to pages of lengthy programs with very different exercises at the edge of the pool during training.

I am a big fan of the keep it simple principle. A plan should be structured simply enough that an athlete can read the program prior to training and is able to commit it to memory. Constantly looking at the plan is distracting and disrupts training. Simple series with simple tasks are more likely to produce the desired effect than highly complex units.

Constant repetition of intervals creates the necessary focus without distraction. Anyone who has swum an 80 x 50 m series knows how challenging it is to be faced with that mountain at the start of a training session.

Such swim sessions make sure the athlete's mind stays in the moment, an essential part of a race. Someone who constantly thinks about what still lies ahead is likely doomed to fail more so than the athlete who is present in the moment and ensures that precisely that moment goes as well as possible. I will come back to this idea later in chapter 12.

Monotonous series or training units have nothing to do with a lack of creativity from the coach, nor do they result from his reluctance to create a more complex program. They have a specific purpose, namely the conditioning of abilities needed during a race (i.e., strokes and mental strengths).

Another important point is that the continuous repetition of crawl intervals also generates improvements in swimming technique and economy.

CONCLUSION

Dull trumps!

6.5.6   Structure of a swim workout

When taking a closer look at the speeds in long-distance triathlon it quickly becomes apparent that there is precisely one moment within the entire 226 km when an athlete has a certain amount of freshness and speed, and that's at the start of the swim. The rest of the course is more of a battle against growing fatigue. But since all participants are fresh at precisely that moment, this intensity is further exponentiated.

In addition to the freshness of competitors there is a highly stressful moment due to the aptly named washing machine, meaning that many swimmers start the race in a small area. The athlete should be adequately prepared for exactly that moment to process the high intensity of the starting swim speed and stress.

There is plenty of evidence that a swimmer can achieve very fast swim times when he is able to get a fast start and then swim in a faster group to take advantage of the water shadow of the swimmers in front of him.

But when looking at training plans from magazines and some other coaches it becomes apparent that they tend to be based on the same pattern. The plan begins with warm-up swimming followed by the technical block, some longer legs, and towards the end a few sprints or units with higher intensities.

By now it should have sunk in that such a structure does not necessarily work. When working on intensity at the beginning of the session the athlete automatically learns to keep on swimming through the signs of fatigue resulting from these segments, just like later in a race. I would therefore suggest the following sequence:

- Warm-up swim
- Short legs at high intensity
- Longer legs
- Strength endurance with paddles and pull buoys
- Warm-down swim

The warm-up can be eliminated in the run-up to a race and the athlete can start directly with a fast tempo. The reason for this approach is that some races don't offer an opportunity for a warm-up prior to the starting gun. Athletes can do a warm-up on land with a pull rope, but often still end up waiting at the edge of the water for the start.

But intensity can still be deliberately built in towards the end of a training when the athlete wants to complete a cycling unit right after swimming, either as a combination unit or temporally separated. Here the idea is to get on the bike with Jell-o legs to simulate race conditions. But in this case athletes should skip the warm-down after the intervals and begin bike training as soon as possible.

6.6 Training Tools

Within a triathlon, swimming is the discipline that requires the least amount of money. Compared to purchasing a bike or different pairs of running shoes, the financial investment in swim training is relatively minor. One doesn't necessarily need anything other than goggles and swimming attire.

But there are some useful tools that, when used correctly, can facilitate an immense performance increase. In this segment, I would like to dispel some myths regarding this topic, explain the pros and cons of some tools, and familiarize readers with their use in training.

Some only-swimmers are amused by the net bag of some triathletes, because it is often filled to the top with implements and looks more like Santa's bag of toys. The following segments explain why it doesn't have to be that full.

6.6.1   Paddles

No other tool is so controversial. Why is that?

Paddles of all kinds have been used in swimming for several decades. Their original purpose was to develop strength abilities via a larger push surface. But paddles have value beyond that form of training.

To me paddle training is technical training. Paddles are often associated with shoulder problems. So how does that fit together?

As we already learned in the content about technical mistakes, when it comes to propulsion, the hand is the most important part of the body. An open palm (i.e., not a shovel) provides several square millimeters additional surface area to push the water back. I continue to wonder why many of the manufacturers' product designers purposefully integrate the convex shovel shape into their paddles.

Based on what I know about biomechanics, that does not make sense because it suggests to the swimmer that he should also hold his hand like a shovel. A paddle with a straight surface is much more conducive to an open-hand position.

In some cases, the position of the fastening straps is also poorly chosen because the hand can be held in only one position. The back closure of the paddle should extend to or beyond the wrist, so the swimmer gets tactile feedback if he folds his wrist at the beginning of the stroke. The back edge would thereby touch the pulse area and send a signal that the elbow has gone up and the forearm should be vertical. When the paddle has too little surface area at the back end, this technique-improving effect is eliminated.

Hence a paddle, no matter its design, should be put on in a way that the fingertips are aligned with the front edge of the paddle to provide as much plastic as possible at the back edge. Athletes who struggle with the high elbow catch can improve their high elbow catch with this tactile stimulus.

When the paddle is used as a technical tool, it makes the athlete aware of the engagement of the latissimus dorsi, the large and wide back muscle. The size of the paddle is not based on the size of the athlete's hand but depends on the athlete's performance level in the water. Hence beginners swim with smaller paddles than experienced swimmers. Since this level can certainly change over the course of the season, purchasing two sets of different-sized paddles is a reasonable investment.

Some coaches promote the use of finger paddles because they allegedly provide a better feel for the pressure against the palms, resulting in improved perception. But here again, a cost-benefit analysis is in order because I see time and again how finger paddles tend to promote breaking at the wrist instead of preventing it. To me as a pragmatist, the stiffness and the corresponding vertical placement of the forearm have significantly more impact on propulsion than feeling the water against the palm. Interestingly finger paddles are used primarily by women and athletes in the Brooder group.

In addition to classic paddles and finger paddles there are many other special types whose acquisition is not necessary. Paddles with a fin on the bottom are supposed to prevent straight immersion and hand tilt during the stroke. But this corrective measure can also be achieved by wearing classic paddles with a straight surface and only the front strap, meaning foregoing a snug fit of the paddle at the wrist.

Paddle models with an extension in the form or a forearm fulcrum are intended to prevent bending the wrist, an effect one can also achieve with correctly worn classic paddles. The wedge shape of anti-stroke or negative paddles is intended to reduce resistance as compared to the normal palm (i.e., promote the conscious vertical elbow placement to generate propulsion via the reduced surface). But the same effect can easily be produced without tools by simply swimming with closed fists.

Paddle swimming is a major power reserve but should be built into training cautiously. I recommend starting with 25 or 50 m legs with an adequate pause so the shoulder muscles can adapt to the increased exertion slowly and without overloading.

CONCLUSION

One appropriate paddle model is enough. You don't need 27 different types in your net bag.

6.6.2   Pull buoy

Swimming with a pull buoy means arm swimming (i.e., consciously eliminating the kick). When looking at the primary importance of the kick in a triathlon it is not propulsion but rather the height of the legs. The kick stabilizes the body's position in the water and facilitates a horizontal position resulting in a smaller front surface.

When the kick has been eliminated the pull buoy takes over this buoyancy function. But most pull buoys used in training are simply too small and offer much too little buoyancy. Often, they are also too wide.

When the pull buoy provides too little buoyancy the swimmer's legs are lower in the water than the upper body. But a horizontal position is necessary to ensure an effective starting situation for a proper vertical forearm position.

TIP

If the swimmer is low in the back, the high elbow catch is out of whack.

Some pull buoy models are so wide in the middle that virtually no muscle tension in the gluteal muscles and hip flexors is necessary to keep them in place. But this muscle tension is essential to ensuring an effective leg height even without the pull buoy.

TIP

When the pull buoy is nice and narrow, you're swim will be like an arrow.

Swimmers with an inferior body position in the water have the option of using air-filled pull buoys made of hard plastic as these offer the most buoyancy. They are rather counterproductive for swimmers with a proper horizontal position as they give the sensation of the legs floating below the ceiling and the upper body being too low.

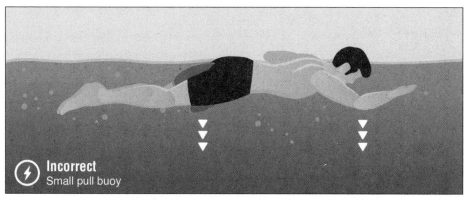

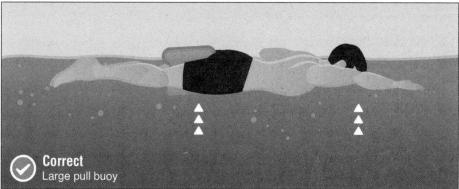

Figure 43: Small vs. large pull buoy.

6.6.3 Band or ankle strap

Pull buoys are wonderful because they promote a good body position in the water. Paddles let the swimmer know right away when he needs to put pressure on the water as they increase a sense of efficiency in the water.

But everyone hates swimming with an ankle strap. There is often a certain amount of ignorance about the use of ankle straps.

* What is it?
* What is it for?
* What does it do?
* Where can I get one?

The basic ankle strap is underappreciated by a large number of triathletes and ranks among the least liked swimming tools because swimming with an ankle strap is hard and intense. Many athletes don't even make it halfway through the pool before deciding: "This is not for me!"

That's because at first glance swimming with a strap feels quite humbling. The first time you wrap a strap around your ankles you feel like you are going to drown, because when the legs are tied together, they sink quite a bit.

But consciously accepting an inferior body position in the water can be very helpful. When starting to swim with a band you will notice that your butt and legs are nearly vertical. It feels terrible and inefficient and is a total waste of energy.

The reason is that tying the feet together eliminates the balancing effect of and propulsion from the kick. This causes the upper body to sink deeper in the water, so the swimmer's body is in a worse position in the water.

Once the swimmer has struggled to survive the first couple lanes and realized that he won't necessarily drown, he should nevertheless carry on and start pushing the T into the water.

The T is the intersection of the trunk's vertical center line and the horizontal line that runs from shoulder to shoulder. To swim more efficiently with an ankle strap, the swimmer must exaggerate the motion of pushing chest and shoulders into the water.

It feels unnatural, which requires some getting used to, but as soon as the swimmer has developed a feel for it, he is on his way to achieving a better position in the water. As soon as the swimmer can put pressure on the water with his upper body, he

Figure 44: T-line

will also do it when he is swimming without the strap, which will subsequently result in some pleasant surprises because the body's position in the water improves significantly.

The use of the strap forces the muscles of the trunk to work harder to connect the upper and lower half of the body. The ability to feel and learn to view the body as one unit consisting of upper and lower body improves significantly.

When swimming with a strap, rotation around the body's long axis will increasingly improve. To rotate while wearing the strap, trunk, hips, and legs must rotate simultaneously and at the same speed, much like a piece of meat on a spit.

The basic ankle strap is a brilliant tool for making balance and rotation errors visible. In contrast to the tools that allow the athlete to swim relatively normally, the ankle strap clearly requires more concentration.

I so often see that the strap helps to synchronize the timing between rotation and pull arm so much so that the athlete might even swim more than one unit. This connection between upper and lower body also reduces the frequently seen mistake of snaking leg movement. Ultimately the increased resistance caused by sinking butt and legs is a fantastic type of swimming-specific strength training.

Using the strap is worth it and its benefits cannot be argued away. For many athletes swimming with a strap means clearly stepping outside their comfort zone where, as we know, not much success happens. An old bicycle inner tube tied in a loop is totally sufficient. No need to buy special straps.

The loop should be tight enough to prevent any leg movement. The valve should be removed. Don't laugh, but I have seen swimmers with a valve in their inner tube finish their swim training with bloody ankles.

Another alternative would be to cut a piece off the legs of a neoprene suit. Two to three inches (5–8 cm) should be enough and can be cut off most suits to make taking it off at a race easier. The cut-off piece works well as a strap and doesn't have to be thrown away.

Forgetting the strap at home, deliberately or accidentally, is no reason to forgo its effect. Crossing the legs achieves a similar effect. Here is a quick tip for all those who think the coach at the edge of the pool can't see if the legs don't remain crossed; I am sorry to disappoint the readers, but you can actually see it quite well.

6.6.4 Snorkel

The biggest advantage of swimming with a snorkel is that it eliminates the head movement for breathing. Particularly athletes who primarily breathe on their sweet side or rather stick to just one side for breathing, benefit greatly because the swimming movement becomes more even, imbalances don't develop, and a bilateral comparison shows symmetry.

Breathing that is too unilateral and the resulting one-sided loading, often causes swimmer's shoulder. Several careers have been cut short by the effects of swimmer's shoulder, which is why this issue should be taken seriously.

A snorkel helps to process the occurring forces evenly and more equally on both sides. Symmetry (if there even is such a thing in the human body) within the movement usually also results in more speed.

One of the most common mistakes in the crawl stroke is that the swimmer tilts his head too far back and looks too far ahead. This causes the legs or rather hips to sink, resulting in a worse body position in the water. This unnatural position puts stress on the neck, on top of most modern people already suffering from smart-phone-related neck pain.

When considering the head position on the subsequent bike ride with the aero bars, holding the head in a neutral position while swimming becomes even more important. Neutral means that the head is an extension of the spine, meaning the gaze is more downward than forward. Forward orientation is a human behavior that must be broken in swimming. A snorkel can significantly improve the head position.

Many athletes continuously turn their head side to side while swimming and afterwards complain of feeling seasick. The snorkel helps to keep the head steady and the athlete learns that propulsion isn't generated by rolling the head from side to side, but with the hip rotation. And this takes us to the next point, namely improving rotation of the body's long axis.

An unfortunately common mistake made when swimming the crawl in triathlon is a lack of or a delayed rotation of the body's long axis or too much rotation, which is promoted in some swimming concepts with low stroke counts. The pig-on-a-spit phenomenon, a chronologically synchronized rotation around an axis without moving side to side, generally occurs when the head remains still due to the snorkel and the gaze is fixed on a point at the bottom of the pool.

The swimmer learns to consciously engage his trunk muscles and allow the swimming movement to be initiated in the hips so he can perform each stroke with more power. In swimming we can only see one brief segment of the movement at a time. By using the snorkel and thereby eliminating the head movement, the athlete can significantly expand his ability to observe his own actions in the water.

Many athletes report that only after wearing a snorkel have, they been able to consciously see what their hands, forearms, and elbows do underwater. It makes it easier to consciously control some technical exercises and execute them with more precision, making them more significant and improving the quality. Warming up with the snorkel is often beneficial so the individual technical characteristics can be mentally solidified, and the athlete is then able to swim the main portion with better quality of movement.

Kick training is not something most triathletes enjoy doing. This is due to, on the one hand, a lack of mobility, and on the other hand, that they continue to hear that kick is not necessary in triathlon. And when they use a kickboard for kick training and the upper body position is a lot higher than the legs, making the body's position in the water even worse, many triathletes can't make any progress and the frustration mounts.

When using a snorkel, the body position improves significantly because the hips are higher, and there is a much better chance that propulsion increases and movements are more relaxed. Here the athlete can consciously extend the arms to get into a streamlined position, or alternatively place the arms against the sides (corpse drill) to markedly improve hip rotation during the kick.

Athletes who suffer from shoulder pain or have very limited shoulder range of motion can do pain-free kick training for the first time, because resting the arms on the board generally causes shoulder pain.

In recent years, while standing at the edge of the pool, I have often observed swimmers exhaling into the water very gingerly. The use of a snorkel gives the swimmer greater acoustic awareness of the air circulating in the tube; flow noise can be heard much better when swimming with a snorkel.

Breathing through a thin tube forces stronger contraction of the main respiratory muscle, the diaphragm. The stronger the diaphragm, the slower respiration fatigues not only during swimming but also on land. For this reason, triathletes should not have a half-hearted approach to swimming and view it as a necessary evil, because swimming offers clear advantages for cycling and running.

When adding a snorkel adapter to deliberately narrow the tube, one can easily conduct hypoxia training. Athletes swimming with less oxygen will swim slower (i.e., stay cooler), when intervals are slower than normal. It is recommended to use a nose clip with a snorkel because when swimming with a snorkel, swimmers often automatically breathe in through the nose.

But since, unlike swimming without a snorkel, the head is in the water while inhaling, the swimmer will suction a ton of water and flood the sinus cavities. So, the snorkel is helpful for warm-up swims, for some technical exercises, or even low-intensity series with increased technical focus but, as previously mentioned, can also be used for hypoxia training.

6.6.5   Metronome

A metronome (e.g., Tempo Trainer by Finis) is helpful when an athlete erroneously believes in a low stroke rate and has trouble with the technical implementation of a higher stroke rate.

The user sets it to a specific stroke rate and then sticks the metronome under his swim cap. The device emits an acoustic signal for every arm stroke, so the swimmer is encouraged to swim a higher rate. The athlete can ascertain the stroke-rate setting by swimming a stroke-rate ladder, more on which can be found in chapter 6.7.

The Tempo Trainer also has a time setting to improve the sense of pace and tempo. For instance, if the athlete plans to swim 200 m intervals in 3:00 minutes, the 50 m intermediate time is 45 seconds. In this case there is an acoustic signal every 45 seconds, letting the swimmer know if he is too fast or too slow.

To me the Tempo Trainer is a much more effective tool than a smart watch, because it gives immediate feedback without the distraction of having to look at the watch.

For some time now, swim goggles have been on the market that track speed and other metrics while swimming. I was a bit skeptical and think that continuous monitoring of these metrics is less likely to develop a sense of tempo than the acoustic method of the Tempo Trainer. But after trying these goggles, I changed my mind because you get details about stroke rate and speed while swimming, which can improve the feel for different swim speeds.

6.6.6   Stretch cord

Stretch cord training can be completed during phases without water access (business trips, pool closures, etc.) as dryland training, but can certainly be incorporated into regular swim training.

Here the athlete should differentiate between four basic purposes.

6.6.6.1   Warm-up

For logistical reasons some triathlons don't have an area available for a warm-up swim. The stretch cord can be used for preparation and warm-up to prepare the swimming-specific muscles for the impending competition workload.

A Thera-band has the advantage of taking up less space compared to a full stretch cord with integrated paddle and therefore fits more easily in the event backpack. But the Thera-band offers a range of warm-up exercises for use before routine everyday swimming (in pool and open water).

6.6.6.2   Technical training

For most late or lateral entrants in triathlon who did not learn the crawl stroke at their mother's breast, the vertical elbow position is the biggest technical challenge. And when the swim coach's frequent calls for a high elbow are misinterpreted and the above-water phase, meaning the upsweep phase, becomes the focus in the swimmer's mind, the whole thing just gets worse.

I think at least 60% of triathletes think that "high elbow" refers to the above-water phase and not the vertical forearm position under water.

Stretch cord training is a very good option for learning this complex motor process called high elbow catch, which is not like any other movement in everyday life. When the water, and therefore the breathing-related stress, is eliminated, the athlete is better able to visually monitor or learn the movement. Standing directly in front of a mirror can make visual monitoring easier.

6.6.6.3   Improving strength abilities

Strength training or rather strength-endurance training is defined as moving approximately 50% of the maximum resistance that must be overcome. But since a stretch cord cannot provide that amount of resistance, the athlete should refer to strength-oriented training (analogous to strength units on the bike). In the end the name really doesn't matter, but stretch cord training in the water with an emphasis on strength endurance and power endurance is highly effective.

6.6.6.4   Cardiovascular training

Cardiovascular training with the appropriately high number of repetitions and low resistance should only be recommended when an athlete has no access to pools or lakes for several weeks.

I think that resistance that is too low only partially promotes activation of the correct crawl stroke muscles and can even be counterproductive when the long series causes the athlete to lose the focus on technique.

As a triathlete one has the great advantage of generating cross-transfer training effects from the other two disciplines for metabolism and cardiovascular system, and therefore can certainly neglect this version of cardio.

6.6.6.5   Equipment

The aforementioned Thera-band is the simplest version of a stretch cord. Athletes who do dryland training not just as a warm-up but would like to add it to their regular training would be better served with a system with a hand strap or preferably a paddle. These systems are much sturdier, the rubber tears less often, and a paddle facilitates technically correct movement execution because the hand remains open and doesn't close into a fist. All three models are available in varying resistance levels, but that presents another big problem.

Many athletes use bands with too much resistance, based on the motto "no pain, no gain," that don't allow a clean technique. Particularly in the beginning, I recommend choosing a band the athlete is still able to barely pull up during the final 10 repetitions in a series of 30.

Since I believe that the primary focus in stretch cord training should be on learning the correct high elbow catch, I have another argument against the use of bands with too much resistance. When using medium-resistance bands, depending on the intended purpose, it is easier to vary the resistance by varying the distance between one's body and the stretch cord's point of attachment. Here it is helpful to mark the spot of the correct distance on the floor to be able to find it again at the next training.

Athletes with a smaller time budget or less access to pools can maintain their level through stretch cord training. In the run-up to a race one can always build in a dry brick session, transitioning from swimming to cycling. Here stretch-cord training is completed immediately prior to cycling while already wearing cycling attire to get on the bike in as little changeover time as possible with prefatigued arms, thereby simulating a race situation. But I would skip wearing cycling shoes because the pedal plate on the cycling shoe positions the forefoot considerably higher than the heel.

Adding bent-over stretch-cord exercises will create a definite strain on the low back, gluteal muscles, and hamstring. But static stretches, as this position suggests, should be avoided prior to actual training because it diminishes muscle tension too much, resulting in sub-optimal muscle performance in the subsequent bike training.

6.6.6.5.1   Starting position

I recommend attaching the band or cord about 4 inches (10 cm) above hip level. When the band is attached too high, the muscle groups used specifically in swimming in a horizontal position aren't properly engaged. When the band is attached too low, it causes low-back problems for many athletes because their ability to hold that pose is limited.

I prefer a standing position with both feet on a level. An astride position is also possible, but here the knees should be slightly bent. The upper body is bent forward so the back is in the line of pull.

As previously mentioned, the cord is not clenched in the hand, rather the hand needs to remain open and should be an extension of the forearm without breaking at the wrist.

6.6.6.5.2 Pull assessment

During the entire pulling motion, the fingertips point downward, elbows are raised, and the cord is pulled until the arms are fully extended. I am not a fan of single-arm pulling and prefer to pull with both arms because in my opinion activation of the latissimus dorsi is less precise during single-arm pulls. After extension the cord is returned to the starting position in a controlled movement.

We can often see athletes or programs that divide stretch-cord training into the individual pulling elements (i.e., putting the focus on the catch and only performing the initial third of the pull) or consciously focus on the rear press phase.

I prefer pulling across the entire range of motion and feel that I am getting a better grinding-in of the motion into my motor memory. Of course, one can focus on just a segment of the movement, but should ideally always pull across the complete amplitude.

On the internet one can always find photos of athletes completing stretch-cord training on an unstable surface because they believe it is a way to functionally ramp up the exercise. I would not do that and would strictly focus on the correct pulling motion with a solid surface beneath my feet.

There is nothing wrong with training proprioception and balance, but one should not necessarily combine these two training units.

EXERCISE

Here is a summary of the main points:

- Back is straight.
- Knees are slightly bent.
- Fingertips point downward.
- Wrist is rigid (the hand is an extension of the forearm).
- Elbows are up!
- Pull to full extension.

I would do a preparatory mobility exercise such as arm circles or jacks to get the blood flowing. Since training with the pull cord is an athletic activity with internal shoulder rotation like swimming the crawl, it is recommended to end this training with an external shoulder rotation exercise to prevent shoulder imbalance and avoid injury.

EXERCISE

Sample program:

5–10 minutes easy warm-up

5–8 sets with 25–40 repetitions each followed by a break of 30–40 seconds.

Three sets of 10 repetitions per side with a Thera-band to strengthen the external rotators.

Such a program can be completed up to five times a week during phases with little to no access to water. Here the resistance should vary, and the focus should be placed on the movement's individual segments as well as working with different movement speeds to create lots of variation.

If normal swim training is possible, I would limit stretch-cord training to two and no more than three units a week as additional dryland training.

Sample warm-up:

5–10 minutes easy warm-up

3–4 sets of 12–15 repetitions each with a 45-second pause

6.6.7   Flippers

Flippers are used very rarely in my long-distance triathlon world. Most athletes have difficulty learning the most effective elements such as the high elbow catch and stroke rate, and struggle enough with that.

When a swimmer wears flippers, his propulsion will come from his kick and it is still necessary to correctly place the forearm in the vertical position and swim with a decent stroke rate. Flippers should be used by beginning swimmers to learn good body position in the water and to gain more ankle flexibility.

But someone who reads a book about long distance should have already moved on from that topic.

6.6.8 Additional aids

In addition to the previously introduced aids there are resistance pants, drag cups, drag parachutes, etc. I think swimmers should use them in training; I don't think age-group triathletes need them.

Based on the aspects, the contents of the net bag are thus limited to paddles, pull buoy, snorkel (with nose clip), and metronome. All together that's not as much as people often claim, or is it?

TRAINING TOOLS FOR SWIMMING AND THEIR USE

Tool	Correct design	Purpose	Notice
Paddles	• Flat, not convex, fingertips line up with the front edge	• Training strength endurance, perception of and feel for vertical elbow position and latissimus dorsi	• Start with short legs • Strap paddles on correctly • Don't use when tired
Pull buoy	• Large pull buoy with appropriate amount of buoyancy • Small center	• Improving the body's position in water • Focus on arms • Unload legs	• Create sufficient tension in hips and butt
Snorkel	• Breathing tube at the front	• Improving head position • Breathing awareness • Improving rotation around long axis • improving the body's position in water, body extension • Visual monitoring of hands	• Wear a nose clip • Beginners often feel constricted
Band/Ankle strap	• Old bicycle inner tube • Tight loop • Remove valve	• Improving the body's position in water • Improving body extension • Improving high elbow catch • Improving strength	• Push the T downward • Keep your head low • High stroke rate • Tighten your gluteal muscles
Metronome	• Acoustic clock	• Increasing stroke rate via acoustic signals • Sense of tempo	• Complete a stroke-rate and speed analysis first to determine target stroke rate

Figure 45: Training tools overview.

6.7 Diagnostics and Testing Methods

As in cycling and running, in swimming there are several testing methods to assess the current performance level. But a test is always just a snapshot that can be impacted by various factors such as stress in everyday life or ill-timed meals and training loads in the run-up to the test.

Many athletes are highly stressed by a scheduled performance test because for many athletes swimming in particular is a horror and an aversion. In club training I therefore prefer to conduct unannounced tests, otherwise participation tends to be minimal.

I rarely prescribe performance tests in remote coaching (i.e., online coaching) without support at the edge of the pool but have the athletes swim specific sets which then act as indirect skill assessments.

6.7.1 Stroke rate and speed analysis

Completing a stroke-rate ladder helps determine the stroke rate and speed at which an athlete will swim most economically. This includes swimming 50 m intervals with increasing stroke rate and speed until the pace cannot be increased any further.

The number of strokes and times in these 50 m segments are recorded and compared to each other. When it is no longer possible to increase the speed, the stroke rate of the last or second to last level the athlete achieved is ascertained as the target stroke rate.

From the start, the number of 50 m segments should be limited to 12 sets. Breaks should be approximately 20–30 seconds long. The results from these tests provide the basis for the settings of the Tempo Trainer metronome, among other things.

EXAMPLE AGE GROUP (IM SWIM TIME 1:04)		
Round	Stroke Rate/min	Time
1	38	50.3
2	40	49.5
3	41	49.1
4	41	48.4
5	43	48.0
6	43	47.1
7	46	46.8
8	49	45.8
9	51	43.9
10	53	43.7
11	56	42.4
12	53	43.9

Figure 46: Example of a stroke-rate and speed analysis in swimming.

133

6.7.2   Thirty-minute test

The name says it all. This test is used to ascertain the distance a swimmer can complete in 30 minutes. The coach on the pool deck can time 50 or 100 m intervals to draw inferences regarding a feel for tempo, stamina, and possibly even the athlete's personality.

An athlete from the Alpha Leader group will almost certainly shine with faster start times than an athlete from the Brooder group. Athletes without a coach at their side should not capture the individual intermediate times manually by operating the stopwatch, but focus exclusively on swimming for 30 minutes.

I use this test relatively rarely. Its purpose is generally to give the athlete some self-confidence. Athletes whose swim technique is not yet well-developed tend to get slower towards the end of the test, which can have a negative effect on their psyche. I would use a different testing method for these athletes like, for instance, the pace-per-100 test.

6.7.3   Pace-per-100 test

A testing method I have been using for at least ten years is the pace-per-100 test. It involves swimming several 100 m segments after a 300–500 m warm-up. The interval pause is 10 seconds. The maximal number is 25 intervals.

If the athlete can swim the 25th interval as fast as the first 100 m, he swam too defensively. The test stops when the segment times get slower than 2 seconds from the first interval. It is important that the break lengths are precise.

During this testing method the athlete learns to estimate his tempo very effectively. Over-pacing becomes relatively obvious; if he swam too slow it means he was too conservative with his tempo structure. Ideally the athlete can maintain the tempo until the 18th to 20th interval before slowing down.

The athlete should not eat or drink during the test. The average tempo for these intervals serves as a predictor for the swim time that can be expected at Ironman.

PLEASE NOTE

Example:
If the athlete swims 20 segments in 1:20 min/100 m with 10-second breaks his anticipated Ironman pace will be approximately 1:24-1:25 min/100 m.

6.7.4   Standard series

Athlete and coach can also determine the performance level or rather performance progression without testing. This requires standard series, meaning training units that are periodically completed over the course of the season. The advantage here is comparability. Since this is not a testing situation but simply a normal training unit in the water, the psychological component is eliminated, and the athlete approaches the unit with an open mind.

The athlete's performance increase is reflected in faster intermediate times, in the ease with which he completes the unit, and the subjectively faster recovery after the intervals. The athlete is able to feel the performance increase and objectively see it on the clock over the course of the season and gains a certain amount of self-confidence regarding the upcoming competition.

Frequently repeated training units in the form of standard series have nothing to do with a coach who is lazy or lacks creativity, but rather serve a legitimate purpose in the training process.

For instance, 40-80 x 50 m, 20-40 x 100 m, or 12-20 x 200 m work well as standard series. Here, too, break times should be strictly adhered to with lengths between 10 and 20 seconds.

6.7.5   Lactate diagnostics

It would also be possible to conduct performance diagnostics by ascertaining lactate values, but most pools don't allow such tests for hygiene reasons, which is why I will not go into further detail here.

6.8   Swimming in Open Water

6.8.1   Goal setting

One common mistake is not swimming enough in open water or with a wetsuit in the run-up to a long-distance race. It differs from everyday swimming in a pool in several ways, which is why the objective has to change accordingly. Some aspects of training would be:

- Getting used to the body's different position in the water in a wetsuit
- Starting on land
- Starting in the water
- Getting out of the water
- Orientation
- Swimming around buoys and changing directions
- Pacing
- Starting in a large group
- Swimming under water with reduced visibility

I recommend finding a lake that offers a 200–500 m lap with at least two directional changes with or without buoys.

EXERCISE

A classic open-water set might look like this:

Ten minutes of an easy warm-up swim to get used to the wetsuit or visibility and water conditions.

Two or three of the laps (leave the water after each lap, take a 1-minute break, and refresh the senses before simulating a land start).

Two to five of the laps (the first 100 strokes fast at racing speed, focus on technique during the middle segment, then back to racing speed for the final 100 strokes, then immediately get out of the water and run one minute on land).

Five minutes of an easy warm-down swim.

Open-water units should also be used to practice putting on and taking off the wetsuit as quicky as possible. To do so, race onto dry land, push the goggles up on the forehead, open the wetsuit zipper, pull the suit down to the hips, stop after 100 m, and quickly pull off the rest of the suit.

With increasing practice and fitness, the number of fast strokes can be increased until the entire lap can be completed at racing speed.

It would be helpful if open-water training included exposure to environmental influences (fog, waves, low sun, wind, etc.) so the athlete is prepared for all eventualities on race day. I recommend completing 6–10 such units in the run-up to the main event.

CONCLUSION

Swimming is about swimming and triathlon swimming is about triathlon swimming.

6.8.2   Converting pool units to open-water training

It is relatively easy to convert pool units into open water sessions and complete them as structured swim training. An endurance unit (approximately 45-60 minutes) can occasionally be incorporated to generate confidence in the distance required in a race. Otherwise, intervals like those in the pool are more productive because the various breaks allow the athlete to swim at higher intensities.

Conversion does not require one-to-one conversion of the length of the laps; a rough approximation is perfectly sufficient. Unlike with pool swimming, a watch or GPS device can be used here.

EXERCISE

Here is a specific example for converting the following pool training for a swimmer with a performance level of approximately 60 minutes at the Ironman distance.

Pool:

300 m easy warm-up
2 x 50 hard, 20-second break
200 m mid-tempo
4 x 100 hard, 20-second break
200 m mid-tempo
6 x 200 m hard, 20-second break
200 m easy

For training conversion, I would convert 100 m in 1:30–1:33 minutes, meaning

4:30–5:00 minutes easy warm-up
2 x 45–60 seconds hard, 20–30-second active break
Three minutes easy tempo
4 x 90 seconds hard, 20–30-seconds active break
Three minutes easy tempo
6 x 3 minutes hard, 30–45-seconds active break
2–3 minutes easy tempo warm-down

Here the focus is on feeling the different speeds and the body's different positions in the water during the different intensities.

6.9   General Suggestions

Before we move on to cycling, I would like to offer a few more basic tips about swimming.

6.9.1   Eating and drinking during swim training

I usually place a lot of importance on an adequate fluid and energy supply during training. But I have a slightly different view when it comes to swimming. During a race there is a continuous network of aid stations along the cycling and running course; athletes can get a continuous supply without major gaps. But not so while swimming.

While there are a few races with a brief period on land—the Australian exit—where fluids are provided, the athletes are generally required to complete the entire distance without fluids or an energy supply. In my opinion, this should be practiced in training.

I always see athletes reaching for their water bottle after every interval to take a small sip. During group training there are usually several bottles at the edge of the pool, which can make grabbing one's own bottle difficult and slow. This in turn is a disruption, athletes lose their focus, and break times are no longer exact, especially when using paddles.

I therefore always prefer proper preparation of the unit, meaning getting enough fluid and energy before training to be able to complete the unit without additional external intake, just like in a race. Athletes who must or want to swim in the early morning as soon as the pool opens and before work can fill their stores on the way to the pool.

6.9.2   Long lanes vs. short lanes

There are always athletes who balk at the closer short lane and instead travel farther for a 50 m lane. But I see no reason why one should absolutely have to train in a long lane in order to have a successful triathlon. Beginners or technically weak swimmers benefit from a shorter lane when incorporating the streamline drill after every turn because it forces them to perform it more often, providing twice the benefit.

The argument of a longer lane without a break during a race, like the long-distance race, is not valid since longer segments should primarily be completed in open water. The effect of properly pushing off the wall, the streamline drill, and the resulting superior quality of movement are factors that should not be disregarded when considering the pros and cons of lane length.

It would be more productive if the athlete in the above example would use the extra time for meaningful regeneration instead of driving farther to the pool.

6.9.3 Understanding swimming as a fitness tool

Triathletes should shed their aversion to swimming and understand that water training does not only improve swimming performance, but also fitness overall. However, many athletes don't care if it takes them 70 or 73 minutes to complete the required 3,800 m in a race.

They argue, and thereby justify to themselves, that they would rather spend less training time in the water. In fact, the three-minute time difference is probably rather irrelevant, but the consequences of a poor swimming technique can be quite serious.

An athlete with good swimming form and the resulting confidence in his own strength will stand at the starting line with noticeably more self-confidence than an athlete who views swimming as an annoying addition to the training process. Ultimately there may only be a three-minute time difference, but the energy expenditure and carbohydrate consumption are much higher in moderately developed swimmers.

Good swimming form results in a better running performance. It sounds paradoxical, but conserving carbohydrates while swimming reserves more energy for running.

6.9.4 Swim goggles

I constantly see athletes pushing their goggles up on their forehead after nearly every interval. Like drinking, this is a distraction and breaks concentration. You are not able to remove your goggles during a race.

This means that the eye socket must be conditioned so the athlete learns to endure the pressure created by the goggles. Additionally, frequently removing and then replacing the goggles causes them to increasingly fog up.

When the coach gives the start signal and the athlete is still messing with his goggles, it lengthens the break and thereby changes the intent of the swimming set.

6.9.5 MP3 player

Before we are born, we grow in our mother's amniotic fluid. Thus, water is a familiar element. Swimming with an MP3 player takes away the calming effect of and the conscious listening to our breathing sounds, particularly since swimming requires a a certain rhythm that can be corrupted by the music's rhythm.

All day long, we are stressed by visual and auditory stimuli. I can only recommend that every athlete reduce sensory overload and consciously utilize water's calming effect to regulate stress, and to forgo musical entertainment.

6.9.6 Group training

Developing swimming performance requires intensities. When someone always swims alone, he will not be forced to swim fast, or rather swim hard, despite the very intrinsic motivation. Swimming as a group inevitably results in comparison. Holding on to the feet of the person swimming in front of you or feeling pressure from the person swimming behind you automatically generates a faster swimming tempo.

Swimming alone produces limited tempo increases because it lacks that extra little bit of intensity. It isn't necessary to join a club or a training group. Even just one swimming partner can do wonders because, as we all know, misery loves company.

6.9.7 Warm-up

Even with a tight time budget and having to squeeze in swim training, athletes should not skip a brief warm-up. It buffers stress and warms up the swimming muscles.

It should not necessarily exceed 5-8 minutes. Prior to training it is recommend to do a dynamic warm-up with arm circles—one arm, both arms, in opposite directions—as a basic exercise.

6.9.8 Expert advice

Not all tips or technical advice from a so-called *expert* such as another swimmer or a coach at the edge of the pool is helpful and correct. One should take that advice with a grain of salt, especially when the person giving the advice does not have an understanding of the triathlon sport. Any triathlon coach who lets his athletes neglect swim training is not an appropriate partner on the path to the season's highlight.

6.10   Health Risks

6.10.1   Chlorine allergy

Some swimmers can develop a chlorine allergy over time. It manifests itself in extended cold symptoms after swimming in chlorinated water. Ordinarily nasal mucous membranes should be swollen for no more than one day after swim training. If symptoms persist beyond that time span, it could be initial evidence of a chlorine allergy.

Swimmers suffering from a stuffy nose after swimming should apply some wound protection ointment (e.g., betamethasone) to the inside of the nose. This ointment will protect the mucous membranes. After training swollen mucous membranes can be soothed with a conventional nose spray.

However, I would like to point out that there is a risk of dependency with long-term use of such a spray. If none of these remedies work, a nose clip might be the only option. There is empirical evidence that nose clips are unfortunately used too soon and too often.

Some athletes simply don't like the feeling of water in their nose and therefore use nose clips. But this eliminates the nose as part of the respiratory system, which can have a negative effect on performance.

6.10.2   Earache

Swimming can cause recurring ear problems in some athletes. For instance, if the shape of the auditory canal prevents water from draining easily, it can stay in the ear canal for longer and can damage the mucous membranes there as well as act as a breeding ground for germs.

Athletes with sensitive ears should therefore use ear plugs that can reduce or prevent water from entering the ear canal. After swimming it is recommended to dry the ears with a hair dryer from a distance of 11–12 inches or tilting the head to the side and shaking out any remaining water.

6.10.3   Swimmer's shoulder

Shoulder problems result from a muscle imbalance of the shoulder and usually surface during phases with high volumes or intensities. They are often associated with the use of paddles, which can be avoided with the previously mentioned swimming dos and don'ts regarding these tools.

Here the internally rotating muscles are more developed than the external rotators. The head of the humerus is therefore no longer optimally centered in the shoulder. This causes some tightness in the acromion, which then irritates the bursae of the shoulder. A recommended remedy is to initially forgo swimming and instead focus on developing and strengthening the external rotators.

Opening the shoulder with backwards arm circles and strengthening the backwards-pulling muscles and scapular stabilizers relieves the acromion and optimizes shoulder stability. Since modern man's everyday forward-oriented work at a desk, and in recent years the increasing use of smart phones, has resulted in a tendency to kyphosis, it is recommended to also perform these exercises as a preventative measure to avoid shoulder problems becoming part of the daily routine.

7   CYCLING

Now that we have mentally left the water, we will focus on the second triathlon discipline, cycling. Cycling represents approximately 50% of the overall duration of a long-distance event. There is a correspondingly great potential for improving this overall performance.

When looking at the evolution of the Ironman triathlon winning times from the past 20-25 years, we can see that back then the times in the water and on foot are barely slower than they are today. By contrast cycling times have downright exploded, not just at the very top but way down into the age-group classes. Nowadays some age-group athletes achieve times on two wheels that 20 years ago would have been enough for an overall win.

Looking at magazines from the 1990s and examining man and machine, the reason is quickly apparent. Increasingly cheaper processing of carbon materials allows the broad masses access to aerodynamically optimized bikes. Unlike the world's governing body for cycling (UCI), regulations for bike form and function in triathlon are relatively loose. This fact allows for panels, integrated drinking systems, monocoque handlebars, etc., to be used in triathlon, greatly improving the aerodynamics of the man–machine system.

Moreover, knowledge about the biodynamics of cycling has significantly improved over the past 15-20 years. From here a completely new line of work developed in the form of bike fitting. What in the past used to be exclusively the judgement of the bicycle dealer and meant a transfer of experience, today is objectively more quantifiable.

Measuring technology to determine the sitting positions has also evolved. Like 3D-motion analysis systems (e.g., Retül), sensors that measure pressure relationships in shoes and on the seat help the fitter to objectively evaluate sitting positions and movements. Nowadays, measuring technology (e.g., Leomo) has evolved to the point that athletes are able to objectively measure or even improve their sitting position in real time during training, meaning outside of a fitting lab.

As a result, not only the bike equipment being used has improved but also the biomechanics and aerodynamics with respect to an optimized sitting position.

Another milestone was the invention of the power meter to ascertain the achieved performance in watts. In the 1990s, training control via the Watts parameter was available to only a very small group of people. The only available system back then was produced by the company SRM in Jülich, Germany, and cost nearly as much as a small car. Here, too, production costs have dropped significantly, resulting in lots of manufacturers on today's market, but unfortunately not always benefitting measuring accuracy. But more on that later.

And finally, we come back to my area of work, because training theory has also changed. New measurable parameters like, for instance, maximum lactate production (Vlamax) have made insight deep into performance physiology possible and thus give the coach the opportunity to fully understand an athlete's metabolism and from there derive interventions for training, nutrition and pacing during a race.

Compared to the two disciplines of swimming and running, technological advances have most impacted cycling. I will examine the important aspects of bike training more closely on the following pages.

7.1   Equipment

It is nearly impossible to keep track of the market for supposedly fast equipment. I just want to touch on a few things, especially since this book is not supposed to include a bike catalog. Rather I would like to point out a few pitfalls and promises made by some manufacturers' marketing departments. Some promise watts conservation as well as increased speed.

What I am trying to say here is that one should be skeptical when it comes to test results and should take a closer look at the comparison or test arrangements, because not every test applies to the reality of a long-distance triathlete. For instance, when wheels are tested at a speed of 50 km/h and only with one particular wind direction, I think it has relatively little to do with the reality of most races and athletes.

The weight of a bike has little effect on races with a normal demand profile, meaning the usual 1,200-1,700 elevation gain on a 180 km to be completed on a bike course.

Bike weight certainly plays a greater role in races like Ironman Wales or Ironman Lanzarote, and even more so in the increasingly popular extreme triathlons like Norseman, Embrunman, etc., and the 4,000–5,000 m elevation gain.

REMEMBER

There is a clock at the finish line, not a scale.

7.1.1   Wheels

Some wheels look quite spectacular and have very deep rims. More important than the rim depth with respect to aerodynamics is the number of spokes on the front wheel. An 80 mm front wheel with 24 spokes is therefore less aerodynamic than a rim with less rim height if it only has 12 spokes.

In recent years I have often seen athletes training using their racing wheels. On the one hand I can understand the desire to use this expensive acquisition more than just the few races in a season.

But I also think that the wheels wear with every kilometer and especially in rain. I therefore recommend purchasing an inexpensive set of training wheels. It's training with a handicap and in a race the athlete can then easily return to using a perfectly intact wheel with all the respective advantages in terms of aerodynamics and low friction.

Of course, such a racing wheel should have been tested in the run-up to master its handling.

REMEMBER

Not every fast-looking racing wheel is actually fast.

7.1.2 Tires

Tires are probably a triathlete's bike's least respected element because many athletes are not aware of their importance. The tire is the only connection between the bike and ground, and thus is a major safety factor because surface adhesion in turns and especially in wet conditions should not be disregarded.

However, not only is safety important but a tire can also make a difference in terms of performance. There are tires with low rolling friction and tires sold by companies with big marketing budgets.

What I am trying to say is that one should be skeptical when it comes to tire tests, especially when the same magazine has a double-page ad by that manufacturer. Tubular tires, clinchers, and tubeless tires all have their advantages and disadvantages, I consider it a compromise between rolling friction, puncture protection, and easy mounting, or rather easy tube swap after a flat tire during a race, and thus make a case for a classic clincher with a latex tube. But the latest generation of tubeless tires have already proven that they have the potential for a new gold standard regarding rolling resistance, protection, and aerodynamics plus offering more comfort because of lower air pressure. If an athlete doesn't get disturbed in his aero position by balancing uneven road surface, fatigue will show up later.

I am always horrified at the large number of athletes who don't know how to change a tube. This should always be practiced so the athlete's hands move with confidence during a race, particularly with the added adrenaline. Otherwise, why even carry a spare tube?

ANECDOTE

Regarding a spare tube, here is a little anecdote from the Ironman Frankfurt several years ago.

Back then a participant from Mexico had a flat tire right in front of me, as a spectator. I watched him change the tube and could hardly believe my eyes. The damaged tube had already been repaired at least four times and was replaced by a tube with at least seven such repairs. Grotesquely, the athlete rode a 10,000 Euro bike.

Please do not use previously repaired tubes in a race! I recommend checking tires and tubes for small cuts before a race, or rather changing them beforehand and riding on them for approximately 100-150 km on training rides. If using tubeless tires, make sure that the tubeless milk isn't older than six months. Otherwise it should be replaced before race week.

Athletes who ride an entire year on the same set of wheels should therefore acquire a set of tires with focus on puncture protection and longevity for training rides and a lighter weight and low rolling friction for racing.

REMEMBER

Make training hard so the race will be easy!

7.1.3   Bicycle drivetrain

The name itself speaks to the importance of the drivetrain. Unfortunately, some athletes don't seem to recognize that, because when looking at some chains, jockey wheels, and front chain rings (sadly even at races), one quickly realizes that the term *bike maintenance* isn't in everyone's vocabulary.

The condition of the drivetrain is extremely important because friction resistance within this system must be minimized. On the one hand athletes go through great lengths to optimize aerodynamics to save a few watts, but on the other hand sacrifice 15 watts with a poorly maintained drivetrain. The chains of some athletes look more like black powertrains, the individual chain links virtually indistinguishable.

But when the chain is clean and treated with oil or wax, friction resistance is significantly reduced. In addition to improved low friction, the durability of chain, rear sprocket, jockey wheels, and front chain rings increases considerably. To play it safe, like changing the tires before a race, I recommend changing the chain and possibly the rear sprocket, so both parts are working safely and trouble-free.

It is unfortunate when an athlete uses expensive ceramic bearings or oversized pulleys, meaning larger jockey wheels with less friction resistance, but then don't take care of the system.

REMEMBER

Chain maintenance is cheaper than aero testing!

7.1.4 Water bottles and stowing options

Most triathlon racing bikes are equipped with aerodynamic drinking systems or stowing options for tools, spare tube, and race fueling supplies.

But there are always athletes who downright destroy their, in many cases expensive, bike's aerodynamic advantages by adding multiple bottle holders and other additions.

Mounted behind the saddle are set-ups for two water bottles and a tool kit along with two additional water bottles in the triangle and a BTA drinking system in the handlebars. In addition, some also attach energy gels and bars to the top tube.

Here not only the bike's weight and esthetics suffer, but the aerodynamics are also greatly affected. Later, I will explain, within the context of race structuring, why these additions are not really necessary.

REMEMBER

Less is more, even if you don't automatically eat less!

7.1.5 Aero helmet

Not every fast-looking helmet automatically has a temporizing effect. What matters is the combination of sitting position, physical proportions, and speed. When an athlete is unable to permanently maintain an optimal sitting position, meaning he noticeably moves his head so the helmet's tail fin points straight up in the air, it will almost certainly have a negative effect on aerodynamics. In this case I would recommend an aero helmet with a short tail.

Most aero helmets have few louvers and ventilation is quite bad compared to a classic road helmet. If it is very hot on race day or the athlete isn't heat tolerant, I would recommend foregoing the watts savings of an aero helmet in favor of better ventilation and less rising of the body's core temperature.

Studies have shown that the difference in the body's core temperature can be as much as one degree. It doesn't sound like much, but ultimately has a major effect on racing performance. It is therefore important to consider whether wearing the aero helmet is truly justified.

REMEMBER

Looking cool or having a cool head?

7.1.6   Cycling shoes

A triathlete must choose between wearing normal cycling shoes or buying shoes that are easier to put on and take off in a transition zones. Since this book focuses mostly on the long-distance race, I would undoubtedly recommend normal cycling shoes. For one, a quick shoe change in a very long race as compared to a sprint, Olympic distance, or even a mixed team relay is almost irrelevant, and secondly, comfort is extremely important.

A triathlon cycling shoe cannot be fitted to the foot as precisely and comfortably since it usually only has a Velcro closure or the like. In that respect the classic road bike shoe offers considerably more options, ensuring comfort and optimal force transmission.

Here I would suggest a wide toe box, because over the course of the race and on a hot day the foot swells noticeably and gets wider and longer. When the toe box is too narrow it can make that final hour of the bike race unpleasant and painful.

REMEMBER

Fast and comfortable is better than just fast!

7.2   Aero Is Everything

Most triathletes are familiar with this tagline from a major American bike manufacturer. Aerodynamics is an important factor with respect to an athlete's travel speed in a race as well as the associated energy savings and resulting faster running performance. I do not wish to delve into the depths of physics, but rather choose to remain close to the surface on this topic.

The amount of wind resistance that must be overcome increases exponentially. Everyone should know what that means after the Covid-19 pandemic, but I will provide a brief outline. The increase in wind resistance with increasing speed is not linear. This means that double the speed does not equal double the wind resistance, but rather eight times as much!

That is precisely where bike manufacturers and bike fitters come in. The idea is to improve aerodynamics according to the increase in speed. Reducing the frontal area or resistance surface is considered critical here. The bike industry is getting increasingly innovative in this area, and nearly every season introduces new equipment with promises of improved aerodynamics.

But even the best material is only conditionally effective if the cyclist doesn't or cannot maintain an aerodynamic position on the bike. When looking at the impact of aerodynamics in cycling in the adjacent figure, one can quickly see how immaterial the shape of the frame, the wheels, etc., become.

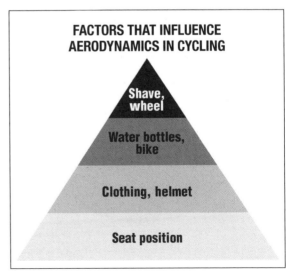

FACTORS THAT INFLUENCE AERODYNAMICS IN CYCLING

Shave, wheel

Water bottles, bike

Clothing, helmet

Seat position

Figure 47: Factors that influence aerodynamics in cycling.

Thus, the greatest influencing factor in reducing the frontal area surface is the athlete himself. Aero helmet and clothing also play an extremely important role. The position and shape of the water bottles mounted on the bike are also an important factor when trying to make a bike faster. Round bottles in the bike's triangle create considerably more drag than an optimally aerodynamic flat aero bottle.

Shaving the legs is supposed to save up to five watts at a speed of 40 km/h. The athlete's sitting position is thus of critical importance. The level of knowledge on this subject has also evolved.

When comparing positions from the 1990s and 2000s to those of today's fastest athletes on two wheels, it is apparent that in the past it was thought that the handlebars should be quite low. Today we know that a low handlebar position can have a negative effect on force transmission and breathing, and that it causes the head to sit relatively high up on the shoulders.

The cyclist Floyd Landis was the first to cause a stir with his praying-mantis position, meaning with aero extensions clearly at an upward angle. This position allows the cyclist to hold his head lower and rotate the shoulders tightly inward. This shoulder shrug significantly reduces the frontal area surface. However, the position must be actively assumed and therefore practiced.

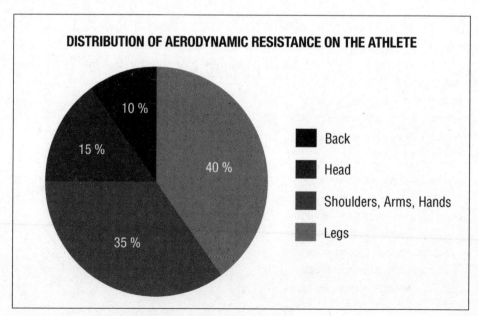

Figure 48: Distribution of aerodynamic resistance on the athlete.

While shoulders, arms, and hands make up approximately 35% of the total attack area, the legs with 40% are even more critical. Here it is recommended to move the legs close to the top tube, providing the athlete's mechanical axis allows it, so the silhouette appears smaller.

Some athletes are severely bow-legged, sit on their racing bike like a cowboy on a horse, and are unable to keep their legs in a narrow position.

Triathlon is always a compromise of various factors. In cycling it is about weighing the aerodynamics, comfort, and force transmission or biomechanics. Top athletes test their position and the materials they use in a wind tunnel to find out where they can save a few watts.

Others do an aero test on a track to get realistic values. These findings should then undergo a confirmation test in the field (i.e., in practice). Because what good is an optimal position if it cannot be ridden cleanly for 180 km?

Especially when it comes to age-group athletes, a spectator at a long-distance event can always see a number of athletes who are no longer able to rest their arms on the aero handlebars after completing two thirds of the course.

Either the chosen sitting position is too aggressive and therefore not sustainable for the total 180 km, or the athlete did not ride enough kilometers in this position during training in the run-up, meaning he did not get used to riding in the aero position.

This point takes up back to my pet issue, which is actual cycling or bike training.

7.3   Posture on the Bike

Before we go into detail about training, I would like to go over some basic information about posture on a bike, because beginning riders tend to make some mistakes that can even result in health issues.

7.3.1   Hands

The hands should not clench the handlebar. Using the thumbs as opportunistic fingers for security is quite sufficient. I always hear about crashes caused by a hand slipping off the handlebar because the hands were resting flat on the racing or drop handlebar. When using the thumb, it acts as a safety hook.

Fingers that feel asleep or are numb result in a tense hand position or a top-heavy sitting position. Both lead to extreme pressure on the nerve canals of the hands or wrists. In aero position the hands should be a natural extension of the forearms. Long-term bending, especially during a race, can cause some very unpleasant pain in that region.

7.3.2   Elbows and arms

When the hands are tense it often leads to straight elbows when using drop handlebars. But bent elbows act as a kind of shock absorber that can absorb irregularities in the riding surface. When the elbows are too straight, the shock from below is transferred from the bike to the athlete's body, which is unpleasant and can cause pain and have a negative effect on the bike's handling.

One can often see approaching cyclists with the arm position of a track sprinter, meaning the elbows point to the outside which, with respect to the aforementioned aspects of aerodynamics, is pretty much an ultimate MCA.

7.3.3   Neck, shoulders, and face

We are all familiar with faces grimacing with pain when looking at race photos. But those tense facial muscles and the baring of one's teeth also cause more muscle tension in neck and shoulders.

It is therefore recommended to relax the face as much as possible, even in a moment of suffering, to not clench the teeth but paradoxically keep them deliberately relaxed.

7.3.4   Upper body

The upper body should ideally be quiet. Bobbing up and down with the upper body is often the result of an awkward force transmission or sitting position but can also be caused by weak core muscles.

7.3.5   Feet and toes

Curling the toes should be avoided because it gradually fatigues the foot and calf muscles. Unfortunately, triathletes need that part of the body for running, which means it is important to not strain the feet on the bike. Consciously pedaling with the midfoot can prevent curling.

7.4   Sitting Position

I don't want to go into too much detail here because after all I am not a bike fitter, nor do I want to be. I only want to point out the possibly biggest mistakes on the subject. As with coaching, there can be very different opinions when it comes to the sitting position.

Bike fitting is still a very new area and standards have not yet been sufficiently established. But some fitters have pretty crude views, which an outsider can catch sight of at a race. My criticism here is focused primarily on seat height and cleat position.

7.4.1   Seat height

Only 20-30% of triathletes ride with an optimal seat height. Most of the athletes sit much too high. It is rather rare to find a seat height that is too low. There is no optimal force transmission when, at the lowest point of the crank turn, meaning in the 6 o'clock position on an imaginary clock, the athlete must tilt his toes far below heel level, especially since the calf muscles have to be tightened significantly.

But since we are talking about triathlon overall, we must also consider the relationships between the three disciplines. When the calves must work too hard during the cycling event the athlete starts the running event in an already fatigued state. A seat that is mounted too high causes the pelvis to considerably tilt right and left so the feet can be pushed down into the crank's 6 o'clock position. This pelvic tilt also causes more movement in the upper body.

One can often see athletes slide back and forth in their seat when the seat is too high, because sitting on the seat's front edge shortens the downward distance the feet must travel. This excessive horizontal movement often causes skin irritations and frequently inflammation of the perineum due to body hair in that region being pulled out, better known among cyclists as saddle sores.

When the seat is too high and the handlebars too low, optimal force transmission may not be possible. The hip angle is too acute and blood flow in the pelvic artery, and consequently in the entire upper leg, is not optimal.

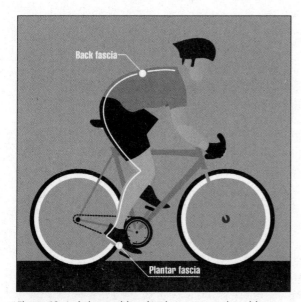

Figure 49: A sitting position that is too aggressive with too much tension on the back fascia.

Something else I have increasingly observed in recent years in this context is that a sitting position that is too aggressive and too low promotes a condition called plantar fasciitis, meaning inflammation of the plantar tendon. One possible reason might be too much tension on the back fascia that runs from the back of the head down the entire back of the body and down to the sole of the foot.

When choosing the seat height, the athlete should consider the difference between seat pad and cycling pants during training and the considerably thinner racing singlet. If the difference is substantial, he might consider lowering the seat slightly for the race.

7.4.2   Cleat position

Over the years, this area has become a matter close to my heart, because I first began to wonder about the work of some sitting-position aggravators back in 2010, when an athlete who was preparing for the Ironman Lanzarote complained of Achilles tendon pain during a cycling block with simultaneously reduced running volume. I read his training journal back-to-back to identify potential overloading.

At that time, I racked my brain until I thought of checking the cleat position of his cycling shoes. The cleats had been mounted to the forwardmost end of the adjustment range by a fitter. Since then, these cleat settings have been repeated with many athletes, so I can no longer call it an isolated case.

As previously mentioned, bike fitting is a relatively new field and there are few current studies and to date no verified standard. But when having ridden a bike, having tested various pedal positions, and felt and understood biomechanics 101, one does not need elaborate studies. And if one has understood the triathlon sport and particularly the long-distance event with its complexity and combination of three individual disciplines and the individual sports' different demand profiles, then one can easily figure out that an extremely forward cleat position cannot be sensible. This position significantly increases the load on the Achilles tendon and calf.

The subsequent running event puts a lot of strain on these two areas, which should then still be halfway fresh after cycling. To me this necessitates moving the cleats all the way back to reduce the strain. Moreover, moving the cleats back considerably improves the ability to put pressure on the pedal during the drive-effective phase.

This places more of the foot over the pedal axis rather than just the front foot as when the cleats are pushed all the way to the front.

Figure 50: Pedaling pictogram.

Feet that have gone to sleep or a burning sensation in the ball of the foot are often the result of cycling shoes that are too tight or cleats that are mounted too far forward, putting too much pressure on the forefoot. This can obstruct blood flow and irritate nerve structures. The accompanying illustration shows the effects of an incorrect cleat position.

But it can always get worse. When some athletes followed up, a few noticed that some bike fitters did not even look at the cleat position on the shoe.

But cleat settings are fundamental, because they determine the other parameters such as seat and handlebar height.

7.5   Bicycle Handling Skills

Fast and successful cycling requires not only a lot of power on the pedals, but also a few other skills which some athletes have not sufficiently developed. The total package of fast cycling includes good cornering technique, good timing with respect to gear changes, and effective out-of-the-saddle riding. Riding downhill also requires a certain performance potential that in some cases is not tapped into.

Another important aspect is cycling in different weather conditions. I always see much-cited fair weather cyclists struggling with bad weather in a race. As with so many things in sports, practice makes perfect.

The increasingly popular indoor training on indoor bike trainers or smart trainers further stunts the often already underdeveloped handling skills. We will come back to the topic of indoor training.

When an athlete can safely control his athletic equipment it increases self-confidence, and as a result he will be more confident on the bike. This psychological component should not be disregarded!

7.5.1   Cornering technique

I find it difficult to describe a particular cornering technique, because every curve angle and the pitch and slope of a road require a different approach. But here I would like to point out that physics in cycling reaches its limits considerably less early than people tend to think.

7.5.2   Changing gears or shifting

For many athletes shifting gears is problematic because they simply don't know when to use which gear. Time and again we can see athletes compensate, meaning the chain wanders completely from right to left. But that takes away any momentum for conquering the climb.

Depending on the length and pitch of the climb, one can leave the gear and push through the rise or briefly ride out-of-the-saddle. On the other hand, a gear change often comes too late, meaning the athlete rides into the mountain for too long in a high gear until all the momentum is lost and a gear change is almost too late.

7.5.3   Out-of-the-saddle

When riding out-of-the-saddle the body must be used effectively to accelerate or climb. To do so the bike must tilt side-to-side under the body (i.e., in the direction of the downward-moving leg). Beginners tend to keep the bike vertical and tilt the body side-to-side.

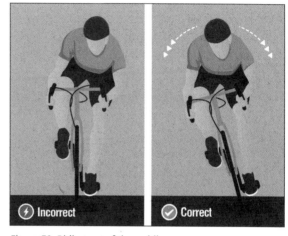

7.5.4   Riding downhill

For some athletes riding downhill is a test of courage. They often don't dare to let the bike roll downhill, thereby giving away precious minutes in the race.

Figure 51: Riding out-of-the-saddle.

Athletes should really work on that and little by little lose the fear of riding downhill. This primarily requires confidence in the material (i.e., the bike). The following aspects should be kept in mind to minimize the fear of crashing.

7.5.4.1   Tires

Using the cheapest tires is not advisable. Some tires have different-color treads. While such tires look good, the color is not conducive to tire adhesion.

The sidewalls can certainly have a different color, but the running surface should be black.

Additionally, tires should be checked regularly before every ride for small cuts in the running surfaces that can lead to a flat, especially when training in the mountains.

7.5.4.2   Tire pressure

The best tires in the world are meaningless when they don't have the appropriate air pressure. Tire pressure should be checked before every ride. Butyl and especially latex tubes lose air over time, causing the filling pressure to drop. However, there is no blanket recommendation for air pressure.

The system's weight consisting of rider and bike, tire width, road surface, and weather conditions all play an important role in choosing the right tire pressure.

7.5.4.3   Quick release skewer

The quick release skewer holds the wheel in the frame and should therefore be closed with a certain amount of pressure. For years I have made it a habit to check the quick release skewers at camps or training events where I am the organizer and responsible person. Making a rough guess, I would say that one-third of all athletes only close the quick release skewer very loosely.

Once the material aspects have been addressed and improved, some of the fear should have been alleviated. In training camps, a surprising number of triathletes keep the crank in a horizontal position while going downhill, meaning the feet are level. Keeping the legs in this horizontal position requires muscle effort, and it greatly diminishes bike control.

Control changes significantly when instead one foot is positioned in the crank's 6 o'clock position, because the weight of the leg is then closer to the road surface. To any cyclists with problems riding downhill I recommend practicing on roads with little traffic and initially without turns. I would consider the following exercise progression.

Practicing hills is particularly expedient when the training plan calls for strength and endurance intervals and the traffic situation permits it.

The interval break is thus efficiently utilized. The following downhill options would be appropriate for building confidence in this area:

* Rolling with crank in horizontal position
* Rolling with crank in 6 o'clock and 12 o'clock position to feel the difference
* Rolling with tense hands
* Rolling with relaxed hands and using the thumbs for stability
* Rolling and simulating breaking hard
* Repeating items 1-5 on a wet road

A frequently asked question is whether to roll and pedal at the same time or just roll. Speed increases linearly while force has an exponential character. This means achieving a higher speed requires more effort. But in a race, downhill passages can be used as recovery phases and for fuel consumption. But the relationship between increased energy expenditure and speed increase isn't always favorable. Here a good rule might be:

* > 50 km/h = let it roll while sitting as aerodynamically as possible
* > 40 km/h = easy pedaling
* > 30 km/h = normal pedaling

7.6   Choosing the Right Bike

A triathlete generally has three different training tools to choose from:

* Time trial bike
* Racing bike
* Mountain bike or cross bike

Every bike has a different area of use and can be used as a specific training tool. As always in triathlon, there are different approaches here as well. Riding exclusively on a time trial bike is often lauded as the best way to match the specific racing position.

But I think this approach has some weak spots that I would like to point out. I tend to prefer a mix of the above bike types if the athlete has access to them. Especially in winter, an all-terrain bike is a good choice. It provides better handling on slippery surfaces and slick roots in woods and fields. It greatly improves correct braking and a safe cornering technique.

I would therefore complete many of the basic endurance sessions in open terrain, particularly during the cold time of year. The slower speed compared to training on the road and partial wind protection from trees are more conducive to training in low temperatures. The opposite approach can be the time trial bike on the roller or smart trainer to get used to the aero position early in the season. Training on the road with the racing bike is also an option when paying attention to a few points and tips.

7.6.1   Bicycle training in winter

Riding a bike on the road in winter might not be everyone's cup of tea but when done right and with the appropriate equipment, it is very doable.

7.6.1.1   Equipment

- The athlete ideally has an old racing bike. The used-up parts of the summer bike migrate to this winter bike and they may still find good use there.
- Mudguards are mandatory. Clip-on guards suffice. The longer they are, the better they keep off moisture and dirt.
- Use 25–28 mm tires. I always take an old tube, cut it open, and tape it with thick tape to the running surface from the inside. While this makes the tire a little heavier, it offers much better puncture protection.
- Attach small blinking lights in the front and rear, because there can be poor visibility even in daylight.
- Use a slightly shorter stem than in summer so the sitting position is less extended and the back is thereby less stressed in the cold.
- A tube bag with a spare tube is mandatory. In winter, I always carry a pair of disposable gloves in that bag because with this repair you always end up with dirty hands.
- A wind vest and rain jacket are mandatory for every ride and useful, even if it doesn't rain. After a bakery stop it is often cold when starting out again and it is nice to have an additional layer.
- Bring two pairs of gloves! Have one thin pair and one thick pair to be ready for any weather.
- Overshoes are also mandatory, because the body loses a lot of heat through the feet.

REMEMBER

Place two layers of aluminum foil under the insole of your cycling shoes. These layers are super thin but offer cold protection from below.

* Wear socks that go above the Achilles tendon to keep it warm.
* Wear a cycling cap under the helmet, preferably with a short shield which can be folded down in rain and act as a splatter guard.
* Pack an emergency gel or bar, because a rider can hit the wall much quicker even on short rides in winter than in summer. The cold also increases energy consumption.
* Bring cash or a credit card, because you never know if the weather or circumstances can take a turn for the worst and you need to have a way to get home.

7.6.1.2   Before riding

* Check the air pressure! That's important because when the pressure is too low and the road is wet, small rocks and pieces of glass will stick to tires more easily and can cause a flat.
* Apply chain oil, because water and salt will cause the chain to rust more quickly. An easy way to oil the chain on the go if it begins to squeak during a ride is with an isotonic drink or an apple spritzer.
* Check the weather!
* Check the wind direction! I recommend choosing rides that allow you to ride into the wind at the beginning of the training session and ride home with the wind at your back, because riding into the wind in winter requires lots of energy and can cause hypothermia, especially when already tired.

7.6.1.3   While riding

* Keep an eye on the sky and if necessary, adjust your route guidance. Fellow cyclists without mudguards MUST ride at the rear. Alert your fellow cyclists to holes in the road surface and especially glass.
* Eat regularly, because in winter the hammer can often drop without warning.
* Find protected areas for pee breaks and repairs and turn your chest towards the sun, providing it is visible, so your chest gets warmed up.

- Stay cool if the speedometer indicates a slow speed. It is perfectly normal for the cold to have a negative effect on material, heavy clothing, and muscles.
- Occasionally take off the gloves to reduce the cold sensation in your hands, because cold temperatures can happen even in the summer and when it's raining like, for instance, during the Ironman Frankfurt in 2011.

7.6.1.4   After riding

- Take off your cold, wet clothes as soon as possible and take a warm shower.
- Dress warmly and maybe even wear a hat indoors.
- Refill stores in a timely manner (open-window effect) with primarily high-energy liquids. In winter, we tend to drink less than in summer due to the cold, but we still sweat and can easily ride ourselves into a state of hypohydration. Cola, hot chocolate, and apple spritzer are good choices. It is not necessary to have a recovery shake after every ride.
- Material maintenance: Clean the bike as soon as possible with warm water, especially the drivetrain (chain, rear sprocket, front chain rings) but also the braking surfaces. When using a chain degreaser to thoroughly remove salt and dirt from the chain, don't forget to lubricate it again afterwards.

CONCLUSION

Riding on roads is very doable with a little planning and logistics. The only exception is riding on a snow-covered or icy road surface, so the progress made over the summer isn't jeopardized by crashes over the winter.

As temperatures rise in spring, the athlete can switch from the MTB or gravel bike to racing bike. The time-trial bike should still be used primarily indoors, especially in bad weather to protect the material. I recommend training exclusively on the time-trial bike during the final eight weeks before the long-distance event to be able to confidently ride in the aero position on longer rides.

However, there is some risk, because as the form tapers and with the aerodynamically optimized material, some athletes tend to turn nearly every ride into a tempo endurance ride. I see all the time that the speeds ridden during training in the run-up to the long distances in the European summer (Ironman Frankfurt, Ironman Hamburg, Challenge Roth, etc.) are very close to the subsequent competition speeds.

To make sure that athletes really ride slowly during some of the preparatory phases I occasionally deliberately use the racing bike as a type of handicap, because that immediately counteracts riding with a specific average (average speed). An important factor about continuously riding in aero position during a race is to ride enough hours in this position in training. If the switch to the time-trial bike is made too late or the athlete did not steadily train on the bike on the roller over the winter, it becomes obvious at the 120–140-km mark in the race, because at that point many athletes are no longer able to maintain the aero position.

7.6.2 Indoor training

When it comes to training many triathletes find the cold and dark time of year particularly challenging. Cycling outdoors in particular can be extremely difficult in some regions because the constant cold temperatures and different types of precipitation greatly increase the risk of infection. Some athletes are tough and ride outdoors in just about any weather, while others have a considerably lower cold tolerance.

Those less cold tolerant can resort to training on the roller, however, not only they, but all triathletes, can hugely benefit from structured and consciously added roller training.

But first a quick digression on material to briefly explain the different indoor trainers.

7.6.2.1 Spinning bike

In the spring, many athletes are surprised that their cycling performance doesn't match their training effort on the spinning bike during winter. The reason is the lack of freewheeling combined with the large, heavy flywheels on stationary bikes. After getting started, the crank is largely moved by this flywheel, considerably reducing the amount of muscular effort required to overcome resistance than would be required during real bike training.

Spinning makes sense when it is consciously built in to improve cadence. But I would not recommend it as the sole form of training over the winter because the athlete learns an incorrect pedaling pattern.

Since, as we have already learned, the actual limiting factor in long-distance isn't the cardiovascular system but rather the muscles, it quickly becomes apparent that using the spinning bike in training should not be a major priority. Spinners train their cardiovascular system and their heat tolerance, but unfortunately not sufficiently their muscles.

7.6.2.2   Roller track

Training on the roller track is closest to cycling on the road because both wheels can move freely. The cyclist can choose from 30–50 cm wide rollers. He must be able to concentrate and have a very good sense of balance.

Accidents on the roller track where athletes ride off the left or right side of the roller are not uncommon. All sharp and valuable items should therefore be removed from the roller's vicinity. Getting on and off the bike requires practice; if necessary, hold on to a fixed object (e.g., door handle, windowsill, etc.) for better balance.

Highly intense intervals should not necessarily be performed on the roller due to the aforementioned accident risk but should be done on the turbo trainer instead.

7.6.2.3   Turbo trainer

On the turbo trainer the rear wheel stays on and is set up against a roller. Resistance can be adjusted manually. A direct-drive version of this trainer became available a few years ago. Here the rear wheel is removed, and the chain runs on a cassette that is attached to the turbo trainer.

These direct-drive trainers make indoor training significantly more realistic, particularly training units that develop endurance strength, because the tire doesn't slide over the roller and the athlete feels like he is pedaling into nothing. Direct-drive trainers are much quieter than most rollers.

7.6.2.4   Smart trainer

Smart trainers are the latest generation of indoor trainers. These are training tools in the turbo trainer category that can be connected via Bluetooth or ANT+ to various software and apps.

The athlete can ride preset interval programs with resistance automatically specified in watts, or he can ride in an imaginary fantasy world and drive his avatar with muscle power.

Figure 52: Wahoo KICKR.

7.6.3 Advantages of indoor training

Training at home is a true gift for all athletes with a smaller time budget. Instead of always getting dressed and undressed the athlete can just jump in his cycling shorts, fill his water bottles, and be ready to go. The gross vs. net training time can be greatly optimized, especially for short training units of 45-75 minutes, because set-up time with airing tires, getting dressed, getting the bike out of the basement, etc., is reduced.

When riding on the road, there are always sections where a cyclist must roll or stop. Both are eliminated on the roller. An hour of training means 60 minutes of pedaling. The fact that the athlete doesn't have to focus on traffic and instead can dedicate himself completely to the training specification is another plus of indoor training. Watt specifications and technical drills are much easier to implement indoors than on the street.

Setting up a mirror in front of the trainer helps reduce the frontal surface area through conscious visualization and practice, resulting in improved aerodynamics. When using a laptop, tablet, or TV screen for training it should be at the right height so the head can be in a realistic position and the cyclist can get used to precisely that head position, particularly while resting the arms on the handlebar.

With respect to getting used to the aero position it is important that the intervals and higher intensities are also ridden in this position. There is an additional factor in urban centers: safety. In recent years, the number of cyclists coming in contact with cars during training rides has increased significantly.

In my experience, in recent years the month of June has been the most accident-prone. When roller training is done without any distractions (music, training apps, movies, etc.) mental toughness is trained as well and helps to keep the focus exclusively on the athlete and his movements.

Last but not least, indoor riding offers great heat adaptation training. More on this topic in chapter 11.

7.6.4   Disadvantages of indoor training

Cycling means freedom. Anyone who has watched children's faces the first time they ride a bike without falling knows what I mean. Unfortunately, the freedom aspect cannot be reproduced on the indoor trainer. Moreover, probably 95% of triathletes spend their professional life primarily inside.

Fresh air is generally a good thing, but roller training can provide that in only a limited way by opening the windows. Another important point is the considerably lower use of the core muscles compared to riding on the road. Cornering, accelerating after cornering, crosswind, etc. facilitate lots of activity of the small stabilizing muscles of the trunk.

Here the main problem is the size of these muscles. As already mentioned, they are small and tend to fatigue more quickly than large muscle groups. In a race the neglect of these muscles from indoor training can have dire consequences when an athlete's core gets tired sooner and he must abandon his aero position.

The main point of criticism with respect to roller training is that bike handling outdoors worsens. When watching some cyclists at the only turnaround point of the Ironman Hawaii, one can see that they can pedal vigorously but they can't really ride a bike. The handling skills must absolutely be integrated into the training plan to counterbalance roller training.

Most triathletes aren't really good technicians, and cornering, getting on and off the bike, choosing the right braking point, and shifting gears correctly are generally poorly developed skills. Even at the highest level on shorter distances (i.e., national events or even the ITU World Cup) one can see crashes not caused by other parties but by the athlete's riding errors. Training on the roller will unfortunately do nothing to improve that.

Another point of criticism is the lack of toughening up. Many triathletes won't ride on the road if it isn't above 53 F (12 C), and then only in good weather. Triathlon is and will remain an outdoor sport, meaning one is exposed to the weather conditions. Someone who only rides in top conditions will have trouble in a race with bad weather. Those athletes tend to struggle mentally during a race, and their cycling times are catastrophic because they simply don't know how to ride in bad weather because they didn't practice it.

Cycling in the single digits toughens you up and increases overall ruggedness. There is a good word for that: *stamina*.

A factor not to be underestimated is increased sweating, even when using ventilation. Sweating causes the body to lose important fluids and electrolytes. If that loss isn't adequately compensated during or after training, regeneration time increases. The lack of the bike's sideways-tilting movements and the relatively rigid sitting position combined with a rising core temperature due to a lack of airflow, make training considerably more intense. If it's not done for heat adaptation, an athlete should really consider these factors in terms of additional load.

Compared to the outdoor watt values, I would recommend pedaling 15-20 watts less on the roller to ultimately get the same training stimulus when combining all the fatiguing factors. If a planned road cycling unit must be switched to the roller trainer due to the weather, I recommend reducing the total time by 30-50%.

But content, meaning intervals or technical exercises, can and should be ridden 1-to-1 indoors. The length of the warm-up and cool-down is shortened correspondingly. In my view the roller trainer is not ideal for working on basic endurance. Units longer than two hours are mentally extremely exhausting.

As the athlete gets hotter, and as a result loses fluids and electrolytes, the cardiovascular load at the same intensity gradually increases and possibly falls short of the planned training unit's original goal.

When an athlete is preparing for a race early in the season, for instance the Ironman South Africa, he can certainly complete some longer sessions on the roller. For athletes whose season peaks in June or July I see no need to complete long rides indoors. To me the major advantage of the modern roller trainer is the precise completion of intervals and the ability to complete technical exercise focused and without interruptions.

Strangely the social media profiles of athletes who completed their outdoor training never show the term *pain cave*, but those of athletes training indoors do, almost excessively. A three-hour ride in the single digits and rain will most certainly be painful. The term *pain cave* is too negative in my opinion and implies that training is automatically linked to pain and can't be fun. That is precisely the impression I have increasingly gotten in recent years.

Some athletes are only about optimization of any kind, and the fun falls by the wayside. An interesting interjection here is that probably 90% of all images of roller training on social media show the athlete riding with drop handlebars, meaning they do not seize the opportunity to effectively focus on training in the aero position. In ancient Rome *cave* meant: Beware!

The following overview (figure 53) is intended to show which of the training tools should be used at which point in the training process.

7.6.5   Training software and apps

At this point I would like to briefly address the pros and cons of the new software options for indoor training.

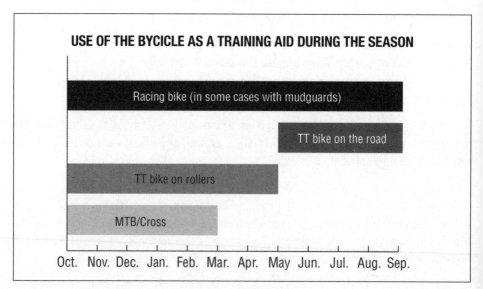

Figure 53: Use of the bicycle as a training aid during the season.

7.6.5.1   Pros

The animated cyclist in a virtual world who chases other athletes makes training sessions pass incredibly fast. These games make sessions that would ordinarily be boring truly entertaining. A simple equation would be that the increase in fun also brings with it training regularity.

This regularity based on the concept of *continuity of a specific stimulus* that I have been preaching for years leads to success. Arranging to meet up for joint training on the same route ensures that roller training can be completed even when motivation is poor due to a lack of daily form because, after all, the athlete has a date, even if it's just virtual.

Longer units on the roller that are necessary for early races like the Ironman® South Africa or New Zealand now can be completed nearly one to one on the roller.

7.6.5.2   Cons

Riding against other athletes, even if it's just in a virtual world, unfortunately often inevitably leads to a competition. No athlete likes to be outpaced and even in normal training mode tries to stay with the rear wheel of the rider in front of him. Here the danger of always missing the purpose of the training session is relatively great. Intensity that is potentially too high unfortunately often leads to the fat metabolism no longer functioning optimally.

Interestingly athletes who prepare for long-distance races almost exclusively on the roller are very often athletes who struggle during the final quarter of the 180 km bike course, because due to their training the lactate production rate is no longer in the desired range and carbohydrate consumption is too high, meaning the body's own glycogen stores are emptying too fast.

These athletes are extremely frustrated after the race because in their view their preparation on the roller was target oriented, but in doing so they often bet on the wrong horse.

Athletes who wish to focus on specific aspects of the pedaling motion can be distracted by the avatars in the animation. Here being at one with oneself, which is so important in long-distance races, also comes up short. Only those who practiced not using external stimuli (music, TV, or even Zwift) as a diversion during training, but consciously focused only on themselves, will be able to stay focused during the race.

CONCLUSION

It is easy to see that a blessing and a curse always exist side by side. I would like to offer the conclusion that neither riding exclusively on the road NOR on the roller is better or more effective.

The old Latin scholars recognized *dosis facet veneum*—that a little bit of everything is better than too much of only one thing.

In short: The mix makes the difference, and those who consciously incorporate both elements (i.e., road and indoor training) will be able to raise their cycling performance to a new level.

7.7 General Suggestions

Before we finally focus on the actual bike training, I would like to offer a few general cycling tips.

7.7.1 Apparel

When comparing cyclists and triathletes during training it is often apparent that triathletes tend to dress more optimistically, meaning their clothes are often too thin or too few. Especially in spring with those first rays of sunshine, and especially on the much beloved island of Mallorca, triathletes tend to already ride in shorts and short-sleeve jerseys during still cool temperatures without first looking at the thermometer.

Training apparel should be based on the onion principle so the rider can react to the respective changes. Arm and leg warmers and a wind vest take up little space. Wearing a functional undershirt significantly reduces the risk of catching cold.

It is common to see the outline of underpants under a cyclist's bike pants. Wearing underpants can cause massive irritation of one's backside, especially if they are cotton and soaked with sweat. Cycling pants should only be worn once and should be laundered after each training. When they are worn more than once, dried salt crystals from perspiration can remain in the padding and cause infections in the perineum.

I highly recommend using a chamois creme to protect the skin in that region. And if you end up getting caught in the rain anyway and didn't bring a rain jacket and it is getting chilly, I recommend buying a newspaper at a gas station or supermarket and stuffing it under your jersey in the chest area (a trick that has been used for decades even in the Tour de France).

REMEMBER

More clothing means less health-related stress and consequently less missed training.

7.7.2 Tools, tube, and pump

Cycling is the discipline with the most risk of a technical problem. The athlete should therefore be prepared for some eventualities. You should always carry a spare tube (with the right valve length or valve extension for aero wheels), tire lever, and a pump or CO_2 cartridge be able to fix a flat.

I unfortunately see time and again that many athletes either don't carry a repair kit or have no idea how to use it. I therefore urgently recommend practicing the tube change, either via the do-it-yourself method or by asking a trusted bike dealer.

Some bike dealers offer basic workshops for hobby mechanics during winter, which is surely a good investment of time and money. If a tire should ever tear and the tube sticks out during training, the hole can be plugged with a gel or bar wrapper. A mini tool with an Allen wrench and chain riveter should also be in the tube bag under the seat.

7.7.3 Water bottles and energy supply

Water bottles should be filled based on the length and intensity of the planned unit. Always bring along a bar or gel to relieve or prevent an unexpected drop in blood sugar or a bonk. Water bottles should be rinsed immediately after training and not hours or days later, or placed in the dishwasher to avoid bacteria or mold forming in the bottle.

7.7.4   Bike computer

Who hasn't had their bike computer fail in the middle of training because the battery was too low? It is particularly annoying when using the computer as a navigation aid. As with rinsing the water bottles, I recommend making it a habit to charge the computer right after training so it is sufficiently charged for the next ride.

7.7.5   Bike maintenance

As I mentioned in chapter 7.1, the bike should always be in perfectly clean and intact condition. This requires some maintenance, especially after riding in the rain. With a little practice, cleaning the bike only takes a few minutes, extends the bike's life, reduces friction and noises, and is considerably more fun than a poorly maintained bike.

Particular attention should be paid to sweat removal after indoor training because sweat causes some parts of the bike to corrode. Either install a sweat catcher between the seat post and the stem or dry the bike off after your ride.

7.7.6   Mobile phone, identification, and money

Nowadays a phone is part of a modern human's basic equipment (i.e., it is always on one's body). Some models are splash-proof while others are easily damaged. Either use a special case or a Ziploc bag. The latter has the advantage of also being able to safely store your ID or a copy of the same, and some cash or a credit card.

One should always carry some form of ID, especially when training alone so police and EMS are able to notify next of kin.

7.7.7   Group training

Some training rides can be completed as a group. Based on the principle misery loves company, the long basic rides become a little more tolerable. Since a sport also has a social component and togetherness is welcomed in sports, I would like to include a few tips and rules of conduct for group training:

- Only use the aero handlebars when riding in front. It is too dangerous while riding further back when to brake, the rider has to first grip the drop handlebars.
- The rest of the group should be alerted to potholes and obstacles via hand signals or verbal warnings.
- It is better to eat and drink at the back of the group instead of the front so as not to endanger the rest of the group.
- No stretching the front wheel, meaning the front wheel nubs should be level with those of the adjacent rider and not a couple inches in front.
- When the front rider relinquishes the lead, the tempo should not suddenly increase, but should stay the same.
- If an athlete in the group experiences a physical problem, the pace must slow down. A simple rule of thumb is: We start together and finish together.
- In case of a breakdown the other group members should help or use the downtime to pee or get some sustenance. It is annoying when the repair has been made and then one of the group members decides he needs to pee when everyone else is ready to resume the ride.
- When the group decides to get back on their bikes after a break everyone should be ready to go. Dawdling should be avoided for the sake of community spirit.
- If the group has more than 15 cyclists, dividing the group and riding a few hundred meters apart is an option.
- During basic training the time a cyclist is in the lead can be limited to 15 minutes, so all group members get to enjoy riding in the wind.

7.7.8   Cycling events

Triathletes have the option of participating in different cycling events. Everyman bike races are becoming increasingly popular, but triathletes also enjoy participating in bike tourism. And then there is the option of racing as a licensed cyclist or doing individual time trials. Each of these events has pros and cons, some of which I would like to list here:

- Bike tourism offers the opportunity of training some place other than the usual routes. Refreshments are provided. These events should not have a competitive feel and should be viewed as a training ride.

- While Everyman races have a Tour-de-France vibe, there is also a major risk of crashing because most participants are not used to riding at close quarters. Sadly, in recent years I have lost a number of athletes on their way to a long-distance race due to broken collarbones, wrists, etc. from crashes. I would therefore argue against doing these races because the risk is too great, especially in poor weather conditions.
- Licensed races are also dangerous, but compared to Everyman cyclists, licensed cyclists can really steer. They are much better able to control their bike in a peloton. In licensed sports the performance level tends to be higher than in Everyman races.
- Individual time trials are naturally the next best option after triathlon and have less risk of crashing. However, some triathlon bikes do not conform to UCI regulations and must be modified accordingly.

7.7.9   Cycling etiquette

And finally, a few tips for dealing with cyclists:

- Approaching motorcyclists usually give a greeting by briefly taking one hand off the handlebar. Cyclists tend to do the same. The question is, what happened to that etiquette in recent years?
- When being passed by one or more cyclists and wanting to ride in their slipstream it is polite to ask if that's alright.
- When a cyclist is broken down at the side of the road it is perfectly appropriate to slow down and ask if he needs help.

7.8   Bike Training

As I mentioned in the beginning, cycling long distances is one of the primary ways to affect overall performance. It therefore becomes quickly apparent that a lot of attention should be paid to training on two wheels when preparing for an Ironman triathlon. The science about target-oriented bike training has only improved in recent years.

During the 1990s and 2000s, most triathletes' bike training looked rather unstructured. Back then, training concepts that are still used today for swimming and running were developed and used successfully. By contrast bike training was treated rather shabbily and primarily consisted of riding on the bike, mostly without content (technique, intensity, etc.). Athletes rode a bike, and that was that.

With the advancement of the power meter and the steadily growing number of people using these systems, the bike training concept has greatly improved.

7.8.1 Advantages of bike training

Cycling is considered a no-impact sport, and unlike running has no impact load. Absorbing the impact energy while running leads to increased orthopedic stress all the way to the risk of overloading. Cycling is therefore suitable for athletes who are orthopedically vulnerable or those who carry a lot of body weight, because training interruptions must be avoided.

But because this requires a proper sitting position, seat height and cleat position must be appropriate for the athlete to avoid accumulating overload with increasing mileage.

Unlike running, the training of highly intense interval loads can be performed in a way that is safer for the locomotor system. Basic endurance training acts like a catapult for aerobic capacity and fat metabolism. Moreover, watt-controlled bike training makes it much easier to quantify and monitor training loads.

7.8.2 Disadvantages of bike training

Sitting and pedaling for hours in a rigid position dictated by the sitting position leads to restricted range of motion of the hip flexors and pectoral muscles. If this is not addressed with mobility training to keep these sensitive areas mobile and functional it can potentially affect the body's position in the water and arm extension after immersion and thus the ability to move the forearm in the correct vertical position.

Cycling requires a lot of energy. During mountainous stages of the Tour de France athletes might burn more kilocalories in 4-6 hours than in eight hours of Ironman triathlon at the world's top level. The two loads can burn up to 9,000 kcal. This energy consumption is approximately 3.5 times higher than that of a normal person in an entire day.

The increased energy expenditure causes more fatigue and requires an adequate regeneration period. Time age-group athletes don't always have due to their everyday obligations. Another important disadvantage of bike training is the rapidly growing accident risk due to increasing traffic. Nowadays, with every additional mile on the road a cyclist has a greater chance of being in an accident.

When taking a closer look at the goal of bike training, three major pillars emerge. We will address the individual points in detail below.

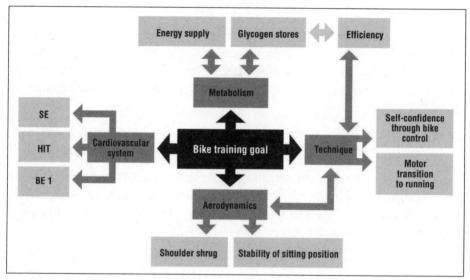

Figure 54: Goal in bike training.

7.8.3 Technical training

Some readers might shake their head because they have never heard of technical training on a bike. While the motor component is less pronounced on a bike than for instance in swimming, it does still exist. The athlete's movements are largely defined or limited by the bike's adjustment.

But here the goal should be to ride within this closed system with as much movement efficiency as possible, to achieve maximum propulsion with simultaneously low energy expenditure so the subsequent running event isn't already negatively affected in the runup. Technical training also includes learning the handling skills, but right now I would like to focus on the pedaling motion as such.

Most triathletes know about the importance of technical training in swimming and the running drills to improve movement economy, motor function, and coordination. But when it comes to cycling, especially roller training during the dark and cold time of year, the wheat quickly separates from the chaff. Most athletes ride boring sessions with little to no variation in intensity, cadence (CAD), or technical components.

Significant differences can be seen in every group road ride in terms of athletes with good and poor movement economy. Movement efficiency, meaning the energy expenditure with which a movement is executed, is critical to a fast cycling time and thus also to the overall triathlon result, because in a race a greater energy expenditure while cycling naturally has a big impact on the subsequent running performance.

Athletes with efficient pedaling function are particularly efficient in the upper portion of the movement. Their transition from moving the pedal back and up to the forward and down portion of the 360° motion is smoother. They perform the opposing transition in the bottom portion of the movement without wasting too much energy.

In terms of timing, cyclists with a poor movement economy tend to be late in the various transition phases and therefore one leg always works against the other. This results in a major energy loss. At a cadence of 80 rpm that's 4,800 movements per hour, and at a riding time of 5:30 h for the 180 km Ironman distance that's a total of 26,400 rotations that are not performed efficiently. Got the message?

Hence the necessity of training pedaling efficiency over the winter, especially for beginners, but also for ambitious athletes who want to increase their performance.

Training on the roller is the most comfortable and most time-effective form of bike training in winter. No pesky getting dressed and undressed, no arduous removal of dirt and ice melt from the bike after a ride. And training in shorts and a short-sleeve jersey and in conditions that are not weather and daylight dependent is also perfect for the working age-group athlete with a family. Another plus is that 60 minutes of riding time really is 60 minutes of training.

When training on the road, especially when living in a large city or congested area, a cyclist pedals only about 50 minutes per hour of riding time. Traffic light stops and rolling segments in turns and on downhill passages have a negative effect on the gross-net riding time. And considering that it's almost impossible to get hit by a car during indoor training and the athlete is therefore able to fully focus on the respective training purpose, roller training is the ultimate.

But many athletes have an aversion to training in a closed environment. They find it mindless and boring and do so rather grudgingly instead of joyfully. To then sweeten their time on the roller they resort to television or a laptop for entertainment and diversion.

But if the idea is to focus on pedaling function, the athlete should really abstain from these sources of entertainment during such rides because he simply won't be able to concentrate. Like running with an MP3 player in your ear, the music's rhythm can have a negative effect on movement frequency.

Studies have shown that an athlete's stride frequency and cadence are influenced by the number of beats per minute. Someone who wishes to properly implement and feel the following drills should complete them without listening to music. Doesn't sound exciting, but it will be a whole lot more effective. Age-group athletes tend to have a limited time budget, which is why every unit should bring a major return on their investment (ROI).

The goals of the technical exercises are:

- Improving pedaling function to be able to achieve a higher cadence during a race. Some athletes have problems with cadences higher than 95 rpms on slight downhill passages. But anyone who can pedal on these passages and not just roll will of course be rewarded with a faster cycling time.
- Improving inter- and intramuscular coordination and strength. In a race both lead to a greater power output (i.e., faster speed).
- Learning how to unload a leg during the pedaling motion. This can be very helpful in a race when cramping.
- Every technical training on the roller should be preceded by an at least 10-minute warm-up. To do so, ride in the BE 1 range in the subjective feeling-good cadence. Measuring the cadence requires a sensor or power meter.

Before we focus on the individual exercises, let us take a closer look at the actual pedaling motion and explain the term *circular pedaling*.

The clock face has become the image of choice for illustrating the actual cycling motion. The pedaling motion can be broken down into four individual segments.

- Power phase
- Gliding phase
- Pulling phase
- Pushing phase

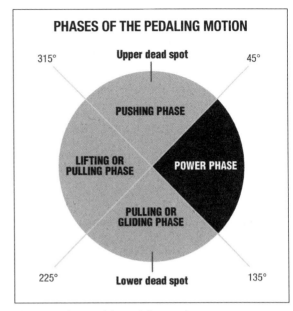

Figure 55: Phases of the pedaling motion.

Within this 360-degree rotating motion there are two dead spots, the top at 12 o'clock or 0 degrees, the bottom at 6 o'clock or 180 degrees. These two sections got their name from the fact that there is no propulsion-producing tangential force in those two areas. The power phase is the section of the rotating motion with the greatest measured tangential force on the crank arm. In theory and in the wishful thinking of many athletes, the leg that isn't in the power phase but in the pulling phase should actively be pulled upward.

Unfortunately, that doesn't really work because, first of all, the cyclist works against gravity and the muscle group necessary for pulling upward, the hamstring at the back of the thigh, is considerably weaker than gluteal and quadriceps muscles used during the pressure phase. Actively pulling upward, as was taught in the past, has turned out to be inconvertible.

Instead, the focus should be on the power phase and quickly overcoming the bottom dead spot by pulling the foot back, and the top dead spot by pushing the foot forward. Oval front chain rings are said to facilitate faster cycling through the dead spots. However, there is little evidence of this for all cyclists. But using oval chain rings may benefit the individual.

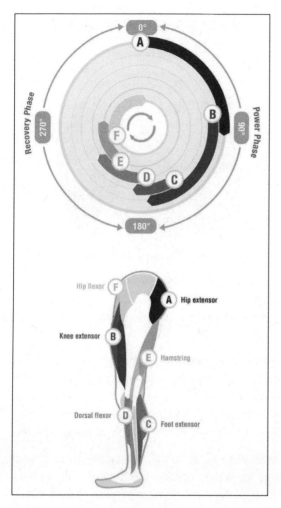

Some athletes report a subjectively improved and smoother pedaling motion. The disadvantage of oval chain rings is decreased shift comfort and more chain vibration that can have a negative effect on drive train friction.

Figure 56: Muscles used during the different pedaling phases.

REMEMBER

My recommendation here: trial educates.

7.8.3.1   Single-leg cycling

The classic among technical exercises. Here one foot is removed from the pedal and rests comfortably on a chair or the like with the knee bent at a 90-degree angle. Please make sure that crank and pedal can turn freely, and you won't get injured.

Now pedal with one leg for approximately 20–60 seconds while maintaining an even and smooth motion throughout the entire 360-degree movement. Then clip the other foot back in for an active recovery of 1–3 minutes of cycling with both legs.

By eliminating one leg the cyclist is forced to actively pull the leg upward and push it forward over the highest movement point. Use caution because this exercise can cause some nasty muscle soreness in the hip flexor.

It is best to use an easy gear at the beginning or reduce roller trainer resistance. Both can gradually be adjusted over the winter once the athlete has gotten used to it.

7.8.3.2   Single-leg dominance

This exercise is similar to single leg cycling, but is done by cycling with both legs. The goal is to focus on one leg and to drag along the opposite inactive leg. In short: the leg performing the drill does all the work. This technical exercise can be incorporated into training all year, even while training on the road.

7.8.3.3   Spin-up

During this exercise the cadence is increased by 5 rpm in one-minute intervals until the cyclist starts to bounce up and down in the seat. Next the cadence is reduced for 45–60 seconds, followed by another gradual rpm increase.

This drill helps the athlete to figure out at which maximum cadence he is able to ride with an efficient technique. After completing this drill several times these cadences can be increasingly pushed upwards.

7.8.3.4 Butt lift

This exercise is performed with both legs. The athlete lifts his butt out of the seat approximately 1-2 inches (3-5 cm) and stays in that position. Ten seconds are enough to start, but these segments can be extended to 1-2 minutes. This drill allows the cyclist to really feel his working muscles. Cadence can be between 90-100 rpm. This drill is not a riding-out-of-the saddle exercise.

7.8.3.5 Push-push-pull

This drill requires a bit more resistance, meaning the chain should be further right or roller trainer resistance should be increased. This exercise emphasizes the pulling phase after every third pedal movement. In practice this should look as follows for approximately 15-30 seconds:

Focus on pushing right / focus on pushing left / focus on pushing right / focus on pulling left / focus on pushing left / focus on pushing right / focus on pushing left / focus on pulling right, etc.

7.8.3.6 Dog-poop drill

We have all stepped in dog poop and tried to clean the bottom of our shoe by dragging it along the edge of a curb or on the grass. Precisely this motion is the goal of this exercise. Here the cyclist is supposed to learn where he should purposefully apply force in the lowest phase (6 o'clock crank position). The focus is supposed to be on pulling the respective foot horizontally back during the lowest phase.

After 30-60 seconds, switch sides and repeat the entire exercise 3-8 times.

7.8.3.7 Toe-touch drill

The purpose of this exercise is to practice the transition phase in the 12 o'clock crank position. Every time the foot is in that position the athlete must try to push his toes to the very front of the shoe. While this can't be done, simply trying to do so leads to improved movement in this segment of the pedaling motion.

Thirty to forty-five seconds per foot are perfectly sufficient before shifting the focus to the other foot. Complete 8-10 repetitions per side. Begin with a moderate cadence and gradually increase the rpm over the course of weeks.

7.8.3.8   Top-only drill

The last drill focuses on the feet one more time. When pedaling normally with both legs the main emphasis is on making sure the instep and the top of the toes are always in contact with the inside of the cycling shoe. This trains the biomechanically less favorable upward movement and therefore also trains and strengthens the hip flexors. This exercise should be performed for 1-3 minutes with 1-3 minutes of normal pedaling in-between sets.

REMEMBER

These drills can be built into any basic training session on the roller. The athlete can pick one exercise per training but can also pack several different aspects into one unit, similar to the aforementioned running drills or the technical portion of swim training.

Roller training can therefore be much more entertaining than many athletes believe. The effectiveness and advantages should not be dismissed.

7.8.4   The ultimate cadence

A wise old bike-racing saying is: big gear x high cadence = high speed.

Cycling can be so simple. But triathlon isn't swimming, cycling, and running, but a standalone sport with the complexity and synergy of these three individual disciplines, so that specialist insights cannot be blindly transferred to the triathlon. Opinions differ when it comes to cadence.

One group advocates for a cadence of 60-70 rpm, another tends to look to the cadences in the cycling sport. But what's right and what's wrong?

As so often in training theory, the answer is: it depends. What I am trying to say is that the cadence depends on the athlete's weight and his athletic background.

There are pros and cons for both theories. I will try to shed some light on the subject.

7.8.4.1   Low cadence (60–70 rpm)

The argument for a low cadence is that these rpm activate fewer fast-twitch muscle fibers. These fast-twitching and explosive fibers have a high rate of carbohydrate consumption. Since long-distance triathlon is the supreme discipline of energy management, this is an important argument.

A low cadence does not cause the heartrate to shoot up, protecting the cardiovascular system so the athlete can be slightly fresher when starting the running portion of the race. In my experience, athletes with a heavy build tend to ride with a lower cadence.

7.8.4.2   High cadence (85–95 rpm)

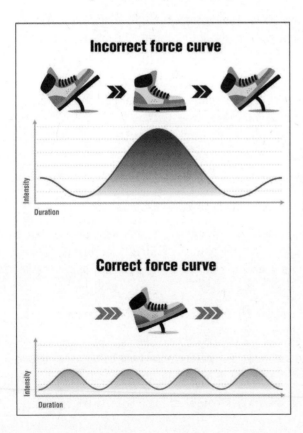

Advocates of pedaling at a higher cadence argue that the load to overcome, meaning the resistance, is spread out over multiple movements (i.e., creating fewer force peaks that fatigue the muscles). It has also been determined that blood circulation in the thigh muscles is not optimal when riding with low cadences in the aero position due to the muscular effort during force peaks.

Figure 57: Force progression using the example of a gas pedal.

Another argument is that athletes with a limited cadence spectrum are often unable to pedal with a high cadence during fast passages (downhill or tailwind), meaning in a high gear, and thereby lose precious time.

Countless analyses of long-distance races have shown me when fatigue starts, because that's when the pedaling speed drops into the basement. When an athlete starts the race with only 70 rpm, he will potentially only ride with 55-60 rpm at kilometer 140, which is then too low because it is uneconomical.

In addition, a cadence of 90 rpm is a neuromuscular trigger for the stride frequency of 180 per minute that is considered ideal in running. The idea is to effectively prepare for the subsequent running event with these 90 rpm.

When cramping occurs during a race, the athlete who can ride higher cadences can get through this impasse by increasing the cadence while simultaneously reducing force peaks.

7.8.4.3   Ultimate cadence (80–85 rpm)

As is so often the case, the solution is a mix. If someone were to ask me what my ideal cadence in the Ironman would be, I would suggest, although sweepingly, 80-85 rpm. To me that's a good mix of both schools of thought with which I have been able to achieve very good race results for several years.

7.8.4.4   Cadence training

So far, we have only looked at cadence in a race, but we should also look at the aspect of cadence training. Based on the principle nothing ventured, nothing gained, many athletes don't tap into the cadence power reserve and do not or only half-heartedly pay attention to it during training. Instead, based on the above calculation, they only train in a big gear.

I absolutely advocate for cadence variations to expand the spectrum, so the athlete has an appropriate response to the respective situations in a race. I would like to introduce a few sessions for that purpose.

7.8.4.4.1 Cadence relay

Relay training takes place in the relaxed basic range. It can be completed on flat terrain, but also indoors. After a brief warm-up, the athlete rides two minutes at 85 rpm followed by one minute at 100-105 rpm. The exercise is completed in a span of 45-120 minutes.

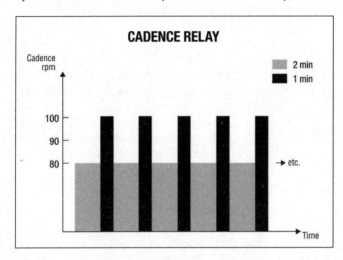

Figure 58: Cadence relay.

7.8.4.4.2 Cadence pyramid

When doing the cadence pyramid, rpm is increased every 3-8 minutes by 5 per minute. After completing the level with 110 rpm the athlete incrementally reduces the rpm by 5 per minute as he comes down the other side of the pyramid.

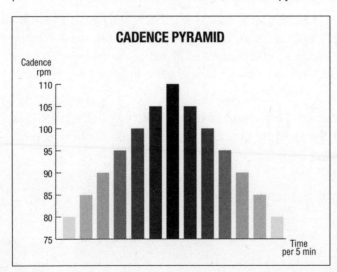

Figure 59: Cadence pyramid.

7.8.4.4.3   Increasing cadence

The name says it all. Rpms are increased every 20–40 minutes by 5 per minute. As with all CAD programs, this unit is also completed in the basic endurance range.

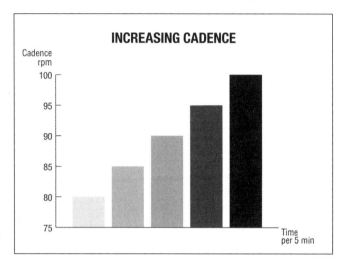

Figure 60: Increasing cadence.

7.8.4.4.4   Increasing cadence at the end

During this unit the athlete first completes 150–300 minutes in the normal BE 1 range with the corresponding feeling-good cadence, also called *freely chosen cadence (FCC)*, before the cadence is then increased to 100–105 rpm for 3–5 minutes during the final hour. In-between the athlete rides 3–5 minutes at FCC.

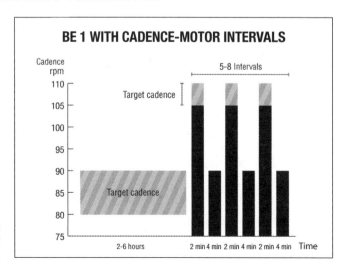

Figure 61: BE 1 with cadence intervals at the end.

7.8.4.5   Controlling the pedaling pattern

Here, too, measuring technology has arrived. The analysis system Leomo makes it possible to measure technical deficiencies during training and to keep the athlete updated. To do so five motion sensors are attached to the body.

The dead spot score (DSS) shows in which area of the athlete's 360-degree movement time delays occur, meaning dead spots, while cycling as well as in the subsequent analysis. This makes it possible to draw inferences about crank length, seat height, chain rings, and cleat position, but also movement execution.

CONCLUSION

Improving movement quality should resonate with all readers by now. In my view, this is a previously barely tapped performance reserve.

7.8.5   Aerodynamic position training

Athletes who worry about their aero position should not just focus their energy on their equipment but also continue to refine their posture and position. This can be done via roller training or in front of a mirror. The latter helps to gain increasing awareness of one's frontal surface area.

7.8.5.1   Aero intervals

Athletes should practice an active aero position with shoulder shrug and a low head position during the winter on the roller. But a deliberately narrow knee position close to the top tube as well as a narrow hand position should also be practiced.

One way to do this is to start with 15 x 1 minute in aero position followed by one minute in a loose and relaxed posture, also on the aero handlebar. As the athlete adapts, these segments can either be extended or the number of aero intervals can be increased. Intensity should start in the basic range.

7.8.5.2   Normal intervals

For some time now, I have followed athletes on their social media profiles. There one can see photos of their pain caves while riding interval programs on the roller trainer. These are often accompanied by details about watt numbers, but I hardly ever see photos of the athletes riding those watt numbers in aero position.

I would therefore recommend pedaling a few watts less, but riding them as much as possible in the race-specific posture, meaning in aero position.

7.8.5.3   Mobility training

Ensuring a solid and sustainable aero position requires the appropriate amount of strength and mobility in shoulders, neck, trunk, gluteal muscles, and hamstring. Regular mobility training is essential.

7.8.6   Cardiovascular and metabolism training

I don't think I need to necessarily explain to the readers the necessity of endurance training to develop the cardiovascular system and the metabolism in preparation of a long-distance event.

But I will address the most important forms of training below.

7.8.6.1   Basic endurance

When looking at the demand profile for a long-distance race, regardless of performance class, one quickly sees that the tempo during the race is equal to BE 1 and BE 2 or zone 1 and zone 2. In a race the goal should be to ride as fast as possible with the lowest possible carbohydrate expenditure to protect the body's own glycogen stores as best as possible, so some carbohydrates in the form of glycogen remain in the tank for the subsequent marathon.

When preparatory bike training isn't optimally regulated the metabolism may not sufficiently develop (i.e., carbohydrate stores empty too quickly). The primary goal during training should therefore be modulating the metabolism in a way that allows the cyclist to realize a superior performance with low carbohydrate expenditure.

In everyday language this means developing a big engine (aerobic capacity or VO_2max) with a very low fuel consumption (low Vlamax).

Training basic endurance is the critical training form for developing both components. But when looking at some training programs or posts circulating in the vastness of the internet, one gets the sense that this all-dominant training form has faded into obscurity. There the focus is primarily on developing maximum oxygen consumption (VO_2max) and less on developing the substrate metabolism. Magazine, blogs, and YouTube channels must understandably generate new content all the time. A 5-hour old-school basic endurance ride is not a good fit here.

What is unfortunately often publicized here are VO_2max rides, HIT training sessions, and other things, while everything else is put aside. Sadly, athletes who primarily look to those parameters very often have their personal Waterloo moment at kilometer marker 130 of a race. Their carbohydrate expenditure is so high that their energy stores are empty at such an early point in the race.

Indoor training is another pitfall on the way to long-distance success if it isn't executed with precision and discipline. Athletes whose indoor training is too intense or who turn every unit into a kind of imaginary competition will certainly increase their VO_2max, but unfortunately also the maximum lactate production rate (Vlamax). By shifting training towards intense intervals and focusing mainly on developing VO_2max, the fact that basic endurance training also increases VO_2max (i.e., not only with intensive intervals) was completely glossed over.

I am certainly no innovation refusenik, but in bike training I am absolutely pro basic endurance training. In my opinion, a solid long-distance performance in the European summer requires at least 4,000 km on two wheels starting with the new year. Compared to running, basic endurance training on a properly adjusted bike is far less orthopedic stress and a much lower injury risk.

The disadvantage is clearly the time component. Cycling requires hours. I would urgently steer clear of promises that make a long-distance race possible with fewer than 10 hours a week of training. It is the nature of things that a 226 km challenge also requires a certain training workload.

I aways ruffle feathers when I say that a long-distance race isn't suitable for every athlete. This assertion is less about physical prerequisites but about concomitant personal circumstances. If an athlete is only able to reliably manage 6–8 hours per week in training time he is better off trying shorter distances. I am hereby also wagging a finger at my professional colleagues. You should really refrain from shepherding athletes with such a limited time budget on the way to long-distance races. As a coach one has a certain amount of responsibility for an athlete's health.

The fact that the Ironman triathlon is no longer viewed as exotic is not necessarily a positive, because it unfortunately opens the door to many athletes who do not have the necessary respect for the challenge (i.e., don't conscientiously prepare for this challenge). I do not want to be responsible for the health-related long-term consequences of an inadequately prepared long-distance race.

Back to the actual training. The importance of basic training rides should have been internalized. The duration of the units can be debated. Some studies show that no additional gains can be made after 4.5 hours on a bike. I would also go primarily by that marker. But I do recommend deliberately exceeding that duration from time to time, even if science argues against it.

Things like mental strength or simply toughening up your backside, neck, and hands are important aspects of preparing for that one day a year. Depending on athlete type and the athlete's history, between one and ten training rides beyond the race length should be planned as over-distance training while making sure that intensity is really low and the athlete has an adequate energy supply during the ride.

7.8.6.2 Strength endurance and power endurance

Another important building block is the development of strength endurance, meaning the ability to overcome high resistance over a long period of time. This ability should be called endurance strength because according to the definition strength training is the ability to overcome at least 50% of the maximum resistance that must be overcome. But since the term *strength endurance* has become mainstream, we will largely stick with it.

Endurance strength can be controlled and trained pretty well. To do so the athlete rides with a high resistance and low cadence (50-65 rpm). These segments can either be performed in 3-15-minute time spans on an incline—a 5-7% incline is ideal—or more specifically on the smart trainer.

Unlike with regular cycling, I recommend placing the hands flat on the handlebar (be careful not to slip off the handlebar!!) to generate greater activity in the necessary muscle loop. When the handlebar is gripped firmly the athlete tends to connect with the shoulder or upper body.

If the athlete rests on the handlebar while performing these intervals, the hands should ideally also hold the handlebar lightly. This training form has been used for decades by cyclists and triathletes.

For a long time, it was not known why this method is so highly effective. Now we know that these intervals affect the distribution of muscle fibers and that fiber type II, which has a high carbohydrate consumption, can be converted to endurance-supporting type I fibers with a lower carbohydrate consumption.

7.8.6.3 VO_2max

Particularly during the cold and dark time of year, training basic rides for hours isn't always a given. A good option during that time is training indoors to tighten the VO_2 screw, instead of long, monotonous change-in-tempo units with VO_2max intervals. The desired target intensity level should be 88–90% of VO_2max.

SAMPLE UNITS

I would like to list two training units as examples.

Session 1

15 min easy warm-up ride
10 x 40 seconds all out/20 seconds alternating active break
10 minutes easy
10 x 40 seconds all out/20 seconds alternating active break
5–10 minutes easy warm-down

Session 2

15 minutes easy warm-up ride
4 x 4 minutes with 3–5 minutes active break between sets
15 minutes easy warm-down

7.8.6.4 Ironman-specific intervals

As previously mentioned, the load range during a race lies in the BE 1/BE 2 transition area. In order to get as close as possible to the specific competition load the athlete needs to complete units with segments in this load range.

The time period approximately eight weeks before race day is a dangerous point in the training process. During this phase the performance capacity is already so high that many athletes unfortunately turn every planned basic endurance ride into a tempo ride, meaning they are working within the Ironman load range. Especially when the weather is good and the legs are tanned and training rides are done on the racing wheels, there is always a major risk of training too fast.

These tempo endurance rides cause major fatigue, and week by week can even catapult the athlete into an overloading-like condition. A better choice would be intervals of 10-30 minutes in this load range in order to get used to that load zone and to largely keep fatigue to a minimum.

When the athlete completes all these sessions too fast and with too much intensity as his form improves, the lactate production rate can potentially worsen. But the goal should be to start the race with an optimally developed fat metabolism (i.e., a low Vlamax). The point at issue here is to continue to optimize the metabolism while also preparing for the specific demands of the competition.

Units to optimize the fiber theory will ensure both. To simplify, imagine the muscle consists of 100% muscle fiber. A minimum percentage of these fibers must be activated for the body to execute a movement.

When an athlete cycles primarily at low intensity he uses approximately 20-25% of the muscle fibers of the entire leg musculature for the pedaling motion. This conscious reduction to a small portion of the musculature is a smart function of the brain to use as little energy as possible. The more we operate in this low-intensity zone the more efficient the brain becomes in targeting that 20-35%.

However, there is a limit to the load these fibers can handle, and precisely that is the point so many athletes have experienced at km 120 on the bike, when the Vlamax and the carbohydrate expenditure are too high. Our trained fibers refuse to work, so the untrained fibers must take over. However, their way of working is much less economical, causing the speed to decrease and subjective effort to be considerably greater.

But how to avoid this phenomenon? How to bypass this point and keep the performance at a high level for the final 60 km?

That means we must find a way to recruit a greater percentage of the musculature, meaning more fibers, during training to further delay the point when fatigue sets in. Weight training uses the following approach: begin weight training with lots of weight, then start reducing the weight and increase the number of repetitions. The goal here is to activate more muscle fibers with the heavy resistance which will then remain activated during the repetitions with less weight. When applying this to bike training, we get the following sample workout.

SAMPLE UNIT

30 minutes easy warm-up
2 x 20 minutes with high resistance (chain all the way to the right) in the upper BE 2 range, break in between of 10 minutes at easy resistance
180 minutes BE 1 with normal cadence
30 minutes BE 2 with racing cadence
10 minutes easy warm-down

The 2 x 20 minutes with high resistance activate a greater percentage of fibers which will then stay activated, or rather will be consciously targeted by the brain with the 30 minutes of BE 2 training at the end of the unit. Those final 30 minutes in particular will feel extremely unpleasant, because towards the end of the three-hour segment activation of fibers in terms of percentage is considerably lower than at the beginning of the BE 1 segment, and the brain has to notch up the performance again.

The following chart (figure 62) offers an overview of when which training units should be used for long distance. The spread of the individual forms of training will become apparent relatively quickly. There is a reason basic training can be called the foundation for success.

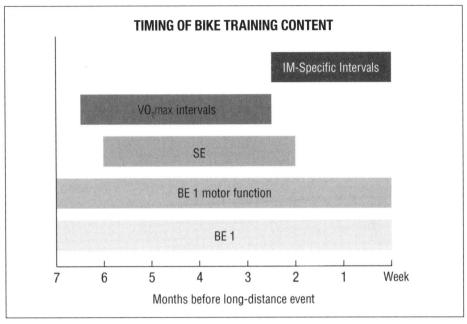

Figure 62: Timing of bike training content.

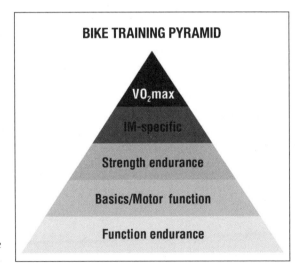

Figure 63 Bike training pyramid.

7.8.7 Training terrain

One common question is about preferred training terrain. Some athletes avoid riding on flat terrain without collecting elevation gain. When looking at the demand profile of a classic long-distance race (except for Wales, Lanazarote, Embruman, etc.) one can quickly see that cumulative elevation gain is between 800 and 1,800 m (i.e., a profile that the Tour de France roadbook would probably list as baseline). It should therefore be apparent which special ability is important in long-distance triathlon: continuous pedaling.

But when training too much in mountainous terrain the athlete might have a better performance pedaling uphill and therefore generates a greater strength stimulus and possibly changes his muscle fiber spectrum from fast-twitch and carbohydrate-consuming type II fibers to type 1 endurance fibers, but subsequently has a much lower load when going downhill. When comparing power meter files from basic rides in mountainous and flat or hilly terrain one can clearly see that most of the time in flat terrain

- performance is continuous and
- the average performance is higher.

Developing strength endurance plays an important role and should be considered in every training plan. To develop Ironman-specific abilities a large portion of the overall kilometers should still be completed in flat terrain with emphasis on constant pedaling and staying in the aero position. For developing strength endurance, I prefer controlled intervals to random topography-based uphill cycling.

Another problem is when athletes from flat regions go to mountainous areas for a training camp and try to conquer every incline in the training camp's region. Knee and back problems due to a lack of orthopedic habituation are inevitable here.

Cooler temperatures come with the risk of hypothermia on rides, which is why the appropriate clothing such as wind vest, jacket, arm warmers and leg warmers should be included in the planning of such a training ride.

TECHNICAL ADVICE

I would like to offer the following technical advice for riding in the mountains:

- Pull the belly button inward to engage the transverse abdominals. This ensures better force transfer in the glutes and quadriceps. Do not hold your breath!
- Hold the handlebar lightly. When the grip is too firm, tension from the forearm spreads to the rest of the body and you become tense.
- Don't lock the elbows.
- Start riding out of the saddle early.
- Alternate between riding in and out of the saddle to spread out fatigue between as many muscle groups as possible.
- Don't use a big gear to ride into the mountain.

7.8.8 Performance-driven bike training with the power meter

The Kona Bike Count shows that the number of athletes with a power meter on their time trial bike has rapidly increased in recent years. When in the past it was just a handful of athletes with mounted sinfully expensive systems who were aware of the advantage of having their performance measured in watts, today athletes almost can't imagine riding without this tool. Meanwhile our knowledge about the advantages of such systems along with plummeting costs have become firmly rooted in triathlon.

In 2009, 256 such systems were counted at check-in the day before the Ironman World Championships in Hawaii. In 2019, it was 1,563 mounted watt meters. But buyer beware! Not every system provides reliable and realistic numbers.

7.8.8.1 Hardware

When looking for the right power meter one is met with a big selection. There are more than 20 suppliers to choose from with different models and technical concepts that determine performance. Not every power meter calculates performance in the same position. Three different measuring concepts have established themselves.

- Capture in the crank or crank spider
- Capture in the pedal axis
- Capture in the rear wheel hub

In addition, there are differences in the way the values are displayed:

- The performance of one leg is captured and the measured value is doubled (e.g., left crank arm or via one pedal).
- The performance of both legs is captured independently of each other and totaled (e.g., both crank arms or both pedals).
- The performance of both legs is captured together (e.g., crank spider or rear wheel hub).

Is a bilateral performance capture even necessary?

I would say yes for the purpose of getting precise data and applying it scientifically, but for everyday use (i.e., during training), I think a unilateral less expensive version is totally adequate.

We unfortunately dream far too much of a perfectly symmetrical human body and wish for equal movement on both sides and a correspondingly equal application of force. But unfortunately, or rather thankfully, man is not a symmetrical machine. Differences in the two halves of the body are normal, which is why in my opinion the idea of a 50/50 side-by-side comparison at all costs is not achievable.

As early as learning to walk as a child, a favored side emerges which, over a normal course of life, remains that way. One exception would be severe injuries to the lower extremities, which then justify the use of a bilateral system so imbalances can be captured and eliminated. The following aspects should play an important role when choosing a power meter.

7.8.8.2   Basic use and handling

Easy use and handling of a performance meter are important. Particularly age-group athletes with little extra time don't like having to spend a lot of time messing with a performance meter before training and checking settings or calibrations each time they use the device. Based on the principle of plug and play, ideally no steps other than switching on the bike computer should be necessary.

The system should be linked to the computer on the handlebar via Bluetooth or ANT+, and both should always find each other again after the initial pairing configuration. Easy handling should also include the user's ability to change the battery himself or simply charge it via a mini-USB.

Nothing is more annoying than a system that must be sent off for a battery change during important phases of training or right before a competition. Here, too, Murphy's Law unfortunately often comes into play.

7.8.8.3 Precise and reliable performance data

To train effectively an athlete must be able to rely on the performance meter to

- provide accurate data: Most manufacturers' stated accuracy is ± 2% or better and should be maintained continuously during training.
- ascertain data reliably: External influences such as weather, temperature, road condition, etc., should not affect the performance meter's measuring accuracy.

With respect to measuring precision, there are unfortunately discrepancies between the information provided by manufacturers and reality. In my experience, pedal systems often fall through the cracks, especially since ascertaining watts numbers on the pedal axis can certainly be physically scrutinized when the only propelling force is tangential force that should really be determined via strain gauges in the crank.

Older pedal systems have shown major differences depending on the amount of torque used to screw the system into the crank. This is particularly tricky when the pedal system is dismantled and in the bike case during flights to training camps or competitions, because very few athletes will have a torque wrench in their luggage, much less have this problem on their screen.

Unfortunately, the trend towards increasingly cheaper systems comes with a certain ambivalence. On the one hand, the number of users is growing, on the other hand, measuring precision very often suffers.

7.8.8.4 Sturdiness

Athletes who ride in all kinds of weather should have a performance meter that is also made of tough stuff. A certain amount of robustness and waterproofness should be assured. The system should not suffer irreparable damage in a crash.

To me this unfortunately is another disqualifier of pedal systems, because the sensors are exposed on the crank and can therefore be easily damaged. The pedal system bearings are often of rather inferior quality. But low friction in the pedal bearing would be desirable to permanently minimize friction resistance.

For rear-wheel systems the athlete must first choose a type of wheel, meaning either a training or a racing bike. The latter would more likely wear out from riding in bad weather during training prior to the race, while a training wheel has some aerodynamics-related disadvantages in a race.

7.8.8.5   Price–performance ratio

Ultimately the sale price should also be a factor in the purchase. Triathlon is increasingly referred to as the new golf game. Sport-related costs are very high, which is why systems with a good price–performance ratio are welcome as long as measuring accuracy does not suffer.

7.8.9   Advantages of watt-based bike training

In triathlon, and especially distances of 70.3 or rather Ironman, energy management plays a critical role when it comes to overall performance. An athlete who optimally manages his energy on the bike and also has an adequate energy supply will generally be rewarded with a solid or fast race.

There are many parameters an athlete believes he can use to stay informed about his training progress, but not all are precise and practical.

For instance, there's the ominous average speed of a ride. It should never, ever be used to monitor performance, because due to the various external influences (wind, topography, slipstream) it cannot reflect the actual performance.

Using the heart rate parameter to manage training due to long-time experience and good and inexpensive HR systems certainly has some value. But it must be noted that in terms of timing, the heart rate always lags behind the actual performance and is simply the body's reaction to the performance.

Training management based on heart rate is certainly an option when training the fat metabolism with the continuous method in the basic endurance range. Precise management of the workload during interval training with short interval durations is difficult to do by pulse rate as its response is delayed and still rises when the interval in question might have already been completed before the heart rate reached its peak.

This often results in the initial load being too high at the beginning of the interval with a drop in performance towards the end.

Moreover, the heart rate is of course not only subject to the organism's load condition, but rather should be viewed as a variable biological parameter that is influenced by digestion, thermal regulation, regeneration processes, stress, etc. Even for that reason alone, training by pulse will certainly result in deviations that in extreme cases can be as much as 10-20 BPM. Depending on an athlete's normal pulse, this can be a deviation of 5-10%.

But it is nevertheless recommended to wear a pulse meter to see the physiological response within the context of physical performance. By contrast, watt-based endurance training measures the athlete's physical performance where it was generated, meaning at the human-machine point of contact.

Unlike control by heart rate, the athlete sees the values measured by the power meter without time delay and has them displayed on the bike computer so the intensities during interval training can be adhered to much more precisely.

Bike training by watts is based on measuring our mechanically generated performance. The power meter measures the torque, the power we use to move the crank, as well as cadence, and calculates the performance based on these two measured values. It then sends this result by radio to the receiver in watts. Compared to heart rate-based measurements the advantage here is that a watt is always a watt regardless of how fit or tired, how relaxed or stressed, or how well or poorly trained an athlete is. The performance measured is precisely the performance given.

Analysis of power meter files shows athletes who tend to just roll through turns and slight downhill passages during training quite clearly how much of their completed training time was spent being lazy or ineffective. There are always athletes who, depending on the training territory, don't pedal during 25% of their training time and just let it roll.

A power meter also allows an athlete to optimize his aerodynamics, because when performance decreases during replicable external conditions but the speed stays the same, or the cyclist can go faster while performance stays the same, it points to significantly improved aerodynamics. Trying out different equipment or sitting positions at the same speed and comparable wind conditions on a regular route can serve as a kind of do-it-yourself aero test.

Another advantage of using a power meter is the fact that results of a performance test produced in a lab can be applied to everyday training. In the past, as is done today, these tests were done with the performance measured in watts. But unfortunately, a corresponding test measured in watts was unavailable in the field.

Looking back on this now, such performance tests were really a waste of time or only helpful for testing performance capacity. But usefulness for subsequent training in terms of determination and reliable implementation of training areas was not clearly evident without the performance meter.

Lab tests today should ideally be done on one's own power-meter-equipped bike to be able to compare the ascertained values to those of the lab ergometer. The diagnostician should mark the difference and should take it into consideration when evaluating the training areas. A manual correction of up to 25 watts is unfortunately not uncommon and is more frequently the case with cheaper pedal systems.

CONCLUSION

In summary, watt-controlled bike training is the most effective method for objectively managing training and competition goals.

Effective and economical bike training is made up of:

- reliable and reproducible performance data,
- detailed analysis of performance, and
- correct pacing during training and competition.

7.8.10   Power meter metrics

In recent years, more and more metrics were created with advances in power meter hardware. But not every value is meaningful and should not necessarily become a focal point.

7.8.10.1   Functional threshold power (FTP)

The functional threshold power (FTP) is probably the best-known value when using a power meter. It is a value that is always listed as a performance indicator and can often be found excessively in athletes' social media profiles. Zwift, the biggest indoor-training platform in the world, also uses FTP to assess a user's performance. If the value is unknown the software even guides the user step-by-step through a testing process to ascertain the value.

FTP is supposed to indicate the maximum performance an athlete can maintain for one hour. The associated test is very popular among athletes because it doesn't require an elaborate test set-up. A smart trainer or a bike with a power meter are sufficient.

Since a 60-minute graded exercise stress test would be a very intensive training session, a second 20-minute test was developed. I would say a one-hour test upon return to training after a season break or off-season is critical.

Theoretically the training areas should be determined based on the ascertained average. This is only conditionally possible. The error in this construct lies in the frequent conflation of the terms *FTP* and *individual anaerobic threshold* (IAT). IAT refers to the metabolic process in which lactate production and breakdown are balanced. This is also referred to as maximal lactate steady state (MaxLaSS).

When intensity increases beyond the IAT point the balance between lactate accumulation and its breakdown unravels. Hence the IAT is not just a specific performance in watts but more of a physiological moment. By contrast, the FTP only reflects a performance value without shining a light on the physiological coherences.

The ascertained FTP value, regardless of whether it stemmed from the 60-minute or 20-minute test, offers no information as to the extent of which this performance was dominantly aerobic or anaerobic.

The following example should offer a transparent explanation of the FTP test's weaknesses. An athlete completes an FTP test and ascertains a value of 330 watts. After 6-8 weeks of training, he tests again with a repeated result of 330 watts. This causes the athlete to feel frustrated.

This testing method will not provide information about the physiological changes that took place during those 6-8 weeks. The athlete will not find out if and how the metabolic dominances within these 330 watts changed. A close look at performance physiology does not permit such an FTP test.

When strengths and weaknesses in the athlete's metabolism are not shown, no reliable assertions regarding training goals can be made. In my view, the FTP test should be used more for training monitoring and less as a predictor for subsequent training zones.

Such a testing method cannot and should not replace a lactate test. I see the FTP test as more wishful thinking, like performance testing for in-home use. The results should be viewed as an approximation and estimation and less as valid test data, especially since the popular 20-minute test is often far from the actual one-hour performance. The FTP test should therefore be taken with a grain of salt. It does not replace a real performance test.

Another point that is critical to long distance is the fact that many athletes bet on the wrong horse when it comes to training. One often reads about training programs with the name "FTP builder" or the like that focus solely on improving that metric. But a very good one-hour performance isn't necessarily decisive for a long-distance performance, but rather a very low carbohydrate expenditure during a high performance. Simply put, this carbohydrate quantity is linked to the lactate production rate (Vlamax).

Lactate burns a large amount of carbohydrates when it accumulates. But since glycogen stores are very limited, during the training process a lot of emphasis should be placed on reducing the Vlamax. In other words, the Vlamax shows how well the athlete can quickly and explosively convert energy into performance.

This ability is irrelevant to the triathlon distance, where diesel engines with low fuel consumption are in demand. The following aspects should be taken into consideration for lowering maximum lactate production:

* regular training
* no high intensities
* training with low carbohydrate stores (FatMax training)
* strength endurance training
* mixed metabolic training (intervals BE 1/BE 2 transition)

Since most FTP-increasing programs include lots of intensity segments, Vlamax will not decrease but may even increase. Athletes who only turn the FTP screw and don't sufficiently focus on developing their fat metabolism or rather reducing Vlamax are traditionally in the athlete group that rides fast until km marker 120–140 in the Ironman®, but then implode because their carbohydrate expenditure is too high for this performance and cannot be covered long term by a supply from the glycogen stores and externally introduced gels or bars.

Training basic endurance and fat metabolism and reducing Vlamax continue to be of critical importance for long-distance events. With the advent of the FTP craze on social media platforms the focus has unfortunately shifted towards intervals that feel hard and productive in training but are not necessarily suitable for athletes with a high lactate production rate.

It is often said that maximum oxygen uptake is increased by training certain intervals. Like the overrated FTP and the attendant workouts, the importance of basic endurance training has gotten increasingly lost. Training large volumes at low intensity, meaning classic basic training, is still a more reliable way to increase maximum oxygen uptake than training the respective intervals.

It seems odd that basic endurance training has gone out of style when we know that it helps to increase VO_2max and reduce Vlamax. In this context we often hear about the quality-over-quantity principle. Here intense intervals are touted as superior, and basic endurance training as an outdated concept.

Back to FTP after this brief digression.

With the knowledge we now have about FTP and this value's lack of validity with respect to an athlete's performance capacity, one can and absolutely should have a different view of such assertions on social media. There we can sometimes read about dizzying values that to me beg the question of why these age-group athletes don't have a pro-tour license in cycling.

Hence a brief guideline from my position to rethink the importance of FTP values:

- Is my power meter accurate enough?
- When was the system last calibrated?
- Does my scale show a realistic body weight?

The competition follow-up of some athletes is particularly interesting. Here one can often read that the athletes were unable to realize the training watt values during the race. Another set of questions for athletes with such race results:

- Is the power meter fully functional after travel (keyword torque for pedal systems)?
- Why do I realize fewer watts in a race than in training? Shouldn't it be the other way around?
- Is my pacing strategy too optimistic or do I assess myself incorrectly?

Once we have understood that FTP is not a very good indicator for determining performance capacity, we can see that the subsequent values should also not be seen as optimal, because some of these metrics are subject to the FTP. FTP turns up in several of these calculation formulas. I am therefore not quite convinced that these values can be reliably and validly used for objective load quantification and evaluation, meaning the actual training load. I therefore view them as more of a resource, and nothing more. I will not base ongoing training plans on one of these values. To me they are merely a not very well thought out attempt to force training into a number construct at all costs.

7.8.10.2 Normalized power (NP)

Watts NP is a performance average used for more accurate representation of changes in ride conditions. It can be used to make acceleration after turns, smaller crests, and inclines visible to gain a more accurate representation of the exertion. In doing so the NP considers the body's reaction to changes in intensity due to changing conditions or resistance.

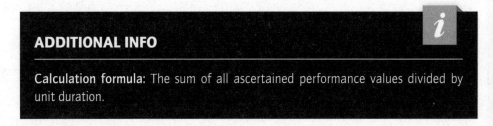

ADDITIONAL INFO

Calculation formula: The sum of all ascertained performance values divided by unit duration.

7.8.10.3 Intensity factor (IF)

The intensity factor should reflect the respective load of a workout relative to the current state of fitness (i.e., FTP). Since FTP is not an indicator for performance capacity, evaluating a training unit via IF makes little sense to me.

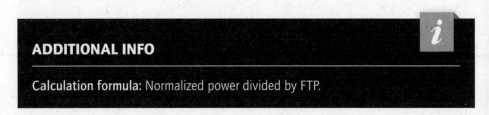

ADDITIONAL INFO

Calculation formula: Normalized power divided by FTP.

7.8.10.4   Variability index (VI)

The variability index provides the relationship between average watts and watts NP and is an indicator for riding smoothness. The closer the value is to 1, the smoother, meaning without performance peaks by accelerating after a turn or pulling over a crest, the training ride. A value of 1.05–1.08 should be realizable in nearly all long-distance races. Exceptions are the Ironman Lanzarote, Wales, etc., meaning races with major elevation differences or many changes in direction and turns.

ADDITIONAL INFO

Calculation formula: Normalized power divided by average watts.

CONCLUSION

He who measures a lot measures a lot of bull, or paralysis through analysis. What I'm trying to say is that not every measured value should be blindly followed!

8   RUNNING

We have now mentally parked the bike in the transition zone and will focus on running as the third triathlon movement pattern. Running is the most natural form of movement but also holds the most risk in terms of injuries and all sorts of overloading.

Due to this disposition and the possibility of getting injured, mistakes in movement execution and training content should be avoided. In a competition the marathon is the phase in which dreams can burst like soap bubbles. Mistakes made in training, pacing on the bike, and a deficient supply strategy of carbohydrates, water, and sodium are mercilessly exposed in the long-distance marathon and have an immense effect on the overall long-distance performance.

Falling short in the running segment of an Ironman triathlon is unfortunately often solely blamed on a poorly developed running technique without considering other error sources.

In this chapter I would like to raise awareness about correct programming and an effective long-distance marathon running technique.

8.1   Equipment

A triathlete can also spend quite a bit of money on this third discipline, but it doesn't require much. I have outlined the important things regarding equipment here.

8.1.1   Shoes

Other than an appropriate pair of shoes one doesn't really need a special arsenal of tools for running. Here, too, we have seen very contrary approaches in recent years. At the turn of the millennium, we saw that shoes with a very big height difference between the shoe's heel and toe and very rigid support elements led to a pretty high injury rate.

Some shoe manufacturers even used this to create a major marketing campaign, resulting in natural running.

Suddenly shoes with 0 mm height difference and flexible sole construction were on everyone's lips, or rather on many feet. The idea was to return runners to a natural running technique without much support from shoes. On principal this approach was correct, leading runners away from heel striking to running on the forefoot, but in doing so made a crucial mistake.

Buyers of natural running or minimalist shoes weren't taught the necessary adjustment to the running technique. Instead, there was faith that the lack of a support element in the heel and no height difference combined with less cushioning would be enough to turn a heel striker into a natural runner with the correct strike. Countless runners surfed this popular wave to end their injury-related martyrdom and finally be able to run pain-free.

Unfortunately, this idea of solely shoe-related transformation did not work very well. The running technique did not aways adapt to the flatter shoes, so that the number of injuries to calf muscles, Achilles, and plantar tendon rose significantly. Today's trend is regressive, meaning away from flat shoes without real cushioning.

Shoes with max cushioning have become popular in recent years, meaning models with lots of cushioning to ease the injury frustration caused by using minimalist shoes. Here, too, it is apparent that people tend to go the path of least resistance, meaning the comfortable path of helpful shoes instead of working on running technique and thereby avoid overloading and injuries to increase running efficiency. In my view it would be much healthier, productive, and sustainable if an athlete changed the way he runs.

Athletes with a lengthy history of injuries tend to view new shoes as the savior and expect to become a better runner with these shoes. But a shoe is only a support tool. The athlete must do the actual running.

I can only partially relate to the reignited debate about prohibiting running shoes with a carbon fiber plate in the sole and the associated catapult action and increased speed. The sport, and particularly the triathlon, live on innovation. The running shoe industry is not spared from that.

Most likely the wearers of these carbon shoes have advantages but prohibiting them in my opinion would be akin to banning disk wheels.

I consider the improper use of some running shoes problematic. Using several different shoe concepts in everyday training is absolutely recommended. This includes conservative running shoes for longer runs and flat, dynamic models for tempo units on the track or road. Minimalist shoes should only be used sporadically and only with the correct running technique.

As with racing wheels, I recommend not using light, dynamic racing shoes for training. These shoes run well, the athlete feels dynamic and naturally wants to use them often and regularly. I would limit that to the competition or test them in training 2–5 times before a race.

Triathletes have a higher-than-average injury rate during a long run when running with racing shoes. On the one hand, I can relate to not wanting to carry an anchor in the form of heavy training shoes, but I prefer a strategy in which training includes a handicap, and the miracle weapon is saved for the big event.

Alternating different models and manufacturers (if the athlete is not tied to a sponsor) may prevent shoe-related overloading. A long-distance athlete should have at least three different pairs of running shoes, because just like the human body, running shoes also need a certain amount of regeneration.

While running, the cushioning material is continuously and increasingly compressed. The shoe should have time to return its cross section and cushioning material to its normal state to ensure properly functioning shock absorption. The shoes will last considerably longer and the risk of injury due to significantly compromised cushioning is eliminated. Apropos longevity, I recommend documenting the mileage completed in the shoes in the training journal. I consider a running performance of 800–1,000 km per shoe as relatively safe. Additional factors that influence a shoe's longevity are bodyweight, running surface, tempo, and the foot's rolling movement during the foot strike.

There is of course a place for racing shoes, but they're not for everyone. Most of these models are intended for fast running of short distances from 5 km to marathons. But an Ironman marathon has very little in common with fast running. Here the tempo will preferably lie in the basic endurance range.

Also, the athlete will be tired when he gets off the bike. Would it therefore not make more sense to use a shoe with adequate cushioning and support to help the athlete, rather than using a super-flat direct shoe designed for a significantly faster tempo range?

When choosing a shoe, many age-group athletes focus too much on the models used in professional sports. The speeds those athletes run justify the use of faster shoes. For age-group athletes I would recommend using a more conservative shoe. Racing shoes should not be too small or too tight because the foot stretches over the course of the race, which can result in pressure spots and blisters.

CONCLUSION

Shoes are important, but do not protect from running injuries or guarantee a faster running speed if the athlete has a poor running technique.

8.1.2   Quick-lacing systems

There are countless quick-lacing systems on the market to avoid lacing up the shoes in the transition zones and ensure fast changeover times. I am not really a fan of using these systems in a race or in training.

It might make sense in shorter races where a quick change from cycling to running can be the difference between victory and defeat. In long distance, I consider stability and comfort more important.

As an outsider on the side of the race course, I always see how little support these rubber laces offer the athletes. There frequently are problems with the plantar tendon when quick-lacing systems are used. The foot has too little support in the shoe which results in the foot muscles frequently cramping.

I have done countless tests on how much time is lost when tying shoes compared to quick-lacing systems, and all the tests showed a maximum time of 18–20 seconds. In a competition that lasts 8–15 hours, that is not a factor to be taken seriously.

When during a hot race the body cools down excessively from sponges and water and shoes get increasingly wet, support inside the shoe becomes even more of an issue in terms of preventing blisters from sliding back and forth inside the shoe. The alleged advantage of a quick-lacing system is invalidated by a lack of support and comfort.

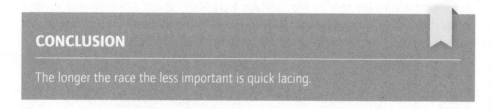

CONCLUSION

The longer the race the less important is quick lacing.

8.1.3   Compression socks

When I first saw compression socks in a race in 2007, I unsuccessfully looked for soccer shin guards. Since then, compression socks have become popular in triathlon as well as in running sports. But why? When doing research for this book, I could not find any manufacturer-independent studies that advocated for the use of compression socks and their positive effect. Hence the lauded benefits seem to stem from the marketing department of the respective manufacturer.

A few years ago, I did a series of tests and ran my regular route in varying conditions and temperatures while wearing compression socks. I was unable to detect a drop in my heartrate or an increase in speed of any kind.

During my test I also timed myself putting on the socks with dry and wet feet. With wet feet, it took between 45-60 seconds to have them on my feet without wrinkles. According to that result, to gain time in a race by wearing compression socks one would have to run 1-1.5 seconds faster per kilometer, which I consider a pipe dream.

Compression calf sleeves that can be put on before the start of the race are an alternative. However, these models have shown that the feet sticking out of the bottom of the sleeves are pretty swollen after cycling because the retrograde venous flow from the foot is inhibited at the calf, meaning the blood remains in the foot.

To me the only justifiable reason for wearing compression socks is if the athlete feels subjectively better. I will forgo offering an esthetic opinion on the subject.

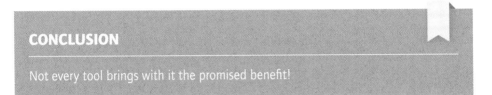

CONCLUSION

Not every tool brings with it the promised benefit!

8.2 Running Technique

Running is the most original of all forms of movement, but as a result of our modern way of working and living, we humans unfortunately have unlearned this ability. Evolutionarily humans have not yet adequately adapted to sitting at a desk for hours on end.

Many runners exhibit the negative side effects of a sedentary lifestyle. Lack of mobility and gluteal muscle atrophy are quite apparent. When looking at children up to age 10, one can see quite normal movement sequences. But due to sitting for hours at school and a lack of exercise, the way children run changes as they get older.

Another factor that has hugely affected running was the development of Nike's first running shoe. Millions of years of human evolution and the associated programming of a natural movement pattern while running was instantly called into question.

Suddenly the runner was supposed to roll off the heel to justify the development of heel cushioning, lots of height difference, and supporting elements. If God had wanted this, he would not have given us calf muscles and foot arches as natural shock absorbers.

With the at that time burgeoning jogging movement in the US, most beginning runners were indoctrinated with this heel run. As a result, several running concepts came along later which teach a movement pattern that has been part of upright walking humans from the beginning. Isn't it sad that the use of a waffle iron to manufacture a running shoe has caused many athletes to bark up the wrong tree?

Matters were complicated further by the fact that in a triathlon, athletes are in a totally different situation than strictly runners. Particularly in long-distance, running while fresh and rested isn't possible and prior fatigue from swimming and cycling is immense. These facts must be considered when evaluating a long-distance triathlete's running technique.

In my view it makes little sense to teach the athlete a running technique he can be successful with over 1,500 m. What he really needs is major focus on economy. He should therefore be taught or rather learn a running technique that is still effective and energy efficient while extremely tired.

To me it is another argument for viewing triathlon as a stand-alone sport and to not blindly implement the approaches of the individual disciplines in triathlon training. A few years ago, I wrote an article for my personal blog about the phenomenon of what back then I referred to as the *Instagram running* technique.

Back then as today I wondered why the photos of influencers in the running sport or triathlon always show them with hugely exaggerated stride lengths and a very vertical component and a foot strike that is miles in front of the body's center of gravity.

These movements are more like the triple jump in track and field, and less like long-distance running. This type of running is probably intended to look especially dynamic; I cannot think of another reason. What I

Figure 64: Body center-of-gravity line.

really don't understand is why shoe manufacturers approve of such photos and equip the influencer crowd with these shoes.

They should be interested in promoting the biomechanically correct running sport and protect athletes from overloading and injuries. I have now already touched on some technical errors but would like to go into more detail.

8.2.1 Stride frequency

Similar to cycling, there is a pretty simple calculation in running that can lead to success, namely:

A high stride frequency plus long strides = high speed.

However, in long-distance we must compromise between energy expenditure and gain (i.e., speed). Hence the athlete should take a close look at which component is easier to implement.

I have seen countless post-Ironman analyses. Today's GPS watches show all the relevant running metrics such as stride frequency, ground contact time, and vertical movement. Looking only at the technical aspect in these files, one quickly identifies the greatest differences between success and defeat when looking more closely at the athlete's stride frequency in the race. Athletes who tackle the Ironman with a stride frequency that is too low are at much greater risk of experiencing a dip in the second half of the 42 km race.

But why is that and why are today's runners still taught a very expansive stride?

Just as in swimming, a long stride along with a low stride frequency, leads to an overly long gliding phase as well as uneven propulsion speed. Here acceleration and deceleration alternate too much and lead to an uneven force progression.

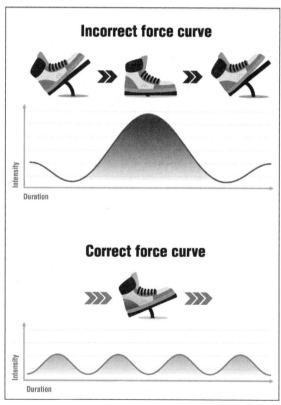

Figure 65: Force progression using the example of a gas pedal.

If the stride is too long the strike takes place in front of the body's center of gravity and usually rolls off the heel. In doing so the foot braces against the direction of movement in a decelerating motion. Here the leg is extended, and calf muscles and arch of the foot are not used optimally to compensate for this impact load. When the foot rolls off the heel the ground contact time increases and the foot remains on the ground longer. But the longer the ground contact time the longer are the support periods, meaning those parts of the movement during which the leg muscles must stabilize the body's ground reaction force.

Unfortunately, these muscles have already been fatigued by 180 bike kilometers, so that the support phase is no longer optimal. This then results in considerably more walking breaks during the second half of the marathon and in some cases in a major loss of speed and time.

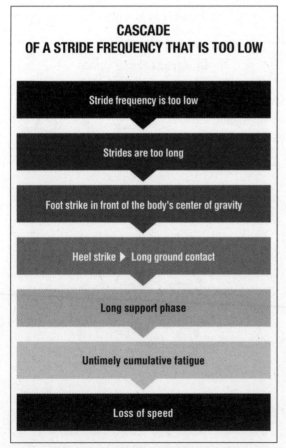

To me the stride frequency is the most important adjustment factor when it comes to running efficiency. When the number of strides per minute is high enough a few other technical aspects tend to regulate themselves.

When analyzing running files, I automatically look at the stride frequency first. If it is greater than 175 strides per minute it is quite likely that the foot strike took place below the body's center of gravity, meaning there is less danger of a stride that is too long.

With the correct number of strides per minute the vertical component of running will also be reduced as the athlete simply has less time to incorrectly move upward while pushing off, but rather runs forward flatter in the direction of movement.

Figure 66: Cascade of a stride frequency that is too low.

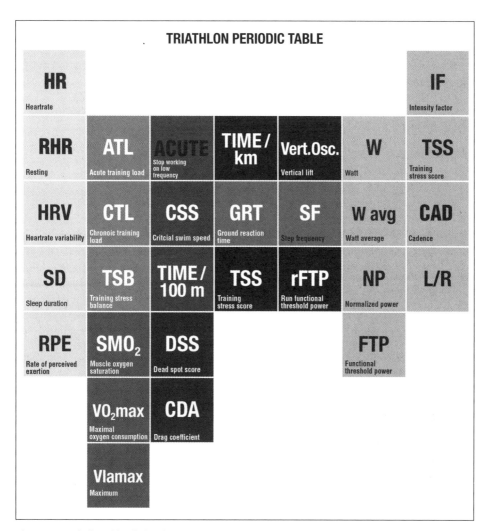

TRIATHLON PERIODIC TABLE

HR							IF
Heartrate							Intensity factor
RHR	**ATL**	**ACUTE**	**TIME/ km**	**Vert.Osc.**	**W**		**TSS**
Resting	Acute training load	Stop working on low frequency		Vertical lift	Watt		Training stress score
HRV	**CTL**	**CSS**	**GRT**	**SF**	**W avg**		**CAD**
Heartrate variability	Chronic training load	Critcial swim speed	Ground reaction time	Step frequency	Watt average		Cadence
SD	**TSB**	**TIME/ 100 m**	**TSS**	**rFTP**	**NP**		**L/R**
Sleep duration	Training stress balance		Training stress score	Run functional threshold power	Normalized power		
RPE	**SMO$_2$**	**DSS**			**FTP**		
Rate of perceived exertion	Muscle oxygen saturation	Dead spot score			Functional threshold power		
	VO$_2$max	**CDA**					
	Maximal oxygen consumption	Drag coefficient					
	Vlamax						
	Maximum						

Figure 67: Periodic table of triathlon running metrics.

The focus in recent years, in my view, has mistakenly been too much on how the foot should strike the ground. Attempts were made to force heel strikers to consciously use a forefoot striking technique because the negative injury-related side effects of heel-striking had become apparent.

This unfortunately resulted in the overloaded or injured structures changing, because when changing the type of strike yet keeping the stride length the same or rather too long, meaning the foot is purposefully pushed down, the plantar tendon is already preloaded before the landing. Another problem is that many runners have a limited ability to feel the difference between heel and toe strike and thus to consciously change it.

I therefore think it would make much more sense to change the running technique for the long-distance triathlon via the completed stride frequency. To me, how the foot strikes is secondary as long as it lands in the correct position, meaning roughly below the body's center of gravity.

A minimum of 180 strides per minute is considered ideal, meaning 90 strikes with each foot in one minute.

Speed formula

To run faster one must understand how running speed is calculated:

Speed = stride length x stride frequency

When the stride length (the distance between two foot strikes) stays the same but the stride frequency is higher, the athlete runs faster. When the stride frequency stays the same but the stride length is longer, the athlete also runs faster. Both components should be improved. But then why is the focus on stride frequency?

The answer is that this change can be more consciously controlled. The frequency is easy to measure and modern running watches display real-time feedback while training.

For instance, when noticing during training or a race that the frequency is dropping one can almost always assume that the pace is slowing as well, because increasing the stride length requires more effort, and with increasing fatigue is nearly impossible to do. Increasing the stride frequency requires less effort but will be accompanied by a slight increase in the heart rate.

Since the cardiovascular system is not the primary limiting factor in long distance, I would always prefer that option. Hence the success formula for running faster is:

Measuring frequency + being able to control the frequency = fast, economical running.

8.2.1.1　Measuring frequency

As previously mentioned, it is easy to measure frequency with a running watch. Runners who don't use a running watch can also assess their frequency by simply counting.

To do so the ground contact of one foot (left or right) should be counted for 15 seconds.

That number is multiplied by two to determine the one-sided contact per quarter of a minute. That number is then multiplied by four to ascertain the two-sided ground contact per minute.

8.2.1.2   Determining the baseline value

To change the frequency, one must first figure out the actual baseline value. This can also be done with a running watch to be able to see the respective average frequencies displayed in the file analysis after completing the units. Measuring the number of ground contacts (as described above) at three specific times during a run has been found to be very helpful. Runners should measure:

*   minute 10

*   minute 40

*   minute 80.

If the run is shorter than 80 minutes, the runner measures only at the first two times. The ascertained frequencies are added and then divided by two or three. This offers a good overview of the average cadence.

8.2.1.3   Stride-frequency training

Ninety percent of all athletes have a low stride frequency as their target frequency. Cadences below 160 strides/min are not uncommon. When coming across such frequencies in the files one has immediate information about the athlete's running technique.

The foot strike will almost certainly be far in front of the body's center of gravity, the stride is too long, the landing takes place primarily on the heel, and the leg is nearly straight. All of these are aspects of a running technique that brings with it a high degree of overloading and propensity for injury.

Changes to the running technique don't happen overnight but require at least 40-60 days. Working towards the target frequency should therefore be done in small steps. The 15/15 or 20/10 running units have proven to be effective methods.

Here the frequency is increased to the target level in 15- or 20-second intervals over a period of ten minutes, followed by a 15- or 10-second drop to the starting frequency. The speed should remain steady. It is strictly an interval-frequency training; running speed is not affected.

ADDITIONAL SAMPLE UNITS

Other strategies are:

- Focusing on stride frequency during the first 5 minutes of every run
- Focusing on stride frequency for the first 10 minutes of every run
- Focusing on stride frequency for the first 15 minutes of every run
- Focusing on stride frequency every 10 minutes for 1 minute
- Focusing on stride frequency every 5 minutes for 1 minute
- Focusing on stride frequency every 10 minutes for 1:30 minutes
- Focusing on stride frequency every 5 minutes for 1:30 minutes

Another alternative to the stride-frequency visual on the watch is using a metronome. Such a clock can be downloaded on a smartphone as an app, but some sports watches also have a built-in metronome function. Athletes who use a tempo trainer for swimming can also use this clock for running.

The athlete receives an acoustic prompt. A step is required for each prompt. However, the constant beeping can become pretty annoying over time. Hence the use of such a metronome should be a conscious choice. Using this tool in group training would probably not be well received.

Athletes whose stride frequency is too low and who recognize the need for action should forego wearing an MP3 player during training as the music rhythm greatly affects movement frequency. Optimizing running technique via stride frequency to me is the biggest performance reserve, because a reduced orthopedic load either enables higher training volumes or lets the athlete achieve a faster speed without major risk of injury.

As previously mentioned, in a race a high stride frequency delays fatigue onset (i.e., the running speed can be maintained for a longer period). In addition to the stride frequency several other aspects should be kept in mind and optimized.

CONCLUSION

The longer the stride, the longer the orthopedic consequences.

8.2.2   Head position and face

The head plays a major role in running, too. At this point I am strictly referring to its posture. The mental component plays a major role in structuring a race, particularly in running. Ideal is a neutral position, meaning the head is an extension of the spine. Here it helps to fix the eyes on a point approximately 6–8 m away.

A frequently seen incorrect posture is the stargazer with his head tilted back, and the shoelace checker who runs with his gaze fixed on his shoes. Both incorrect postures have a negative effect on running technique.

When the head is tilted too far back, in almost all cases the stride is too long as well. When the head is held too low, the pelvis has to be tilted back or the hips tilted forward for balance, so the runner doesn't fall forward. Moreover, in both cases the windpipe is not in an optimal position, which can have a negative effect on inhalation.

Clenching one's teeth during physical effort is a common reaction, but when the facial muscles are too tight and rigid, that tension is gradually transferred from jaw to neck to shoulders.

To maintain an efficient and relaxed running technique in a race the face should be relaxed as well.

8.2.3   Shoulders, arms, hands

As previously mentioned, the shoulders should be as relaxed as possible. But in a race one can often see what I call the turtle posture. I am not talking about the speed but the fact that the shoulders are pulled up and the head sinks increasingly into an imaginary shell.

To ensure that arms and shoulders swing loosely the distance between shoulders and ears should be as big as possible. The arms can be used as a metronome for the stride frequency. But to do so the elbows must be bent. Many athletes carry their arms too long, meaning the elbow angle is too wide.

The longer the arms, the greater is the lever effect of the arms. The greater the lever, the greater is the upper body's rotation relative to the leg, which means the runner's core muscles must work harder. The better option is to actively move the arms backward and to perform that pendular motion in running direction in a relaxed manner driven by gravity in order to conserve energy.

Athletes with a very expansive forward pendular motion are a pretty common sight. I call these athletes pear pickers. Moving the elbow back allows for an easier leg swing on the opposite side. Hands should be moved in front of the chest at nipple level.

Just like long arms, excessive arm rotation with elbows sticking out to the sides should also be avoided. I like to refer to these athletes as underarm razor carriers. The waiter drill can help fix this problem. Here the runner's palms face the ceiling like a waiter carrying a tray, with the thumbs pointing to the outside. The elbows move close alongside the body. As with the facial muscles, hands should be relaxed. Hands should be closed into loose fists with thumbs resting on the index fingers.

Another category in my coaching world is the karateka, who runs with open hands like a sprinter and at any given moment is ready to perform a karate chop. Another phenomenon is what I call the clock arm.

When doing a side-by-side comparison of athletes' arms one can see differences in movement in many of them. Often the arm that wears the watch is very rigid and does not swing as freely as the other arm. It is therefore a good idea to occasionally wear the watch on the other arm to counter this imbalance. When the arm is particularly constrained, I like to engage in a little wordplay in the form of *"G-ARM-in"* or *"Pol-ARM."*

8.2.4   Posture

Posture is critical to speed development. Here the upper body can be referred to as the gas pedal. The more the upper body bends forward, the more speed the athlete can gain with the help of gravity without having to employ more effort.

Figure 68: Effect of the upper body on speed development using the example of a gas pedal.

But we can always see athletes with a very erect posture and in some cases leaning back, whom I refer to as stick swallowers. This posture causes the foot to strike in front of the body's center of gravity to maintain balance. But when the body is allowed to fall forward like a ski jumper's, the foot will strike directly below the body's center of gravity and the runner kills two birds with one stone.

The most common mistake made when leaning forward with the upper body is bending at the hip, meaning pushing the butt and hips back. The hips must be pushed forward to facilitate the falling forward in a straight line. When the upper body breaks at the hip and the hips don't move forward, the center of gravity changes significantly.

Sitting hips due to fatigue can be seen in probably 90% of athletes at kilometer mark 30 of the Ironman marathon. When the hips drop back, I like to refer to this as toilet

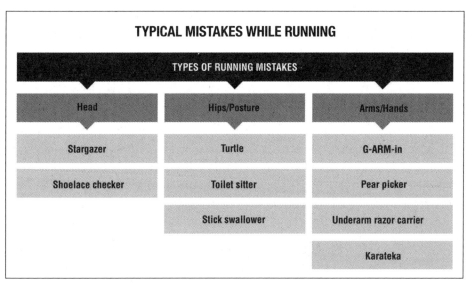

Figure 69: Types of running mistakes.

sitter, the center of gravity changes and the foot will strike almost certainly far in front of the body.

When adding a stride frequency that is generally too low, it increases the loss of speed, but I won't go back to talking about stride frequency again.

8.3 Noticing Technical Errors

In addition to external corrections by a coach or via video analysis of the running technique and by rating the running indexes (stride frequency, vertical movement, etc.) there is also the option of identifying mistakes or problems through self-observation.

8.3.1 Muddy calves

The expression *muddy calves* indeed refers to mud and dirt on the inside of the calves. It is an indication of weak gluteal muscles. The gluteus medius controls the mechanical axis during the supporting phase, meaning when the foot has firm contact with the ground.

Another reason could be insufficient hip extension (i.e., running in the toilet sitter position). Both weaknesses combined lead to destabilization of the pelvis, which then manifests itself in an unstable mechanical axis or rather dirt and mud on the inside of the calves. Here the solution would be to focus on strengthening the gluteal muscles was well as stretching the hip flexors.

8.3.2 Side-by-side comparison of differences in sole wear

When looking at the bottom of one's shoes and noticing that one of the two soles is more worn than the other, there are generally two reasons.

The easy-to-fix problem is the slope or crown on some running routes. Some roads are considerably higher in the center than at the outside edges. There can be a significant difference when running on the left side of a public road facing traffic. It is therefore best to avoid such routes or, if possible, regularly switch sides.

Another reason can be the difference in leg length. However, this requires a very close look because most differences in length are not due to a structural problem. In approximately 90% of cases these differences stem from a blockage in the pelvis, sacroiliac joint, or lumbar spine, which an osteopath or physical therapist can easily treat.

It really gets tricky when a bike fitter wants to eliminate a difference in length that he noticed while standing, by adding inserts or wedges under the cleats. This problem regulates itself by sitting in the saddle and letting the hips hang freely.

8.3.3   Calluses

When palpitating the soles of the feet the athlete should look closely for differences in calluses, which provides information about various things. Particular attention should be paid to the area of the metatarsophalangeal joint of the big toes.

If differences are detected it could be evidence of less flexible calf muscles in one calf or a blockage in the ankle. The latter would have to be examined by a physical therapist. Although it can be painful, the athlete can also massage his tight calves with a fascia roller.

8.3.4   Bouncing visual field (oscillopsia)

When an athlete has trouble focusing his eyes on the horizon because it continuously jumps up and down, the reason might be that his stride frequency is too low and his strides too long along with a major vertical component, meaning that he pushes off the ground too forcefully.

8.4   Training

After having learned about the equipment and the most important aspects of running technique, we will now focus on the training with its content, and dos and don'ts in preparation of a long-distance event. As previously mentioned, running is the discipline with the greatest risk of overloading and injury.

Many athletes have had the unfortunate experience of an injury from running or of doing far worse than expected in a race. Unfortunately, these experiences rarely generate the correct conclusions, but instead the wrong measures.

When an athlete experiences an alleged failure in a competition, he will pay particular attention to his training runs in the form of increased volume for fear of another negative experience. Hence many athletes believe that a successful Ironman marathon necessitates many running miles in the run-up.

But particularly in running, it quicky becomes apparent that a triathlon isn't the coincidental stringing together of three individual disciplines. In fact, it becomes obvious that there are definite synergies between the individual disciplines that must also be considered in training. For running this means that the athlete benefits from swimming and cycling.

I notice all the time that athletes who swim well also tend to run very well. I would like to suggest the stronger diaphragm and the massaging effect of the hydrostatic pressure on the abused leg muscles as the reason. With the correct sitting position, cycling is a very good way to develop overall endurance, fat metabolism, and cardiovascular system with a simultaneously lower orthopedic load due to the lack of impact load as compared to running.

Athletes with a predisposition to injury or a history of previous injuries should consciously reduce their running volume to be able to stay healthy during race preparation. In the 1990s, as part of the Ironman Europe in Roth, I was able to hear the six-time Hawaii winner Dave Scott speak. In a training lecture he used an example that has stuck with me ever since:

"Finishing an Ironman isn't difficult. It is much more difficult to be healthy at the starting line!"

That sentence had a big impact on my approach to training and especially running, because fast marathon times don't necessarily require massive mileage in the run-up. Since the beginning of my coaching career, I have consistently argued for fewer running miles and more time on the bike, even if bike training requires more training hours by comparison.

But I thereby make sure that Dave Scott's quote finds application, and athletes are fresh, uninjured, and motivated at the starting line. Conversely, this does not mean that we should operate according to the laziness principle because a modicum of training is definitely important. I like to describe this as running minimax, meaning minimal effort and maximum gain.

I try to prescribe the minimum required training dose because any excessive mileage or intensity in running can lead to missed training due to overloading or injury.

In recent years, I have read the training notes of countless athletes or looked at their activity on Strava. For probably 80–90% of athletes, the volumes and some of the running intensities are not in line with their race performances, because in some cases the long runs during the winter are completed faster in training than later in a race during the summer. Somehow that doesn't make sense to me.

It is ok to experiment in training to set new stimuli. But when the same things that clearly did not lead to success on race day are repeated year after year, the athlete should take a close look at his own actions and training. Below I will try to address possible mistakes and how to avoid them.

8.4.1   Overall running volume

As I already mentioned, I believe that many long-distance athletes complete too much of their training volume on foot. In doing so some look to the training contents of top professional athletes that are constantly circulated in magazines and on the internet, and while deducting a few percentage points, at the end of the day, in most cases it is still too much.

I have countless times seen age-group athletes complete 70–80 km as a weekly average throughout their preparation for a long-distance event, and still fail in the race. Instead of focusing primarily on bike training and an orthopedically safer preparation, in most cases athletes invest too heavily in running.

I was able to coach several very successful athletes who stayed below the magic three-hour mark in an Ironman or even won races with a 45–50 km weekly average. If every single run in a training week fulfills a purpose and no additional unnecessary kilometers, also called junk miles, are run, the volume can be reduced significantly. Blanket recommendations about running miles are not really practicable. The following table should therefore serve as a rough orientation for age-group athletes.

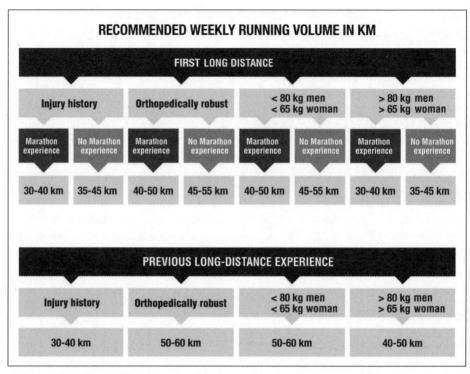

Figure 70: Recommended volume for running.

If a first-time long-distance athlete has previous marathon experience, he has most likely completed effective training for that purpose. In this case I would reduce the volume slightly compared to that of an athlete without marathon experience. Likewise, athletes who tend to be heavier or tend to have overloading responses should reduce the volume or complete some of it in the water in the form of aqua jogging, but more on that later. The following four items should prompt athletes to reflect on their running volume.

8.4.1.1   Injury history

An athlete with a history of injuries should be particularly vigilant. Recurring overloading is a sign that the body isn't ready to adequately absorb the volume. Initial signs of this should not be ignored.

Instead, the athlete should take advantage of not competing in a single sport by training more in the other two disciplines and completing running training with the lowest volume necessary.

8.4.1.2   Build

Due to their higher weight, heavier athletes naturally experience greater impact forces during the foot strike. The eccentric load in thighs and calves is distinctly higher than in a lighter athlete. The often-quoted passive structures (ligaments, tendons, joints), but also the muscles, experience a higher degree of damage and thus require more recovery time.

A sensible way of increasing volume by, for instance, five minutes every week for long runs and documenting the physical state after training is a very good method for determining which volume can still be safely tolerated. We now also know that different types of muscle fibers have different regeneration times.

Athletes with a large amount of fast-twitch type-II fibers should complete smaller volumes than athletes with type-I diesel fibers. Sprinter fibers need more time for adequate recovery.

A performance test to determine Vlamax could be called the ordinary man's muscle biopsy, because a high maximum lactate production rate can point to a larger number of type-II fibers.

8.4.1.3   Age

Our physical condition changes with increasing age. The loss of testosterone and growth hormones leads to longer regeneration times because these two hormones play an important role in the repair of muscles damaged during training. The older an athlete, the more the focus should shift away from absolute volumes towards training frequency and improved mobility, strength, and movement execution.

8.4.1.4   Life mileage

When an athlete has been largely injury-free for many years as a runner he will be able to handle higher volumes, because his motor function and movement efficiency should have economized over the years. Beginning runners should start by working on movement frequency (steps per minute) and their foot strike, improve their running economy, and only then incrementally increase the volume.

8.4.2   The long run

The long run is one of the basic pillars of long-distance training. But how long is long, or is there a too long here as well? Here opinions differ. Some camps need to have at least 6-8 runs of more than 30 km in their legs before an Ironman, while others think the long run should end at two hours.

Most athletes focus too much on the preparatory training of strictly marathoners. These plans have more volume and more tempo training than a plan for a long-distance run in a triathlon. The approach to an Ironman marathon is completely different than that of a standalone marathon race. Anyone who has ever stood at the side of the road at kilometers 25-30 understands what I mean when I talk about zombie mode.

Due to fatigue, the running technique downright collapses, the posture can become quite unattractive, and it looks more like a battle against further physical deterioration than economical, purposeful running.

As triathletes we try to push this decline in technique, posture, and tied to that the running speed, as far back as possible towards the finish line. In a standalone marathon the objective is different because the idea is to run as fast as possible from start to finish. This difference in approach also necessitates a different training plan.

The sense and purpose of the long run is to train the metabolism, cardiovascular system, and orthopedics. The first two can be very well trained in an orthopedically more agreeable manner by cycling. I therefore see no reason to let athletes run longer than 2-21/4 hours during long-distance training. Recovery time after an even longer run is also considerably longer, which means that subsequent sessions on the same or following day cannot be completed in optimally recovered condition.

To me long-distance running fitness is more the result of running frequency, continuity, adequate stimulus processing and regeneration. As I have already mentioned several times in this book, the Ironman engine is built by the meaningful interplay between all three individual sports and sensible alternation between loading and unloading. Continuity in running training and the resulting orthopedic stability leads to less downtime due to injury and can thus be considered more sustainable and productive than expanding the volume of the long run at any cost.

Athletes with orthopedic problems can choose to do the double-run version of the long run. To do so the athlete should complete 80% of the intended volume during the day's first run. There should be at least a 5–6-hour break with an adequate carbohydrate supply after the first run. In the run-up to the competition the long run can also be combined with cycling. In this case I would not plan more than 60 minutes of cycling. More about brick runs later.

The running tempo during the long run in my view cannot be slow enough. But if the chosen tempo is too intense the load increases and merely long becomes long and hard. The primary focus should be on toughening up with impact loads. Tempo and tempo endurance should not be the focus of this unit.

The final-acceleration version of the long run, meaning with increasing tempo towards the end that is still within the basic endurance range, gives it a mental zest. This version promotes mental toughness without undermining the true intention of its training purpose.

REMEMBER

Running long without gasping!

8.4.3 Training pace for intervals

When looking at the long-distance marathon demand profile, one quickly realizes that intensity is clearly in the basic range, although in the upper range or rather the transition to the BE 2 zone. For instance, if an athlete wants to run the marathon in a competition in 3:30 hours it is at an average pace of 5:00 m/km.

The time difference between a marathon and a long-distance marathon can be about 15–35 minutes. The following table is based on empirical observation of more than 1,100 long-distance races coached by me.

"TIME OF DEATH"	
Marathon in hours	Long-distance marathon in hours
2:30	2:45-2:48
2:40	2:57-3:03
2:50	3:04-3:10
2:55	3:11-3:18
3:00	3:19-3:28
3:05	3:25-3:32
3:10	3:34-3:43
3:20	3:40-3:49
3:30	3:52-4:03
3:40	3:59-4:10
3:50	4:08-4:22
4:00	4:24-4:40

Figure 71: "Time of death" marathon vs. long-distance marathon.

To stick with our example, let us deduct 20 minutes from the anticipated 3:30 hours. So, we assume that the athlete in this example can achieve 3:10 hours in a marathon without previous swimming and cycling, which would be a pace of 4:30 min/km. This average speed is the intensity he needs to specifically train for the Ironman marathon.

But that does not mean that every training, whether it is a long run and intervals on the track, should always be done at this tempo. The long run should be completed at 5:21-5:28 min/km intervals to increase VO$_2$max and 1,000 m at 3:35-3:40 min/km. To me it makes little sense to choose faster running speeds even if the athlete has the necessary basic speed.

Every second faster per kilometer means an increased risk of injury and a longer regeneration time. Here, too, the horse should only jump as high as necessary. All that's needed is a strong Ironman marathon time, not insanely hard workouts on the track.

Here, too, we can see that it is not an isolated form of training or unit that catapults an athlete to a higher level, but the sum of all training sessions that ensures the necessary sustainable performance development.

LONG-DISTANCE MARATHON RUNNING SPEEDS

Target time long-distance marathon in h	Avg. pace competition min/km	Tempo long run in min/km	Tempo 1000 m VO_{2max} in min/km	Tempo 800 m Yassos in min/km	Tempo 800 m Yassos in min/800 m	Tempo 800 m Yassos 200 m jog break in min/km
2:55	4:09	4:25-4:30	3:15	3:50	3:04	5:00
3:00	4:16	4:30-4:35	3:20	3:53	3:06	5:03
3:05	4:23	4:35-4:40	3:25	3:57	3:09	5:07
3:10	4:30	4:40-4:45	3:30	4:06	3:16	5:18
3:15	4:37	4:45-5:00	3:35	4:11	3:20	5:22
3:20	4:44	5:08-5:15	3:40	4:17	3:25	5:29
3:25	4:51	5:13-5:23	3:50	4:22	3:29	5:34
3:30	4:59	5:21-5:28	4:00	4:29	3:35	5:41
3:35	5:06	5:26-5:35	4:10	4:35	3:40	5:48
3:40	5:13	5:32-5:40	4:20	4:44	3:47	5:55
3:45	5:20	5:40-5:48	4:25	4:51	3:53	6:08
3:50	5:27	5:45-5:55	4:30	5:00	4:00	6:19
3:55	5:34	5:53-6:00	4:35	5:08	4:06	6:26
4:00	5:41	6:00-6:09	4:45	5:17	4:13	6:32
4:05	5:48	6:08-6:15	4:55	5:29	4:23	6:38
4:10	5:55	6:14-6:22	5:05	5:41	4:32	6:58
4:15	6:03	6:20-6:30	5:15	5:47	4:37	7:03
4:20	6:10	6:32-6:36	5:20	5:55	4:44	7:09
4:25	6:17	6:34-6:40	5:25	6:00	4:48	7:16
4:30	6:24	6:43-6:50	5:25	6:06	4:52	7:22

Figure 72: Training tempo table for running.

8.4.4 Brick runs

The purpose of brick runs is to simulate the motor transition from cycling to subsequent running and to economize. Here, too, there are different opinions as to length, frequency, and timing. Since a brick run isn't always completed in rested condition there is also a certain risk of overloading. The use of this form of training should therefore be purposeful and take place at the right point of the season.

Some commercial training-camp programs offer nearly daily brick sessions or in some cases also multi-brick workouts (i.e., multiple changes of bike-run-bike-run-bike-run). As previously mentioned, these runs are usually not performed with an optimal technique.

During a phase with a large cycling volume (i.e., at spring training camp), muscular effort from longer cycling is usually much higher.

When completing such a multi-combination training, the already stressed muscles are further negatively affected. Such a training should therefore not be done during this time period.

Experience has shown that athletes can easily destroy themselves for several weeks with such a workout that can unfortunately quickly turn into a competition. A conscientious athlete should avoid such a training offer to ensure linear form building. I see no reason to implement multi-combination training in a long-distance plan since the motor transition isn't as critical, or rather the race is still very long after the change in disciplines.

A combination of a long bike ride and a long run is also not listed in the below table, because in my view that is one of the biggest mistakes an athlete can make in the run-up to a long-distance race since the loads of, for instance, 150 km on two wheels and 25 km on foot are almost two thirds of a long-distance event and require a very long recovery period.

In general, combined runs can be separated into direct and indirect brick runs. Indirect would mean a training day when the athlete first gets on the bike and then starts running training 60-90 minute later. The direct brick run, similar to a competition, starts immediately after bike training.

A seamless transition isn't always a given because not every athlete can set up a transition zone at home. I suggest that a 5-10-minute break to carry the bike to the basement, etc. can be seen as tolerable.

FORMS OF COMBINATION TRAINING FOR BIKE–RUN

Bike		Run		
Duration in minutes	Intensity range	Duration in minutes or distance	Direct/indirect	Intensity
120-360	BE 1	10-40	Direct	BE 1
30-60	BE 1	80-120	Direct	BE 1
120-240	BE 1	4–10 x 800 m + 200 m jog break	Direct	BE 2
120-140	BE 1	6–12 x 200 m + 200 m jog break	Direct	DZ
120-140	BE 1 increased	10-40	Direct	BE 1
120-240 (30-60 min)	BE 1 with BE 2 strength focus at the end	10-40	Direct	BE 1
120-240 (30-60 min)	BE 1 with BE 2 strength focus at the end	4–6 x 800 m +200 m jog break	Direct	BE 2
45-90	BE 1	4–8 x 1000 m +200 m jog break	Direct	BE 2/DZ
90-180	BE 1/BE 2	10-20	Direct	BE 1
90-150	BE 1 with DZ intervals	10-20	Direct	BE 1

Figure 73: Forms of combined training.

I would limit brick runs to once—and no more than twice—a week because brick runs diminish movement quality due to the aforementioned fatigue.

The following graph shows when which forms of combined training make the most sense in terms of timing.

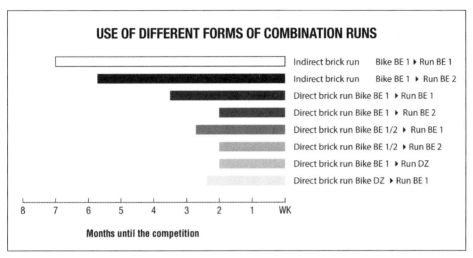

Figure 74: Use of different forms of brick training during the season.

8.4.5   Choosing a surface

Choosing the right surface is another parameter in addition to duration and intensity in order to affect the effectiveness of a training run and largely avoid injuries. Most long-distance events are largely run on an asphalt surface. That is why an athlete needs to sufficiently adapt to precisely that surface.

Athletes who only train on soft ground (i.e., in the forest) can experience muscular problems in a race because they did not sufficiently include the hard surface in their training program.

On the other hand, training on asphalt and concrete does bring with it some risk of overloading. A combination of units on soft surfaces and runs on asphalt would be appropriate if the athlete's home location allows, to avoid injury and not miss the necessary adaptation.

Here, too, is a timeline to visualize tapering towards the competition as well as use of the right surface.

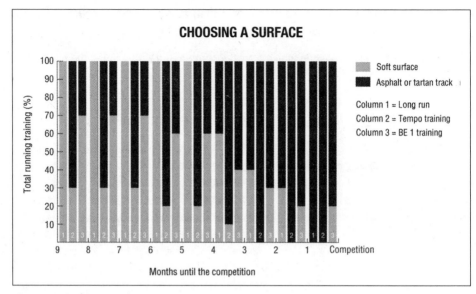

Figure 75: Choosing a surface.

While climate change is upon us, there are still regions where it snows in winter. Not everyone has access to a treadmill and many don't enjoy running indoors. When considering a few factors, training over the winter can also take place injury-free outdoors.

As a coach I can practically set my watch by the first complaints about injuries coming in two weeks after the first snow. By the way, I can report that same phenomenon after summer vacation, when athletes run on the beach.

When running on ice and snow or on the beach, the foot strike is no longer optimal, the heel sinks into the snow, and the foot slides on the slick surface. This often causes a lot of tension in the plantar tendon, Achilles tendon, and calf muscles. This tension often leads to a blockage in the head of the fibula—to me a classic winter injury.

Another crucial point about running in the snow is that running feels cushioned. The ground contact increases significantly. As we already learned, injury risk increases with increased ground contact time because the lower leg must stabilize the total bodyweight. Since the ground contact time is an important factor in terms of speed, permanently training on a soft surface is a performance killer.

When training on soft surfaces the muscles are no longer asked to do the cushioning or rather the static work. Here the surface to some extent takes on that job. Athletes should never train on a surface where snow melts during the day and then refreezes overnight because the ground becomes too uneven.

Runners in rural regions should avoid frozen tractor tracks. If it is extremely slick or heavy snow, the best option is to find a largely plowed and salted route to minimize the injury risk. There are probably more exciting things than a long run on a 300 m circuit, but as we know, the end justifies the means.

While we are mentally in the cold time of year, here is a cross reference regarding running in cold temperatures. Temperature perception tends to vary from athlete to athlete, so blanket recommendations about when not to run outside anymore cannot be given. With the proper clothing, a scarf to warm up the inhaled air, running even in temperatures as low as minus 15–20 C (5 to -4 F) does not pose a health risk.

Another point is the partially exposed Achilles tendon when wearing very short socks and running tights that are too short. While it may be in line with current fashion, it does significantly stress these areas. Since flanking has become a trend, I see increased problems with the Achilles tendon and calves in winter.

8.4.6   Training sessions

I would like to share the training sessions I have considered most important for many years. The possibilities are endless. Listing all the units would be outside the scope of this book. I don't think I need to say much more about basic endurance training; every long-distance-focused athlete should already be familiar. Instead, I would like to introduce the various ways an athlete can optimize technique, that can be built into a basic run.

8.4.6.1   Acceleration runs

Acceleration runs are a perfect opportunity to briefly step outside the normal endurance-run shuffle. In doing so, the running speed is increased over a distance of 60-100 m without going into a sprint at the end of the stretch. These short segments can be built into a normal BE 1 run every 5 or 10 minutes to periodically loosen up motor function.

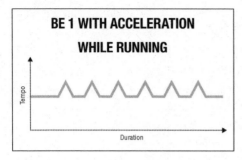

Figure 76: BE 1 run with acceleration
in the middle.

Another option is to do acceleration runs at the end of a unit. The athlete ends his normal endurance run, and at the end builds in a series of 6-10 60-80 m acceleration runs. Walking back to the starting point represents the break. Here the idea is to reinvigorate and improve a running technique that is worsening from cumulative fatigue.

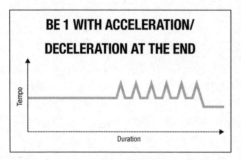

Figure 77: BE 1 run with acceleration at the end.

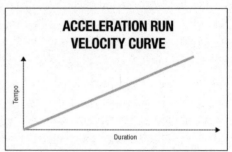

Figure 78: Acceleration run velocity curve.

8.4.6.2 Deceleration runs

Deceleration runs are built in at the end of a run based on the same pattern as acceleration runs, but with the opposite speed progression. To do so, the athlete finds a fixed starting point and momentarily stands still to then start at a fast speed (No sprint here as well!) and gradually slows down over the 60-80 m distance.

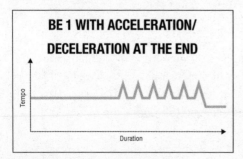

Figure 79: BE 1 run with deceleration
runs at the end.

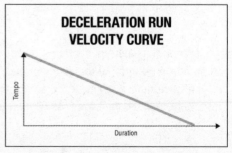

Figure 80: Deceleration run velocity curve.

8.4.6.3   Jumping rope or ankle jumps

Boxers aren't the only ones who benefit from jumping rope. Long-distance athletes can make their running more efficient and improve their technique. Because when jumping rope, one automatically lands directly below the body's center of gravity and more likely on the forefoot than the heel.

Short segments of 20-30 seconds before a run activate all of the muscles involved in running. When jumping rope barefoot or with flat shoes without cushioning, it benefits the athlete's proprioception.

Proprioception refers to an athlete's perception in a space. Jumping rope can improve physical awareness and develop awareness of the accurate foot strike. Jumping rope at the end of a unit can loosen up motor function. If the athlete doesn't have a jump rope, he can simulate the jumping movement without a rope as ankle jumps.

8.4.6.4   Technical elements as intervals

It is generally a good option to build individual technical elements into a basic run as intervals. For cohesion purposes the athlete can alternate between four minutes of normal running and one minute of technical focus (3-2, 2-2, 2-3, etc., would be other possible sequences).

Technical elements could be something like consciously running with high hips, but also a conscious arm position and other construction sites.

8.4.6.5   Nose breathing

Nose-breathing runs are another way to liven up BE 1 runs. To do so the mouth is closed for a previously determined period and the athlete breaths exclusively through the nose to increase oxygen utilization.

These segments can be 30-90 seconds long. Breaks with normal breathing should be about three times as long as the nose-breathing interval. When an athlete is clearly the strongest in running group-training, he can use this method to make his life difficult, meaning putting on the brakes a bit so he can still utilize the tempo that is too slow for him. However, conversations with fellow runners will be more difficult.

8.4.6.6   100 m or 200 m intervals

A successful training plan includes the right mix of loading and unloading that closely relates to the demands of a planned competition.

I am not a big fan of very high intensities for long-distance age-group athletes during running training, because the anticipated race tempo is merely a basic tempo and intense intervals create a higher injury risk.

One exception are 100 or 200 m intervals. I call these sessions leg speed boosters because they are a pretty safe way to improve running performance.

ADDITIONAL INFO

The advantages and benefits of these short intervals are:

VO$_2$max

During these sessions the relationship between loading and unloading is one-to-one and allows for training at an intensity near the VO$_2$max.

Improved technique

These short and fast intervals improve the high stride frequency necessary for economical running. Especially as a combined session or the day after a very long bike unit, these short intervals help to improve movement frequency and as a result also keep the foot strike close to the body's center of gravity.

Hormone balance

Long-term endurance training lowers the body's own testosterone level. At the same time training is deliberately generated stress and leads to an increase in the stress hormone cortisol.

When there is a continuous imbalance in favor of cortisol due to long units in the BE 1 range, athletes are at risk of not being able to adequately process the training stimulus due to a lack of testosterone.

Short, intense intervals verifiably lead to a rise in the testosterone level.

SAMPLE SESSION

As previously mentioned, these runs can be built in as a brick run or as a separate session.

10 min easy warm-up
Depending on level and time of year:
10–30 x 100 m with 100 m jog or a passive break of 20–30 seconds, or
10–25 x 200 m with 200 m jog break
Maximum five minutes easy warm-down

It is not necessary to sprint like Usain Bolt, rather the athlete should always keep a security reserve. With maximum exertion comes the risk of injury. In the beginning, the tempo should be in the range of the current 5,000 m performance, but once the athlete has adapted it can be gradually increased. As an alternative, these workouts can also be completed on the treadmill.

Athletes who can barely do more than 160 steps per minute in basic training and have trouble reaching the ideal frequency of 180 should set the treadmill on 0% incline, which corresponds to a slight slope downhill on a road.

The slow phases should then be completed with 1–1.5% incline.

Here the focus on technique lies in achieving a frequency of 180 and high hips, meaning the pelvis is pushed forward.

REMEMBER

Wall-sit version:

To create a certain amount of tension in the thighs and thereby simulate cycling, the 100s or 200s can be combined with the wall sit.

To do so the athlete sits in an imaginary chair by leaning against a wall or the like. After 20-30 seconds the athlete immediately transitions to running the interval. Here the total number should not be higher than 15 wall-sit intervals with subsequent 200 m run.

8.4.6.7   Uphill runs and uphill sprints

The limiting factor in long-distance is not the cardiovascular system but the muscles. It is therefore important to condition them accordingly. Running in hilly terrain is one option. Either by doing a strength-focused BE 1 run or by using the topography for an interval workout.

ADDITIONAL INFO

Hilly runs are an outstanding opportunity for working on technique because

- stride frequency,
- forward upper body position,
- gluteal and hamstring strength, and
- neurological activation of the movement pattern

are significantly improved.

SAMPLE SESSION HILL SPRINTS

Short (30-40 seconds) sprints at max speed are combined with walking breaks back to the starting point. Ten to twenty repetitions at a 6-8% incline truly accelerate strength and technique.

SAMPLE SESSION HILL INTERVALS

During this form of training the athlete completes 3-4-minute intervals at a 3-5% incline. The tempo is much slower than during hill sprints and the focus is on developing strength endurance. Here it is nearly impossible to take strides that are too long, and leads to a considerably improved running technique on the flat.

SAMPLE UNIT FARTLEKS IN HILLY TERRAIN

Fartleks are a playful type of hill training. The athlete changes intensity as he sees fit and adapts it to the respective terrain. This form of running training is usually a lot of fun and is an excellent simulation of a race for athletes whose competition takes place in hilly terrain.

Some races, like the Ironman Wales or the Powerman Zofingen, have a pretty demanding route profile, which means the athlete has to not only practice running uphill, but must also focus specifically on downhill phases during training. It is therefore a good idea to include this in the training plan when preparing for such a race.

However, running downhill is an eccentric form of movement. The thigh muscles must do more static work, which can also cause more knee stress. Downhill training must be integrated into a training plan very carefully and gently and with conservative progression. Athletes who can let loose going downhill in a race are able to gain time and ground on their competitors.

REMEMBER

When used correctly, the treadmill is a useful training tool to simulate uphill running. Especially for athletes living in regions without any appreciable hills, running on the treadmill is a wonderful alternative.

8.4.6.8   Yasso 800s

Bart Yasso is a journalist at *Runner's World* magazine. While preparing for a marathon a few years ago, he discovered that by running 800-m intervals he could predict his marathon time, or rather that the aimed-for target time determined the tempo for precisely these intervals. Thus, if an athlete wants to complete the marathon distance in 3:30 hours, he must be able to run 10 x 800 m with a slow phase of 200 m in a time of 3:30 min/800 m.

But we are talking about triathlon and not strictly running, meaning this formula finds only limited application because, as we already know, there is a certain time of decay (i.e., a time difference) between individual marathon and triathlon marathon. Since the triathlete, unlike the strictly runner, must train in two additional sports, I would slightly mitigate the Yasso formula and add a few seconds, as was previously shown in the tempo table.

The advantage of this workout type, which can certainly be ramped up to 30–35 x 800 m via the number of intervals, lies in its low orthopedic demand. Coming back to our athlete example with a target time of 3:30 hours in the Ironman, which translates to an average pace of 5:00 min/km. If he runs the Yasso intervals at a 4:29 min/km pace or 3:35 min/800 m, he runs at a faster average speed than his race speed. So far, so good.

If he then runs 20 x 800, that's 16 km total that he runs faster than race pace. He has thereby set a good tempo stimulus. The secret of these intervals lies in the orthopedic loading or (better yet) unloading in the form of the 200 m slow phase. If that phase is consciously completed slowly, meaning in terms of tempo even slower than the pace of the long run, he uses other areas of his leg muscles in this recovery phase due to a modified stride frequency, stride length, and posture. The primary driving muscles are rested and remain fresh longer.

If, instead of 20 x 800 m with a 200 m jog break, he would complete this unit at a pace of 4:29 min/km as a 20 km endurance run, he would have trained this tempo stimulus for 20 km but would have also built up considerably more fatigue (i.e., could expect a longer regeneration time).

When completing this run on the tartan track he will have two advantages free of charge. First, the tempo feel will develop extremely well, so the athlete will be able to determine his pace with relative certainty in a race without his GPS watch. And second is that certain amount of mental zest, because there isn't much that will shock an athlete who has run 30 km in a circle.

I frequently hear from athletes that the Yasso 800 helped them to mentally divide up the remaining distance in a race into small 800 m/200 m segments. The big danger with this unit is choosing the wrong tempo, both during the actual interval as during the jog break.

The athlete must be disciplined to stay in his tempo range and not make this unit too intense. For some athletes the 800 m intervals take the place of the long run if the number of intervals to be completed is high enough.

Increasing the number of intervals should be done carefully. No more than two intervals should be added from one week to the next. This is also why these runs should be built in early on. I generally start 16-18 weeks before race day.

8.4.6.9   The Galloway run-walk-run method

Another concept that promotes alternating between running and deliberate walking phases is the *Galloway run-walk-run method of running*. This concept was developed by Jeff Galloway, one of the best-known running gurus in the United States, and he has written many books on using his method in training.

Regardless of the athlete's performance level, he recommends that the athlete plan in the run-up to alternate between running and walking. Just like my interpretation of the Yasso 800, the idea is that the running muscles briefly recover during the walking phase and the time-related cumulative fatigue can be pushed back farther.

Interestingly, the 1,600-2,000 m Galloway promotes usually coincide with the distance between aid stations in most long-distance races. They fit precisely this pattern, meaning the athlete runs from one aid station to the next but walks at the aid station, which also ensures better fueling and cooling than while running.

But the critical point of the matter is that the athlete must adhere to this pattern from the start of the running discipline and not begin when he already feels very fatigued. This requires some self-confidence because when you are walking at the first aid station and competitors run past you, it is hard to stick to this concept.

The alleged loss of time is not at all excessive, especially since it prevents the athlete from having to take longer walking breaks 25-35 km later when the loss of time really goes through the roof.

8.4.6.10   Running drills

Like swimming and cycling, there are also coordination exercises for the third triathlon discipline. Here we can see the same problems as in swimming. Everyone has heard of or read about the running drills or has completed them at club training or training camp. But with a profusion of exercises, it is often difficult to choose the right exercises, particularly since many athletes rarely know the reasons and purpose of the various exercises.

When an athlete doesn't know the purpose of the exercises, a technique-improving effect is unlikely. I would therefore not prioritize the running drills and complete it at most once a week for only 10-15 minutes.

Many athletes spend 30-60 minutes completing these exercises. In my view that is way too much and implies a coordination overdose. In the end the athlete won't even know what he did and especially not why he did which exercises. I would suggest sticking with the basic exercises:

- high knee skips,
- skipping backwards,
- high-knee sprints,
- heel-to-butt running, and
- ankle work,

doing each exercise 1-2 x for 30-50 m, so the total time is not more than 10-15 minutes.

I like to build technique-enhancing elements into the normal basic training to make training time more effective. Another aspect is that many athletes are almost embarrassed to do the running drills and don't have the self-confidence to do these exercises in public.

The following chart shows which of the listed forms of training should be used when preparing for a long-distance event.

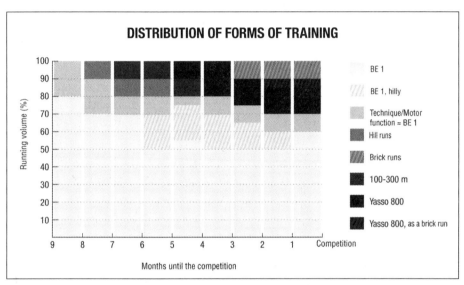

Figure 81: Distribution of forms of training during the season.

8.4.6.11 Aqua jogging

Long-distance training can be described as a ride on a razor blade, because the risk of overloading increases along with the increased training volume, especially in running. Aqua jogging is an orthopedically gentler alternative to minimize this risk.

To do so the athlete needs a flotation belt or vest to be able to simulate walking in deep water, but without ground contact. With the correct technique, all training units done on land can be done in the water. Athletes at the brink of an injury, those frequently dealing with a minor ailment, or athletes carrying a little more bodyweight can complete part of their training in the water.

In case of an acute injury the massaging effect from the hydrostatic pressure can accelerate healing. However, athletes should proceed with caution, because in the water particular strain is placed on the dorsal chain, specifically the hamstring muscles. When running on land, this muscle group's function is to actively pull up the lower legs, but is underdeveloped in nearly all triathletes. Hence aqua training can certainly be called running-specific strength endurance training.

Since water is 800 times denser than air the leg must be moved against a greater resistance than on land. For beginners the greater hamstring activity usually causes sore muscles, which is a definite sign of that region's weakness. But that also means that periodically running in water all year round would be beneficial so the athlete can permanently get used to that strain.

I have often seen athletes shift all their running training to the water while injured, which then led to massive hamstring problems. During training with a comparable load, the heart rate should be approximately 20–25% lower than on land, but cumulative lactate will be considerably more concentrated because the legs must move against the water's resistance in every direction.

Another area that benefits from aqua jogging is breathing. As in swimming, when taking a breath, the ribcage must expand against the water's resistance, which strengthens the diaphragm. This alternative training can be used both during an endurance run or interval training. Aqua jogging can be done in a pool or in open water.

But athletes should cover their head when training in the fresh air in summer and put sunscreen on the parts of the body that stick out of the water (i.e., shoulders and neck).

ADDITIONAL INFO

Advantages of aqua jogging include

- optimization of the running technique;
- dynamic strengthening of the dorsal chain;
- improved pulling phase;
- static strengthening of the trunk muscles; and
- strengthening of the diaphragm.

8.4.6.12 Treadmill training

In recent years, indoor training on the bike has gotten more and more popular. Runners also train increasingly on the treadmill. This development was almost certainly inspired by images of top athletes on the treadmill and in videos on social media. But I am more ambivalent when it comes to treadmill training and would like to bring some awareness to this issue.

Running is the most original form of movement of humans and can be done just about always and anywhere. Exceptions are icy conditions and poorly lit streets in winter that don't permit secure running, especially at a faster running pace. Another aspect is safety. Women in particular should not be running alone in the dark in some areas.

If none of the above factors apply, running training should take place primarily outside, because running also means a bit of freedom, especially since triathlon is still an outdoor sport and will remain that way for the foreseeable future. Experiencing the change of the seasons with the different weather conditions should always be preserved so the athlete is able to also handle them during race conditions.

But the treadmill can be purposefully used as a training tool. Athletes can work on their stride frequency on the treadmill when the band is set at 0% incline, as that corresponds to a slight slope downhill on a road. You could say that the athlete runs at a higher tempo with the same cardiovascular load. On a neuromuscular level, it allows him to simulate running faster without increasing the cardio load.

ADDITIONAL INFO

Another alternative developed in recent years is the AlterG anti-gravity treadmill. Here the athlete is up to his hip in a kind of air sack, which allows him to gradually reduce gravity so he can gradually return to running after an injury with only partial weight-bearing.

But initial studies have shown that knee strain does not decrease as desired when using such a band. Hence its use should be carefully considered and only after consultation with a physical therapist or physician.

Otherwise, the band should be set at a 1-1.5% incline to simulate running on a flat road. Athletes from regions without hills or mountains to speak of can train mountain running on the treadmill. A mirror set up in front of the treadmill can help optimize the running technique.

8.4.7 General suggestions for running training

Finally, I would like to offer a few tips about running in general that make safe, injury-free, and successful running possible. Running is the most dangerous discipline in triathlon. The athletes can feel quite clearly when they make mistakes in training. Overloading, major fatigue, injuries, and performance setbacks are just a few things that can result from incorrect programming. When an athlete is aware of this and recognizes the mistakes, he has a good chance of standing at the starting line fresh and injury-free.

8.4.7.1 On–off running schedule

I have had great results training age-group athletes with a day of running followed by a day of no running. This on–off schedule reduces the orthopedic load on the off day and avoids the risk of incremental overloading.

Such a schedule is a good option particularly at the start of the training year, meaning after the off season, but can also be abandoned once the athletes have developed some resilience.

8.4.7.2 Running rested vs. running tired

In a race an athlete never starts to run in a rested condition, which is why athletes should practice running with tired legs in training. However, I would wait until the final 10-14 weeks before a long-distance event to build this aspect in, and prior to that always try to run fresh and halfway rested.

For instance, when several sessions are on the day's schedule I would, if possible, try to run as the first workout of the day during the critical final three months before day X, to ensure that the technique is clean and thus ideally biomechanically optimal to avoid overloading.

Particularly in spring training camps that are still a long way off from the main competitions and during which the athlete's body experiences a big overall load, athletes should try to run only in a fairly rested state.

Injury-prone athletes should try to run fresh during the entire long-distance preparation period to make sure they get to even see the starting line.

8.4.7.3 Weekly volume increases

Magazines and training literature always refer to 10% as the magic number for weekly volume increases. I do not think this number can be applied across the board because it considers neither the running training load from completed intensities or impact of the other two disciplines, nor the athlete's individual orthopedic load tolerance. I would therefore take this blanket recommendation with a grain of salt and say: it depends!

8.4.7.4 No pain, no gain!

The assumption that running training is always linked to pain is simply false. The tempo should be chosen appropriately and athletes should adhere to a polarized training approach. This also means that longer runs are completed at a slow tempo.

To me training frequency, meaning the number of runs per week, is more important than the volume of a particular unit because it is a more reliable way of working on running technique and resilience, and endocrine balance between testosterone and cortisol is a more likely.

Short 20–30-minute units are just as valid as long runs or tempo sessions and have a performance-stabilizing purpose. Such short runs help to improve movement quality through regular repetition of the running technique because consistency is key.

8.4.8 Running competitions

Running competitions are a very good opportunity to breathe some competition air and ascertain the current performance level. However, here, too, the number matters.

Too many running competitions prevent the athlete from building sustainable form and potentially are a mental drain, because even when the race is used as training, pinning on the bib number and standing at the starting line automatically creates psychological stress. Particularly in winter, the opportunity to train during daylight hours should be used for riding the bike outside.

An ideal race scenario in the run-up to a long-distance race in July would therefore look like this.

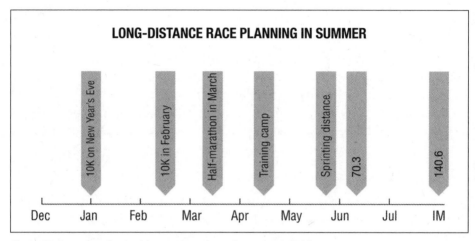

Figure 82: Race planning in the run-up to a long-distance competition.

When taking a closer look, one does not see a spring marathon, and rightly so. In all my years as an active athlete and coach, I have never seen a spring marathon that led to a successful long-distance summer. A marathon just is a marathon, and even at a considerably slower tempo than PR range, those 42 kilometers leave their mark.

The race must be prepared by tapering and requires a subsequent recovery phase. Depending on the athlete's performance level, the athlete will lose 2-5 precious weeks of training time since after the race he can only train in moderation or at a very reduced rate.

Unfortunately, most spring races fall into a time period that should be used for lots of cycling volume, risking the possibility that the bike kilometers necessary for the long-distance race in the summer are not being completed.

PLEASE NOTE

My take-home message here: fast marathon in spring = slow Ironman in summer

9 NUTRITION

The subject of nutrition is an extremely broad field with, in some cases, very controversial views. I am not a nutritionist and don't wish to be. I can only assess nutrition as it pertains to training, regeneration, and competition. I must therefore disappoint those readers who expected nutritional information tables and recipes in this chapter. I also don't want to open a can of worms regarding vegetarianism and veganism, as that would start a war of opinions.

When looking at how scientists of highest renown argue with each other on, for instance, Twitter about their theories, it is difficult for me as a coach, but also as a person, to figure out what's right and what I should no longer eat.

I also don't want to recommend any super foods that have become increasingly popular in recent years. I think that a balanced diet with freshly prepared—ideally seasonal and regional foods—is the best approach. I tend to be more critical of a trend towards a very specific diet.

I cannot shake the feeling that many athletes who subscribe to a particularly healthy diet almost develop a kind of eating disorder, because at some point eating is no longer about pleasure and social interaction, but only about efficient nourishment and energy intake to improve performance. But based on my experience with Olympic champions, world champions, and Ironman winners I can say that their diet isn't particularly complex or extremely sophisticated. They tend to eat colorfully, meaning across the entire spectrum of food groups, and focus more on quality and freshness.

As in many other aspects of life, balance plays an important role here as well. Athletes who worry too much about calories and ingredients lose that balance. They are no longer able to value eating as pleasurable togetherness and therefore develop an eating disorder.

Just like in training, it is interesting to always see new trends being promoted in magazines and on the internet that are blindly followed by athletes. I call it diet hopping.

As the saying goes "An army marches on its stomach", and I would like to delineate for you what that means in terms of the chow that is required within the context of training in my coaching world.

Good nutrition for athletes should generally be divided into four supply segments:

1. Fueling (calory consumption during training and competition)
2. Everyday diet
3. Fluids outside of the sport
4. Fluids in the sport

9.1 Fueling

- Training sessions < 60-minute duration: no calory intake.
- Intense training > 60-minute duration: primary fuel is sugar; gels and bars are a good source.
- Basic training > 60-minute duration at low intensity: real food, meaning fewer gels and bars and instead a break with coffee and cake.
- After every training, regardless of duration and intensity, a carbohydrate intake should occur within 30 minutes of the workout's completion to ensure quick recovery and an intact immune system (keyword *open window effect*). It should include protein, carbohydrates, and sodium to accelerate recovery processes.
- Rule of thumb for bike training > three-hour duration: 60–70 g carbohydrates per hour.

9.2 Daily Diet

- Regular meals throughout the day.
- Distribution of macronutrients should be 40% carbohydrates, 30% protein, 30% fat.
- Meal size should decrease over the course of the day.
- The carbohydrate share should decrease with each meal over the course of the day.
- Dinner should consist primarily of protein, fat (oils), and vegetables.

Diets should be avoided and the emphasis should be on a healthy lifestyle. The metabolism can be influenced with the proper distribution of the macronutrients to increase the effectiveness of certain training units.

Largely skipping carbohydrates during the last four hours before a training unit or the evening before can be very helpful when the fat metabolism needs optimization.

But many athletes misinterpret this FatMax training method. They automatically associate FatMax with fasting training, meaning morning training without any previous nutrient intake. Athletes who engage in this form of training excessively and too often might optimize their metabolism, but the utilization of exogenic energy in the form of nourishment during physical exertion should also be practiced.

I have seen countless times how athletes who train while fasting gradually trained themselves backwards because the lack of carbohydrates results in longer regeneration times.

In recent years, the low carb high fat (LCHF) concept has become increasingly popular in sports. Here the idea is to raise the fat oxidation rate so that in a race, the athlete metabolizes fewer carbohydrates at the same load, and will draw his energy primarily from nearly unlimited fat stores.

There is certainly evidence to support this ketogenic diet. The athlete consumes only 50-150 g of carbohydrates per day. There are certainly different strategies to apply this metabolism-modulating effect. But there are also studies that show that a long-term lack of carbohydrates can also cause problems with the utilization of this nutrient during a competition when it is suddenly being used in large quantities but was not integrated into training and sufficiently practiced.

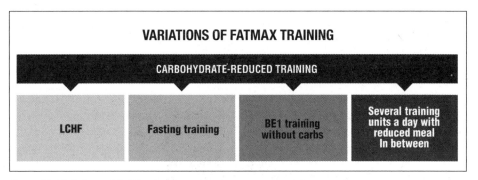

Figure 83: Variations of FatMax training.

I prefer to use fuel from both worlds, meaning on the one hand it can certainly make sense to eat LCHF-compliant during some phases, but the athlete also needs phases with larger amounts of carbohydrates.

When food consumption is divided up accordingly, the athlete can get an optimal energy supply from both supply methods. As I have already said multiple times in this book: it depends!

When completing session longer than three hours, it is recommended to work with 70-90 g of carbohydrates per training hour to ensure an optimal supply. But this quantity can only be permanently absorbed when using a mix of glucose and fructose.

The reason is the limited absorption capacity of the human body's various transport paths. The maximum absorbable amount of glucose is 60-70 g per hour; the *sodium-glucose-linked transporter-I (SGLT I)* does not permit a higher amount. By contrast fructose is absorbed via the GLUT5 transport path. There the upper limit is 30-40 g of fructose per hour.

When both forms of carbohydrates are combined, the athlete can permanently achieve 90 g or even more per hour during a race.

The science behind correct fueling has dramatically changed over the years. In the 2000s, there was a recommendation of 1 carb per kg of body mass per hour. With ongoing research, higher amounts of carbohydrate intake in combination of glucose and fructose was discovered. The ratio of 2:1 between glucose and fructose was established, but nowadays the latest scientific papers show larger intakes by switching to a ratio of 1:0.8

The below bar graph shows which form of carbohydrates should be used when or in which combination.

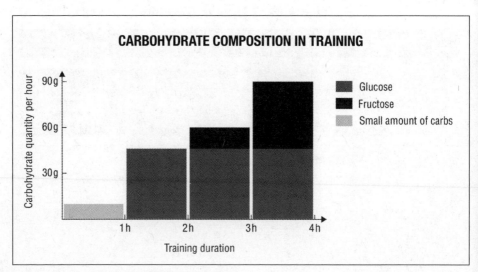

Figure 84: Carbohydrate composition in training.

9.3   Fluid Intake Outside of the Sport

- Sugary drinks daily should be avoided. Water is and remains the primary fluid source.
- Carbonated water is fine.
- Rule of thumb: consume 350-400 ml of water per 10 kg of bodyweight per day.
- Drink two glasses of water with every meal.
- In the morning, drink a glass of water with a generous pinch of cooking salt in it to quickly balance the loss of fluid that occurred overnight, particularly when the first training session is immediately after getting up.
- Coffee is not harmful, but the athlete should forego drinking coffee after 3 pm to avoid impacting sleep quality.
- Alcohol is a diuretic, meaning it dehydrates. It interferes with sleep patterns, recovery time, and fat metabolism. I don't want to argue for an alcohol ban; it is up to the individual athlete.

9.4   Fluid Intake During the Sport

A brief digression into the animal world. The fastest animal on land is the cheetah. It can achieve speeds of more than 100 km/h and is considered an excellent hunter. However, the amount of muscular work necessary to achieve such speeds causes the body's core temperature to rise extremely high, which is why the cheetah can sustain this performance only very briefly. If the hunted prey manages to get through that time with clever evasive maneuvers, it has a good chance of surviving the attack because the cheetah has to break off his hunt to cool down in the shade.

By contrast, the human does not possess such excellent sprinting skills, which is why he had to adapt evolutionarily to the various conditions. Unlike the cheetah and most other animals, a human can reduce the body heat generated by physical effort.

Here the magic word is *sweating*. In doing so, fluid is transported to the skin's surface and a cooling effect is created through evaporation that helps us humans to keep the body's core temperature constant at 36-38 degrees C (96-100 F).

Unfortunately, some athletes ruin this cooling effect by getting large tattoos. This process damages the sweat glands so much that their productivity drops by up to 53%. Cooling by sweating will be correspondingly worse in the tattooed areas.

Apart from the esthetic effect, athletes who wish to command a certain performance should really reconsider the trip to the tattoo parlor. Thermoregulation and cooling sound terrific but have the disadvantage that the amount of fluid we sweat out has to be replenished, because our fluid reservoir for sweat production is not limitless.

Approximately 65–70% of the human body is water. About one third of that is stored outside the cells in the extracellular space. Blood contains approximately 5 liters of fluid in the form of blood plasma, and that plasma is what an athlete sweats out. In terms of quantity, the human body usually loses the electrolyte sodium most with this fluid.

Sodium is a critically important electrolyte that helps with the absorption of food in the stomach via the aforementioned SGLT I transporter, with muscle contraction (keyword: *sodium-potassium pump*) and also helps maintain the blood plasma volume. With respect to fluid and sodium supply in sports, opinions have greatly evolved in recent decades.

When back in the 1960s and 70s, in many sports (e.g., cycling), it was considered a weakness to hydrate, but opinions swung completely in the opposite direction in the 1980s. Suddenly athletes were told they needed to consume at least 1,200 ml/h and to do so continuously.

Other sources recommended drinking as much as the athlete could tolerate. This recommendation resulted in the phenomenon of hyponatremia (literally: too little salt in the blood) that is a health risk and unfortunately still causes athletes to die. After a few years, this effect was recognized, recommendations for fluid consumption were adjusted, and the new recommendation was to consume enough fluid to prevent more than 2% of weight loss from sweating.

Theoretically that was a good approach, but it is hardly practicable because the athlete doesn't carry a scale during a race to check his weight loss.

9.4.1   Hyponatremia

Before we talk about which strategy is the right one, I would like to offer a more detailed explanation of the hyponatremia condition, because that's where the fun ends. The blood's normal sodium level is between 135 and 145 mmol per liter of blood. When this concentration drops to less than 135 mmol due to excessive fluid intake, it is referred to as hyponatremia.

Sodium in a beverage or in energy gels or bars serves as a transportation molecule to make the GI tract permeable so the consumed fluid can get to where it needs to go, namely the bloodstream to replenish the loss of blood plasma caused by sweating.

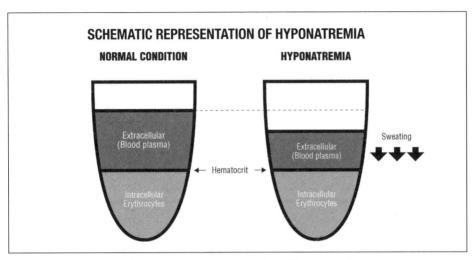

Figure 85: Blood-plasma volume: a schematic representation of hyponatremia.

If the supply strategy's chosen amount of sodium is too low, too much of the consumed fluid remains in the stomach. This phenomenon can be visualized as a kind of funnel. The fluid is poured into the top, but the fluid does not properly drain out of the bottom, meaning from the GI tract into the bloodstream. Only sodium makes this process possible by opening up the SGLT I transport path.

PLEASE NOTE

Initial symptoms of hyponatremia might be:

- Feeling of abdominal fullness
- Nausea
- Shortness of breath because the bloated stomach pushes on the diaphragm
- Stomach gurgling while running
- Trouble concentrating
- Vision problems
- Headache

At a long-distance race, a spectator with trained eyes and ears can notice the bloated stomach and the gurgling. Next to the unpleasant feeling of fullness there is also another negative effect, because the athlete will be unable to take in any more energy and thus risks a carbohydrate deficiency.

Athletes often projectile vomit the excess fluid, which only provides temporary relief. Since the urge to urinate is reduced during the physical exertion, little relief can be expected from urinating. But since water, as we know, always finds a way through, so the water infiltrates from the extracellular space into the cells, causing them to swell.

At some point during the race the athlete notices that the band of his GPS watch is getting tighter on this wrist. This edema isn't too much of a concern. But it becomes a problem in the brain, because the firm boundaries of the cranial bones don't allow for any fluid displacement, which leads to a headache.

But if the pressure continues to significantly increase there is a risk of ruptured blood vessels, which can potentially result in death. An athlete tragically died from precisely this issue at the Ironman Frankfurt in 2015.

A study showed that between 2005–2013, 10% of participants at the Ironman Frankfurt exhibited symptoms of hyponatremia. Next to preserving good health, sodium and fluids have a considerable effect on race performance.

I first observed the effect of hyponatremia in a race back in 2010. Back then, I took a closer look at the athletes' notes and race files while asking myself why the bottom suddenly falls out of their running performance.

If it was certain that the athletes trained properly in the run-up and tapered correctly and did not make any pacing mistakes in the race and had an adequate carbohydrate supply, such a drop should not have happened.

Here is a sample progression that took place over and over.

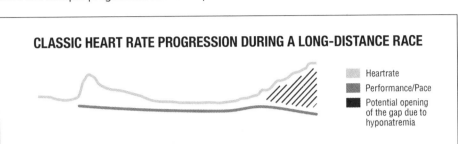

Figure 86: Sample heart rate progression during a long-distance race.

After some pondering, it occurred to me that it could be caused by a loss of sodium or rather the blood's increasing viscosity. Increased sweating and a simultaneously deficient fluid supply with sodium, change the ratios in the blood. Fluid decreases and blood thickens.

Cardiovascular effort increases and blood pressure goes up, and due to the slower blood flow rate, an optimal oxygen supply to the muscles is no longer guaranteed. Back then, I pointed out to the athletes that the cause might be a lack of sodium and recommended a more generous sodium supply.

9.4.2   Determining the sodium concentration in sweat

A few years ago, a method emerged for measuring the concentration of sodium loss per liter of sweat. With more than 15,000 tests worldwide, it was determined that the spread can be between 230 to 2,300 mg per liter of sweat. The average number is approximately 950 mg, which shows that a blanket recommendation with respect to dosage is not really possible.

In the process, athletes were tested for several years in completely different conditions (e.g., competition season, off-season, in the heat, in the cold, at sea level, at altitude, pre- and post-competition) and it was determined that the concentration only varies 5-8 %. The reason given was that sweat concentration depends on a certain protein on the cell membrane, the cystic fibrosis transmembrane regulator (CFTR).

The amount of these CFTR molecules is determined genetically. Therefore, one can cautiously extrapolate that the amount of sodium in sweat is also to some extent determined by genetics.

ADDITIONAL INFO

Three different categories can be differentiated for classification:

1. Low sweater 200-750 mg
2. Medium sweater 750-1,100 mg
3. High sweater > 1,100 mg per liter of sweat

9.4.3 Calculating sweat loss

When calculating the total loss amount, there is another value to be considered in addition to the sodium concentration, and that is the rate of sweat loss, meaning the amount of sweat in ml that an athlete loses per time unit X, specifically per hour. In contrast to the relatively fixed concentration, this amount is rather volatile and subject to several external factors:

• Temperature
• Intensity of physical activity
• Training condition
• Humidity
• Stimulants (caffeine)
• Duration

When taking a closer look at these factors one can see that the entire amount of lost sodium and sweat cannot be calculated with a single test, but that the sweat quantity must be measured under varying conditions.

To do so, the athlete should use the restroom before training. Next, he should get on a scale in the nude to establish the starting weight. After training, the sweaty clothes are removed, the top layer of sweat is wiped off the skin, and the athlete then gets back on the scale to determine the difference in bodyweight.

For longer sessions that include fluid intake, water bottles, bars, or gels are weighed before and after training. Consequently, the amount of excreted urine during a pee break should also be quantified. I have heard of athletes who capture their urine by peeing into an empty water bottle. But that might be going a little too far.

Figure 87: Doing a sweat rate test to determine the sweat rate.

If the athlete then records the intensity, duration, ambient temperature, type of sport, and date, he will be able to predict accurately the amount of sweat he will lose per hour in certain conditions.

A tip here regarding measuring during indoor training. During roller training the athlete should record whether he trained with or without cooling from a fan. The amount of sweat loss will vary from 0.7-2.8 l.

Scientific literature also lists losses on a scale from 3.5-4.0 l per hour. I personally have so far not seen such values in practice.

The following overview is a good example of what such a table can look like.

TABLE FOR DETERMINING SWEAT RATE

Training time (min)	Start weight (kg)	End weight (kg)	% weight difference	Start weight fluids (kg)	End weight fluids (kg)	Fluids consumed (l)	Temp (C)	Avg. power bike (w)	Indoor or outdoor	With or without fan	Sweat amount total (l)	Sweat rate (l/h)
90	65	64	-1.5%	1	0.6	0.4	20	255	Indoor	With	1.40	0.93

■ Example row　　■ To be filled in　　■ Automatically filled in

Figure 88: Sample table to determine the sweat rate.

The two factors of sodium concentration and sweat loss amount can now be used to calculate the total sodium-loss amount.

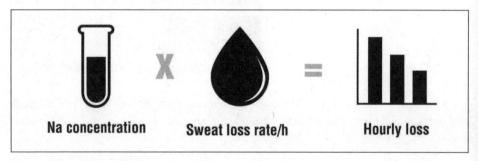

Na concentration　　**X**　　**Sweat loss rate/h**　　**=**　　**Hourly loss**

Figure 89: Formula to calculate total sweat loss.

9.4.4　Application in running practice

To establish an appropriate supply strategy for the competition the athlete can now look up the expected temperature and intensity on this table and multiply them by the measured sodium concentration. Athletes who don't know their individual sodium concentration should work with an average value of 950 mg per liter of sweat as a reference point.

SAMPLE CALCULATION

Athlete A has a concentration of 1,000 mg and an anticipated sweat rate of 1.5 l per hour, which means that he has a total sweat loss of 1,500 ml per hour.

Athlete B has a concentration of 750 mg and an anticipated sweat rate of 2.5 l per hour (i.e., a total loss of 1,875 ml per hour).

Athlete C sweats out 1,800 mg per liter, but only has a total sweat loss of 0.81 l, thus loses 1,440 mg.

These examples show well how important it is to consider both factors. An athlete is not a better or worse athlete if he has a higher or lower value.

The excitement mounts, because now I would like to talk about the practical application, especially in a race. At a competition the goal is to avoid hyponatremia to prevent health consequences. Another goal is to minimize performance loss as much as possible by protecting the blood-plasma volume for as long as possible, meaning keeping the blood from increasingly thickening.

Regardless of the measured optimal sodium concentration, it is a good idea to drink 750 mg of sodium dissolved in 500 ml of water the night before the race. The athlete should drink the same mix again on the morning of the race to fill his salt stores and to increase the plasma volume with the slightly higher intake.

In 2010, I worked up a salt-loading schematic that provided for a dose of 3,000 mg the night before and 1,500 mg on the morning of a race, based on the principle "more helps more."

But the quantity on the night before was too concentrated because it generated a lot of thirst. That in turn led to drinking a lot of water. The increased fluid consumption then resulted in several trips to the restroom during an already not-so-stress-free night before a race.

But back to the race. Once the athlete is back on solid ground after swimming and has left the transition zone, it is best to wait a few minutes before starting nourishment so the stomach can first recover from swimming and the stress of the transition zone.

From then on it is important to stick with a previously calculated schedule, beginning with an intake on the bike of 70-80% of the total loss per hour.

SAMPLE CALCULATION

For athlete A, 70-80 % means 1,050-1,200 mg sodium intake per hour. For athlete B it means approximately 1,300-1500 mg. For athlete C, it is approximately 1,000-1,150 mg.

The goal should be the disciplined consumption of this amount during the bike segment of the race, so the athlete can ideally start the run optimally hydrated and with an adequate blood plasma volume. To err on the side of caution it is often best to increase the amount to 90% during the last quarter of the 180 km.

The amount of fluid consumed per hour should be calculated based on the amount of sweat listed in the table. If an athlete sweats less than 1,000 ml/h, water consumption should be 350-750 ml/h. For 1,000-1,500 ml of sweat loss the athlete should consume 700-900 ml/h. For losses of more than 1,500 ml of sweat per hour the recommended water consumption is 1,000 to no more than 1,200 ml/h.

Those 1,200 ml/h should not be exceeded even in very hot temperatures, as the GI tract cannot adequately absorb a larger amount. External cooling plays a major role during hot temperatures, but more on that later.

This external amount of sodium and water is no longer required during the run. For one, water intake from paper cups is difficult to do accident-free, and for that reason it is also difficult to calculate a precise amount of fluid. An athlete doesn't know how much water the volunteers put in the cups, and it is impossible to quantify how much of the cup's contents end up in the athlete's mouth and on the race kit.

If the athlete did not build any mistakes into his strategy during cycling, 30-50% sodium intake is sufficient to reach the finish line safely and quickly. Another advantage of a lower intake amount is that the athlete continues to lose bodyweight during the race and gets increasingly lighter due to sweating, which will have a positive effect on running speed during the second half of the marathon.

The following chart shows an ideal running progression within the context of sodium intake.

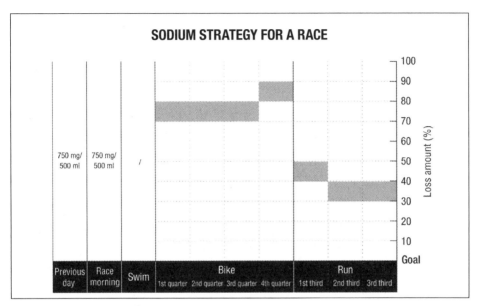

Figure 90: Sodium strategy for a race.

The athlete should use a calculator to calculate the amount of sodium and check the packaging or nutritional information of the gels, beverages, and bars he plans to consume during the race. The greatest pitfall here is confusing sodium and sodium chloride, or salt.

Sodium is only 39% the amount of salt or sodium chloride, which is very important to know when calculating the intake amount. Frighteningly, today there are still manufacturers of gels who put a laughable 10-50 mg of sodium in one package unit. The athlete then consumes 2-3 of those per hour to cover the carbohydrates, which still only provides 150 mg of sodium per hour total.

I can only insist that athletes research the gel market, read labels, and test them in training. To me, the question of why no manufacturer has marketed a gel with 300-400 mg of sodium remains unanswered.

The fact is, when an athlete only consumes just over 150 mg of sodium per hour from his gels, he should compensate with salt tablets. Those contain between 100–250 mg of sodium per tablet. With a gel with low content and a high intake amount the total amount is large, and continuously consuming that amount can get stressful during a race.

Here I would like to address the matter of a possible overdose. Everyone knows what it's like when a meal was too salty. The result is usually excessive thirst, and that's really the only problem when having consumed too much in a race as well.

The hypothalamus in the brain realizes that the concentration was too high and sends the message to dilute the concentration with water. There unfortunately are no comparable safety mechanisms when it comes to hyponatremia.

Of course, we not only sweat during a competition, but also while training. As was mentioned in the race strategy for running, the human body can tolerate some losses and therefore does not always require a certain schedule or sodium supply strategy in training.

In my view, in training it would be much more important to prepare the sessions by preloading. Workouts that are completed in a less than ideal state of hydration can be very challenging and also require a longer recovery time. In general, the unit's weight loss should be replenished with a 1.5 ratio of water.

To allow faster transport of the consumed fluid to the bloodstream the recovery drink after the session should not only contain water, carbohydrates, and protein, but also sodium as a transporter of the fluid.

When it is very hot and the training plan lists a 4:30-hour bike unit with 3 x 40 minutes at racing tempo and ends with a short combination run, it is wise to adhere to a strategy like that of a competition to

a)   have simulated the same in training and
b)   to ensure that good quality will be maintained until the end of the respective unit.

A shorter regeneration time should be another positive side effect since the loss during training is correspondingly less.

Indoor bike training is another peculiarity. Particularly during the cold time of year, many athletes train exclusively on the roller. Some don't use a fan, which results in heavy sweating. To increase the quality of roller training and to quickly restore the fluid balance, athletes should diligently turn this screw.

Based on experience, some athletes have trouble deciding when which strategy is the right one. The below chart is intended to assist in this process.

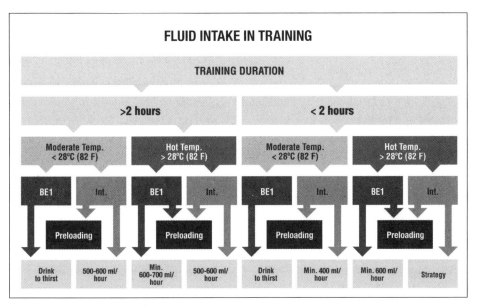

Figure 91: Fluid intake in training.

9.5 Cramps

Many athletes regularly suffer from cramping, but why? When a muscle must work for an extended period of time or is simply overloaded, it stops working, which can cause nasty cramps.

Cramps are extremely painful and will cause even the toughest dog problems. They generally occur after long and hard training units, during or after a race, and especially if the athlete also sweated a lot. Muscle camps can be divided into two categories.

9.5.1   Heat cramps

Heat cramps result from an electrolyte imbalance in the circulating blood. Electrolytes are positively and negatively charged elements that are essential to muscle effort. As we just learned, when the athlete sweats he loses primarily sodium, and this loss can throw off the electrolyte balance.

When this balance unravels, muscle effort is no longer economical. Individual muscle fibers, but also muscle groups, work against each other instead of working together. This conflict leads to cramps.

9.5.2   Cramps due to fatigue

Cramping due to fatigue is less connected to an electrolyte imbalance but is more likely the result of long-term effort in a specific body position. Cramps in the soles of the feet and calves during swimming are caused by the foot's extended plantar flexion, meaning a ballerina-like hyperextension of the foot.

Add an energy deficit, meaning an insufficient carbohydrate supply to muscles, and the muscle stops doing its job, is overloaded, and cramps up. A consistent supply with adequate energy during intense training or in a race is essential to preventing cramps.

What can an athlete do when he is cramping during exertion?

Briefly stopping and stretching the cramping muscle causes it to relax. For instance, when experiencing calf cramps while swimming, the athlete must improvise, grabbing the foot or toes and pulling towards the shin. If this cannot be done comfortably, hold on to a support kayak.

Another technique to relieve cramps is flexing the antagonist, meaning the opposing muscle group. This also brings relief to the cramping muscle. For instance, flexing the quadriceps during a hamstring cramp will reduce cramping in the affected area.

A last resort when it comes to battling muscle cramps, and probably not everyone's cup of tea, is penetrating the cramping muscle with a safety pin. To do so, the athlete removes a safety pin from his starting bib and rams it into the cramping muscle. The sudden pain causes an extreme contraction of the muscle followed by a relaxation phase; the muscle stops cramping. But it takes a lot of resolve to jam a needle into a muscle.

A slightly gentler and more hygienic method is to pound the muscle with a clenched fist. It works the same way as the needle. A very high dose of sodium can also relieve muscle cramps.

Soy sauce has a high sodium content and works well in such a case. Sushi lovers are familiar with the small plastic envelopes of soy sauce that come with meals. They are perfect for a race, are small, and the packaging is sturdy enough to carry them in the back pocket of the racing attire.

Cramps are not caused by a magnesium deficiency. Athletes should therefore definitely not take magnesium during a race because that often proves to be a bad idea. Magnesium virtually guarantees diarrhea. If at all, magnesium should be taken at night before bed as a muscle relaxer and to prepare for the next day's training.

9.6   Ideal Weight and Racing Weight

For years I have noticed that at the beginning of the year, every internet forum, triathlon magazine, Facebook page, etc., is full of articles intended to help us triathletes reach the ideal competition weight. But I don't think that in long distance the lowest weight is necessarily the ideal racing weight.

When looking at specialists in the individual disciplines one can see differences in physiognomy. Marathon runners tend to be lighter. When they find their way to the triathlon, they tend to have major problems with swimming and cycling, and even in the race, run far below their performance level as strictly runners.

But swimmers tend to have more subcutaneous fat that serves as natural insulation during frequent swimming in water temperatures below body temperature.

When looking at the cyclists, more precisely the triathlon-related, the time-trial cyclists, one can see that they are usually more muscular than GC or uphill riders in professional cycling. In long-distance triathlon, cycling is of critical importance. Strong, muscular athletes often not only cycle better, but they also tend to have more left in the tank for the subsequent run.

Thin, very light athletes potentially can't adequately meet their energy needs during cycling and therefore are no longer able to exploit their perceived advantage over heavier athletes during the running segment. But age-group athletes should not look to the body type of some top professionals. They are absolutely exceptional athletes with exceptional bodies that are unachievable for Aunt Gerda from next door. A slightly higher body fat percentage usually leads to better swimming and cycling performance, as well as being better for overall health.

A six pack or huge biceps can certainly be visually appealing but should definitely not be the highest priority in training. Nowadays there are countless athletes who look extremely fit but aren't when it comes to the anticipated demands of a long-distance event.

Athletes who permanently consume too little energy, particularly carbohydrates, run the risk of experiencing negative adaptations with respect to training stimulus and immune system. The situation becomes perilous when athletes at spring training camp in the South try to lose the holiday fat by castigating themselves about eating.

Particularly during peak training phases, the body needs all forms of energy to be able to quickly initiate repair processes between units so the athlete can be restored for the next unit.

Traditionally this works well for the first 3-4 days of training camp, but then fatigue and maladaptation take over and the training performances worsen day by day. Training camp with those big cycling volumes requires energy. There is nothing wrong with a coffee break; even professional athletes take them. A slice of cake or a bocadillo on Mallorca come with the territory.

Athletes who only drink black coffee and water because they want to optimize their fat metabolism will complete training camp on empty, come away with poorer adaptations, and significantly increase their risk of infection.

The following chart shows a temporal view to reliably and safely reach competition weight. Restricting calories over an extended period can have a negative effect on various body functions.

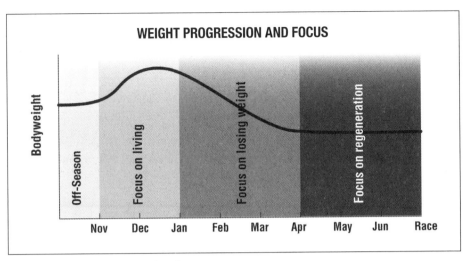

Figure 92: Weight fluctuation during the season.

9.6.1 Immune system

For optimal functioning the immune system requires energy in the form of carbohydrates. Permanently consuming too little of this nutrient leads to increased susceptibility to infection.

9.6.2 Training adaptation

On a biochemical level various signaling molecules require energy for the implementation and adaptation of the training stimulus. When an athlete eats too little, he will not be successful on that level.

9.6.3 Hormonal balance

Too little energy means stress for the body. Stress typically leads to a rise in the stress hormone cortisol, which in turn leads to a testosterone imbalance.

Paradoxically, high cortisol levels over an extended period do not, as many people think, lead to weight loss but rather weight gain, because the fat metabolism is suppressed by the reduced release of the growth hormone (HGH). Female athletes in particular, often tend to consume too little energy to chase after a perceived beauty ideal.

Their desire to lose weight causes them to walk into a trap. They wonder why they don't lose weight despite calorie restrictions and training. Their weight stagnates or even increases. As a result, some eat even less, and the downward trend in their performance is difficult to stop. Here the body continuously thinks it is in an emergency situation.

Mother Nature is smart and therefore won't allow reproduction of life (i.e., the menstrual cycle is abnormal, periods change, and become irregular or even stop).

Disruptions to menstrual cycles can be reversed, meaning a normal cycle can often be restored after reducing the training volume, but not always. This topic is unfortunately still taboo.

9.6.4 Bone health

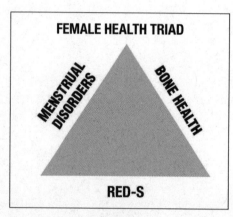

Figure 93: Female health triad.

When female athletes eat too little for an extended period of time, this energy deficiency can have a negative effect on bone health. The body's reduced fat mass causes a lower estrogen and progesterone release. Estrogen is critical here because a deficiency of this hormone leads to an impaired bone metabolism and consequently a higher risk of osteoporosis. If bone density continues to decrease, there is a risk of developing a bone marrow edema or a stress fracture. The term *female health triad* was created in this context. It describes the relationship between lack of energy, menstrual disorders, and the risk of osteoporosis.

The subject of menstrual cycle-driven training in which phases of particular trainability occur within the menstrual cycle to date has been assessed as empirical. I have been able to observe that, for instance, strength training was processed very well during the follicle phase, while endurance stimuli seem to be effective during ovulation. Studies in endurance sports are still pretty sparse, which is why I do not want to delve deeper into this subject in this book. The subject is highly complex and highly individual and differs from athlete to athlete.

But I would like to impress upon all female athletes to talk to their coach if changes in the menstrual cycle occur. Advice with respect to contraceptives, etc., is clearly something to discuss with a gynecologist.

A missed period should not be dismissed and is always the first sign of a hormonal imbalance. Here the athlete's health is a top priority and should absolutely be considered to prevent possible long-term harm.

9.7   Nutritional Supplements

The dietary supplement market is a billion-dollar industry. Manufacturers promise increased performance and effects that are not always based on valid evidence. Instead of taking questionable supplements, as I already mentioned earlier, I would argue for an everyday diet of diverse, seasonal, regional, and fresh ingredients that covers all aspects of human nutrition, and thus makes the addition of supplements obsolete.

Empirically speaking, exceptions would be vitamin D during the winter months, magnesium as a muscle relaxant right before going to bed, and colostrum for immune and GI support.

An important point here is the potential contamination of supplements which can potentially cause a positive doping test. It is wise to test the product before taking it for the first time. The National Anti-Doping Agency (NADA) will test such products.

CONCLUSION

As previously mentioned, I am not a nutrition specialist and can view diet only from a coach's perspective. But experience has shown me that the most successful athletes are those who consume enough energy from food. Here it is often not so much what they eat, but that they consume the necessary number of calories.

A low power-to-weight ratio on race day is certainly an advantage, but only if the health-related price isn't too high, and the athlete made sure before the event that optimal training adaptations and an intact immune system for performance development exist due to an adequate amount of energy.

10 INJURIES AND ILLNESSES

Unfortunately, it is necessary to also address this subject, because a preparation period of several months with massive training volumes does leave its mark. During that time both the immune system and the orthopedic apparatus are significantly stressed.

Both areas can largely be removed from the line of fire by skillfully balancing loading and unloading, but unfortunately not completely. A cold or a GI virus over the winter are pretty much a standard feature of the training process for a long-distance event in the summer.

In this chapter I would like to point out the most common problems, but also methods of prevention and therapy, whereby my competencies in this area are limited since I am neither a physical therapist nor an osteopath. I will therefore refrain from making diagnoses, or the like.

10.1   Taking Care of the Immune System

The immune system as a defensive bulwark against germs, bacteria, and viruses is challenged every day. During training we are exposed to extreme factors such as car exhaust, solar rays, germs in the water while swimming, heat, and cold, etc. To be prepared and avoid missed training sessions due to illness, we should protect ourselves accordingly. I designated maintenance tips to the respective disciplines as follows.

10.1.1   Swimming

- No swimming with cold symptoms, because damaged mucous membranes are a perfect entrance for any germs present in the water.
- If the water is cold, take a long warm shower after swimming to raise the body's core temperature.
- Hair should be blow dried after swimming, because the body loses lots of heat through the head.
- Athletes with a tendency to develop ear problems should use ear plugs and after swimming dry out the ear canal with a blow dryer.

- If the nasal mucous membranes are swollen for an extended period after swimming, it helps to rub a nose ointment into the nostrils and to use a nose spray after swimming to reduce swelling. But nose sprays should be used with caution due to the risk of addiction.
- Wear shower sandals at the pool to prevent foot fungus.

10.1.2   Cycling

- The athlete is most exposed to the weather conditions and airflow while cycling, which is why he should be prepared for all eventualities. It is better to dress too warm than too cool. Even in good weather, a wind vest should be on board.
- During single-digit temperatures, wearing a scarf or bandana over the mouth warms inhaled air a little and thereby minimizes bronchial stress.
- Sunburns should be avoided. Always apply sunscreen before training in summer. Carry a small tube of sunscreen on long rides to reapply as needed.
- Always wear freshly laundered pants and apply chamois cream to avoid skin irritation and inflammation of the perineum.
- Riding for hours and consuming the corresponding amounts of sugary fluids and foods affects the teeth. It is therefore recommended to brush the teeth right after training because health begins in the mouth!
- Sweaty clothing should be removed as quickly as possible after training, followed by a shower.

10.1.3   Running

- The same recommendations regarding sun protection, covering the mouth with a cloth to warm inhaled air when cold, and showering as soon as possible after training apply to running.
- Regularly trimming the toenails or a visit to a podiatrist help prevent infections of the nail bed.

If an infection occurs despite the protective measures, athletes should determine the source of the problem, its severity, and how much of an effect it will have.

I prescribe absolutely no sports in cases of fever and use of antibiotics. Even after colds and GI problems, athletes should return to training in moderation. The following chart should be viewed as a rough guide but not a blanket recommendation.

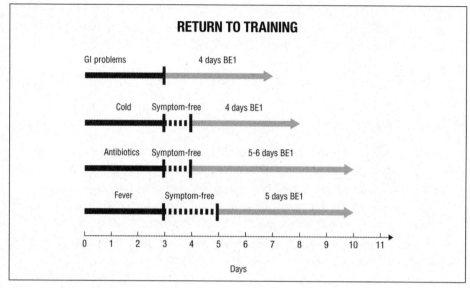

Figure 94: Return to training after illness.

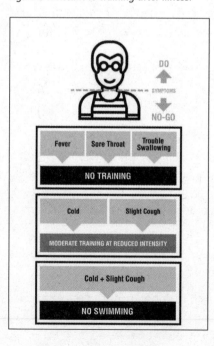

If health restrictions aren't so severe that the body reacts with fever or the doctor prescribes an antibiotic, the athlete can proceed according to the above-the-neck rule, which I have successfully used since I first began coaching. This rule is also a guide to show the athlete when he should take a break.

When it comes to resuming training, it is generally better to be more cautious than too aggressive. Waiting another symptom-free day is more beneficial than starting back too soon, too intensely, and too long.

Figure 95: Above-the-neck rule.

PLEASE NOTE

When in doubt, leave it out!

10.2   Orthopedic Problems

All three triathlon sports—swimming, cycling, and running—have cyclical and recurring loading patterns. A biomechanically poor movement execution therefore creates a significant potential of overloading.

This means that motor function and movement execution must be of high quality and the training equipment used must be adjusted to the athlete using it.

In addition to technical training, the training process should include workouts that improve strength, overall athleticism as well as mobility, and prevent injuries. Almost every triathlete is familiar with the often-cited stabilization exercises to increase core strength and knows about the importance of flexibility training through stretching and fasciae training, but often there is a lack of regular practical application. Since the needs and problems in this area are highly individual, it is very difficult for me as the author of this book to make sweeping recommendations for exercises in these areas, and I have decided not to do so.

I can therefore only offer general tips on the subject. There is probably no right or wrong when it comes to athletic or strength training. A few years ago, I still recommended classic stationary strength training with the basic exercises of squats, deadlifts, and pull-ups, but have since moved away from that.

For one, these exercises have an immense injury risk when performed incorrectly, and I am unable to eliminate those mistakes from afar if I am unable to stand next to the athlete to correct him. That assessment can certainly be different in a situation with a set-up where an athletic trainer or physical therapist can make corrections on site.

And secondly, I did not always see positive results in terms of performance development. The described strength training places major demands on the muscles, so they require longer regeneration times after such a training. But that means that the athlete is unable to train effectively for 2-3 days after the strength workout. But since I consider continuity of a particular stimulus to be the highest priority, meaning nearly daily training of the core sports of swimming, cycling, and running, purposely accepting 2–3 less effective training days is a direct contradiction.

Instead, I advocate for bodyweight exercises, balance exercises, and lateral movement because that direction of movement is not required in triathlon. Here, too, regularity is the key. Three 20-minute sessions a week in this area is better than working out once a week for a whole hour at the gym.

Here the advantage is temporal effectiveness, because those 20 minutes can be easily built in after or before the actual training, since the athlete is already in sport mode and appropriately dressed. Here, too, in recent years training science has consistently been unnecessarily overcomplicated. Nowadays basic exercises are considered not fancy enough, instead exercises with circus-like artistry are chosen. But when people aren't even able to correctly perform basic exercises like push-ups, there is really no need to build in unnecessary higher degrees of difficulty.

When working on overall athletic skills and strength, I recommend a more basic approach. Sport-specific strength in my opinion is trained better and more safely by swimming with paddles, cycling uphill with a low cadence, and running in hilly terrain, because it poses less risk of injury. Since most age-group athletes sit all day at work, those athletes in particular should pay attention to a strong and healthy back to avoid health-related side effects from sitting on a daily basis (i.e., build in classic core stability exercises).

The subject of mobility training is close to my heart. There is no clear evidence that static stretching improves mobility and thus protects from injuries. But what to me is crucial about stretching is the psychological component. The athlete almost always feels subjectively better after such a mobility unit.

A sense of well-being, and maybe even the fact that he appears to become more flexible, are important aspects of my approach to triathlon training, because when an athlete feels good, he will train more often and with more enjoyment, which then brings us back to the previously mentioned continuity of a certain stimulus.

Like athletic training, success comes with regularity. Here, too, three 20-minute workouts beat one 60-minute session a week in terms of effectiveness. But static stretching should never be done before a training sessions, because holding the positions for an extended period reduces tension (tonus) in the muscles. The idea is to activate before a unit instead of sedate. Static training therefore is more of a regeneration measure after training.

I will let the athlete decide whether he wants to stretch right after training or build in a separate stretch workout a little later. Dynamic warm-up exercises should be done before training to warm up the muscles, activate breathing and metabolism, and to prepare the mind for the subsequent activity. With increasing age, the warm-up should play a more important role and should at least be done before every run and before more intense units.

Fasciae training with foam rollers should primarily be used as a regenerative measure but can also be helpful before a workout if the athlete notices a tight spot in a muscle that must be loosened up. Rolling the lower legs before swimming, for example, can provide relief to athletes with regular calf cramps while swimming.

To date there is still no real reliable evidence with respect to the rolling direction, rolling amplitude, and the amount of time between fasciae training sessions. The discovery of the fasciae or rather their importance and function within the movement apparatus is only a few years young and the science in this area is still in its infancy.

10.2.1   Frequent injuries

Like the measures to protect the immune system, I have listed the most common injuries according to the individual disciplines.

10.2.1.1   Swimming

With a good technique, swimming poses almost no orthopedic stress. Yet athletes do complain about problems with the neck, shoulders, or elbows, which can all be eliminated via corrections to the technique.

10.2.1.1.1   Neck

Changing the breathing direction from time to time, consciously allowing the head to hang, and if necessary, swimming with a snorkel can ease stress in the neck.

10.2.1.1.2 Shoulders

Forego the use of paddles or take a temporary break from swimming if necessary. Build in exercises with a Thera-band to strengthen the external rotators, hang from a pull-up bar with different hand positions and open the shoulders with the use of gravity, massage/fasciae work of neck, chest, and trapezius.

10.2.1.1.3 Elbows

Forego the use of paddles or if necessary, take a temporary break from swimming. Massage/fasciae work of neck, chest, and trapezius can be beneficial.

10.2.1.2 Cycling

In cycling problems with the locomotor system typically only surface due to a poorly chosen seat height and cleat position of the shoes. Increasing cycling volumes too quickly, particularly at spring training camp, can cause problems in the knee area.

10.2.1.2.1 Neck

Neck problems tend to increase in spring when athletes switch from a racing bike to the time trial bike, and not enough time was spent training on the bike indoors over the winter to get used to the sitting position.

An overly aggressive handlebar position can also cause problems in that area, but the frames of some cycling sunglasses are also too large. The athlete must potentially lift his head too high to maintain his field of vision, which can also lead to problems.

10.2.1.2.2 Knees

Most knee problems don't originate in the knee itself as so many people falsely believe but are the result of overly tight and inflexible thigh muscles, and therefore can be treated quite easily by the athlete himself by stretching the quadriceps; massaging the area with a fasciae roller will also bring relief.

10.2.1.3 Running

Running is the discipline with the highest orthopedic load and the risk of injury is correspondingly high, particularly when the running technique leaves something to be desired.

To avoid problems from arising in the first place, training should include focus on prevention. This includes regular stretching and rolling of the lower leg muscles, but also strengthening the feet and especially working on sufficient mobility of the metatarsophalangeal joints of the big toes.

It has been my observation that many problems with lower legs and feet are related to the big toe. The reason is that while running the force transmission at the moment the foot pushes off takes place precisely via that toe.

If the metatarsophalangeal joint isn't extremely flexible or even has a case of Hallux valgus, this force transmission can no longer proceed in the best possible way, which then causes other structures in the foot and lower leg to have to also take on this function that they are not intended for.

When adding too many kilometers, the problem worsens. About 80% of all overloading symptoms in the lower legs and feet can be treated with increased mobility in the big toes.

This does not require expensive inserts or painful shockwave therapy. In cases of acute problems such as shin splints, plantar fasciitis, or an irritated or inflamed Achilles tendon I would forego running on the street and, if the problem permits, resort to aqua jogging until the problem has been resolved.

10.2.2 Resuming running after injuries

Just like returning to training after illness, training after an injury should be conservative and cautious. Particularly when it comes to running, it is wise to run a shorter route to avoid having to limp home for a long distance if the injury worsens. The warm-up time should be twice as long as before the injury. The athlete must be patient and not return to training like a sledgehammer.

Here is an example of a defensive restart after an injury to a lower extremity.

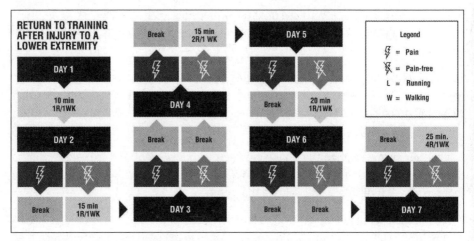

Figure 96: Return to training after injury to a lower extremity.

10.2.3 Use of pain medication

In conversation with some athletes, I often hear that they regularly use pain medications in training and at competitions. A study completed with the participants of the Ironman Brazil in 2008, revealed that 50% of participants regularly took pain meds.

There is a stubborn preconception that all triathletes, and especially professionals, would do that anyway, particularly since over-the-counter pain medications are not on the doping list. To me it is a frightening development that has taken root.

There is a place for pain meds when they are medically indicated, but that's it! Pain fulfills a purpose in the human body; it is a protective measure. Pain signals that a situation is getting critical. Suppressing that signal puts the individual at risk of permanent damage.

Chronic use of these pain medications frequently results in kidney problems, heart attack, liver failure, or heart failure. I am therefore strictly opposed to the use of these medications without a medical reason.

Particularly after injuries, an athlete should not resort to taking pain meds because in this phase it is important to feel any potentially occurring pain and as shown in the chart, make a decision about how to structure the impending training day. When the pain is suppressed, the athlete might make the wrong decision and the injury returns.

10.2.4   Relative energy deficiency syndrome (REDS)

REDS syndrome refers to impaired physiological function. The alleged cause is an energy deficiency, which has a negative effect on metabolic turnover, immune system, and endurance performance, among others.

REDS is caused by an undersupply of energy in the form of food. Here the energy intake is insufficient for ensuring energy consumption for health, body function, and everyday life when adding the additional demand from training. Since many athletes think they need to be light, some simply eat too little. Along with the negative side effects listed above, there are worse adaptations after training stimulus and a worsening metabolic rate.

REDS is one of the main reasons stress fractures (fatigue fractures) occur. The body resorts to using bone substance and muscles to cover its energy budget.

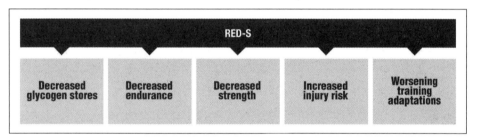

Figure 97: RED-S.

In women REDS has a negative effect on bone health and menstruation. Together these three factors form the female athlete triad. Clearly the diagnosis must be made by a physician. But a vigilant coach should be aware of this problem and if necessary, seek a conversation with the athlete or encourage her to seek medical help.

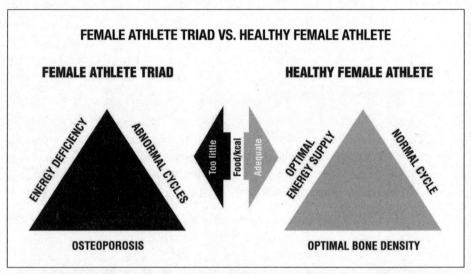

Figure 98: Female athlete triad vs. healthy female athlete.

11 TRAINING AND COMPETING IN HOT CONDITIONS

Everyone has seen images from the Ironman Kona, where athletes have to excessively cool themselves due to the prevailing temperatures. But such high temperatures are not only found in Hawaii or Asia. As a result of global climate change, athletes are exposed to high temperatures during summer competitions in previously temperate climate zones.

In 2019, for instance, temperatures during the Ironman Frankfurt were nearly 10 degrees C higher than those at the world championship race in the Pacific Ocean. However, when assessing the racing conditions, one needs to look at more than just the temperature.

The wet bulb globe temperature (WBGT) considers humidity, wind speed, and visible infrared radiation in addition to temperature. When all these factors are included a more precise picture of the weather's influence emerges.

Special measuring devices calculate a score based on the ascertained values. The International Triathlon Union (ITU) has published a table to serve as a guideline for race organizers so they can modify or even cancel a race during extreme weather conditions.

11.1 Environmental Conditions

The athlete is continuously interchanging his body heat with his environmental conditions. This heat exchange is based on the following four mechanisms.

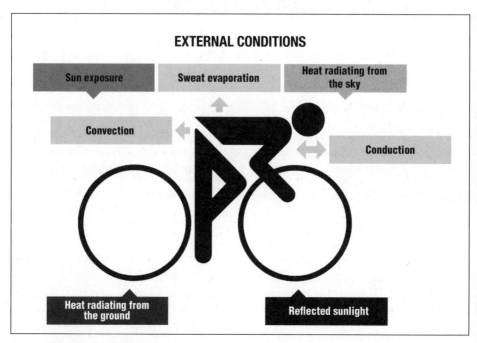

Figure 99: External conditions.

11.1.1 Evaporation

Unlike many animals, we humans have outstanding thermoregulation, meaning we can largely keep our body's core temperature in an ideal range of 36.5–37.5 degrees C (97.7–99.5 degrees F). This brings fluid to the skin's surface, and the evaporation of that sweat provides the necessary cooling.

11.1.2 Conduction

Conduction refers to heat exchange through direct contact with an object (clothing, handlebar, seat, running shoes, etc.).

11.1.3   Convection

Convection refers to heat exchange via a medium (air or water). Naturally, unlike cycling, when running there is less cooling due to the lack of airflow.

11.1.4   Radiation

Radiation refers to heat radiation from electromagnetic waves, direct sun exposure, or reflected heat from asphalt. All long-distance athletes should be familiar with Hawaii's legendary energy lab in this context.

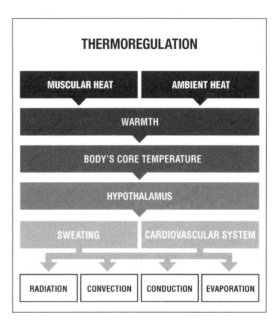

Figure 100: Superficial thermoregulation.

11.2   What Happens Inside the Body When It's Hot

Along with the aforementioned factors, as a side effect of the muscle work, an immense heat production takes place inside the body that must be cooled by sweating. It is the only way to ensure that the body functions optimally and the body's core temperature remains constant and does not rise.

When the body's core temperature rises due to extreme physical exertion, such as a long-distance event, and additional hot ambient conditions, it can happen that the compensating mechanisms to lower the temperature lapse. Certain symptoms occur as a result of exceeding this critical temperature limit.

Dizziness, nausea, excessive sweating, and cold, pale skin are initial signs of heat exhaustion. Further heat exposure and continuing physical activity can lead to heat stroke, which will manifest itself in headache, no additional sweating, nausea, and an extreme rise in the body's core temperature, and can lead to unconsciousness and even death.

Beyond the health risks, major heat or rather critical WBGT affects race performance. The shorter the race, the less impact due to heat can be expected on the anticipated performance. But since we are talking about long-distance triathlon, we should take a closer look at this subject as it can certainly be the difference between success and failure. But first some good news. This can be alleviated with the appropriate interventions and by purposefully planning one's race objectives.

But before trying to control the situation it is best to take a closer look at the coherences. In addition to the previously mentioned symptoms, the athlete can experience a massive drop in performance during a race in hot conditions. The GI tract is less well-supplied with blood when stressed since blood is needed primarily in the muscles involved in propulsion. When it's hot, more blood is moved to the periphery because sweat is produced from blood plasma which then provides cooling on the surface of the skin through evaporation.

But when there is insufficient blood flow in the stomach the ability to absorb carbohydrates diminishes and the muscles are then no longer adequately supplied, which can further decrease performance. Poor blood flow in the stomach also raises another issue, leaky gut syndrome.

This change in the stomach lining leads to GI problems that can cause the athlete to lose even more valuable time because he must frequently relieve himself.

Another phenomenon is cardiac drift, which can be observed during analysis of a heart rate curve after longer training units or a hot race. Here the heart rate increases. The cause can also be attributed to the increased amount of blood in the periphery to cool the human system.

The rising core temperature causes the blood to move to the outside for cooling. But this also means that there is reduced retrograde venous flow to the heart. When a smaller amount is enriched with fresh oxygen, the oxygen supply to the muscles with precisely this oxygen is then no longer ensured. The heart must beat considerably more to ensure blood flow and thereby an adequate oxygen supply.

I have seen exactly this effect hundreds of times in the files after a race. The circle now closes and the importance of sodium as part of the supply strategy should sink even deeper into the awareness. Sodium makes sure the consumed fluid amount returns to the blood stream and the sweated-out blood plasma is replenished, meaning the amount of blood is maintained.

Adequate sweating also has a major effect on subjective heat perception. Many athletes lose their sense of well-being in the heat and are then mentally preoccupied with braving the heat instead of keeping their mind on themselves and completing the race in the best possible condition. Heat tolerance varies from athlete to athlete.

When it comes to the reasons for these differences, body composition plays a major role. Athletes with slightly more body fat are more likely to have a low heat tolerance. Large athletes with a high body mass index (BMI) also tend to suffer in the heat. The less tissue that needs cooling, the less heat stress can be expected.

There is a reason that lighter and thinner athletes have an advantage in Hawaii and tend to be more successful. Body composition isn't the only factor that influences heat tolerance, but also physical performance capacity. It can be said that athletes with a higher maximal aerobic capacity (VO$_2$max) have better heat tolerance than less fit athletes.

There are two optimization methods to beat the heat and its negative side effects. One, heat tolerance can be developed during certain training phases, and two, cooling strategies during a race are a good way to curb the amount of heat produced in the body.

The adjacent figure shows which measures can reduce the generated heat.

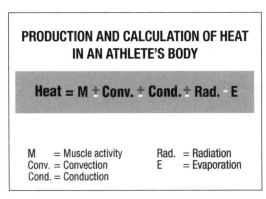

PRODUCTION AND CALCULATION OF HEAT IN AN ATHLETE'S BODY

Heat = M + Conv. + Cond. + Rad. - E

M	= Muscle activity	Rad.	= Radiation
Conv.	= Convection	E	= Evaporation
Cond.	= Conduction		

Figure 101: Heat formula.

11.2.1   Strategies for reducing the heat load

The following methods can be used to reduce heat load:

- Reducing radiation by covering the skin. Wearing a hat and protecting the neck with a legionnaire cap can lessen heat generation from direct sun light.
- Cooling via convection by squeezing out wet sponges or pouring cups of water over the head.
- Cooling through conduction by holding ice cubes or sticking them inside the racing suit.
- Reducing the metabolic load (i.e., decreasing tempo and intensity) which would be a rather undesirable state during a race.
- Cooling through evaporation (i.e., sweating).

We will come back to the first three items later. Physiological adaptations to heat are addressed below.

11.3   Heat Acclimation

With steadily rising temperatures and athletic events being awarded to locations with extreme weather conditions like, for instance, the Track & Field and Cycling world championships in Qatar or the Olympics in Rio or Tokyo, science has focused more urgently on the subject of heat and sports. The approach to long-distance training has changed with the acquired knowledge.

Only in the past few years has the topic of heat adaptation been on the screen of some coaches. There are frequent anecdotes about athletes training on the roller in the sauna or coaches having their charges ride their bike wearing a neoprene suit. I also experimented a little in this area and had some pretty good results that approximate today's level of knowledge.

The goal of adapting to heat is to delay the rise of the body's core temperature for as long as possible before a critical temperature is reached that can result in abandoning the race, and possibly even health-related consequences. But this critical temperature differs from one individual to the next and should be ascertained in the run-up as a baseline. A more detailed explanation of the testing process will follow later.

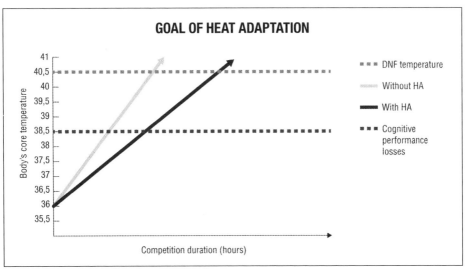

Figure 102: Goal of heat adaptation.

Heat adaptation refers to purposefully exposing oneself to higher temperatures to achieve an adaptation response of the body to this stimulus. Here we differentiate between proceeding in a natural environment or in artificially produced heat.

Heat adaptation in a natural environment is much more difficult to plan because weather can only be predicted to a point. Not every athlete has the necessary financial means or number of vacation days to complete such climate training to prepare for conditions close to those on race day.

Phases of artificial heat are easier to produce during the normal training process. Here we again differentiate between active and passive heat application. Sitting in the sauna or taking warm baths is considered passive heat. To do so, the athlete sits in the sauna for 30-40 min at 60-80 degrees C (140-176 F) or gets in a bathtub with 38-40-degree C (104 F) water for the same amount of time, immediately after a traditional endurance workout.

The athlete should take normal nourishment during training but should forego fluids for the last 15-20 minutes of the training session. No fluids should be consumed while in the sauna or bathtub. Fifteen minutes after heat exposure, the athlete can begin to replenish his fluids and enhance the process by adding sodium as an accelerator.

If the athlete wants to adapt to heat conditions during physical activity (i.e., training), he has several options. Many countries, or rather their national associations, now have special climate chambers in which every climate in the world can be simulated. But not all athletes have access to such a chamber, which is why they must improvise a bit.

The simplest option is indoor training on the treadmill as well as the Smart Trainer. When an athlete does so without the use of a fan, the heat load increases massively. Keeping windows closed and turning up the thermostat in the room will ramp it up considerably.

Workouts completed this way should not be important key units with high intensities but should be performed in the lower basic endurance range. Those sessions should be between 30-60 minutes long. Athletes should forgo fluid intake for the first 20-30 minutes, then drink only minimally for the remainder of the session.

Such a heat session should not take place on a day of rest that is intended for true unloading, because even such a short workout combined with heat will put a lot of stress on the entire organism.

Another option is wearing a special sauna suit. These suits are used in sports with different weight classes (weightlifting, combat sports, boxing, etc.) to cut weight right before a competition so the athlete can start in the next lighter weight class. Such a climate chamber for the average man certainly meets its purpose at least with respect to temperature adaptation. But it does not simulate conditions with high humidity.

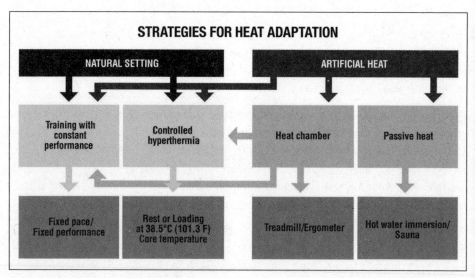

Figure 103: Strategies for heat adaptation.

11.4   Adapting Through Heat Training

Training in hot conditions causes various changes in the human body. For example, the ability to sweat is boosted significantly. The athlete starts to sweat sooner and thereby increases the amount of sweat via the sweat glands' increased work capacity. And when including the electrolyte sodium in the supply strategy before or during training, the blood–plasma volume increases further.

The sweat flow rate and the increase in plasma makes heat degradation in the form of sweating more effective, which in turn mitigates or delays the cardiac drift effect (i.e., cardiovascular stress decreases).

Moreover, the subjective perception of heat stress noticeably decreases, allowing the athlete to develop confidence about competing in hot conditions. After a successful adaptation, the subjective feeling of thirst decreases and so does fluid consumption.

11.5   Implementing and Periodizing Heat Acclimation

Training in hot conditions does harbor some risks that should be considered when planning a long-distance race in hot temperatures. For me personally, a period of 10-14 days has been ideal. Here intensities should be moderate for the first 3-5 days.

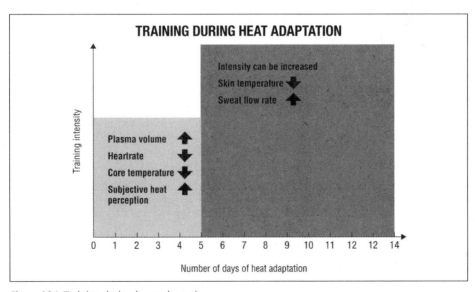

Figure 104: Training during heat adaptation.

During this time heat means more stress for the body, which is why intense training sessions would be counterproductive. After this phase and initial signs of adaptation, the intensity can be gradually increased.

Since heat adds stress, training should be carefully controlled, and during this phase even more importance should be placed on precise documentation of the entire process in the training journal. Too much heat can lead to greater exhaustion and worse training adaptation, and subsequently to undesirable development of the athletic performance.

This stress can potentially also lead to an increased risk of infection, and at worst missed training due to illness. But if the ambient temperature is too low the previously learned about and aspired to competitive advantages do not materialize, meaning the heat adaptation is inadequate.

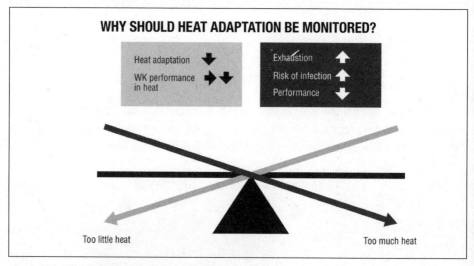

Figure 105: Why should heat adaptation be monitored?

Several parameters should be documented during heat adaptation training to be able to assess the load objectively and precisely.

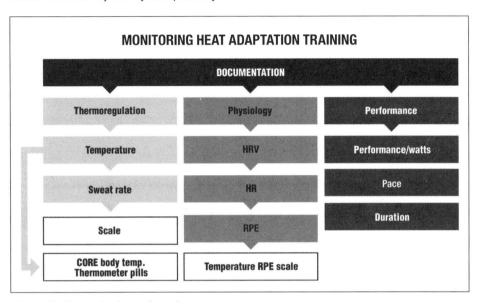

Figure 106: Monitoring heat adaptation.

Further documentation in addition to the known values, performance (watts), pace, and duration is important. The body's core temperature should be measured for better assessment of thermoregulation. A normal fever thermometer can be used for this. Those who want a more precise temperature can take the rectal temperature. The temperature should be taken right before and right after training.

The measuring technique has also gotten more sophisticated. Previously there were only thermometer pills the athlete would swallow to continuously track the body's core temperature without interruption. However, these systems are very expensive and the pills are useless once expelled.

Newer systems (e.g., CORE by the company greenTeg, Inc.) have a sensor that attaches to the skin. This sensor can send the ascertained values to the bike computer, smart phone, or GPS watch via ANT+. The athlete thus receives feedback regarding the body's current core temperature in real time, as well as a display of the trajectory along with the known performance data in the recorded file and is then able to put them into context.

To document sweat loss, each unit should include a test to determine the sweat rate. To determine cardiovascular stress, each training unit should be completed with a heart rate monitor to evaluate performance with respect to the cardiovascular load.

Measuring heart rate variability (HRV) in the morning provides inference about load tolerance. But that only makes sense for creating a reliable baseline in the runup if this measurement was also taken before the heat adaptation phase. Changes in this area will only be made visible when starting with this baseline.

In addition to the parameters that must be measured objectively the athlete should be sensitized through subjective evaluation. He should explore the way he feels in this specific heat situation and learn to feel the changes and adaptations.

Filling out a special heat RPE chart is one way to be able to bridge the gap between data and physical awareness.

SUBJECTIVE EVALUATION OF HEAT ADAPTATION

	Temperature perception	Thirst	RPE based on Borg scale
1	Very cold	Not thirsty at all	Very easy
2	Cold	Not thirsty	Very doable
3	Cool	Not very thirsty	A little strenuous
4	Neutral	Neutral	More challenging
5	Warm	Thirsty	Hard
6	Hot	Very thirsty	Very hard
7	Very hot	Very, very thirsty	Very, very hard

Figure 107: Subjective evaluation of heat adaptation.

Since training in hot conditions adds more physical stress, particular attention should be paid to intensity control in training.

There are again several ways to do so. For one, a specific core temperature can be set as the goal. A ramp test on the ergometer can be used to identify the individual critical temperature. But this requires the use of a CORE measuring device that can ascertain information about the body's core temperature in real time.

ADDITIONAL INFO

Test arrangement:

There is a protocol available from CORE (corebodytemp.com). I tried to establish my own way of doing the heat ramp test because I've seen more precise results with it, but that doesn't mean my way is necessarily the best. This topic is so new; there are only a few hints and empirical observations, but I'm sure we'll see more of this in sport-science research in the upcoming years. For now, it's fine to follow this test:

The athlete rides on an ergometer without the use of a cooling fan and fluids. Here the FTP should be watched to control intensity. Intensity is increased by 8% every five minutes, starting with 55% of the FTP.

When a core temperature of 38.5° C (101.84 F) has been reached, the corresponding performance in watts as well as the measured heart rate are recorded. After reaching this temperature mark the athlete continues to ride at the same heart rate and cadence until the performance drops by approximately 15% or the subjective perceived exertion is higher than 9 on a scale from 1–10. Upon test termination the core temperature is also recorded.

To determine the critical temperature limit 0.4–0.5° C (32.72–32.9 F) is deducted from the ascertained termination temperature. This value should be used as the temperature to control heat adaptation training.

Thus, this temperature should be targeted during heat adaptation training without overshooting the mark. However, practical implementation is difficult without the appropriate measuring device. Another option would be to control the training via a certain cardiovascular load. To do so a target frequency is set that should not be exceeded. The disadvantage to this is that the performance or pace will be slightly below training performance under normal conditions, which can have a negative effect on the athlete's mindset because he is training slower than usual.

To avoid a psychological hit it is essential to first educate the athlete and explain to him that the purposefully slower speeds are necessary to prevent the overall load from going through the roof.

However, a lower intensity also means a lower training stimulus. The extent to which the performance during hot conditions should be below the stimulus during a normal setting must therefore be considered carefully.

A third option for training control would be to specify the performance in watts or the speed in min/km for running. The disadvantage here lies in the higher anticipated cardiovascular stress and the athlete's greater sense of perceived exertion.

This form of control poses an immense risk to the already built performance because the increased overall load could cause non-functional overreaching or eventually overtraining.

The final option would be that the athlete controls intensity strictly according to his subjective perceived exertion. This can work very well and accurately for very experienced athletes. However, athletes from the Alpha Leader group run the risk of interpreting the body's signals incorrectly and potentially training too hard, especially since the danger of heat exhaustion or heatstroke should not be ignored.

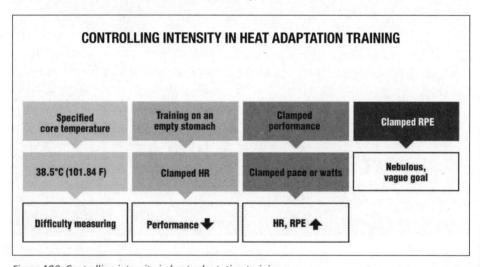

Figure 108: Controlling intensity in heat adaptation training.

I hesitate to make a wholesale recommendation as to which form of control is indicated, because that topic is too complex and because the adaptation responses are very individual and cannot be accurately predicted.

REMEMBER

A few basic guidelines must be adhered to in order to achieve highly effective heat adaptation:

- 10–14 consecutive days.
- Significantly reduced volume for the first 4–5 days.
- If possible, train as closely as possible to the conditions expected at the race location.
- Never train in hot conditions when feeling poorly or during illness.
- Consistently prepare and follow up every session with adequate fluid and sodium.
- Consistently monitor, especially the cardiovascular system.
- Accept a low performance and pace in heat training.
- No heat training the day before traveling.
- After arrival at the race location, train at a moderate tempo for the first 2–3 days and consistently monitor the load, and don't let the local atmosphere tempt you into an overly high training tempo.
- No heat training on the final days before the race.

Finally, there remains the question of which time of year is ideal for such heat adaptation. Pro athletes can certainly build more such heat phases into their program. Age-group athletes are usually limited by the number of available vacation days, and therefore tend to have to resort to artificial heat.

The following graph shows a frequently used schedule that produced the desired adaptations in nearly all cases without risking performance development in the run-up to the competition.

The 14-day heat block with slightly reduced intensity and slightly lower volume is followed by a final three-week training block under normal conditions, before departing for the race location. There the athlete re-adapts to the prevailing climate, at which point adaptations take place considerably faster.

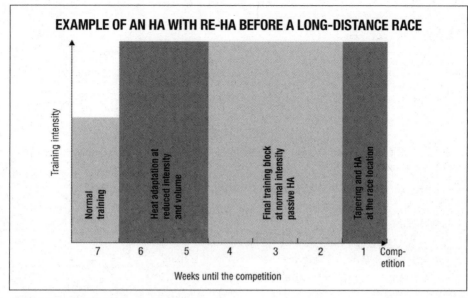

Figure 109: Example of a heat adaptation sequence.

To me improved heat tolerance is an immense performance reserve that can be integrated into the training process more easily and practicably than training at elevation. This stimulus during reduced oxygen in the inhaled air is intended to stimulate red blood cells to respond with improved oxygen transport.

But achieving an optimal level of efficiency really requires several stays for an elevation chain, which for many athletes is simply not doable. The effectiveness of elevation training varies greatly from athlete to athlete. Some athletes benefit very little from elevation training.

I would therefore opt for heat adaptation, because

a) it is easier to implement and
b) there are significantly fewer non-responders.

Interestingly studies have shown that such a training does not only improve race performance in hot conditions, but athletes can also expect faster times in cooler temperatures. In my view it is well worth exploring this topic in the run-up.

11.6   Cooling Strategies

Next to the already introduced approaches to increasing heat tolerance in the run-up to a competition, athletes can also use different cooling strategies during a race. Here the idea is to delay a rise in the body's core temperature to minimize the possible negative effects on racing performance. In doing so the athlete has to decide when to start cooling.

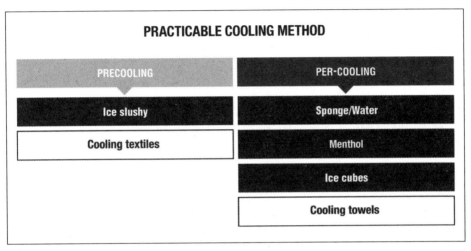

Figure 110: Pre- and per-cooling

11.6.1   Precooling

Precooling, meaning cooling before the activity, is used more so in shorter races like a sprint or the Olympic triathlon. Here the idea is to keep the increase in temperature very low or in the normal range before the start of the race despite the necessary warm-up, because due to the higher speed and shorter race duration, cooling during the race isn't always practicable.

Precooling before a long-distance event isn't necessary since most of the cooling isn't needed until the last discipline, the marathon, at which time any cooling applied before the race would be ineffective.

It might be better to consider precooling during check-in on the previous day when a long line forms at the transition zone and there is no shade and heat stress is very high. But I would consider that less precooling and more of an overheating preventative measure.

But back to the actual topic that is long distance. Precooling has been eliminated, so that leaves cooling during the race, or per-cooling.

11.6.2   Per-cooling

Here we once again differentiate between internal and external application. Inner cooling includes drinking sufficient amounts of fluids based on the sweat loss rate (more on that in chapter 9).

Cool drinks tend to be more readily available along the course than slush beverages. The consistency of these slushies is somewhere between ice and water.

Producing these slushies requires special machines and a reliable way of keeping them cold, which explains why they are not offered along the course. They have a considerably greater cooling effect than traditional liquids. One alternative to drinking basic water is sucking on ice cubes to cool down the inside of the mouth and thereby improve heat perception.

Regardless of their form, athletes should test drinking very cold fluids in the run-up to make sure this form of cooling is well tolerated. If a test shows that an athlete does not tolerate cold fluids well, a good alternative is to rinse the mouth with ice water and then spit the water out. This stimulates the receptors in the lining of the mouth that perceive a certain amount of cooling.

These same receptors are also stimulated by menthol. When mixing menthol into beverages and slushies the cooling sensation intensifies, but from a physiological standpoint the body's core temperature is not reduced. Some manufacturers now produce energy drinks with a certain amount of menthol.

Before producing mentholated beverages, the necessary mixing ratio should be thoroughly tested beforehand, because too much menthol can have a negative effect on the GI tract. Mentholated chewing gum is another alternative for generating a cooling effect.

Athletes who tend to supply themselves with fluids or gels during a race benefit from chewing this type of gum because chewing promotes better blood flow in the skull and therefore has an invigorating effect. But temperature can not only be affected from the inside, but also from the outside.

To do so, long-distance athletes have always used sponges and cups of water that are wrung out or poured over head and body. Especially when it is really hot, athletes can often get a bit erratic and randomly pour any fluids over their bodies in the hopes of lowering the temperature. Due to excessive external cooling the water, thanks to gravity, runs down the body.

Particularly when cycling, a wet stomach combined with the airflow can be very unpleasant and tends to cause stomach problems. When running, the water travels down lower (i.e., to the feet). Wet shoes and socks can cause blisters, which is why this side effect must be diminished.

I would therefore recommend cooling those regions of the body with the highest thermoreceptor density instead of wetting the entire body. These receptors are largely located in the forehead, neck, chest, the pulse regions, and the palm. The below illustration shows the individual regions and offers options for cooling them.

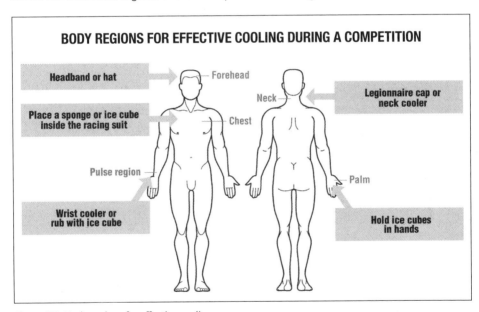

BODY REGIONS FOR EFFECTIVE COOLING DURING A COMPETITION

Headband or hat — Forehead

Neck — Legionnaire cap or neck cooler

Place a sponge or ice cube inside the racing suit — Chest

Pulse region

Palm

Wrist cooler or rub with ice cube

Hold ice cubes in hands

Figure 111: Body regions for effective cooling.

Special cooling textiles that originated in occupational healthcare and in jobs with extreme heat exposure (fire fighters, smelting furnaces, road construction, etc.) can be frequently reactivated by wetting them at aid stations. The moist coolness on the skin's surface reduces the temperature via evaporation and simulates the natural cooling process, namely sweating.

Some athletes also get creative with their racing attire and sew small pockets to the inside of their jersey in the collar bone area, and then fill the pockets with ice cubes from the aid stations.

The following table provides a quick overview of the various cooling strategies and their respective effect. I assessed the various effects, and in some instances measured them with a CORE body temperature system.

COOLING STRATEGIES AND THEIR EFFECT

Measure or Strategy	Precooling	Per-Cooling
Cooling Cap	+	++
Wrist Cooler	+	++
Neck Cooler	+	++
Ice Vest	+	++
Holding ice cubes in hand	x	++
Sponge/Cup	x	++
Cold Beverages	+	++
Ice Slushies	++	+++
Menthol	+	+

x = impracticable
+ = minor effect
++ = noticeable effect
+++ = major effect

Figure 112: Cooling strategies and their effectiveness.

11.7 Adapting the Pace Strategy for a Hot Race

A few things should be able to persevere in a race in hot conditions and not be in for a nasty surprise.

11.7.1 Ego

After all those tough weeks and months, most athletes struggle to deviate from the original pacing and target times. I know that it is difficult to abandon the hope of somehow still getting a fast time.

Athletes who can reconcile a slower time with their ego and don't view it as a failure but rather consider it out of their control will be successful.

11.7.2 Inexperience

Unfortunately, there are still athletes who don't inform themselves about the problems that can occur with respect to heat. These athletes draw a blank when confronted with terms like *sweat flow rate, thermoregulation, hyponatremia*, etc.

11.7.3 Lack of troubleshooting

Athletes familiar with troubleshooting strategies in case they lose their personal race provisions or sodium preparations will be much more likely to reach the finish line than athletes who never thought about the possible eventualities in the run-up to the race.

11.7.4 Adjusting the necessary carbohydrate intake

Heat has a negative effect on carbohydrate stores. As a result, more carbohydrates are metabolized at the same intensity. The athlete either reduces the intensity to complete the race with the same carbohydrate amount, or he tries to maintain the intensity and increases the carbohydrate amount in his supply strategy. Athletes with a tendency to experience GI problems are better off reducing the intensity rather than increasing the amount of ingested energy.

11.7.5 Limiting the fluid amount

Many athletes tend to consume too much fluid and thereby are at risk of hyponatremia. In very hot conditions the amount of fluid per hour should be limited. I consider 1,000– maximally 1,200 ml of water per hour perfectly adequate. For very hot conditions I recommend painstakingly cooling from the outside and limiting the amount of fluid intake per hour.

CONCLUSION

Stay cool!

12 THE RACE

A successful long-distance race begins long before the starting gun and absolutely depends on choosing the right race. Nowadays, there are countless races on every inhabited continent on this earth, year-round.

Back in the 1990s, there was only a limited number of races, but that has massively changed today with more than 100 events around the world with distances of 3.8-180-42 km. Next to the Ironman and Challenge race series there are lots of smaller events, and in recent years more and more races with an adventure character, meaning outside of cities in sometimes rugged wilderness with special climatic and topographical challenges.

Since many races are surrounded by a lot of hype, it is important to start planning early and keep an eye on the registration process, because some races like, for instance, Challenge Roth, are fully booked within minutes.

When it comes to success or failure, choosing the right race is one of the biggest factors. Not every athlete has the right abilities for a particular race.

12.1   Choosing a Race

A coach should therefore be able to assist his athletes with choosing a race.

ATHLETES' QUESTIONNAIRE AND DECISION GUIDE FOR CHOOSING A RACE

When it comes to success or failure, choosing the right race is one of the biggest factors. The below table is intended as a decision aid. Please rate your responses on a scale from 1–6, with 1 meaning "does apply" and 6 meaning "does not apply."

Brainstorming	1	2	3	4	5	6
Do you have previous experience as a long-distance athlete?						
Ironman?						
Challenge?						
No-logo races?						
Are you willing to travel to the race by plane and do you own an appropriate bike case?						

Have you had experience with overcoming jetlag before a trip?

Do you have ambitions regarding a Kona slot?

Are you hunting for a new best time?

Do you get energized by crowds of spectators?

Do you prefer being out on your own?

An early race means lots of roller training. Are you prepared to do so?

An early race means early training camp. Is that possible?

An early race means lots of training in the dark. Are you prepared to do so?

A late race means that you must train longer than your club mates, etc. Are you prepared to do so?

A late race means that you will potentially be less fit in the spring and summer than your club mates. Can you ignore that?

A late race means that you might have to consider family vacation plans. Is your partner on board?

Do you consider yourself a strong swimmer?

Have you ever panicked during a mass start?

Are you comfortable in neoprene?

Do you get cold easily?

Are you afraid of fish and other ocean creatures?

Have you ever had problems from saltwater?

Do you feel stronger on the bike in flat terrain (Roleur)? Do you have access to the appropriate training areas and equipment?

Do you feel stronger on the bike in undulating terrain? Do you have access to the appropriate training areas and equipment?

Do you feel stronger on the bike in mountainous terrain? Do you have access to the appropriate training areas and equipment?

Are you a good technician, good at cornering, and confident riding downhill?

Are you mentally strong in very windy conditions?

Are you mentally strong in bad weather conditions?

Are you able to cope with extreme heat on the bike?

Do you feel stronger running in flat terrain? Do you have access to the appropriate training areas?

Do you feel stronger running in undulating terrain? Do you have access to the appropriate training areas?

Do you feel stronger running in mountainous terrain? Do you have access to the appropriate training areas?

Do you feel secure on uneven surfaces?

Are you heat resistant?

Have you ever had stomach problems while running?

Can you make do with the organizer's provisions?

Do you provide your own provisions?

Figure 113: Questionnaire for choosing a race.

This questionnaire helps athletes, but also coaches, to gain an overview of the abilities even if purely subjective from the athlete's point of view.

This table lists the most common questions when choosing a race. From swimming with or without neoprene to the elevation profile of the bike route all the way to temperature preferences, it prompts the athlete to contemplate his abilities. A race that corresponds to the athlete's preferences and abilities can then be chosen based on the responses.

12.1.1 Time of year

Nowadays there are long-distance races nearly year-round all over the world. An athlete should inform himself about the particularities associated with a specific race date.

If the date is very early in the year, the previous year's season break or rather transition period should be adjusted accordingly. A fall marathon or a late long-distance race with the subsequent recovery phase can potentially be counterproductive, because the preparation period for the long-distance race might be too short. In central Europe, races during winter or spring tend to necessitate a big indoor training volume due to the prevailing climatic conditions and lack of daylight.

At some point the athlete needs to plan a training camp to generate the necessary cycling volume on the road. A race scheduled late in the triathlon season offers the opportunity to take advantage of summer with more pleasant temperatures and better light conditions. But that also requires mental toughness when the athlete, unlike club mates and training partners, is still training in the fall, when most athletes have already ended their season.

The time change from summer to winter and fall weather setting in can also have a negative effect on psyche and motivation. A later race also means that, due to the later season development, there is limited opportunity to train with other athletes because in the northern hemisphere their racing climax is often in the summer.

12.1.2   Race format

As previously mentioned, there are races in the Ironman or Challenge series but also competitions that are not part of a series. It is the nature of the thing that an athlete who wishes to qualify for an Ironman Hawaii shouldn't compete in a race without the Ironman's M-dot logo.

The races in the Ironman series have a nearly identical organizational standard worldwide. For athletes who are very agitated during a race week, this standardized process can offer some certainty provided the athlete has some previous experience with races in this series. Smaller races sometimes have organizational flaws.

The most important points here are route closures and fueling stations during the race. Supposedly bigger races often draw more spectators to the race course. Athletes who tend to prefer the solitude of the course and are unable to draw energy from the cheers of encouragement should therefore choose smaller races.

12.1.3   Qualification for Ironman World Championships in Hawaii

Participation in the legendary Ironman Hawaii can surely be called the Wimbledon of triathlons. For many athletes being part of the illustrious circle of those who were able to secure one of the sought-after slots is a lifelong dream come true. However, performance density at the qualifying races has become so great that one must consciously think about when and where this Kona slot can be secured.

Those thoughts should include whether to try for an early qualification or a later one. An early slot means the qualifying race is between the end of August to the end of April. The advantage here is that the period of time between qualifying races and Hawaii is long, the athlete is thus obligated to follow up with a long regeneration period and can arrive on Kona fairly refreshed. Another plus is that the athlete will have enough time for another attempt at qualifying if the previous qualifying races were unsuccessful.

If the athlete is looking at a slot during fall of the previous year, he should not plan any other long-distance races in the run-up so he can enter the qualifying races in fresh condition. Athletes with such ambitions should be careful when training with partners, because if they are focused on considerably earlier season climaxes there is a risk of getting in shape to soon when training content and volume converge.

The advantage of a late race in the second half of the season is that the athlete can dedicate himself to working on identified weaknesses in training without time pressure. He can thereby focus on improving motor function, movement technique, mobility, and strength since the phase with large volumes will be delayed. The big foundational blocks (especially on the bike) can be completed in summer weather, and a spring training camp or climate training course is not necessary for a late race with slot ambitions.

From a mental or motivational point of view, it is important to begin training a little later to ensure the athlete will even make it to the second half of the season, won't peak too soon, and will still have that often-quoted bite in training during the critical 6–8 weeks before the planned qualifying race. Particularly when club mates, friends, or training partners reach their peak in June and July and subsequently slow down a bit, athletes who begin to train too early and with too much intensity tend to become lethargic.

If the qualifying race was successful, the strategy in the run-up to the Hawaii race can be applied again. Races scheduled for November or December will require that some important hours of training will have to be completed in fall weather and less daylight.

A training camp in the South is definitely a good choice for preparing for a race like Ironman Mar del Plata, Arizona, Cozumel, or Busselton. If such a camp is not an option, the athlete should work on heat adaptation. The ideal time for such a training camp is during the third or fourth week before day X.

If the race is scheduled for spring, meaning at an earlier time as per the above definition, training should begin correspondingly earlier. For instance, if the athlete is aiming to qualify for the Ironman South Africa, the training break after the previous season should be considerably earlier.

Starting training at the beginning of October allows enough time to prepare for this race both in terms of quality and quantity. The one difficulty here is that in central European weather the lion's share of training will have to be completed indoors on the roller trainer. A training camp or climate training course with focus on accumulating basic kilometers on the bike is an option.

Training partners with identical competition goals help to make training easier based on the principle a sorrow shared is a sorrow halved. If the environment cooperates, initial larger training blocks can already be built in over the holidays. Challenges like, for instance, the Rapha Festive 500 help to accomplish larger volumes at that time.

Opportunities for a test race in the spring before the long-distance event are slim or rather hardly viable. Particularly athletes without prior long-distance experience should skip such an early major race. One advantage is the fact that travel arrangements and bookings for the Ironman Hawaii can be made earlier and often at a much lower cost.

The biggest disadvantage of a qualification that is close to the Ironman Hawaii date is the shorter regeneration time and less time for preparatory training for the world championships. On the other hand, races during the European summer are much easier to prepare for. Training can begin in November or December with a training camp planned for spring.

With the large number of European races in summer an athlete is able to choose a race that is appropriate for his abilities. Logistics and costs for such a race tend to be easier to manage than a race overseas or somewhere outside of Europe.

On the other hand, a race in June or July also means that if the qualifying race was unsuccessful, it is only conditionally probable that the athlete will have a second chance to try again during that calendar year. Often the races are already fully booked and completing two long-distance races in quick succession is not easy to do. If the athlete had to complete two races in quick succession for a slot, it will considerably lessen the chances for success at the Ironman Hawaii.

The increased travel costs are another disadvantage since prices for lodging and flights will go up significantly by October. One way to minimize costs would be to book lodging and flights with a cancellation option before successfully qualifying. For instance, if an athlete gets a slot in August in the Ironman Copenhagen, he will have less than eight weeks to book the trip, recover, or rather resume training.

Another point is that performance density in age groups is often very dense in European summer. European age-group athletes are considered the highest-performing contingent in the world. That means that qualifying with off-peak times is often more likely outside of Europe than, for instance, for the very crowded Ironman Frankfurt.

Those with the appropriate financial means should consider trying for a race during the second half of the season but should aim for a second race during European summer as a backup.

Finally, I should mention that races that are chosen strictly on rational grounds as potentially offering the best chances for successfully qualifying, at the end of the day aren't always the right choice. When opening a race application, an athlete has to emotionally connect with that race.

If that connection and the desire aren't there it will be difficult to develop the motivation for this race. One can rationalize the general conditions, but ultimately the gut should decide.

12.1.4   Travel logistics

A factor not to be underestimated is the arrival at the race location. When an athlete is less nimble fingered and unable to disassemble his bike, store it in a bike case, and then reassemble it to good working order at the race location, he should rethink traveling by plane.

REMEMBER

A tip for all those flying with a bike. If the frame has an exchangeable mech derailleur hanger, I recommend bringing a replacement. Particularly with non-traditional bikes, it is often not possible to find a suitable mech derailleur hanger in situ. Stress, loss of training, or even canceling a long-planned race can thereby be avoided.

When traveling across multiple time zones it is recommended to plan an appropriate amount of time before the race for jetlag recovery. A good rule of thumb is to arrive one day early for each hour of time change.

An additional day should be planned for every five degrees C of anticipated temperature change. For races in a different time zone with more than four hours difference from the home location, the athlete should begin a modified sleep-wake-eat cycle approximately two weeks before day X to minimize the adjustment after arriving at the race location.

If personal circumstances permit (job, family, etc.), training during the final 2–3 weeks before the race should be scheduled for the same time of day as the start of the race. For instance, if the race starts at 7 am local time, which in the case of Kona would be 7 pm central European time, the athlete should try to shift major portions of his training to the evening hours.

Here are a few tips to make travel to the competition less stressful.

12.1.4.1   Before the trip

- **No late dinners:** The last meal of the day should be consumed no later than two hours before bedtime to ensure a restful last night in the athlete's own bed.
- **Carbohydrates:** Yes, but correctly: Consume as little simple sugar as possible, instead choose fiber-rich meals with vegetables if traveling to the race location more than 48 hours before race day.
- **A light breakfast on travel day:** I recommend a low-carb meal high in protein and fats. An omelet with vegetables and cheese is my top choice on travel day.
- **Provide your own provisions:** I remember well from my days as a professional athlete that gas station and airline food isn't always ideal. Instead plan to prepare and pack some of your meals or have nuts and almonds on hand. They are easy to transport, wholesome, and very energy dense.
- **Trip planning:** Nothing is worse than too much stress during an already tense situation. It is therefore wise to plan for plenty of time to get to the airport and check beforehand for possible construction or other unexpected hindrances.

12.1.4.2   During the trip

- **Compression socks:** Unlike wearing them during physical exertion, here these socks make absolute sense. They keep the legs from swelling and hugely minimize fluid retention. Otherwise, loose and airy clothing is the best choice. Comfort over appearance!
- **Hydration:** It is important to have your own water supply when flying and purchasing water at the airport (while overpriced) after going through security is necessary to make sure you don't dehydrate in the dry cabin air.

- **Eating:** On intercontinental flights food is served. The first meal should be higher in protein and low in carbs because carbohydrates increase fluid retention in tissue. The meal prior to landing can contain more carbohydrates.
- **Movement:** During the flight, stand up every 45-60 minutes and walk up and down the aisles. If driving, take a break at least every 90-120 minutes and walk around at the rest stop. Briefly stretch calves, hip flexors, front of thighs, and shoulders.
- **Avoid alcohol and sugary drinks:** Alcohol causes increasing hypohydration and sugary drinks make blood sugar go through the roof.
- **Protect the immune system:** Wear a mask during the flight (already recommended before Covid), wash your hands regularly, and carry a disinfectant. Carry a bandana or scarf as well as a hat in your carry-on bag, because air conditioning on some flights can be quite cold.

12.1.4.3   General suggestions

- If the budget allows, consider upgrading to business class or an XXL economy seat on the flight to the race location. Legroom is a definite plus on long flights. The athlete arrives at the race location less folded up.
- If possible, book direct flights or keep transfers to a minimum. Changing planes is stressful and there is a risk of missing flights or bags and bike cases not making it on the flight. Mark your luggage with an Apple Air Tag, so you can track your back in case it doesn't arrive at your destination.
- Preferably pack all individual items needed for a successful race in your carry-on bag. That includes cycling shoes, pedals, racing suit, running shoes, and goggles. Anything else can be provided by the airline at the race location if the suitcase or bike case get lost.
- When planning to travel after the race it is wise to find out beforehand if the bike can be shipped home as a package or can be held somewhere in the interim.

12.1.4.4   Travel documents

- Make sure your passport is valid and check your destination's entry requirements.
- Vaccinations should be administered at least 6-8 weeks before departure.
- Verify travel medical insurance.

12.1.4.5   Continuing travel by car

Not every competition can be reached directly by plane. Often longer distances must be traveled in a rental car.

Plan for one additional day ahead of the race for every three hours in the car.

12.1.5   Weather conditions

Triathlon is an outdoor sport and thus is subject to very different weather effects. Triathletes respond differently to the various stimuli. Some athletes adapt to heat better than others.

Often tall and heavy athletes are at a disadvantage in hot and humid conditions because their cardiovascular system must work harder to cool the body than that of smaller athletes with less skeletal muscle.

Compared to heavier athletes, lighter athletes are at a disadvantage on very windy cycling courses with little elevation gain. Athletes with little body fat have less of an insulating layer and often get cold faster during low temperatures.

When choosing a race, the athlete should therefore look at climate databases to be able to at least anticipate a weather trend, whereby the weather will always be an unpredictable factor.

A good example here is the 2011 Ironman Frankfurt with 12 degrees C (53 F) and steady rain, and the 2019 race with temperatures above 40 degrees C (104 F). Races with a high likelihood of rain should be avoided by athletes with subpar bike control.

12.1.5.1   Swimming

Less proficient swimmers often benefit more from wearing a neoprene suit than former competitive swimmers. When choosing a race, athletes should therefore keep an eye on the expected water temperature. Race organizers can provide that information.

Currents and waves should also be considered. The start of the swimming leg is a very stressful moment for many athletes. When choosing a race those athletes should consider the start (mass, wave, or rolling start).

12.1.5.2   Cycling

The biggest differences in the demand profile are probably in cycling. In terms of time, cycling takes up the biggest share in a long-distance triathlon and has a very big effect on the subsequent performance. That is why the choice of race should be in line with the athlete's cycling abilities.

When planning, the athlete must therefore consider the elevation gain, wind effect, and route. Routes with lots of directional changes and resulting acceleration phases after a turn should be chosen by athletes with good bike control and cornering technique.

Developing these accelerations will also be considered in preceding training.

Mountainous routes require specific equipment. The first to come to mind are gear ratio, wheels, and choice of helmet.

On routes that are particularly prone to drafting the athlete should keep this unsportsmanlike behavior of some competitors in mind beforehand and mentally prepare for such cheating behavior, so it won't cause him to lose his focus during a race.

12.1.5.3   Running

Elevation gain also plays a critical role in running. However, weather tends to have a bigger effect on an athlete's running or rather overall performance. Differences in running surface conditions, directional changes, the number of fueling stations, etc., should also be taken into account.

12.1.6   Racing in Asia

Athletes face a series of peculiarities during long-distance races in Asia that must be considered. The weather conditions tend to not be easy. Along with very hot temperatures there is often extremely high humidity, which doesn't really allow cooling through evaporation of sweat on the skin. The extreme weather conditions do not allow optimal training before the race, which puts the athlete in a bind.

For one, jetlag when traveling east is a little more severe so that training to return to one's own rhythm would be helpful, but on the other hand, in situ training is only conditionally viable. Depending on the destination, safe bike training on the road may not be possible. The athlete should therefore consider bringing along a roller.

I have often seen athletes already have GI problems before the race. The reason can be unfamiliar food but also poor water quality in open water. It is therefore advisable to stick to the provisions brought from home and possibly swim in the pool instead of on the race course.

GI problems can also be avoided by regularly washing hands and foregoing tap water.

Results from the previous year should not be a factor in trying to choose a race in Asia. One should not be confused by the considerably slower finish times. The climatic conditions usually don't permit faster times.

Generally speaking, I would probably not participate in premier events in Asia because the organizational standard is not like those at European or North American races. I have received multiple adventurous race reports from athletes after premiere events.

Swimmers who strongly benefit from neoprene suits should probably not choose Asian races, because due to the warm water temperatures athletes tend to swim without wetsuits. Nevertheless, a trip to Asia is very appealing, and when keeping in mind the items I mentioned, nothing should stand in the way of a successful long-distance experience in Asia.

12.2   The Final Four Weeks Before the Long-Distance Race

After addressing choice of race and travel arrangements, I would now like to outline the final four weeks before the long-distance race. I have observed the following phenomenon for many years.

Four to five weeks before day X, I start to get lots of emails from athletes who feel insecure about their performance level and question their current training. No significant improvements to performance in terms of strength and speed before day X are possible at this point.

Only endurance and metabolism can be maintained, both of which are important factors for a successful long-distance finish. On the other hand, all the hard work of the past weeks and months can be destroyed in the last four weeks with too much training.

12.2.1 Tapering

Ironman is an extreme form of long-distance effort. I think that the generally accepted tapering schedule is not a good fit for a long-distance marathon. This tapering was adopted by sports with a rather more anaerobic character and considerably shorter duration (i.e., mid-distance running or swimming). Other than the same type of movement, it has little to do with a long-distance demand profile.

We should therefore focus on cycling. There is no real tapering. Athletes train until day X more or less without reducing the load. Triathletes who work with a traditional three-week tapering schedule, meaning they reduce the volumes week by week, will be considerably less fit at the starting line on day X.

On the other hand, there are those crazy chickens that panic about their performance in the last 3-4 weeks and start to search for last-minute form. Those athletes then have to do another 30+ km run or another six hours of 4 x 40 minutes at Ironman tempo, but by doing so unfortunately often ruin their form with just one of those sessions and are frustrated on race day because they still can't meet their goals in the race, in spite of those last-minute training sessions.

But how to do it right? Humans are creatures of habit who tend to have trouble dealing with uncertainty and panic. The desired routine should also be continued in training. It means that athletes should stick to the same training regimen as the previous weeks and months. If the athlete went on a long run every Wednesday and spent a lot of time on the bike on Sundays, he should continue to do so during the final month, even if the training volume gradually decreases as the race approaches.

We want to retain the training principle while simultaneously building in a little more rest and relaxation. The required amount of rest varies for different individuals and should be viewed within the context of the athlete's everyday stress as well as his performance capacity.

Athletes who have completed the past months with lots of continuity and few missed trainings are often mentally burned out 4–5 weeks before the race and would benefit from more rest. On the other hand, those are athletes who greatly depend on the established routine. They quickly lose self-confidence and think that tapering is not really to their advantage.

As coach, I would lay up such athletes with considerably reduced training for 5–8 days about four weeks before the race. Most of them feel refreshed after this phase and are less likely to lose confidence in their performance because the race is still four weeks away. The purpose of this week of rest is to complete workouts with more or less normal volumes and intensity until the race.

Athletes who (for whatever reason) occasionally had to skip training days during preparation, are better able to physically and mentally handle 1–2 days of rest during the final 10 days because they were used to having such days without training during preparation.

Athletes should know that rest during this final phase does not necessarily help them feel fit and fresh. Often periods of rest make athletes feel more tired or make them sluggish. Many respond to this state by panicking and see their performance go down the drain. They then go back out, train too long and too hard, but actually need more rest.

Correct tapering should take all these aspects into consideration and cover the athletes' individual peculiarities. In my experience, tapering for 7–10 days is totally adequate. When rest periods are too long, some athletes lose too much endurance capacity. Those athletes potentially still ride up to three hours at an easy tempo on Monday of race week.

Other athletes must recover orthopedically. They will complete runs of no more than 40 minutes so their muscles can recover. The classic three-week pattern probably only works for 3–5% of athletes. I have not had positive experiences with it while coaching more than 1,100 long-distance races. Athletes should know that they will feel poorly during the final 10 days up to 2–3 days before the race and should still stay calm and not go on a search for last-minute form.

The example of a racehorse describes correct tapering quite well. The horse is stabled and is dying to get out on the track after having been confined to its stall. Athletes who properly taper and rest are spoiling for the race and can hardly wait for the starting gun. Athletes with a dysfunctional interplay of loading and unloading will usually feel burned out during race week and not meet their expectations in the race.

Since tapering is very individual, I can only recommend carefully documenting the last 3-4 weeks before the main event. Next to routine entries the athlete should also take notes about everyday stress, sleep, weather, and diet. If the race is successful, that tapering schedule can be used again when preparing for the next competition.

If the race result is not ideal, the schedule should be analyzed so the athlete can see which parameters need to be adjusted. In general, each athlete should ask himself if he is training to train or if his training is intended to produce a race performance.

12.2.2   To-do list for the final four weeks before the long-distance race

There are a few things that must be taken care of during the final four weeks from an organizational or logistical standpoint.

12.2.2.1   Massage

Regular muscle care in the form of a massage or physical therapy really should be a part of every long-distance preparation. Myogeless, meaning adherences in the muscles and fascial tissue, inhibits the function of these structures. When these muscular side effects, that are inevitably caused by the tapered large training volumes, are treated early and regularly by a therapist, the athlete can make sure that his muscles will also work optimally in the race.

But getting one massage during race week without previous regular muscle care won't do anything. Because in that case the therapist will have to work on those structures fairly vigorously to release the adherences, which can cause sore muscles and muscle weakness, and during race week that would have a rather negative effect on the psyche.

The athlete should therefore start this process early, with the last treatment no later than Tuesday of race week, so he will have sufficient time to regain his muscle tonus. The financial investment is a factor, but in my view makes much more sense than buying a carbon bottle cage.

12.2.2.2   Pedicure

In addition to muscle care the athlete should also pay attention to his feet and get a pedicure. Some athletes complain of blisters, ingrown toenails, or infected nail beds. To avoid these problems, I would make two appointments for a medical pedicure during the final four weeks, so the nails are optimally trimmed to prevent any such problems.

I would avoid going to a beauty parlor or nail studio, and instead see someone with a medical background in this area. It significantly improves your chances of not losing your toenails after the race.

12.2.2.3   Bike check-up

It is a good idea to have an appointment for a professional check-up with your trusted bike dealer two weeks before the race. It is best to make that appointment several weeks earlier.

PLEASE NOTE

That check-up should include the following:

- Check the bottom bracket for low friction.
- Check all screw connections for correct torque.
- Change the chain and possibly the rear cassette.
- Check the jockey wheels in the derailleur mechanism.
- Prepare racing wheels (tires, tubes, sealant).

After the check-up I recommend riding the bike for another 150–200 km total before race day to be able to fix any problems that might crop up. The following timeline summarizes the things that need taking care of during the last four weeks. The pattern shown there is based on a race with arrival by car. It would have to be modified for travel by plane.

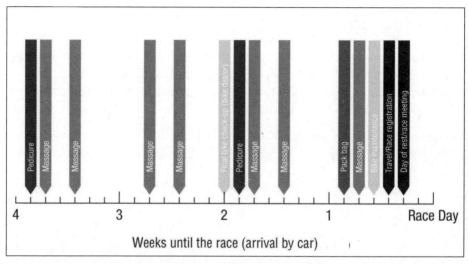

Figure 114: Logistics of the final four weeks before the long-distance race.

12.3 Race Week

In my experience, the final days before a long-distance race are filled with tension, logistics, travel, and stress. Creating checklists can help ease at least that last part. Sounds stuffy but makes a lot of sense.

First-time long-distance athletes in particular can relieve much uncertainty and nervousness by checking off their list. Packing all the necessary items for the race help make for a smooth race day.

12.3.1 General rules of conduct

- Get enough sleep and don't go to bed too late.
- Try to avoid any additional stress.
- Try to avoid crowds at the race location to prevent a viral infection. Also regularly wash your hands and potentially wear a mask.

- Do not plan any last-minute training sessions.
- Only do familiar mobility exercises; avoid anything new.
- Pay a brief visit to the triathlon expo, but don't spend hours going from booth to booth.
- Try to avoid sun exposure as much as possible and train during the cooler hours.
- Don't take any last-minute dietary supplements. Avoid anything new!
- Immediately follow up every training unit with fluids, carbohydrates, sodium, and protein.
- Don't let yourself get hungry.
- Don't let yourself get thirsty, but also don't drink excessive amounts of water.
- Consume alcohol in moderation.
- Register early and pick up your starting documents.
- Check the weather report every day and adjust your material choices accordingly.
- Try to avoid triathlete gatherings, because fit-looking athletes, futuristic bikes, etc., cause some athletes to feel awestruck and make them lose self-confidence.

Absolutely do not allow yourself to be influenced by the algorithms on your sports watch. The tapering during the final days before the race also changes the input the watch ordinarily gets from training.

It might show a decreasing VO_2max, an unproductive state, or a drop in the possible marathon time. During race week, do not pay the slightest bit of attention to those values and data!

12.4   The Final 48 Hours Before the Start Gun

It's getting exciting and the countdown has started. Mentally the final 48 hours have begun for which I would like to offer a guideline to avoid potential mistakes.

When the athlete receives his bib number, he is given the three changing bags, which he must fill.

- Swim-to-bike
- Bike-to-run
- After the race
- Optional special needs (the racer's own race provisions)

If it should rain on race day, put the contents of the bike-to-run bag in a plastic bag before putting them in the change bag to keep the items as dry as possible.

12.4.1   Two days before check-in or handing over the bike

- Check all screw connections on the bike, possibly retighten with a torque wrench. Don't use brute force!
- Check brake position.
- Securely close the quick release skewer on the wheels and position the lever so you can remove the wheel if you get a flat.
- Fully charge the electronic shifting system.
- Switch on the bike computer so it can find the satellite position at the race location more quickly on race day. Check all connections to the power meter, heart rate measuring device, cadence measuring device; set the display to the correct profile and calibrate the power meter.
- Attach the frame number to the bike, possibly trim the corners with nail scissors so the number has an aerodynamic fit and doesn't flutter in the wind. Cave: race sponsors must be visible on the bib number. Failure to do so can result in disqualification.
- Attach drinking systems to the handlebar, squeeze the bottle holder together for a more reliable hold during the race, especially when stretches of cobblestone (e.g., Ironman Frankfurt) or rough road surfaces are expected.
- Attach the repair kit consisting of 1 or 2 tubes, valve extensions for aero rims or rather disk wheels, tire lever, multi tool, and pump or CO_2 cartridge.

PLEASE NOTE

Addition for tubular tire rims: Securely attach the sealant, possibly carry a small cutter (to cut open the damaged tire if needed). Spare tubular tire should already have been put on a rim to ensure a specific size.

REMEMBER

Use a waterproof marker to mark all of the items used in the race with your name or initials, so you can retrieve them from the lost-and-found box if you lose them.

12.4.2   Swim-to-bike bag

This bag should contain very few items. To speed up the changeover it is wise to have as many things as possible, within competition rules, already attached to the bike to avoid losing too much time in transition zone 1 (T1).

BAG CONTENTS

- Helmet with affixed bib number
- Cycling shoes (check the screw connection of the cleats)
- Sunglasses
- Those with vision problems: spare contact lenses or glasses
- Race number belt (attach starting number with four safety pins)

Particularly for cycling, racing attire should be appropriate for the weather conditions. The following table shows the different versions.

COMPETITION CYCLING ATTIRE

Normal version	Comfort version	Rain & cold version	Heat version
Race suit	Cycling pants	Race suit	Race suit
Optional socks	Cycling jersey	Wind vest or tight wind-resistant jersey	Arm coolers
	Optional undershirt	Arm warmers	Helmet-cooling inlay
	Socks	Possibly knee warmers	
	Cycling gloves	Under-helmet cap	
		Socks	
		Overshoes	
		Rubber household gloves that can be disposed of at an aid station if temperatures rises.	
		A newspaper might be sufficient to block the wind and can be disposed of at an aid station if temperatures rise.	
		Bike glasses with clear lenses	

Figure 115: Competition cycling attire.

12.4.3   Bike-to-run bag

Just like the swim-to-bike bag, these contents should be kept small.

I recommend packing all individual items like gels, salt tablets, etc., in a Ziploc bag and putting that in the change bag. The athlete can quickly grab it, everything is together and waterproof, and after leaving the second transition zone (T2), it can be emptied out and the contents stored in the back pockets of the tri suit.

The amount of time saved with a quick changeover can be as much as 2–3 minutes. Making up that amount of time running would most likely hurt a lot more.

BAG CONTENTS

- Running shoes (Laces are open; I recommend not using elastic laces, because they provide too little support and stability!!)
- Running socks (rolled up with one sock stored in each running shoe; check left and right).
- Vaseline or a similar lubricant to prevent chafe marks.

CONTENTS OF ZIPLOC BAG

- GPS watch, if a different watch was used for cycling. It is wise to turn it on once before the race so it can find satellite reception more quickly.
- Energy gels
- Salt tablets

COMPETITION RUNNING ATTIRE			
Normal version	Comfort version	Rain & cold version	Heat version
Visor or cap	Visor or cap	Hat	Visor or cap
Socks	Fresh socks	Fresh socks	Socks
	Possibly compression socks	Wind vest	Cooling cap/Head band
	Running pants	Arm warmers	Wrist cooler
	Singlet		Neck cooler

Figure 116: Competition running attire.

12.5   The Day Before the Race

The day before the race usually proceeds according to the following schedule. Since sleep tends to be very restless the night before the race it is important to get a good night's sleep on the previous night. The remaining day's schedule is based on the timetable.

Version 1

If check-in at the transition zone is early, the athlete should complete a 30-minute bike pre-race activation after breakfast. He should run through all the gears for a last-minute check-up. He can either cycle from his lodgings to the check-in and get picked up there or take the shuttle bus back, or he can do the pre-activation ride and later drive to T1 by car.

In any case, any remaining dust and dirt should be wiped off the bike with a rag after completion of the bike unit. After check-in the athlete returns to his lodgings, and if temperatures are warm, should spend the rest of the day in the shade or a darkened room, preferably lying down.

Version 2

If check-in is in the afternoon or early evening, also complete pre-activation after breakfast and clean the bike. But afterwards stretch out on the sofa or bed, and drive to check-in.

REMEMBER

If the previous day is very hot, make sure to hydrate sufficiently and wear a hat. Lines are often long and it's not possible to wait in the shade to protect yourself from direct sunlight.

Once it is your turn and you can enter the transition zone after the security check of bike and helmet as well as wrist ID or race participant wristband, it is time to set up your transition spot. Hang up your bike by its seat and let a little air out of the tires. Particularly in hot temperatures and direct sun exposure, this prevents the air from expanding, avoiding a burst tire before the race.

Water bottles, nutrition, cycling shoes, sunglasses, helmet, and bag should not be put on the bike on the previous day because, for one, there are thieves among athletes, too, and secondly, overnight winds can blow the material away.

To remember your transition spot in the sometimes crowded and large T1, take photos to jog your memory. Next, it's important to check out the swim course. When possible and permitted, some athletes swim for 10-20 minutes on the course after checking in.

A few years ago, I also still advocated for doing so, but now think that for most athletes pre-activation on the bike and checking in is stressful enough, and some activation in the water isn't really necessary. I recommend also taking photos of the water exit and the way to the transition zone.

After the work is done, the goal should be to quickly return to the lodging and lie on the couch or bed. Athletes often run into acquaintances or friends and waste precious time by chatting here and there.

Once back at home base, it's time to pack those last items needed for the race. To make sure that nothing is left behind I always recommend putting everything by the door so you will, figuratively and not literally, trip over it. This includes the timing chip, cycling shoes, helmet, bike computer, and race provisions.

12.6   The Backpack on Race Day Morning

This backpack should be able to hold everything needed before the race, during the race, or after the race. Here the athlete needs to make sure that it will fit into the after-race bag, because that is the only way to ensure that after crossing the finish line it will be returned as part of the after-race bag.

Since it is not allowed to put floor pumps in the after-race bag, the athlete should arrange to meet a supporter at a specific meeting spot so he can hand off the pump after airing up the tires on the morning of the race.

BAG CONTENTS

- Race suit
- Cycling shoes
- Organizer's official swim cap and a second swim cap to wear under it if the water is cold (wear a neoprene cap in very cold water)
- Swim goggles with reflective or clear lenses, depending on the light conditions
- Neoprene, or swimsuit if neoprene is not allowed.
- Plastic bag to make putting on the wetsuit easier
- Lubricant to rub on the neck to prevent chafe marks on the neck from the wetsuit
- Earplugs and nose clip if necessary
- After-race bag to store the backpack before the start
- Timing chip
- Flip-flops or disposable slippers from the hotel that can be removed right before the start signal to avoid cold feet.
- Possibly a head lamp to have sufficient light when setting up the transition spot
- Bike computer with charged battery
- Full water bottles
- Gels, bars, etc.
- Provisions for race morning (gel, bar, banana, etc. for the period before the start signal)

REMEMBER

Emergency items can be packed in a separate bag in case the bike was damaged overnight.

- Tube
- CO_2 cartridge
- Pump adaptor to pump up the rear disc wheel
- Multi tool
- Small towel to dry off the bike if it rained overnight
- Tape
- Cable tie

CONTENTS OF AFTER-RACE BAG

- Shower gel
- Towel
- Fresh clothes
- Comfortable shoes
- Phone to arrange meet-up with the support crew
- Possibly medical certificate or TUE (therapeutical use exemption) for a doping test if the athlete takes certain medications or uses an asthma inhaler

12.7 Checklist on Race Day Morning (Still at the Hotel or at Home)

Planning is everything! Planning the morning of the race with plenty of foresight allows the athlete to stand at the starting line stress-free. It is important to allow plenty of time to get to transition zone 1 or the start, because many of the feeder roads tend to be on the small side and lots of spectators and supporters arrive along with the participants.

Athletes should absolutely use the restroom at their lodgings, because in my experience the number of restrooms at the race location is very limited, and after a certain amount of time their condition is anything but appetizing.

REMEMBER

It's better to get there early than late. Any type of stress should be avoided.

- Set your alarm to three hours before the start of the race.
- Take a warm shower, which stimulates blood circulation and the appetite, which some nervous athletes lack on race-day morning.
- Put on the timing chip (secure Velcro with safety pin).
- Tape the nipples to protect them from chafing.
- Apply chamois creme, sunscreen, etc.
- Put on the HR meter chest strap.
- Use the restroom.
- Put on race suit.
- Put on warm clothes over race suit and wear a hat if temperatures are cool.

12.7.1 Chronological order after arrival in transition zone 1 (T1)

After a largely stress-free and early arrival at T1, the athlete should right away find a port-a-potty. Next, it is time to attach and turn on the bike computer and make sure that the GPS satellites have been located so later during the race the athlete can receive reasonable information regarding speed and the number of km covered.

While the bike computer establishes satellite reception it is time to check tire pressure and if necessary, add air. Next the chain is put on the correct sprocket. At the mount line one can often see athletes with their chain in a high gear struggling to accelerate and weaving back and forth, thereby putting other cyclists at risk.

Once the correct gear has been chosen, the cycling shoes are clipped into the pedals and attached with rubber bands to the forward derailleur and rear quick-release skewer.

REMEMBER

Taking off with the feet on the already attached pedals absolutely needs to be practiced beforehand because a long-distance race is not the time to learn how to do so.

Next the water bottles are placed in the bottle holders, the drinking system (if used) is filled with fluid or a gel/water mix, and the other necessary items such as energy bars or salt tablets are stored in the top-tube bag. After that the helmet is placed top down on the aero bar with straps open and folded to the side. The sunglasses are placed inside the helmet (if the helmet doesn't have a built-in visor), and finally it is time to memorize the way through the transition zone to the bike, and to the T1 exit and the mount line.

Since the transition zone is usually very cramped with frantic activity, it is wise to leave it as quickly as possible. As the athlete leaves T1, he turns in his after-race bag and hands over anything he needs after the race to his support crew.

A brief warm-up is recommended after handing off the floor pump to a supporter. Three to five minutes of easy jogging, skipping, and butt kicks followed by some dynamic mobility exercises is sufficient. The entire warm-up process should take no more than 10 minutes.

Afterwards, the athlete should visit the restroom one more time, if possible, then put on his racing suit and wet suit or swimsuit. Covering hands and feet with small plastic bags or freezer bags helps the body to easily slip into the wetsuit.

Next, the athlete should apply lubricant to the neck. Lubricants in stick form keep the lubricant off the hands. If the athlete gets Vaseline on his palms he needs needs to wash them thoroughly. Otherwise, the hand will slide through the water and offer considerably less resistance against the water while swimming.

Next, the athlete lines up for the start or goes to the designated area for a warm-up swim while eagerly awaiting the start signal. A warm-up swim isn't always possible; in some races there isn't sufficient space or no opportunity. But while waiting in the starting line-up athletes should get their engines warmed up by doing limbering exercises and little jumps

If a warm-up swim is possible, it should be done with caution, because most of the time swimmers in this area swim in all directions. Collisions between swimmers are part of the race and are certainly not good for pre-start nerves.

12.8   Race Strategy

Issuing a blanket recommendation as to a generally applicable race strategy is difficult. Course profiles, weather conditions, and the athletes' competition goals are too different to bring down to a common denominator.

Hence an attempt at a recommendation for a race in normal summer temperatures and with a moderate degree of difficulty and no specific demands (Kona slot, age-group or overall win). The charts show the normal speed progression as well as the stress-progression curve.

I would now like to more fully explain three terms.

12.8.1   Body inventory phase

This phase can be found in all three disciplines. It describes the moment when there are no particular stresses and the athlete is alone with himself. During this phase it is important to proceed with a high quality of movement.

Here I always imagine the athlete seeing himself from a bird's eye view and evaluating his actions. While swimming the athlete would have to continuously answer the following questions for himself:

* Am I swimming the ideal line?
* Where can I find water shadow to save strength?

- What does my stroke rate look like?
- Is my head in the right position?
- Are my forearm and elbow in a vertical position?
- Do I have enough stroke length and extension?
- Am I inhaling and exhaling effectively?

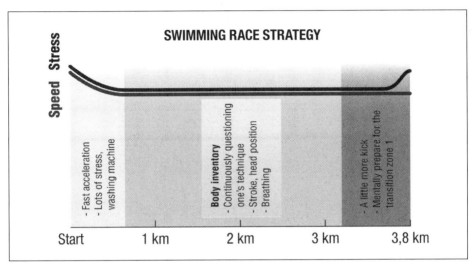

Figure 117: Swimming race strategy.

The questions for cycling are completely different:

- Am I riding the ideal line?
- Can I take that turn a little tighter?
- Am I sitting correctly?
- How is my head position? Am I doing the shoulder shrug?
- Does my gear match the topography?
- Are watts, cadence, speed, and variability index appropriate?
- Do the numbers on my bike computer match the way I feel or do I have to make an adjustment?
- Am I still outside the wind-shadow box?
- Do I have a handle on my fueling strategy?
- When is the next aid station?
- Do I need to cool externally?
- What time can I achieve if I keep riding like this? Is it realistic?

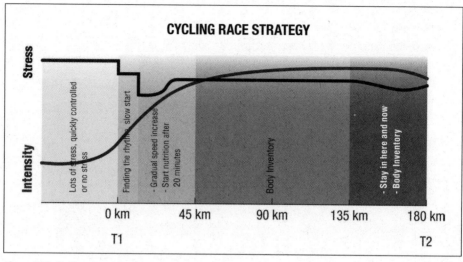

Figure 118: Cycling race strategy.

For the final discipline, running, there are some items with respect to self-regulation that must be continuously checked and if necessary adjusted or stopped:

- Am I running the ideal line?
- Are my facial muscles relaxed or am I already grimacing?
- Are my shoulders relaxed and down?
- Are my arms and hands relaxed?
- Are my hips high enough?
- What does my stride frequency look like?
- Is the pace appropriate?
- Where can I catch wind shadow?
- Is the pace of my competitors appropriate so I can mentally latch on to them?
- Where is shade?
- Is my nutrition strategy still appropriate?
- When is the next aid station?
- Where are my supporters?

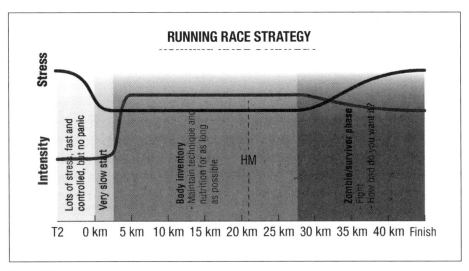

Figure 119: Running race strategy.

12.8.2 Stay-in-the-here-and-now phase

If an athlete manages to stay focused and can continuously check off his body-inventory list, he will be busy and will stay in the moment. By doing so his mind will rarely wander and he will be able to do his best in a given situation. It is important advice to stay in the here and now and not think about the remaining distance, elevation, etc.

An athlete who at km 30 already thinks about the remaining 150 km, plus the 42 km marathon that awaits him will potentially begin to doubt himself early on. This also means that the athlete should not judge his own race while he is still in it but should wait to retreat into himself after he crosses the finish line and then evaluate his race.

Someone who judges split times early on, or placement in his age group and the overall results is at risk of believing too soon that his race is lost.

Swimming in particular is often a kind of surprise bag. The athlete doesn't know precisely how the course was measured or how much current there was, and he also has no way of checking if he is swimming fast or slow. As the old saying goes, one should not count one's chickens before they hatch. The same is true in a race.

12.8.3   Zombie phase

This phase describes the moment in the race when the fun really starts. The point at which the race is run purely on willpower and attitude, depends on the athlete's performance level or mistakes he made in pacing and nutrition. I would say the average running kilometers 20-28 mark the beginning of the zombie zone. That's where the wheat separates from the chaff.

Athletes who are most likely to accept that it will hurt from that point forward are also more likely to reach the finish line without many lows. Athletes who don't realize that an Ironman is no walk in the park will suddenly be surprised by how strenuous and unpleasant such a race can become. During this phase the question "How bad do you want it?" determines success or failure.

Athlete types from the groups Count, Alpha Leader, and Social Media Athlete tend to struggle most during this phase. But not only does the mental component play an important role during this phase, so does the training beforehand.

When an athlete continuously surpasses himself in training, completed epic training sessions, and in doing so put pressure on himself, it can happen that these actions during the run-up cost too much physical and mental energy. Energy that at this point is critically necessary. This phase of the race like no other sums up my guiding principle of many years: Be strong when it matters!

12.8.4   Realistic power-meter pacing in the Ironman

Many athletes are familiar with the problem of not being able to accurately assess their pacing strategy on the bike or have only a limited understanding of the advantages of a power meter.

Objective measuring of the performance in watts provides immediate feedback in training and allows the athlete to objectively compare progress in training or performance. In addition, the power meter can help structure the race tempo, but this requires some understanding of how the performance should be evaluated in different race situations.

Literature and the internet offer many formulas that calculate a pacing guideline based on functional threshold power (FTP). Based on that, a race like the Ironman should require approximately 75-81% of this FTP. Based on this formula, 70.3 km races result in values between 81-89% of the value previously ascertained with the 20-minute critical power test.

However, stubbornly sticking to this bandwidth of values isn't enough. Environmental conditions must also be considered.

For example, let's say a course has 3-5% elevation gain and a corresponding downhill passage. When the athlete tries to keep his performance as constant as possible in this segment, meaning forcing a baseline in the analyzed file that looks like a flatline on an EKG, it will not be the fastest way to complete this segment. It is the nature of physics that it is easier to achieve higher watt numbers going uphill than on the flat, which also means greater speed with commensurably less additional effort.

If the athlete forces himself to also achieve those specified values while riding downhill, he must accept an enormous amount of metabolic stress in order to achieve minimally faster speeds. The power meter is an excellent feedback tool, but it is not a shackle to which the athlete is mercilessly bound.

Below are a few examples of sensible power meter use.

12.8.4.1 Different gradients

Every athlete has a comfort gradient, meaning a gradient that makes it easier for him to generate high watt numbers. When trying to achieve those same watt numbers on flat terrain the athlete usually looks dumbfounded because it is much more difficult to achieve. It is therefore best not to ride the same numbers in flat terrain as when climbing!

12.8.4.2 Head- and tailwind

Unlike riding in heavy headwind, maintaining the previously specified values on flat stretches with heavy tailwind is extremely challenging. In heavy tailwind a 1 km/h speed increase is not proportional to the generated performance.

If the athlete now stubbornly sticks to his selected watts he may have to put in an enormous amount of effort for minimal reward, but on the stretches with headwind might be too tired to ride these segments fast and steady. What matters in the end is who rides fastest and ultimately runs fastest, and not who produced the most wattage.

12.8.4.3   Rolling hills

In training camp on Mallorca or in training on hilly terrain, one can often see lots of athletes shift their chain far to the left for every little bit of sand on the road to keep the power output as steady as possible. Here the loss of speed is immense. It would be smarter and faster to push away the rise faster than is specified, meaning maintaining performance over the crest and then ride downhill with a little less on the pedal.

That doesn't mean riding every hill and every incline all out based on the burning matches strategy, but rather doing so judiciously, just a little faster. For years, I have therefore been issuing very different guidelines for flat and for hilly or mountainous sections. The body tends to handle slight variations better than a constant performance.

A power meter is a great tool, but nothing more. Successful use of this tool requires understanding of how the different natural occurrences can influence the athlete's power output. Pacing guidelines are thus merely a criterion that can be influenced by external factors.

12.8.4.4   Practical example for power-meter pacing

The average pedaled performance can be an interesting indicator but offers only a very superficial insight into effectiveness and the resulting speed. Let us use as an example a two-lap course like the Ironman Frankfurt, with classic wind out of the southwest, meaning there is tailwind at the beginning of each lap, and headwind on the way back towards downtown Frankfurt.

We now choose two athletes with the same build, same system weight, same material, and same sitting position and identical power meter function and look at their files after the race.

Athlete A achieved an average 250 watts, athlete B 235 watts. One would probably assume that athlete A was faster than athlete B. But actually, athlete B ended up being a few minutes faster. How is that possible? Let's look at the individual sections of the course.

During the first half of the lap

Athlete A was asked to maintain a steady 250 watts during tailwind. Here the amount of expended energy and the neuro-motor load are immense while the speed increase is barely perceptible.

Athlete B slowly built his speed and let himself be guided by the anticipated average speed (the coach specified 4h 55, meaning approximately 37 km/h) and rode about 38-40 km/h, but with considerably lower watt numbers on the pedal.

The second half of the lap

Athlete A was asked to maintain a steady 250 watts with the same cadence in headwind. During the second bike lap athlete A was no longer able to maintain the 250 watts because he had wasted too much energy in the previously mentioned tailwind section.

Athlete B was able to realize more wattage with a greater gear transmission ratio. His gain in time, compared to athlete A, was immense.

On balance athlete B was considerably faster in T2 than athlete A. Some downward AND upward deviation from the average value ascertained beforehand leads to success. That does not mean one should take every little rise standing with a big gear and maximum effort or to simply roll downhill, but to put the external conditions into context and adjust the watt numbers situationally. The body often tolerates these minor variations better than a steady cycling performance.

The watt meter is a very helpful tool, but many athletes unfortunately depend too heavily on this technology. In the run-up to an Ironman the average athlete completes approximately 4,000 training kilometers, and during that time should have developed a good feel for the respective effort. As a coach I have often seen athletes unable to tap into their true potential in a race because their actions were greatly limited by the power meter. I know several athletes who achieved their best bike splits because the bike computer or power meter failed.

12.8.5 Pacing while running

The most dangerous moment while running is definitely the first two kilometers. The athlete cycled 180 km at a significantly higher speed than is possible while running. Realizing the different speeds takes time. And the atmosphere at the T2 exit is also heated up due to the narrow lane formed by crowds of spectators, putting the athletes at risk of starting out too fast.

The athlete needs 10-15 minutes for his motor function to transition from cycling to running. This transition requires quite a bit of effort. And when he also starts out too fast, that energy expenditure increases.

I therefore recommend a deliberately slow start for those first two kilometers. As a rule of thumb, the first kilometer should be 40-45 seconds slower than the anticipated average tempo, the second kilometer 25-30 seconds slower. This requires a good amount of self-confidence, because 99% of athletes start too fast, meaning they pass the athlete who starts more slowly.

But later in the race the slow starter will make up the amount of time allegedly lost during those first two kilometers. Interestingly the performance of athletes who start out too fast usually drops suddenly between kilometers 8 and 12.

The energy expenditure in the form of a very high carbohydrate consumption during this phase can also exact vengeance at a later point. Another one of my observations is that athletes with a fast starting tempo tend to be more likely to experience hamstring cramps. This observation manifests itself particularly at competitions where the course goes slightly downhill at the start of the third discipline. So, start slow!

12.8.6   Troubleshooting during the race

In the process of analyzing more than 1,100 coached long-distance races and subsequent conversations, I have heard countless stories about incalculable factors during a race. Just when I think I've heard it all, I am always surprised yet again.

Fistfights, broken stems, and a stress fracture during the race are certainly not the order of the day, but I guess here, too, the Ironman marketing slogan applies: Anything is possible!

I have created a timeline of the most common mistakes along with some solution approaches.

TROUBLESHOOTING

	Issue	Solution
-3:00	Fatigue, too little sleep	Coffee
-2:30	Problems eating	Energy through liquid nutrition
-1:30	Nervousness, doubts	Faith in completed training
-1:00	Problems with bowel evacuation	If necessary, elimination via Microklist
-0:30	Doubts, problems with motivation	Visualization, music
-0:10	Last energy intake/gel	Carry a disposable bottle with 200 ml water
0:03	Breathlessness, lactate in arms	Focus on controlled breathing and technique
0:10	Swimming rhythm	Simulate fast swim start in training
0:35–	Poor movement execution, lack of focus	Body inventory (head position, breathing rhythm, etc.)
0:48–2:00	Water exit	Simulation in training or rather visualizing transition during the final meters of the swim
T1	Too chaotic	Inspect the competition area
km 0–1.5	Finding the rhythm	Consciously defensive start, powermeter/ watts are ideal for self-braking
km 15–35	Building temp, start nutrition strategy	Watch or speedometer with countdown (e.g., set a reminder for every 20–24) minutes)
km 35–130	Building tempo, optimal movement execution, and sitting position	Body inventory, consciously check performance (ideally via watts parameter)
km 130–180	Cramping	Carb intake too low, core fatigue, keep cadence above 78 rpm
km 130–180	Problems with maintaining aero position	Adjust cadence (not < 80 rpm)
km 20–180	GI problems	Avoid consuming high-calorie energy sources too soon (start no earlier than 20 minutes after the swim), reduce carb intake, possibly dilute by drinking take it a little slower, drink a soda like Coke
km 170–180	Loosen up legs and back	Ride out of the saddle to loosen up low back and glutes
T2	Too chaotic	Simulation in training, visualization during the final bike km
km 0–2	Low back issues	Mobilization
km 0–4	Started too fast	Cardinal error! Homeostasis at high risk, deliberately controlled start (GPS), start subjectively too slow
km 0–42	Optimal movement execution	Body inventory: head position, hip extension, backward arm movement, relaxed hands, straight foot placement
km 0–42	Cramping	Reduce speed, increase carb and sodium intake, eventually stretch
km 0–42	GI problems	Reduce carb intake, if necessary dilute by drinking more water, take it a little slower, drink soda like Coke
km 20–42	Lack of focus	Rinse mouth for 30 seconds with high-carb fluids, provides essential stimulation
km 20–42	Blisters on feet	Press on regardless
km 20–42	Knee problems	Stretch hip flexors, massage m. tensor fasciae latae

Figure 120: Troubleshooting during the long-distance race.

12.8.7   Behavior at the aid station on a bike

Before we focus on the important topic of food and refreshments during a race, here are some more tips about conduct at the aid station.

On race day, one of the greatest risks of falling in the entire race is riding through the aid stations. There are other race participants, volunteers, bottles dropping on the ground, wet roads, etc.

But another bigger problem is when the athlete is unable to grab the amount of previously calculated fuel or fluids at the aid station. Energy and fluid management are particularly challenging in a long-distance race. When an athlete must skip an aid station on a hot day it can definitely lead to a deficit that cannot be compensated. It can mean a drop in performance or even an aborted race (DNF).

Athletes should therefore be aware of aid station conduct. Athlete guides offer information about where and at which kilometer aid stations are located. Those who have trouble remembering this information should write it down and tape the note to the handlebar or top tube to keep an eye on it.

As soon as the sign at the side of the road indicates that the aid station is within reach the athlete should drink the remaining water in the bottle on his bike. He then throws the empty bottle into the net at the beginning of the aid station, and must only throw it there because otherwise he is subject to a time penalty or even disqualification due to littering.

The speed while entering the aid station should be reduced enough to be able to communicate with the volunteers there and to safely grab what is being offered. Here the hands should be on the drop portion of the handlebar to be ready to brake anytime. The right hand signals the volunteers that the athlete would like something from the offered items. This gives subsequent riders timely notice that the athlete is about to receive bottles, bars, or gels.

Big races usually have water stations at the entrance and exit of aid stations, giving the athletes another opportunity to get fluids. I recommend grabbing water at the first opportunity. If that bottle drops or the athlete is unable to grab it, he still has another chance to fuel up with water. The bottle should then be quickly and safely stowed in the bottle holder without taking the eyes off the potentially dangerous situation of passing the aid station.

It is important to stay focused on the road, make eye contact with the volunteers, and communicate with them verbally. Here I would like to offer another reminder that these helpers volunteer to spend their day on the race course, and a thank you from an athlete's lips is more appropriate than an insult if a bottle should fall down. After grabbing the first bottle this process can be repeated to pick up an isotonic beverage, Coke, or another water bottle.

The athlete should take another big drink from that bottle like he did before he entered the aid station. It can be as much as 200–400 ml. Then the half-full bottle is thrown into the designated litter zone still within the aid station.

With such a refreshment strategy, there is no need for four bottle holders on the bike, which significantly worsen aerodynamics and weight and thereby the bike's handling, especially since they don't really improve the esthetics of a time trial bike. Hence, two holders are enough, one bottle with the previously calculated quantity of gels and one bottle holder for water.

If the athlete proceeds in the aforementioned manner and ensures that he is adequately hydrated when leaving the aid station and has a full bottle on board, he should not fail because of his hydration status.

This strategy makes even more sense considering that an athlete's aerodynamics worsen every time he reaches for a bottle because he must abandon his aerodynamic position. When the athlete rides through the aid station at a slow speed and gets the necessary supplies, he only loses a few seconds compared to his normal speed. But by doing so he doesn't have to abandon his aerodynamic position to drink as often on the faster stretches outside the aid station, which he can then complete with his arms resting on the aero handlebar.

REMEMBER

Important rule of thumb: The athlete must drink any remaining water in his water bottle before reaching the aid station and then take another big drink at the end of the aid station. He thereby ensures that he is adequately hydrated even if he loses the bottle between aid stations, and thereby avoids having a personal Waterloo.

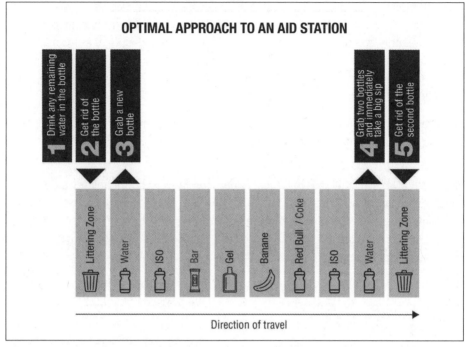

Figure 121: Conduct inside the aid station.

12.9 Fueling for the Long Distance

A long-distance race is a continuous balance. The entire race can be called a single compromise. It is about the perfect balance between energy expenditure and output (i.e., speed). In this book we have already addressed the bulk of influencing factors via the previously introduced methods of metabolic modulation during training (increasing VO_2max, lowering the lactate production rate), but also optimization of material and aerodynamics.

Another important aspect is the energy supply during a race in the form of carbohydrates. Sadly, I so often see athletes behaving not as conscientiously in this area as they do when it comes to training and material. But carbohydrate intake plays an important role in a race and has a huge impact on success or failure.

In no other race format are mistakes in fueling and pacing more apparent than in the Ironman. The 226 km race can be considered an energy-related ride on a razor's edge. The thing could also be described as a mistake-avoiding sport, because athletes who, separate from training, make the fewest mistakes will almost always be faster in the end and will reach the finish line with fewer complications, in a vertical position, and looking halfway dignified.

As a coach, I have unfortunately seen countless athletes with an excellent training record and great sacrifices (time, social contact, and money) in the run-up, completely unravel in the race due to fueling mistakes.

Many call the transition the fourth triathlon discipline but, at least with respect to a long-distance race, think of it as the fifth triathlon discipline that plays a rather inferior role. Number four is clearly a functioning fueling strategy.

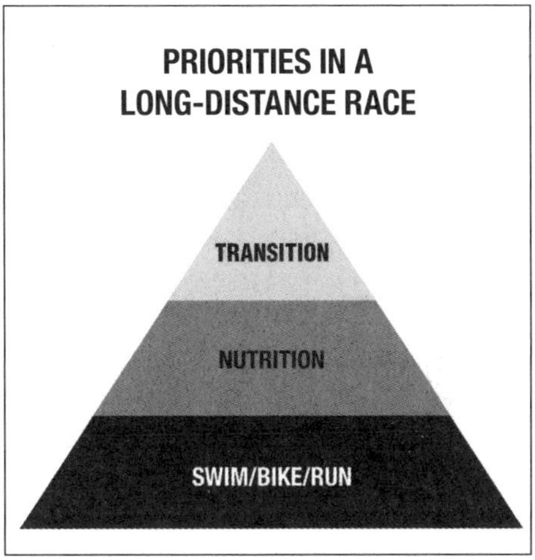

Figure 122: Priorities in a long-distance race.

12.9.1 Race week and carb loading

Long-distance-specific fueling begins days before the actual start signal. Athletes who make mistakes in their nourishment during race week can potentially jeopardize their success before the sound of the starting gun. During race week the objective should be to supply the body with sufficient energy and fluids, so the engine is well lubricated and adequately fueled up.

Carbohydrates are stored in the muscles as glycogen. We know that maximal storage is about 20 g of carbohydrates per kg of muscle. Depending on body composition, height, and gender, 300-450 g of carbohydrates are available in the form of glycogen as an energy amount.

In this context, for years a stubborn myth circulated that claimed storage capacity can be increased by first depleting theses stores in training, and then replenishing them with a larger amount of carbohydrates. While doing so, athletes should train normally, but largely forgo carbs. This form of race preparation is widely referred to as the Saltin diet.

But glycogen stores cannot be completely depleted because our brain is very sensitive to a lack of sugar. The human brain relies on this fuel, so there is always a certain safety reserve. Foregoing carbohydrates as part of a Saltin diet usually results in worsened performance that can then have a negative effect on the athlete's psyche. As a result, the athlete often loses faith in his abilities, and doubt begins to creep in.

But these negative thoughts must be avoided during race week; the athlete should stand at the starting line with lots of self-confidence and belief in his own strength. Another negative aspect of this form of carb loading is that excess carbs are not burned and thus turn into fat, which increases body weight and changes the athlete's appearance. The latter tends to also have a negative effect on the athlete's psyche when he thinks he looks unathletic, bloated, and not ready to compete.

Instead, during race week I prefer gently increasing the amount of carbohydrates day by day. Radical changes and dogmatic self-denial during race week tend to have a rather negative impact and affect the athlete's psyche.

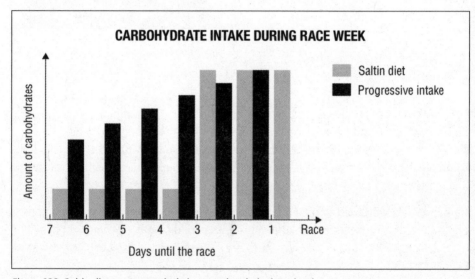

Figure 123: Saltin diet vs. progressively increased carbohydrate intake.

12.9.2 Fiber and sodium

In addition to the right amount of carbohydrates, I would like to mention two other aspects: fiber and the electrolyte sodium. Fiber should always be part of a healthy diet but should be balanced during race week.

Fiber-rich vegetables and cereals should largely be avoided or balanced in the run-up to race day, because they can cause bloating and GI problems during the race. By contrast, the athlete should increase sodium intake in the run-up to day X to increase the blood–plasma volume.

As a quick anecdote here, the example of a female athlete I coached, who a few years ago qualified for the Ironman Hawaii. We had a final video call 3–4 days before the world championship race, and at first glance I was quite shocked because her face was bloated and swollen.

My first thought was an allergic reaction, which turned out not to be the case. The cause of the massive water retention was that she had consumed an excessive amount of water. Sure, it's warm on Hawaii, but she thought she needed to drink more water to fill her stores. I asked her to show me the water's nutrition label and was able to identify the culprit.

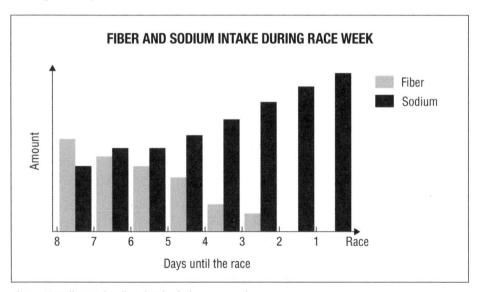

Figure 124: Fiber and sodium intake during race week.

The water had an absurdly low sodium content of 35 mg per liter. The athlete drank herself into a state of hyponatremia with the excessive consumption of nearly sodium-free water. By increasing her sodium intake and reducing the amount of water, we were able to improve her condition, so her face was back to normal without water deposits the day before the race, and she was able to complete a successful race with a daylight finish.

12.9.3 Suggestions for race week

*   Start every training session in an adequately hydrated condition and afterwards follow up with a sufficient amount of fluid. For quicker regeneration the athlete should add at least 500–750 mg of sodium per liter to the amount of water or fluid.
*   For the fastest possible recovery after workouts the athlete should consume quickly available carbs immediately after training. Gummy bears are a good option that are also low in fiber.
*   The athlete should avoid feeling hungry.
*   No experimenting, meaning not eating unfamiliar foods.
*   Largely forgo alcohol.

12.9.4 Last meal the night before the race

With respect to the meal on the evening before the race, there are different approaches that are certainly also dictated by an athlete's taste preferences. Athletes should skip fiber, meat, and large portions to ensure reliable bowel elimination. I have had good results with ice cream as the last meal. The advantages here are that it can be easily purchased in a local supermarket and it doesn't require time-consuming cooking.

But the biggest advantage is its very high energy density (i.e., it contains lots of carbohydrates (but also fat) in a relatively reasonable quantity or volume). Unlike with traditional meals, the athlete doesn't have the stress of having to empty his bowels multiple times on race-day morning and doesn't feel bloated, which would have a negative effect on breathing while swimming.

As an alternative to pasta or rice, the athlete should then consume 800–1000 ml ice cream. To make sure that this form of energy intake is also well-tolerated, the athlete should test this form of carb loading in training before long and intensive units or before a test race. No matter what dinner looks like, the athlete should drink 500 ml of water with 750 mg of added sodium with dinner to increase the blood–plasma volume.

12.9.5   Morning of the race

There is a reason race day is called the longest day of the year. The alarm should be set at least three hours before the start signal so the athlete's circulation gets into gear and he does not have to travel to the starting line in a state of logistical stress. Some athletes are hungry or feel like they can't eat a bite due to the large amount of tension and nervousness.

A brief warm shower can be helpful here and can stimulate the appetite. Like the last meal, food preferences differ greatly here as well. Some athletes prefer easily digestible oatmeal, others like 2–3 slices of toast with jam.

As on the previous few days, athletes should largely forego fiber. A cup of coffee with breakfast stimulates bowel activity and ensures a first trip to the restroom at home or at the hotel.

Just like the night before, I recommend drinking another 500 ml of water with an added 750 mg of sodium during the final 90 minutes before the start. Right before entering the water, athletes should consume an initial small dose of carbohydrates in the form of an energy gel with an additional 200 ml of water.

12.9.6   In-competition strategy

An individually calculated supply strategy that was tested in training can be the difference between success and failure. Unfortunately, many athletes pay too little attention to this important topic and step up to the starting line starry-eyed and naïve.

12.9.6.1   Planning the strategy

Planning such a strategy requires checking the race's athletes guide for the products the organizers will hand out during the race. To ensure that those products won't literally end up in your pants it is advisable to try them out during a few training sessions before the race.

Even if an athlete plans to have an independent energy supply of bars or gels during the race, athletes can lose their supply due to potholes, uneven road surfaces, or carelessness.

That is precisely why athletes should test the official race supplies beforehand. I always recommend storing his self-sufficient energy supplies where the athlete can see them, meaning not storing the bottle with the gel and water mix in the bottle cage behind the saddle, because a loss here would not be noticed.

If the athlete still ends up losing his independent fuel supply, he must decide situationally whether it's worth stopping to retrieve the bottle or just keep going. If choosing to retrieve the bottle, it is critical to look out for oncoming athletes and to never ride against the direction of traffic, but rather stop and go back on foot. Otherwise, there is a chance of instant disqualification by the race marshal.

When planning for the race the athlete should think about how he will transport his fuel supplies. There are athletes who must open gel or bar wrappers during the race, while others squeeze the entire amount of gel needed for the 180 km distance into one water bottle beforehand, avoiding opening wrappers and sticky fingers. The latter method would mean that the athlete only needs water from the organizers.

For a visual of the entire amount, I recommend putting all the gels and bars in a pile before the race. It quickly becomes apparent just how large that quantity is due to the packaging alone, and that storage capacity on the bike is quickly exhausted and some athletes must get creative. One can always see photos of countless gels taped to top tubes, which makes me wonder why those athletes spent thousands of dollars on highly aerodynamic bikes.

12.9.6.2   Fueling per se

Now that we have discussed the transport requirements, let us come back to the fuel supply. The highest priority when it comes to the fueling strategy is an ideally steady and continuous intake, particularly 5-6 hours into the race. Like the fluid and sodium supply, the athlete should ride as disciplined as possible so he can start the running segment without an energy deficit.

Here I would like to offer another example from my practice to show how some athletes can think laterally and not see the forest for the trees. A few years ago, at the Ironman 70.3 Kraichgau, an athlete I coached ran a full 20 minutes slower than I had originally planned.

On the night after the race, I received an email from him telling me that he absolutely needed to add a running block to his training before the Ironman Frankfurt just four weeks away, his main event for that season, since his running form was obviously lacking.

When I asked how he had fueled on the bike he replied that he had consumed two gels, meaning a total carb intake of 54 g, during the entire 90 km. Back then the athlete weighed 82 kg and, based on performance diagnostics, had a carbohydrate expenditure of around 150 g per hour at the prespecified pace.

When I pulled out my calculator and showed him that he wasn't able to run fast purely due to an energy deficit, he was quite sheepish. When considering that he only had to complete half an Ironman in Kraichgau, one can imagine that the long-distance race would have been a disaster.

Instead, he used the time between races to focus intensely on nutrition. He was rewarded with a slot at the Ironman Kona.

12.9.6.2.1 Bars or gels

The form in which carbohydrates are consumed depends entirely on the athlete's preferences. Some athletes need solid food and therefore eat bars or bananas, while others find it difficult to chew during exertion. That is also why it is difficult to make a blanket recommendation of one product group (gel, bar, energy chips, etc.) or even one product in particular.

Tolerability is simply too individual to be able to categorize all athletes. A few years ago, a recommendation circulated that an athlete should consume 1 g of carbs per kg of body weight per hour. Today we know that carb intake is not determined by the athlete's body weight but rather by the GI system's ability to absorb them.

Currently the assumption is that 90 g of carbs via a mix of fructose and glucose can be steadily realized. More recent studies in the area of ultra-running already mention 120 g per hour.

In my work as a coach, I have so far never seen or heard of an amount greater than 100 to 110 g per hour. The intake is easier to manage while cycling because the quantity can be transported more easily and running causes more stress to the stomach due to the running-related jolting. Athletes who prefer solid fuel in the form of bars should chew each bite for at least 15 seconds and should not swallow big pieces because those can cause stomach problems.

Gels are mixed more uniformly and are easier to ingest. I have had good experiences with athletes using bars in colder temperatures and gels when it is warmer.

It doesn't matter how an athlete consumes his fuel as long as he manages to do so steadily. I would absolutely agree that there is a definite correlation between the amount of carbohydrates an athlete consumed and success or fast finish times. Especially on the bike, the goal should be to keep the difference between carbohydrate expenditure and carbohydrate intake as small as possible to protect the glycogen stores, since ingestion while running is more difficult.

Here there are two parameters. One is to reduce consumption by training the metabolism (i.e., another reason for basic endurance training), and the other is to increase the carbohydrate intake through fueling.

12.9.6.2.2 Training the gut

The stomach can certainly be called a trainable organ. We now know that SGLT and GLUT5 transporters, and thus the intake amount, can be increased with a regular intake of large amounts of carbohydrates. But when training the GI tract the athlete should occasionally also consciously get out of his comfort zone.

To do so he can use the following training interventions:

*   Train immediately after a big meal.
*   Consume large amounts of carbohydrates during training, meaning consciously taking in the 90 g per hour or more.
*   Consume large amounts of fluids during training.
*   Consume large amounts of highly sugary drinks (e.g., sweetened iced tea) during training.
*   Test different gel products.
*   Last but not least: Test the planned race strategy.

The following chart is a sample overview of four different supply strategies during a race.

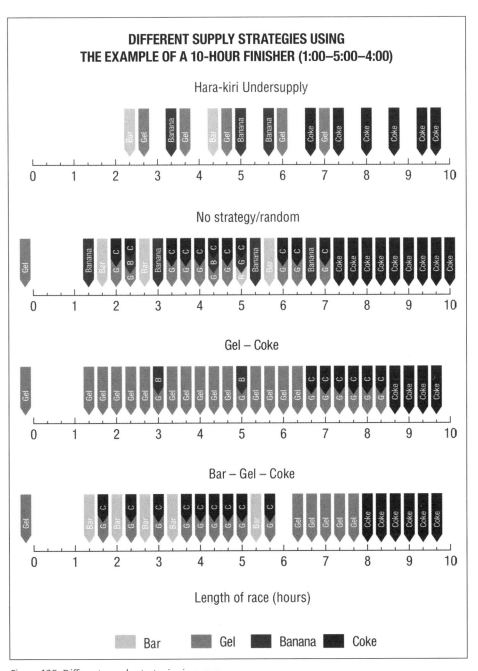

Figure 125: Different supply strategies in a race.

12.9.6.2.3 GI problems during the race

A few years ago, I began collecting feedback from athletes with a questionnaire after races. I now have a data set of more than 600 athlete feedback forms. Over a period of five years, nearly 80% of the athletes had complained of GI problems during a race. The most common causes are listed below:

- Did not adequately test race energy supplies
- Fluid intake was too low compared to the amount of carbohydrates
- Carbohydrate intake was too irregular
- Sodium intake was too low
- Carbohydrate intake was too low

The last item in particular should give some readers pause, because previously it was thought that only an excessive amount could be the cause. Here a brief digression on the subject.

GI PROBLEMS IN TRIATHLON AND THEIR POTENTIAL CAUSES

Symptom	Cause
Nausea and vomiting	• Dehydration • Hyponatremia • Hypoglycemia bonk • Too much caffeine • Too much high-fat food right before training or the race • Drinking and eating too much • Large amount of hypertonic fluids
Abdominal fullness and bloating	• Dehydration • Hyponatremia • Consuming too many carbs during the sport • Drinking and eating too much • Large amount of hypertonic fluids
GI cramps	• Large amount of hypertonic fluids • Consuming too many carbs during the sport • NSAIDs (Ibuprofen, Diclofenac, etc.)
Diarrhea	• Large amount of hypertonic fluids • Consuming too many carbs during competition • Too much caffeine • Had previous GI problems • Runner's gut, triggered by the impact load

Figure 126: GI problems during a race.

During the race, blood is primarily present in the working muscles or rather the periphery, because the sweat that cools the body through evaporation at the surface of the skin is produced from blood plasma.

When there is an undersupply of carbohydrates during the race, blood flow in the stomach decreases further and the gastric mucosa becomes more susceptible to endotoxins. Here we also refer to leaky gut syndrome.

Carbohydrates and fluid in the stomach provide better blood flow in the gastric mucosa and can minimize the emergence of this problem.

The chart lists the most common problems and their causes. I can only stress that athletes should memorize the chart to be able to solve such problems during a race, because when we know the possible cause, we are able to eliminate the problem. If energy intake is no longer possible due to existing GI problems, mouth rinsing can be used to bridge such a phase.

To do so, liquid carbohydrates are kept inside the mouth and gargled for about 10 seconds, and then spit out. This tricks the body into thinking that carbohydrates are available. The parts of the brain that signal fatigue are tricked, allowing the body to maintain performance for a period of 30-60 minutes through mouth rinsing without an actual carbohydrate intake.

Particularly when it comes to caffeine, athletes should be careful. Athletes who reach for caffeinated gels from the start risk consuming excessive amounts of this performance-boosting substance. Everyone is familiar with the effects of caffeine. It wakes you up and stimulates the metabolism. But on the flip side, it dehydrates and raises the blood pressure.

Some manufacturers add up to 150 mg caffeine per serving to their gels. If an athlete consumes three servings per hour of running to cover his energy requirement, he simultaneously takes in 450 mg of caffeine. This amount is equivalent to 2-3 espressos. When adding the time factor, meaning the athlete consumes this quantity for several hours, it becomes quickly apparent that it is often too much of a good thing.

I therefore recommend not using caffeine until kilometer marker 130-140 when fatigue cumulates, and to increase the amount during the last 40-50 km on the bike to possibly avoid diarrhea problems caused by an excessive dose of caffeine.

Athletes who squeeze all their gels into a bike bottle before the race, while cycling cannot differentiate whether they took a drink of gel with or without caffeine. I would therefore suggest using caffeine tablets to ensure some calculative certainty, because with every tablet he takes the athlete knows precisely how much he ingested.

In the early 2000s, some sports had a permitted caffeine limit. If that was exceeded and the athlete had to submit to a doping test, he tested positive. Athletes who use caffeine gels throughout the entire race back then would have certainly tested positive. That limit no longer exists, but with this retrospection I would like to make athletes aware that caffeine as a performance-boosting substance should not be used excessively.

I have had positive experiences with guarana as a stimulant during races. Guarana's effects are more subtle, but last longer. The company Biestmilch offers a booster that contains 4 g of guarana and colostrum. Studies have shown that colostrum could significantly reduce the onset of leaky gut syndrome.

So, if he can avoid all the listed mistakes the athlete can look forward to the chute as the reward for all those hours of hard work..

12.9.7   The finish line

It might sound a bit dramatic, but crossing the finish line permanently changes a person. I often hear reports that the first long-distance race made a particularly big impression on most athletes. The pain is great, but the joy predominates.

Once the athlete has reached the finish line, he should get sufficient nourishment in the finish area, the athlete's garden.

After the sugar orgy during the race, athletes often have a major craving for salty or hearty foods. If the overall physical condition at the finish is poor and the athlete has to vomit or did so during the race, I recommend notifying the medical staff to potentially be given a saline solution for a quicker recovery.

After a shower the athlete should put on warm clothes because the immune system is significantly weakened after the race, and the open window can easily become an open barn door.

That is also why alcohol consumption should be kept to a minimum, and only after consuming adequate amounts of food and fluids. I would advise against getting a massage because the muscles are pretty irritated and many athletes do not tolerate external pressure on the muscles very well at this point.

12.9.8　The day after: What happens next?

The night after the race is a mix of complete exhaustion and feeling super pumped. The body is still so full of adrenaline that it isn't always possible to wind down, but alcohol or even sleeping pills should not be used. Both add more stress to an already stressed body. To me, one of the best moments of the year is the awards ceremony the day after the race. Looking at the tired but jubilant warriors always reminds me of the performance they achieved on the previous day.

When looking in the mirror or at the scale during those first days after the race, athletes will notice that they gained weight or even have a swollen face. This swelling results from an increased creatin kinase level (CK). For men the normal range is < 170 U/l, and for women it is < 145 U/l. But after a long-distance race that value can be as high as > 2000 U/l.

This parameter reflects the advanced degree of muscle damage. Unfortunately, this marker is also extremely elevated after a heart attack. Therefore, anyone getting bloodwork done after the race should mention that he recently finished a long-distance race.

12.9.8.1　Resuming training

Depending on plans for the rest of the season, training should resume, but with prudence and with the following rules:

- **Frequency trumps duration.**
  Returning to training with shorter (20-30 minutes) but more frequent sessions, 1-3 times a day, rather than one 60-90-minute unit.
- **Energy trumps FatMax.**
  The time period right after a long-distance race is not the time to complete carbohydrate-reduced sessions in the FatMax range. Every workout should be completed with full energy stores.

- **Intensity is poison.**
  Training during the week after the race should be considered active recovery. Those longing for intense units apparently did not give it their all in the main event.
- NO running during the first week after the race.

No matter what the continuing running schedule looks like, athletes should take at least a one-week break from running after the long-distance race. There is no such thing as regenerative running! Due to the impact load, running is not suitable for recovery.

12.9.8.2   Regeneration protocol after the long-distance race

In the week after the race, euphoria from the previous accomplishment often overshadows physical symptoms, but during the following week athletes are regularly overcome by general fatigue. This is part of the normal regeneration process after an Ironman.

12.9.8.2.1   Days 1–4

Those first days tend to be marked by muscle soreness and prevent smooth movement. Muscle soreness is caused by damage to muscle fibers. The body then often responds with increased fluid retention to flush out the inflammatory processes. Athletes frequently gain several kilos after the race, primarily due to swelling. Not a reason to go on a diet or start fasting during the first week after the race!!

I have had good results with gentle non-impact sports (swimming, cycling, aqua jogging, or ellipse trainer) on those first days after the race instead of stopping all activity. Here I recommend volumes of 20 minutes in the water and 30–40 minutes on the bike. Intensity should not exceed the lower BE1 range.

Running is absolutely contraindicated, because the eccentric impact load when the foot strikes the ground will further irritate already stressed muscles. Athletes often crave junk food and a cold beer after crossing the finish line. This reward should absolutely take place, but after 2-3 days the athlete should resume a healthy diet.

Junk food is a catalyst for additional inflammatory processes that the organism is trying to reduce. To promote regeneration, I recommend skipping fasciae training and massages for the first four days to avoid additional stress to the muscles.

Cold and ice baths are a good alternative for reducing the body's inflammatory responses. Sauna sessions are also considered contraindicated since the fluid balance, particularly after a hot race, has not yet been fully compensated.

12.9.8.2.2 Days 5–7

The muscle soreness goes away, but overall fatigue increases. Motivation and the desire to train return. However, during this phase the athlete should still abstain from running. The length of training sessions (without any intensity) can be extended to 60 minutes on the bike and 40 minutes in the water.

Cold applications should continue, and massages or fasciae training can be included individually.

Even on those days some athletes report that they want to pass because their muscles are still too sore. To be safe, I would also recommend waiting at this time.

12.9.8.2.3 Days 8–12

During this phase fatigue hits like a brick, and any type of movement is hard. Some athletes misinterpret this and think they need to train considerably more because they are losing their form. But fatigue and shortness of breath are symptoms of continuing regeneration.

Those training too much during this phase risk significantly extending their recovery period or not having any more successes in the current season. Running can resume during this phase, but without intensity and for no more than 20-25 minutes.

12.9.8.2.4 Days 13–18

At this time recovery is usually complete, but the athlete should still self-reflect and check himself 2-3 hours after training. If he continues to feel good after training, regeneration seems to be complete. If the athlete feels heavy and lethargic after training, he should adjust his training program and make downward corrections.

12.9.8.3   When can I race again?

If an athlete correctly navigated the above phases, regeneration should have advanced to a point that he is able to participate in another race three weeks after the long-distance triathlon. When giving the system that is man the chance to process the immense stimulus of a long-distance race, he will be able to enter more races invigorated and refreshed.

Empirically speaking, the aforementioned three, but also five or seven weeks between two long-distance races has proven to be the best interval. But these close intervals are only realizable if the athlete has made no mistakes both in training and before the first long-distance race as well as the recovery protocol.

The below chart shows when training can and should resume in which sport. Here the athlete must decide if he is ready to tackle another 70.3 km or even longer long-distance race so soon (3–8 weeks) after a successful long-distance event.

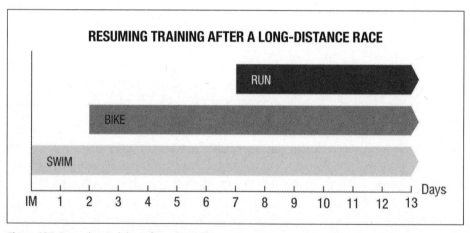

Figure 127: Resuming training after a long-distance race.

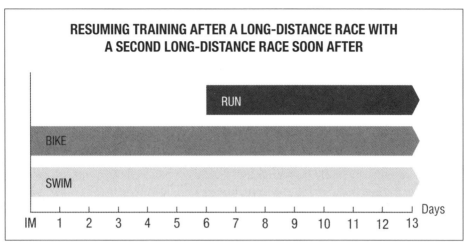

Figure 128: Resuming training after a long-distance race with the goal of competing in another race soon after.

CLOSING REMARKS, ACKNOWLEDGMENTS, AND DEDICATION

It is my sincere hope that my knowledge and experience will help many athletes get past their fear of the gargantuan task of a long-distance race. As I mentioned at the beginning of the book, there are almost certainly other approaches that can also lead to success. This book can therefore never lay claim to offering the only correct concept.

It is based on my current level of knowledge and experience that has made more than 1,100 successful long-distance races possible. I am particularly grateful to Meyer & Meyer Publishing for fulfilling my long-time dream of writing an entire book.

At this point I would like to thank some people who are very important to me, who greatly influenced me during my time as a coach and left a mark on my coaching style.

I would like to name just a few.

Dennis Sandig was and is my greatest mentor and brother-from-another-mother. We have known each other since the last millennium and our paths crossed many times. He always helped me to sharpen my senses, to be alert, to form my own opinion about triathlon, and fed me literature and knowledge. Thank you for always lending an ear and for enduring many moments of self-doubt! To me Dennis personifies the application of sports science in practice.

Lothar Leder is the real record breaker. He is the first human to complete a long-distance race in less than eight hours in 1996, as part of what was then the Ironman Europe. His wealth of experience from countless top successes and his estimations regarding the current triathlon, to some extent intuitively, make sense and continue to impress me today.

Thank you also to *Claudia Klasing Pandolfi* of thetimedrop.com for the very successful graphic representation of my hieroglyphic sketches, and Dustin Nicolai for the illustrations.

I would also like to thank all the athletes I was able to advise, guide, and coach on their path to long-distance races since 2004. Some influenced my coaching style. Thank you for your leap of faith and for allowing me to live my dream as a triathlon coach.

Finally, I would like to thank my wife *Therese*, without whom I would never have had the opportunity to grow into my profession. She always brings me back down to earth, gives me a piece of her mind, and helps me organize my thoughts. Without her we also would not have our four amazing daughters *Luise, Mathilda, Paula, and Käthe*. I would also like to thank my *parents* who always supported me in my development and my dreams, and who believed in me.

I would like to dedicate this book to Julia Mai. We walked the same path for many years. I coached her as a professional athlete and we ultimately became colleagues. She passed away on October 7, 2018, at the age of 38, tragically and much too young after a very brief illness.

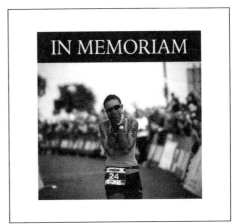

In memoriam Julia Mai.

APPENDIX

1 Sample 16-week training plan

LEGEND

Legend	Definition
Comp. tempo	Competition tempo
70.3 tempo	Mid-distance race tempo
OD tempo	Olympic-distance tempo
B	Break (in minutes)
m	Meters
C	Cadence (U/l/min)
SF	Stride frequency (steps/min)
STF	Stroke frequency
WU	Warm-up in swimming, cycling, running
WD	Warm-down in swimming, cycling, running
PBO	Pull buoy only or arm swimming
PD/PB	Paddles, pull buoy
PD/PB/AS	Paddles, pull buoy, ankle strap
CR	Crawl stroke
BR	Breaststroke
BA	Backstroke
A	Arms
L	Legs
RI	Right
LE	Left
CHO	Carbohydrates
RB	Road bike
TT	Time trial bike
SE	Strength endurance/endurance strength
Easy	Relaxed tempo
All out	Sprint

As previously mentioned, I would like to provide a sample training plan for the final 16 weeks of preparation for a long-distance race. But this framework should be viewed strictly as a rough orientation and an example of how an athlete might prepare for such a competition. Such a very general plan does not take into account individual strengths, weaknesses, an athlete's athletic history, gender, and life circumstances. I would define the performance level of the fictitious male athlete in this general plan as an anticipated race time of between 9:30 h and 10:10 h.

WEEK 1

	Monday	Tuesday	Wednesday	Thursday	Friday	Saturday	Sunday
Unit 1	**Swim** 12 x 50 m, every 6th one fast, B 0:10 / 8 x 50 m, every 4th one fast, B 0:10 / 6 x 50 m, every 3rd one fast, B 0:10 / 4 x 50 m, every 2nd one fast, B 0:10 / 4 x 100 m, (25 m catch-up, 75 m fast) CR, B 0:15 / 100 m CR easy / 3 x 100 (50 m single arm, 50 m fast CR) B 0:10 / 100 CR easy / 2 x 100 fast CR, B 0:05 / 400 m PBO WD	**Run** 10 min WU 8 x Yasso, 800 m + 200 m jog break, 5 min WD	**Swim** 200 m WU 15 x 100 m mid-tempo, B 0:20, 200 m WD	**Run 40 min** BE1 with focus on high SF, end with 5–10 min running drills	**Run 100 min** Easy jog with 100 min acceleration every 5 min	**Bike 180 min** Flat or hilly terrain, BE1, C 80–100	**Bike 210 min** Flat or hilly terrain, BE1, C 80–100
Unit 2	**Core stability** 20 min		**Bike 50 min** 10 min WU, 4 x 3 min SE, B 3 min each, remainder BE1 WD	**Swim** 800 m CR easy, B 1:00 / 600 m CR easy, B 0:45 / 400 m CR easy, B 0:45 / 200 m CR easy, B 0:30 / 2 x 100 m CR, B 0:20 / 8 x 50 m CR mid Tempo, B 0:15 / 100 m WD	**Core stability** 20 min		
Unit 3	Mobility 10 min	Mobility 20 min	Mobility 10 min	Mobility 10 min	Mobility 10 min	Mobility 10 min	Mobility 10 min

WEEK 2

	Monday	Tuesday	Wednesday	Thursday	Friday	Saturday	Sunday
Unit 1	Swim 200 m WU 4 x 700 m as follows: 50 m catch-up, B 0:15 50 m BR A CR L, B 0:10 300 m PBO, B 0:30 200 m PD/PB, B 0:20 100 m All out, B 0:45 200 WD	Run 10 min WU, 10 x Yasso, 800 m + 200 m jog B, 5 min WD	Swim 200 m WU 20 x 100 m mid- Tempo, B 0:20 200 m WD	Run 40 min BE1 with focus on high SF, end with 5–10 min running drills	Run 100 min Easy jog with 100 m accelerations every 5 min	Bike 180 min 90 min BE1 with C 90–100, 3 x 8 min Comp-tempo, in bet- ween 10 min each BE1, remainder of time WD	Bike 240 min Flat/hilly terrain, BE1, C 80–100
Unit 2	Core Stability 20 min		Bike 50 min 10 min WU, 5 x 3 min SE, B 3 min each, remainder BE1 WD	Swim 800 m CR easy, B 1:00 600 m CR easy, B 0:45 400 m CR easy, B 0:45 200 m CR easy, B 0:30 2 x 100 m CR, B 0:20 8 x 50 m CR mid- Tempo, B 0:15 100 m WD	Core stability 20 min		
Unit 3	Mobility 10 min	Mobility 20 min	Mobility 10 min	Mobility 10 min	Mobility 10 min	Mobility 10 min	Mobility 10 min

WEEK 3

	Monday	Tuesday	Wednesday	Thursday	Friday	Saturday	Sunday
Unit 1	**Swim** 10 x 50 m, every 5th one fast, B 0:10 6 x 50 m with every 3rd one fast, B 0:10 3 x 200 m PB0, B 0:30 6 x 50 m with each 3rd one fast, B 0:10 4 x 50 m with every 2nd one fast, B 0:10 3 x 200 m PB0, B 0:30 6 x 50 m with every 3rd one fast, B 0:10 10 x 50 m PD/PB with every 2nd one fast, B 0:10 200 m WD	**Run** 10 min WU, 10 x Yasso 800 m + 200 m jog break, 5 min WD	**Swim** 300 m WU 6 x 50 m BR A CR L, B 0:20 40 x 50 m CR, B 0:10 200 m WD	**Run 40 min** BE1 with focus on high SF, end with 5–10 min running drills	**Run 120 min** Easy jog with 100 m acceleration runs every 10 min	**Bike 180 min** 90 min BE1 with C 90–100, 3 x 10 min comp. tempo, in between 10 min each BE1, 20 min WD	**Bike 240 min** Flat or hilly terrain, BE 1, C 80–100
Unit 2	**Core stability** 20 min		**Bike 55 min** 10 min WU, 6 x 3 min SE, remainder BE1 WD	**Swim** 800 m CR easy, B 1:00 600 m CR easy, B 0:45 400 m CR easy, B 0:45 200 m CR easy, B 0:30 2 x 100 m CR, B 0:20 8 x 50 m CR mid-tempo, B 0:15 100 m WD	**Core stability** 20 min		
Unit 3	Mobility 10 min	Mobility 20 min	Mobility 10 min	Mobility 10 min	Mobility 10 min	Mobility 10 min	Mobility 10 min

WEEK 4

	Monday	Tuesday	Wednesday	Thursday	Friday	Saturday	Sunday
Unit 1	**Swim** 400 m WU, 10 x 50 m (10 m hard/40 m easy), B 0:10 10 x 50 m (15 m hard/35 m easy), B 0:10, 10x 50 m (20 m hard/30 m easy), B 0:10, 10 x 50 m (25 m hard/25 m easy) B 0:10 3 x 400 m PBO, B 0:45, 100 m WD	**Run** 10 min WU, 10 min runningdrills 15 x 100 m at a brisk Tempo (please NO sprinting), B 100 m easy jog 10 min WD	**Swim** 300 m WU 6 x 50 m Br A Cr L, B 0:20 40 x 50 m Cr, B 0:10 200 m WD	**Run 60 min** BE1 with focus on high SF and clean technique	**Run 80 min** BE1 with focus on high SF and clean technique	**Bike 180 min** Flat or hilly terrain BE1, C 80–100	**Bike 240 min** Flat or hilly terrain BE1, C 80–100
Unit 2			**Core stability** 20 min	**Swim** 200 m WU 15 x 200 m mid-Tempo, B 0:30 200 m WD	**Swim** 200 m WU 5 x 500 m PBO, B 1:00 100–200 m WD	**Core stability** 20 min	
Unit 3		Mobility 10 min		Mobility 10 min	Mobility 10 min	Mobility 10 min	Mobility 10 min

WEEK 5

	Monday	Tuesday	Wednesday	Thursday	Friday	Saturday	Sunday
Unit 1	**Swim** 300 m WU 6 x 50 m BR A CR L, B 0:20 40 x 50 m CR, B 0:10 200 m WD	**Run** 10 min WU, 12 x Yasso 800 m + 200 m jog break, 5 min WD	**Swim** 10 x 50 m, every 5 one fast, B 0:10 6 x 50 m, every 3 one fast, B 0:10 3 x 200 m PBO, B0:30 6 x 50 m, every 3 one fast, B 0:10 4 x 50 m, every 2 one fast, B 0:10 3 x 200 m PBO, B 0:30 6 x 50 m, every 3 one fast, B 0:10 10 x 50 m PD/PB, every 2 one fast, B 0:10 200 m WD	**Run 40 min** BE1 with focus on high SF, end with 5–10 min running drills	**Run 120 min** Easy jog with 100 m acceleration run every 10 min	**Bike 210 min** 160 min BE1 at C 90-100, 20 min comp. tempo, 10 min 70.3 tempo, 20 min WD	**Run** Fasting run, easy tempo in BE1
Unit 2	**Core stability** 20 min		**Bike 90 min** 20 min WU, 60 min alternate between 2 min at C 80 and 1 min at C 110 in BE1 10 min WD	**Swim** 200 m WU 5 x 500 PBO, B 1:30 100–200 m WD	**Core stability** 20 min		**Bike 240 min** Flat or hilly terrain. BE1, C 80-100
Unit 3	**Mobility 10 min**	**Mobility 20 min**	**Mobility 10 min**	**Mobility 10 min**	**Mobility 20 min**	**Mobility 10 min**	**Mobility 10 min**

WEEK 6

	Monday	Tuesday	Wednesday	Thursday	Friday	Saturday	Sunday
Unit 1	**Swim** 300 m WU 8 x 100 m (25 m waterball/25 m catch-up/50 m CR), B 0:20 8 x 100 m (25 m Br A Cr L/50 m CR/25 m BA L), B 0:20 8 x 100 m Pbo (25 m fist LE/25 m fist RI/25 m both fists/25 m CR), B 0:20 10 x 50 m Pd/Pb/As mid-tempo, B 0:10 100 m WD	**Run** 10 min WM, 15 x Yasso 800 m + 200 m jog break, 5 min WD	**Swim** 10 x 50 m, every 5th one fast, B 0:10 6 x 50 m, every 3rd one fast, B 0:10 3 x 200 m PBO, B 0:30 6 x 50 m, every 3rd one fast, B 0:10 4 x 50 m, every 2nd one fast, B 0:10 3 x 200 m PBO, B 0:30 6 x 50 m, every 3rd one fast, B 0:10 10 x 50 m PD/PB, every 2nd one fast, B 0:10 200 m WD	**Run 40 min** BE1 with focus on high SF, end with 5–10 min running drills	**Run 100 min** Easy jog with 100 m acceleration runs every 10 min	**Bike 210 min** 140 min BE1 with C 90–100, 30 min comp. tempo, 20 min 70.3 tempo, 20 min WD	**Run** Fasting run, easy Tempo in BE1
Unit 2	**Core stability** 20 min		**Bike 90 min** 10 min kickstart, meaning w/o WU at OD pace, 80 min BE1 to the end	**Swim** 200 m WU 5 x 600 m Pbo, B 1:30 100–200 m WD	**Core stability** 20 min	**Bike 240 min** Flat or hilly terrain, BE1, C 80–100	
Unit 3	Mobility 10 min	Mobility 20 min	Mobility 10 min	Mobility 10 min	Mobility 20 min	Mobility 10 min	Mobility 10 min

WEEK 7

	Monday	Tuesday	Wednesday	Thursday	Friday	Saturday	Sunday
Unit 1	**Swim** 200 m WU 5 x 700 m as follows: 50 m catch-up, B 0:15 50 m BR A CR L, B 0:10 300 m PBO, B 0:30 200 m Pd/Pb, B 0:20 100 m all out, B 0:45 200 m WD	**Run** 10 min WU, 18 x Yasso 800 m + 200 m jog break, 5 min WD	**Swim** 200 m WU 8 x 100 m (25 m all out/75 m easy), B 0:15 8 x 50 m (25 m catch-up/25 m Cr, B 0:15 400 m alternate 25 m 5- or 6-stroke-breathing/25 m 2- or 3-stroke-breathing 12 x 50 m PB and AS, B 0:10 4 x 200 with PD/PB/AS, B0:30 100 m WD	**Run 40 min** BE1 with focus on high SF, end with 5–10 min running drills	**Run 110 min** Easy jog with 100 m acceleration runs every 10 min	**Bike 210 min** 120 min BE1 at C 90–100, 40 min comp. tempo, 30 min 70.3 tempo, 20 min WD	**Run 40 min** Fasting run, easy tempo in BE1
Unit 2	**Core stability** 20 min		**Bike 90 min** 15 min kickstart, meaning no warm-up, at OD pace, 75 min BE1 to the end	**Swim** 200 m WU 5 x 600 m PBO, B 1:00 100–200 m WD	**Core stability** 20 min		**Bike 240 min** Flat or hilly terrain, BE1, C 80–100
Unit 3	Mobility 10 min	Mobility 20 min	Mobility 10 min	Mobility 10 min	Mobility 10 min	Mobility 20 min	Mobility 10 min

WEEK 8

	Monday	Tuesday	Wednesday	Thursday	Friday	Saturday	Sunday
Unit 1	Rest day	**Run** 10 min WU, 10 min running drills 15 x 100 m at a brisk tempo (please NO sprinting), B 100 m easy jog 100 m WD	**Swim** 200 m WU 15 x 200 m mid-tempo, B 0:30 200 m WD	**Run 60 min** 50 min BE1, final 10 min 6–8 x 50 m acceleration runs	**Swim** 200 m WU 10 x 100 m (25 m catch-up/75 m Cr) B0:20, 10 x 100 m (15 m fast start/85 m easy) B 0:20 10 x 100 m PB0, B 0:10 200 m WD	**Run 50 min** 5 min WU 10 min alternate 15 sec increasing SF/ shortening stride length + 15 sec easy jog 5 min normal BE1 10 min alternate 15 sec increasing SF/ shortening stride length + 15 sec easy jog 5 min normal BE1 10 min alternate 15 sec increasing SF/ shortening Stride length + 15 sec easy jog 5 min WD	**Bike 180 min** 30 min WU 3 x 10 min BE 2 at C 55–65 sitting climb, in between 10 min each active break Remainder WD
Unit 2			**Core stability** 20 min		**Core stability** 20 min	**Bike 120 min** 30 min WU, 60 min alternate 2 min at C 80 and 1 min at C 110 in BE1 30 min WD	
Unit 3		Mobility 20 min	Mobility 10 min	Mobility 10 min	Mobility 20 min	Mobility 10 min	Mobility 10 min

WEEK 9

	Monday	Tuesday	Wednesday	Thursday	Friday	Saturday	Sunday
Unit 1	**Swim** 400 m WU, 10 x 50 m (10 m hard/40 m easy), B 0:10 10 x 50 m (15 m hard/35 m easy), B 0:10, 10 x 50 m (20 m hard/30 m easy), B 0:10, 10 x 50 m (25 m hard/25 m easy), B 0:10 3 x 400 m PB0, B0:45 100 m WD	**Run 100 min** 35 min BE1 WU 3 x 20 min w/o B 5 min BE1 12 min 70.3 tempo, 3 min OD tempo, 5 min WD	**Swim (pool)** 200 m WU 8 x 400 slow tempo, clean technique, B1:00 100–200 WD	**Run 60 min** BE1 with focus on high SF and clean technique	**Swim (pool)** 400 m easy WU 4 x 100 m (25 m single arm LE/25 m single arm RI/25 m catch-up/25 m CR), B 0:20 20 x 100 m mid-tempo, B 0:20, 10 x 100 m PD/PB, B 0:20 200 m WD	**Bike 240 min** 20–30 min easy WU 3 x 15 min comp. tempo, in between each 10 min easy Remainder in BE1	**Bike 300 min** BE1 with lots of segments in aero position; ensure sufficient CHO supply
Unit 2	**Core stability** 20 min			**Core stability** 20 min	**Run 70 min** BE1 with focus on high SF and clean technique		**Combined run 10 min** BE1, start easy
Unit 3	Mobility 20 min	Mobility 10 min	Mobility 10 min	Mobility 10 min	Mobility 20 min	Mobility 10 min	Mobility 10 min

WEEK 10

	Monday	Tuesday	Wednesday	Thursday	Friday	Saturday	Sunday
Unit 1	Swim (pool) 300 m WU 6 x 50 m BR A/Cr L, B 0:20 50 x 50 m CR, B 0:10 200 m WD	Run 100 min 10 min WU, 20 x Yasso 800 m + 200 m, jog break, 5 min WD	Swim (pool) 200 m WU 6 x 500 m slow Tempo, clean technique, B 1:00 100–200 WD	Run 40 min BE1 with focus on high SF, end with 5–10 m runningdrills	Swim (pool) 600 m WU 20 x 50 m (40 m easy/10 m hard), B 0:15 10 x 50 m Pd/Pb (30 m easy/20 m hard), B 0:20 10 x 50 m Pd/Pb (25 m easy/25 m hard), B 0:20 100 m easy 3 x 400 m WD, B 1:00	Bike 240 min 25–30 min easy WU 3 x 20 min Comp. Tempo, 10 min easy in betweeneach. Remainder in BE1	Bike 360 min BE1 with lots of segments in aero position: ensure adequate CHO supply
Unit 2	Core stability 20 min		Bike 60 min Lower BE1 with strictly regenerating character, ideally on RB not TT	Core stability 20 min	Run 60 min 50 m BE1, final 10 min 6–8 x 50 m acceleration runs		Combination run 10 min BE1, only easy starts
Unit 3	Mobility 20 min	Mobility 10 min	Mobility 10 min	Mobility 10 min	Mobility 20 min	Mobility 10 min	Mobility 10 min

WEEK 11

	Monday	Tuesday	Wednesday	Thursday	Friday	Saturday	Sunday
Unit 1	Rest day	Run 100 min 30 min BE1 WU 3 x 20 min w/o break (5 min BE1 10 min 70.3 tempo, 5 min OD tempo) 5 min WD	Swim 300 min WU 6 x 50 m Br A/Cr L, B 0:20 30 x 50 m Pd/Pb/As, B 0:20 200 m WD	Run 90 min BE1 with focus on high SF and clean technique	Swim (pool) 400 m easy WU 4 x 100 m (25 m single-arm LE/25 m single-arm RI/25 m catch-up/25 m CR, B 0:20 20 x 100 m mid- tempo, B 0:20, 15 x 100 m PD/PB, B 0:20 200 m WD	Swim (open water) NO WU, 3 x 20 min (4 min hard start/ 15 min easy/1 min all out), B1:30	Bike 300 min 30 min with at least 95 C, 4 x 40 min without break (10 min BE1, C 100, 25 min BE1/BE2, transition zone C 80, 5 min BE2 C 90) remainder in BE1
Unit 2			Bike 60 min Lower BE1 with regeneration charac- ter, ideally on RB nof TT	Run 30 min Double-run day, BE1 with focus on high SF and clean technique	Core stability 20 min	Bike 210 min BE1 with lots of segments in aero position; ensure adequate CHO supply	Combined run 20 min BE1 with focus on high SF and clean technique
Unit 3	Mobility 20 min	Mobility 10 min	Mobility 10 min	Mobility 10 min	Mobility 20 min	Mobility 10 min	Mobility 20 min

WEEK 12

	Monday	Tuesday	Wednesday	Thursday	Friday	Saturday	Sunday
Unit 1	**Swim (pool)** 1,000 m CR, B 1:30 / 800 m CR, B 1:00 / 800 m CR, B 0:45 / 400 m CR, B 0:45 / 200 m CR, B 0:30 / 2 x 100 m Cr, B 0:20 / 8 x 50 m CR, B 0:15 / 100 m WD	**Run** 10 min WU, 25 x Yasso 800 m + 200 m. jog break, 5 min WD	**Bike 90–120 min** Lower BE1 with regenerating character	**Run 40 min** BE1 with focus on high SF, end with 5–10 min runningdrills	**Swim** 400 m WU / 400 m PBO / 6 x 50 m CR fast, B 0:10 / 6 x 150 m (100 m Cr fast/50 m CR easy), B 0:30 / 6 x 50 m CR L easy, B 0:15 / 400 m PBO / 400 m WD	**Swim (open water)** NO WU 3 x 20 m (4 min fast start/15 min easy/1 min all out), B 1:30	**Bike 240 min** 30 min with at least 95 C, 4 x 40 min w/o a break (5 min BE1 C 100, 25 min BE1/BE2. transition zone C 80, 10 min BE2 C 90) 10 min WD
Unit 2				**Core-Stability** 20 min	**Run 60 min** 50 m BE1, final 10 min 6–8 50-m deceleration runs	**Bike 180 min** BE1 with lots of segments in aero position; ensure adequate CHO supply	**Combined run 20 min** NO WU 8 x 200 OD-Tempo, B easy jog per 200 m, remainder with focus on clean technique in BE1
Unit 3		Mobility 10 min	Mobility 20 min		Mobility 10 min	Mobility 10 min	Mobility 10 min

WEEK 13

	Monday	Tuesday	Wednesday	Thursday	Friday	Saturday	Sunday
Unit 1	Swim (open water) 4 x 10 min easy with focus on orientation, getting used to wetsuit and high STF, B 1 min	Swim (pool) 800 m WU (Alternate 75 m CR/ 25 m BR A CR L) 12 x 50 m (every 4th all out), B 0:15 8 x 50 m (every 4th all out), B 0:20 4 x 50 m (every 2nd all out), B 0:25 2 x 50 m (all out), B 0:30 200 m CR easy 200 m CR PBO easy 200 m WD	Bike 90 min 20 min WU, 2 x 5–8 min at comp. tempo with 8–10 min active break, remainder in BE1	Swim (pool) 300 m WU, 10 x 100 m PBO easy, B 0:10 min, 10 x 50 m hard, B 0:30 min, 300 m WD	Run 25 min 10 min WU, 3 x 1 min 70.3 tempo, B 1:30 min jog, 10 min easy WD	Bike 60 min 10 min WU, 3 x 1:30 min at comp. tempo, B 2–3 min in between, remainder easy WD	70.3 race
Unit 2		Run 40 min 15 in WU, 3 x 1,000 m in 70.3 tempo minus 15 sec/km, B 3 min passive, 5 min WD	Combination run 20 min Deliberately easy tempo, focus on high SF			Swim (open water) 5 in easy WU, 3 x 1:00 min at comp. tempo, B 1:00 easy, 5 min WD	
Unit 3	Mobility 10 min	Mobility 10 min	Mobility 20 min		Mobility 10 min	Mobility 10 min	

WEEK 14

	Monday	Tuesday	Wednesday	Thursday	Friday	Saturday	Sunday
Unit 1							
Unit 2	Swim (pool) 30 x 50 m PBO, B 0:20 with regenerating character	Day of rest	Swim (pool) 200 m WU 10 x 50 m (25 m catch-up/25 m CR medley), B 0:20 10 x 50 m (15 m ultra-hard start/35 m easy) B 0:20 10 x 50 m PBO, B 0:05 10 x 50 m PD/PB 4- or 5-strokebreathing, B 0:10 200 m WD	Swim (open water) 5 min Wu, 3 x 15 min (12 min hard start/12 min easy with focus on high STR, 1 min hard) B 2 min 5 min WD	Run 40 min Easy tempo in BE1 with focus on clean technique and high SF	Bike 240 min Flat or hilly terrain with adequate CHO supply, ideally on RR instead of TT, lower BE1	Bike 330 min Flat or hilly terrain with adequate CHO supply, ideally on RR instead of TT, lower BE1
Unit 3			Bike 90 min Lower BE1 with C > 90	Core-Stability 20 min	Bike 150 min BE1 with C > 85		Combination run 20 min BE1
Unit 4			Mobility 10 min	Mobility 20 min	Mobility 10 min	Mobility 10 min	Mobility 10 min

WEEK 15

	Monday	Tuesday	Wednesday	Thursday	Friday	Saturday	Sunday
Unit 1	**Swim (pool)** 12 x 50 m, B 0:10, every 4th sprint 2 x 1,000 m, every 4th 25 fast, B 1 min 12 x 50 m, B 0:10, every 4th sprint	**Run** 10 min WU, 20 x Yasso 800 m + 200 m jog break, 5 min WD	**Bike 90 min** 40 min BE1, 30 min comp. tempo, 20 min 70.3 tempo	**Swim (pool)** 200 m WU 15 x 200 m comp. tempo, B 0:30, 200 m WD	**Run 90 min** 70 min in BE1, 10 min BE1/BE2 transition zone, 10 min WD	**Swim (open water)** 5 min WU, 8-10 x 2 min at comp. tempo, B 0:30 min, 5 min WD	**Bike 150 min** BE1 with focus on consistent performance
Unit 2	**Core stability** 20 min		**Combination run** BE1	**Core stability** 20 min		**Bike 120 min** 30 min BE1 WU, 2 x (15 min Comp. tempo/ 10 min 70.3 tempo/ 5 min DO-tempo), in between 10 min easy, 20 min easy WD	**Combination run 15 min** First 10 min at 70.3 tempo, then 5 min easy WD
Unit 3		**Mobility 20 min**	**Mobility 10 min**	**Mobility 10 min**	**Mobility 20 min**	**Mobility 10 min**	**Mobility 10 min**

WEEK 16

	Monday	Tuesday	Wednesday	Thursday	Friday	Saturday	Sunday
Unit 1	Day of rest	**Swim (pool)** 300 m WU, 10 x 100 m PBO easy, B 0:10 min, 10 x 50 m hard, B 0:30 min 300 m WD	**Bike 75 min** 20 min WU, 2 x 5–8 min at Comp. Tempo 5–10 min active break, remainder BE1	**Run 30–45 min** Easy tempo with 5 x 100 m acceleration runs	Day of rest	**Bike 45 min** 10 min WU, 3 x 1:30 min Comp. Tempo, B 2–3 min in between, remainder easy WD	Long-distance race
Unit 2		**Run 40 min** 15 min WU, 3 x 1,000 m at comp. tempo minus 15 sec/km, B 3 min passive, 5 min WD	**Combined run 10 min** Deliberately easy tempo, focus on high SF	**Swim (open water)** 5–10 min easy WU, 3 x 1:30 min Comp. Tempo, in between 0:30 min easy, 5–10 min WD		Mobility 10 min	
Unit 3		Mobility 10 min	Mobility 10 min	Mobility 10 min			

2   References

Science and practice belong firmly together. Here is a selection of interesting sources that I use in my day-to-day work as a trainer and whose content helped shape this book. I would be very happy if I could inspire some readers to browse and thus improve their understanding of the science behind the training.

Allen, H., Coggan, A. & McGregor, S. (2020). *Wattmessung im Radsport und Triathlon* (8., aktualisierte Auflage 2020 Aufl.). Delius Klasing.

Amann, M., Wan, H. Y., Thurston, T. S., Georgescu, V. P. & Weavil, J. C. (2020). On the influence of group III/IV muscle afferent feedback on endurance exercise performance. *Exercise and Sport Sciences Reviews, 48* (4), 209-216. https://doi.org/10.1249/jes.0000000000000233

Arellano, R., Terrés-Nicoli, J. & Redondo, J. (2006). Fundamental hydrodynamics of swimming propulsion. *Portuguese Journal of Sport Science – Suppl. Biomechanics and Medicine in Swimming X, 6,* 15-20.

Armstrong, L. E. [L. E.], Curtis, W. C., Hubbard, R. W., Francesconi, R. P., Moore, R. & Askew, E. W. (1993). Symptomatic hyponatremia during prolonged exercise in heat. *Medicine & Science in Sports & Exercise, 25* (5), 543-549.

Armstrong, L. E. [Lawrence E.], Casa, D. J., Maresh, C. M. & Ganio, M. S. (2007). Caffeine, fluid-electrolyte balance, temperature regulation, and exercise-heat tolerance. *Exercise and Sport Sciences Reviews, 35* (3), 135-140. https://doi.org/10.1097/jes.0b013e3180a02cc1

Arnal, P. J., Lapole, T., Erblang, M., Guillard, M., Bourrilhon, C., Léger, D., Chennaoui, M. & Millet, G. Y. (2016). Sleep extension before sleep loss: Effects on performance and neuromuscular function. *Medicine and Science in Sports and Exercise, 48* (8), 1595-1603. https://doi.org/10.1249/mss.0000000000000925

Bachl, N. (Hrsg.). (1991). *Advances in ergometry: With 85 tables.* Springer. https://doi.org/10.1007/978-3-642-76442-4.

Baker, L. B., Chavez, P. J. D. de, Ungaro, C. T., Sopeña, B. C., Nuccio, R. P., Reimel, A. J. & Barnes, K. A. (2019). Exercise intensity effects on total sweat electrolyte losses and regional vs. whole-body sweat Na+, Cl-, and K+. *European Journal of Applied Physiology, 119* (2), 361-375. https://doi.org/10.1007/s00421-018-4048-z

Baker, L. B. & Jeukendrup, A. E. (2014). Optimal composition of fluid-replacement beverages. *Comprehensive Physiology, 4* (2), 575-620. https://doi.org/10.1002/cphy.c130014

Baker, L. B., Stofan, J. R., Hamilton, A. A. & Horswill, C. A. (2009). Comparison of regional patch collection vs. whole body washdown for measuring sweat sodium and potassium loss during exercise. *Journal of Applied Physiology (Bethesda, Md.: 1985), 107* (3), 887-895. https://doi.org/10.1152/japplphysiol.00197.2009

Barber, J. F. P., Thomas, J., Narang, B., Hengist, A., Betts, J. A., Wallis, G. A. & Gonzalez, J. T. (2020). Pectin-alginate does not further enhance exogenous carbohydrate oxidation in running. *Medicine and Science in Sports and Exercise, 52* (6), 1376-1384. https://doi.org/10.1249/MSS.0000000000002262

Barnes, K. A., Anderson, M. L., Stofan, J. R., Dalrymple, K. J., Reimel, A. J., Roberts, T. J., Randell, R. K., Ungaro, C. T. & Baker, L. B. (2019). Normative data for sweating rate, sweat sodium concentration, and sweat sodium loss in athletes: An update and analysis by sport. *Journal of Sports Sciences, 37* (20), 2356-2366. https://doi.org/10.1080/02640414.2019.1633159

Barnes, K. R. & Kilding, A. E. (2019). A randomized crossover study investigating the running economy of highly-trained male and female distance runners in marathon racing shoes versus track spikes. *Sports Medicine (Auckland, N.Z.), 49* (2), 331-342. https://doi.org/10.1007/s40279-018-1012-3

Barry, N., Burton, D., Sheridan, J., Thompson, M. & Brown, N. A. T. (2015). Aerodynamic performance and riding posture in road cycling and triathlon. *Proceedings of the Institution of Mechanical Engineers, Part P: Journal of Sports Engineering and Technology, 229* (1), 28-38. https://doi.org/10.1177/1754337114549876

Barwood, M. J., Gibson, O. R., Gillis, D. J., Jeffries, O., Morris, N. B., Pearce, J., Ross, M. L, Stevens, C., Rinaldi, K., Kounalakis, S. N., Riera, F., Mündel, T., Waldron, M. & Best, R. (2020). Menthol as an ergogenic aid for the Tokyo 2021 Olympic Games: An expert-led consensus statement using the modified Delphi method. *Sports Medicine (Auckland, N.Z.), 50* (10), 1709-1727. https://doi.org/10.1007/s40279-020-01313-9

Bates, D., Mächler, M., Bolker, B. & Walker, S. (2015). Fitting linear mixed-effects models using lme4. *Journal of Statistical Software, 67* (1). https://doi.org/10.18637/jss.v067.i01

Bellinger, P., Desbrow, B., Derave, W., Lievens, E., Irwin, C., Sabapathy, S., Kennedy, B., Craven, J., Pennell, E., Rice, H. & Minahan, C. (2020). Muscle fiber typology is associated with the incidence of overreaching in response to overload training. *Journal of Applied Physiology (Bethesda, Md.: 1985), 129* (4), 823-836. https://doi.org/10.1152/japplphysiol.00314.2020

Bentley, D. J., Millet, G. P., Vleck, V. E. & McNaughton, L. R. (2002). Specific aspects of contemporary triathlon: Implications for physiological analysis and performance. *Sports Medicine (Auckland, N.Z.), 32* (6), 345-359. https://doi.org/10.2165/00007256-200232060-00001

Berger, M. A., Hollander, A. P. & Groot, G. de (1999). Determining propulsive force in front crawl swimming: A comparison of two methods. *Journal of Sports Sciences, 17* (2), 97-105. https://doi.org/10.1080/026404199366190.

Bernard, T. (2003). Effect of cycling cadence on subsequent 3 km running performance in well trained triathletes * Commentary. *British Journal of Sports Medicine – BRIT J SPORT MED, 37*, 154-159. https://doi.org/10.1136/bjsm.37.2.154

Best, R., Payton, S., Spears, I., Riera, F. & Berger, N. (2018). Topical and ingested cooling methodologies for endurance exercise performance in the heat. *Sports (Basel, Switzerland), 6* (1). https://doi.org/10.3390/sports6010011

Billat, L. V. (2001). Interval training for performance: A scientific and empirical practice. Special recommendations for middle- and long-distance running. Part I: aerobic interval training. *Sports Medicine (Auckland, N.Z.), 31* (1), 13-31. https://doi.org/10.2165/00007256-200131010-00002

Björklund, G., Pettersson, S. & Schagatay, E. (2007). Performance predicting factors in prolonged exhausting exercise of varying intensity. *European Journal of Applied Physiology, 99*, 423-429. https://doi.org/10.1007/s00421-006-0352-0

Bonacci, J., Saunders, P. U., Alexander, M., Blanch, P. & Vicenzino, B. (2011). Neuromuscular control and running economy is preserved in elite international triathletes after cycling. *Sports Biomechanics, 10* (1), 59-71. https://doi.org/10.1080/14763141.2010.547593

Bongers, C. C. W. G., Hopman, M. T. E. & Eijsvogels, T. M. H. (2017). Cooling interventions for athletes: An overview of effectiveness, physiological mechanisms, and practical considerations. *Temperature (Austin, Tex.), 4* (1), 60-78. https://doi.org/10.1080/23328940.2016.1277003

Bouchama, A. & Knochel, J. P. (2002). Heat stroke. *The New England Journal of Medicine, 346* (25), 1978-1988. https://doi.org/10.1056/NEJMra011089

Bramble, D. M. & Lieberman, D. E. (2004). Endurance running and the evolution of Homo. *Nature, 432* (7015), 345-352. https://doi.org/10.1038/nature03052

Brisswalter, J., Hausswirth, C., Smith, D., Vercruyssen, F. & Vallier, J. M. (2000). Energetically optimal cadence vs. freely-chosen cadence during cycling: effect of exercise duration. *International Journal of Sports Medicine, 21* (1), 60-64. https://doi.org/10.1055/s-2000-8857

Brodie, M., Walmsley, A. & Page, W. (2008). Comments on "Runners do not push off but fall forward via a gravitational torque" (vol. 6, pp. 434-452). *Sports Biomechanics, 7* (3), 403-5; author reply 406-11. https://doi.org/10.1080/14763140802255804

Brown, M. B., Haack, K. K. V., Pollack, B. P., Millard-Stafford, M. & McCarty, N. A. (2011). Low abundance of sweat duct Cl – channel CFTR in both healthy and cystic fibrosis athletes with exceptionally salty sweat during exercise. *American Journal of Physiology. Regulatory, Integrative and Comparative Physiology, 300* (3), R605-15. https://doi.org/10.1152/ajpregu.00660.2010

Buchheit, M., Laursen, P. B. & Ahmaidi, S. (2007). Parasympathetic reactivation after repeated sprint exercise. *American Journal of Physiology. Heart and Circulatory Physiology, 293* (1), H133-41. https://doi.org/10.1152/ajpheart.00062.2007

Burke, L. M., Hawley, J. A., Jeukendrup, A., Morton, J. P., Stellingwerff, T. & Maughan, R. J. (2018). Toward a common understanding of diet-exercise strategies to manipulate fuel availability for training and competition preparation in endurance sport. *International Journal of Sport Nutrition and Exercise Metabolism, 28* (5), 451-463. https://doi.org/10.1123/ijsnem.2018-0289

Burke, L. M., Hawley, J. A., Wong, S. H. S. & Jeukendrup, A. E. (2011). Carbohydrates for training and competition. *Journal of Sports Sciences, 29 Suppl 1*, S. 17-27. https://doi.org/10.1080/02640414.2011.585473

Burke, L. M., Ross, M. L., Garvican-Lewis, L. A., Welvaert, M., Heikura, I. A., Forbes, S. G., Mirtschin, J. G., Cato, L. E., Strobel, N., Sharma, A. P. & Hawley, J. A. (2017). Low carbohydrate, high fat diet impairs exercise economy and negates the performance benefit from intensified training in elite race walkers. *The Journal of Physiology, 595* (9), 2785-2807. https://doi.org/10.1113/JP273230

Burke, L. M., Whitfield, J., Heikura, I. A., Ross, M. L. R., Tee, N., Forbes, S. F., Hall, R., McKay, A. K. A., Wallett, A. M. & Sharma, A. P. (2021). Adaptation to a low carbohydrate high fat diet is rapid but impairs endurance exercise metabolism and performance despite enhanced glycogen availability. *The Journal of Physiology, 599* (3), 771-790. https://doi.org/10.1113/JP280221

Burrows, M. & Bird, S. (2000). The physiology of the highly trained female endurance runner. *Sports Medicine (Auckland, N.Z.), 30* (4), 281-300. https://doi.org/10.2165/00007256-200030040-00004

Campbell, J. P. & Turner, J. E. (2018). Debunking the myth of exercise-induced immune suppression: Redefining the impact of exercise on immunological health across the lifespan. *Frontiers in Immunology, 9*, 648. https://doi.org/10.3389/fimmu.2018.00648

Carmigniani, R., Seifert, L., Chollet, D. & Clanet, C. (2020). Coordination changes in front-crawl swimming. *Proceedings of the Royal Society A: Mathematical, Physical and Engineering Sciences, 476* (2237), 20200071. https://doi.org/10.1098/rspa.2020.0071

Carr, A. J., Sharma, A. P., Ross, M. L., Welvaert, M., Slater, G. J. & Burke, L. M. (2018). Chronic ketogenic low carbohydrate high fat diet has minimal effects on acid-base status in elite athletes. *Nutrients, 10* (2). https://doi.org/10.3390/nu10020236

Carrard, J., Kloucek, P. & Gojanovic, B. (2020). Modelling training adaptation in swimming using artificial neural network geometric optimisation. *Sports (Basel, Switzerland), 8* (1). https://doi.org/10.3390/sports8010008

Carter, J., Jeukendrup, A. E., Mundel, T. & Jones, D. A. (2003). Carbohydrate supplementation improves moderate and high-intensity exercise in the heat. *Pflugers Archiv: European Journal of Physiology, 446* (2), 211-219. https://doi.org/10.1007/s00424-003-1020-4

Carter, J. M., Jeukendrup, A. E. & Jones, D. A. (2004). The effect of carbohydrate mouth rinse on 1-h cycle time trial performance. *Medicine & Science in Sports & Exercise, 36* (12), 2107-2111. https://doi.org/10.1249/01.mss.0000147585.65709.6f

Casadio, J. R., Kilding, A. E., Cotter, J. D. & Laursen, P. B. (2017). From lab to real world: Heat acclimation considerations for elite athletes. *Sports Medicine (Auckland, N.Z.), 47* (8), 1467-1476. https://doi.org/10.1007/s40279-016-0668-9

Casado, A., Hanley, B., Jiménez-Reyes, P. & Renfree, A. (2020). Pacing profiles and tactical behaviors of elite runners. *Journal of Sport and Health Science.* Vorab-Onlinepublikation. https://doi.org/10.1016/j.jshs.2020.06.011

Castell, L. M., Nieman, D. C., Bermon, S. & Peeling, P. (2019). Exercise-induced illness and inflammation: Can immunonutrition and iron help? *International Journal of Sport Nutrition and Exercise Metabolism, 29* (2), 181-188. https://doi.org/10.1123/ijsnem.2018-0288

Cejuela, R. & Esteve-Lanao, J. (2020). Quantifying the training load in triathlon. In S. Migliorini (Ed.), *Triathlon medicine* (pp. 291-316). Springer International Publishing. https://doi.org/10.1007/978-3-030-22357-1_18

Chang, Y. H., Huang, H. W., Hamerski, C. M. & Kram, R. (2000). The independent effects of gravity and inertia on running mechanics. *The Journal of Experimental Biology, 203* (Pt 2), 229-238.

Cheung, S. S., McGarr, G. W., Mallette, M. M., Wallace, P. J., Watson, C. L., Kim, I. M. & Greenway, M. J. (2015). Separate and combined effects of dehydration and thirst sensation on exercise performance in the heat. *Scandinavian Journal of Medicine & Science in Sports, 25, Suppl 1*, 104-111. https://doi.org/10.1111/sms.12343

Cheuvront, S. N., Carter, R. & Sawka, M. N. (2003). Fluid balance and endurance exercise performance. *Current Sports Medicine Reports, 2* (4), 202-208. https://doi.org/10.1249/00149619-200308000-00006

Chidi-Ogbolu, N. & Baar, K. (2018). Effect of estrogen on musculoskeletal performance and injury risk. *Frontiers in Physiology, 9*, 1834. https://doi.org/10.3389/fphys.2018.01834

Chorley, A. & Lamb, K. L. (2020). The application of critical power, the work capacity above critical power (W′), and its reconstitution: A narrative review of current evidence and implications for cycling training prescription. *Sports (Basel, Switzerland), 8* (9). https://doi.org/10.3390/sports8090123

Chrzanowski-Smith, O. J., Edinburgh, R. M., Thomas, M. P., Haralabidis, N., Williams, S., Betts, J. A. & Gonzalez, J. T. (2020). The day-to-day reliability of peak fat oxidation and FATMAX. *European Journal of Applied Physiology, 120* (8), 1745-1759. https://doi.org/10.1007/s00421-020-04397-3

Cipryan, L., Plews, D. J., Ferretti, A., Maffetone, P. B. & Laursen, P. B. (2018). Effects of a 4-week very low-carbohydrate diet on high-intensity interval training responses. *Journal of Sports Science & Medicine, 17* (2), 259-268.

Close, G. L., Kasper, A. M. & Morton, J. P. (2019). From paper to podium: Quantifying the translational potential of performance nutrition research. *Sports Medicine (Auckland, N.Z.), 49* (Suppl 1), 25-37. https://doi.org/10.1007/s40279-018-1005-2

Collie, J. T. B., Massie, R. J., Jones, O. A. H., LeGrys, V. A. & Greaves, R. F. (2014). Sixty-five years since the New York heat wave: Advances in sweat testing for cystic fibrosis. *Pediatric Pulmonology, 49* (2), 106-117. https://doi.org/10.1002/ppul.22945

Costa, R. J. S., Gaskell, S. K., McCubbin, A. J. & Snipe, R. M. J. (2020). Exertional-heat stress-associated gastrointestinal perturbations during Olympic sports: Management strategies for athletes preparing and competing in the 2020 Tokyo Olympic Games. *Temperature (Austin, Tex.), 7* (1), 58-88. https://doi.org/10.1080/23328940.2019.1597676

Couto, J. G. M. D., Franken, M. & Castro, F. A. d. S. (2015). Influência de diferentes padrões respiratórios na cinemática do nado crawl. *Revista Brasileira de Cineantropometria e Desempenho Humano, 17* (1), 82. https://doi.org/10.5007/1980-0037.2015v17n1p82

Crewe, H., Tucker, R. & Noakes, T. D. (2008). The rate of increase in rating of perceived exertion predicts the duration of exercise to fatigue at a fixed power output in different environmental conditions. *European Journal of Applied Physiology, 103* (5), 569-577. https://doi.org/10.1007/s00421-008-0741-7

Crowcroft, S., Duffield, R., McCleave, E., Slattery, K., Wallace, L. K. & Coutts, A. J. (2015). Monitoring training to assess changes in fitness and fatigue: The effects of training in heat and hypoxia. *Scandinavian Journal of Medicine & Science in Sports, 25, Suppl 1,* 287-295. https://doi.org/10.1111/sms.12364

Da Rosa, R. G., Oliveira, H. B., Gomeñuka, N. A., Masiero, M. P. B., Da Silva, E. S., Zanardi, A. P. J., Carvalho, A. R. de, Schons, P. & Peyré-Tartaruga, L. A. (2019). Landing-takeoff asymmetries applied to running mechanics: A new perspective for performance. *Frontiers in Physiology, 10,* 415. https://doi.org/10.3389/fphys.2019.00415

Da Rosa, R. G., Oliveira, H. B. de, Ardigò, L. P., Gomeñuka, N. A., Fischer, G. & Peyré-Tartaruga, L. A. (2019). Running stride length and rate are changed and mechanical efficiency is preserved after cycling in middle-level triathletes. *Scientific Reports, 9* (1), 18422. https://doi.org/10.1038/s41598-019-54912-6

Daanen, H. A. M., Racinais, S. & Périard, J. D. (2018). Heat acclimation decay and re-induction: A systematic review and meta-analysis. *Sports Medicine (Auckland, N.Z.), 48* (2), 409-430. https://doi.org/10.1007/s40279-017-0808-x

Dickhuth, H. H., Huonker, M., Münzel, T., Drexler, H., Berg, A. & Keul, J. (1991). Individual anaerobic threshold for evaluation of competitive athletes and patients with left ventricular dysfunction. In N. Bachl (Ed.), *Advances in ergometry: With 85 tables* (pp. 173-179). Springer. https://doi.org/10.1007/978-3-642-76442-4_26

Doherty, C., Keogh, A., Davenport, J., Lawlor, A., Smyth, B. & Caulfield, B. (2020). An evaluation of the training determinants of marathon performance: A meta-analysis with meta-regression. *Journal of Science and Medicine in Sport, 23* (2), 182-188. https://doi.org/10.1016/j.jsams.2019.09.013

Downs, N. J., Axelsen, T., Parisi, A. V., Schouten, P. W. & Dexter, B. R. (2020). Measured UV exposures of ironman, sprint and olympic-distance triathlon competitors. *Atmosphere, 11* (5), 440. https://doi.org/10.3390/atmos11050440

Du Plessis, C., Blazevich, A. J., Abbiss, C. & Wilkie, J. C. (2020). Running economy and effort after cycling: Effect of methodological choices. *Journal of Sports Sciences, 38* (10), 1105-1114. https://doi.org/10.1080/02640414.2020.1742962

Düking, P., Giessing, L., Frenkel, M. O., Koehler, K., Holmberg, H. C. & Sperlich, B. (2020). Wrist-worn wearables for monitoring heart rate and energy expenditure while sitting or performing light-to-vigorous physical activity: Validation study. *JMIR Health and Health, 8* (5), e16716. https://doi.org/10.2196/16716

Düking, P., Zinner, C., Reed, J. L., Holmberg, H. C. & Sperlich, B. (2020). Predefined vs data-guided training prescription based on autonomic nervous system variation: A systematic review. *Scandinavian Journal of Medicine & Science in Sports, 30* (12), 2291-2304. https://doi.org/10.1111/sms.13802

Earhart, E. L., Weiss, E. P., Rahman, R. & Kelly, P. V. (2015). Effects of oral sodium supplementation on indices of thermoregulation in trained, endurance athletes. *Journal of Sports Science & Medicine, 14* (1), 172-178.

Egan, B. & Zierath, J. R. (2013). Exercise metabolism and the molecular regulation of skeletal muscle adaptation. *Cell Metabolism, 17* (2), 162-184. https://doi.org/10.1016/j.cmet.2012.12.012

Egan-Shuttler, J. D., Edmonds, R. & Ives, S. J. (2020). The efficacy of heart rate variability in tracking travel and training stress in youth female rowers: A preliminary study. *Journal of Strength and Conditioning Research, 34* (11), 3293-3300. https://doi.org/10.1519/jsc.0000000000002499

Ehlert, A. M., Twiddy, H. M. & Wilson, P. B. (2020). The effects of caffeine mouth rinsing on exercise performance: A systematic review. *International Journal of Sport Nutrition and Exercise Metabolism*, 1-12. https://doi.org/10.1123/ijsnem.2020-0083

Elliott-Sale, K. J., McNulty, K. L., Ansdell, P., Goodall, S., Hicks, K. M., Thomas, K., Swinton, P. A. & Dolan, E. (2020). The effects of oral contraceptives on exercise performance in women: A systematic review and meta-analysis. *Sports Medicine (Auckland, N.Z.), 50* (10), 1785-1812. https://doi.org/10.1007/s40279-020-01317-5

Emmonds, S., Heyward, O. & Jones, B. (2019). The challenge of applying and undertaking research in female sport. *Sports Medicine – Open, 5* (1), 51. https://doi.org/10.1186/s40798-019-0224-x

Etxebarria, N., Anson, J. M., Pyne, D. B. & Ferguson, R. A. (2014). High-intensity cycle interval training improves cycling and running performance in triathletes. *European Journal of Sport Science, 14* (6), 521-529. https://doi.org/10.1080/17461391.2013.853841

Farley, C. T. & González, O. (1996). Leg stiffness and stride frequency in human running. *Journal of Biomechanics, 29* (2), 181-186. https://doi.org/10.1016/0021-9290(95)00029-1

Festa, L., Tarperi, C., Skroce, K., La Torre, A. & Schena, F. (2019). Effects of different training intensity distribution in recreational runners. *Frontiers in Sports and Active Living, 1*, 70. https://doi.org/10.3389/fspor.2019.00070

Figueiredo, P., Zamparo, P., Sousa, A., Vilas-Boas, J. P. & Fernandes, R. J. (2011). An energy balance of the 200 m front crawl race. *European Journal of Applied Physiology, 111* (5), 767-777. https://doi.org/10.1007/s00421-010-1696-z

Filipas, L., Gallo, G., Pollastri, L. & La Torre, A. (2019). Mental fatigue impairs time trial performance in sub-elite under 23 cyclists. *PloS one, 14* (6), e0218405. https://doi.org/10.1371/ journal.pone.0218405

Fiorenza, M., Gunnarsson, T. P., Hostrup, M., Iaia, F. M., Schena, F., Pilegaard, H. & Bangsbo, J. (2018). Metabolic stress-dependent regulation of the mitochondrial biogenic molecular response to high-intensity exercise in human skeletal muscle. *The Journal of Physiology, 596* (14), 2823-2840. https://doi.org/10.1113/JP275972

Fletcher, G., Bartlett, R., Romanov, N. & Fotouhi, A. (2008). Pose® method technique improves running performance without economy changes. *International Journal of Sports Science & Coaching, 3* (3), 365-380. https://doi.org/10.1260/174795408786238506

Flood, T. R. (2018). Menthol use for performance in hot environments. *Current Sports Medicine Reports, 17* (4), 135-139. https://doi.org/10.1249/JSR.0000000000000474

Forbes, S. C., Candow, D. G., Smith-Ryan, A. E., Hirsch, K. R., Roberts, M. D., Van Dusseldorp, T. A., Stratton, M. T., Kaviani, M. & Little, J. P. (2020). Supplements and nutritional interventions to augment high-intensity interval training physiological and performance adaptations – a narrative review. *Nutrients, 12* (2). https://doi.org/10.3390/nu12020390

Fuchs, C. J., Gonzalez, J. T. & van Loon, L. J. C. (2019). Fructose co-ingestion to increase carbohydrate availability in athletes. *The Journal of Physiology, 597* (14), 3549-3560. https://doi.org/10.1113/JP277116

Garcia, A. M. C., Lacerda, M. G., Fonseca, I. A. T., Reis, F. M., Rodrigues, L. O. C. & Silami-Garcia, E. (2006). Luteal phase of the menstrual cycle increases sweating rate during exercise. *Brazilian Journal of Medical and Biological Research = Revista brasileira de pesquisas medicas e biologicas, 39* (9), 1255-1261. https://doi.org/10.1590/s0100-879x2006005000007

García-Pinillos, F., Roche-Seruendo, L. E., Marcén-Cinca, N., Marco-Contreras, L. A. & Latorre-Román, P. A. (2021). Absolute reliability and concurrent validity of the Stryd system for the assessment of running stride kinematics at different velocities. *Journal of Strength and Conditioning Research, 35* (1), 78-84. https://doi.org/10.1519/JSC.0000000000002595

García-Pinillos, F., Soto-Hermoso, V. M., Latorre-Román, P. Á., Párraga-Montilla, J. A. & Roche-Seruendo, L. E. (2019). How does power during running change when measured at different time intervals? *International Journal of Sports Medicine, 40* (9), 609-613. https://doi.org/10.1055/a-0946-2159

Garvican-Lewis, L. A., Clark, B., Martin, D. T., Schumacher, Y. O., McDonald, S., Stephens, B., Ma, F., Thompson, K. G., Gore, C. J. & Menaspà, P. (2015). Impact of altitude on power output during cycling stage racing. *PloS one, 10* (12), e0143028. https://doi.org/10.1371/journal.pone.0143028

Gibson, O. R., James, C. A., Mee, J. A., Willmott, A. G. B., Turner, G., Hayes, M. & Maxwell, N. S. (2020). Heat alleviation strategies for athletic performance: A review and practitioner guidelines. *Temperature (Austin, Tex.), 7* (1), 3-36. https://doi.org/10.1080/23328940.2019.1666624

Gibson, O. R., Willmott, A. G. B., James, C. A., Hayes, M. & Maxwell, N. S. (2017). Power relative to body mass best predicts change in core temperature during exercise-heat stress. *Journal of Strength and Conditioning Research, 31* (2), 403-414. https://doi.org/10.1519/JSC.0000000000001521

Gil, J. M., Moreno, L.M. G., Mahiques, J. B. & Muñoz, V. T. (2012). Analysis on the time and frequency domains of the acceleration in front crawl stroke. *Journal of Human Kinetics, 32*, 109-120. https://doi.org/10.2478/v10078-012-0028-2

Gilgen-Ammann, R., Buller, M., Bitterle, J. L., Delves, S. K., Veenstra, B. J., Roos, L., Beeler, N. & Wyss, T. (2018). Evaluation of pulse rate measurement with a wrist worn device during different tasks and physical activity. *Current Issues in Sport Science (CISS)*. Vorab-Onlinepublikation. https://doi.org/10.15203/CISS_2018.011

Giorgi, A., Sanders, D., Vicini, M., Lukaski, H. & Gatterer, H. (2018). Body fluid status, plasma volume change and its relationship to physical effort during a multistage professional road cycling race. *International Journal of Performance Analysis in Sport, 18* (5), 679-685. https://doi.org/10.1080/24748668.2018.1514564

Girard, O., Brocherie, F., Goods, P. S. R. & Millet, G. P. (2020). An updated panorama of "living low – training high" altitude/hypoxic methods. *Frontiers in Sports and Active Living, 2*, 26. https://doi.org/10.3389/fspor.2020.00026

Gonzalez, R. R., Cheuvront, S. N., Ely, B. R., Moran, D. S., Hadid, A., Endrusick, T. L. & Sawka, M. N. (2012). Sweat rate prediction equations for outdoor exercise with transient solar radiation. *Journal of Applied Physiology (Bethesda, Md.: 1985), 112* (8), 1300-1310. https://doi.org/10.1152/japplphysiol.01056.2011

González Parra, G. C. (2009). Optimization of swimming performance in triathlon. *Journal of Human Sport and Exercise, 4* (1), 69-71. https://doi.org/10.4100/jhse.2009.41.08

González-Alonso, J., Crandall, C. G. & Johnson, J. M. (2008). The cardiovascular challenge of exercising in the heat. *The Journal of Physiology, 586* (1), 45-53. https://doi.org/10.1113/jphysiol.2007.142158

Gottschall, J. & Palmer, B. M. (2002). The acute effects of prior cycling cadence on running performance and kinematics. *Medicine & Science in Sports & Exercise, 34*, 1518-1522. https://doi.org/10.1249/01.MSS.000002771.03976.B6

Gourgoulis, V., Aggeloussis, N., Vezos, N. & Mavromatis, G. (2006). Effect of two different sized hand paddles on the front crawl stroke kinematics. *The Journal of Sports Medicine and Physical Fitness, 46* (2), 232-237.

Griffiths, A., Shannon, O. M., Matu, J., King, R., Deighton, K. & O'Hara, J. P. (2019). The effects of environmental hypoxia on substrate utilisation during exercise: A meta-analysis. *Journal of the International Society of Sports Nutrition, 16* (1), 10. https://doi.org/10.1186/s12970-019-0277-8

Guezennec, C. Y., Vallier, J. M., Bigard, A. X. & Durey, A. (1996). Increase in energy cost of running at the end of a triathlon. *European Journal of Applied Physiology and Occupational Physiology, 73* (5), 440-445. https://doi.org/10.1007/bf00334421

Guy, J. H., Deakin, G. B., Edwards, A. M., Miller, C. M. & Pyne, D. B. (2015). Adaptation to hot environmental conditions: An exploration of the performance basis, procedures and future directions to optimise opportunities for elite athletes. *Sports Medicine (Auckland, N.Z.), 45* (3), 303-311. https://doi.org/10.1007/s40279-014-0277-4

Halsey, L. G. & Bryce, C. M. (2021). Are humans evolved specialists for running in the heat? Man vs. horse races provide empirical insights. *Experimental Physiology, 106* (1), 258-268. https://doi.org/10.1113/ep088502

Halson, S. (2013). Sleep and the elite athlete. *Sports Sci, 26,* 1-4.

Halson, S. L., Burke, L. M. & Pearce, J. (2019). Nutrition for travel: From jet lag to catering. *International Journal of Sport Nutrition and Exercise Metabolism, 29* (2), 228-235. https://doi.org/10.1123/ijsnem.2018-0278

Halvorsen, F. A., Lyng, J., Glomsaker, T. & Ritland, S. (1990). Gastrointestinal disturbances in marathon runners. *British Journal of Sports Medicine, 24* (4), 266-268. https://doi.org/10.1136/bjsm.24.4.266

Halvorsen, F. A. & Ritland, S. (1992). Gastrointestinal problems related to endurance event training. *Sports Medicine (Auckland, N.Z.), 14* (3), 157-163. https://doi.org/10.2165/00007256-199214030-00002

Hansen, E. A., Emanuelsen, A., Gertsen, R. M. & Sørensen S, S. R. (2014). Improved marathon performance by in-race nutritional strategy intervention. *International Journal of Sport Nutrition and Exercise Metabolism, 24* (6), 645-655. https://doi.org/10.1123/ijsnem.2013-0130

Hanstock, H. G., Ainegren, M. & Stenfors, N. (2020). Exercise in sub-zero temperatures and airway health: Implications for athletes with special focus on heat-and-moisture-exchanging breathing devices. *Frontiers in Sports and Active Living, 2,* 34. https://doi.org/10.3389/fspor.2020.00034

Hausswirth, C., Bigard, A. X., Berthelot, M., Thomaïdis, M. & Guezennec, C. Y. (1996). Variability in energy cost of running at the end of a triathlon and a marathon. *International Journal of Sports Medicine, 17* (8), 572-579. https://doi.org/10.1055/s-2007-972897

Heikura, I. A., Burke, L. M., Hawley, J. A., Ross, M. L., Garvican-Lewis, L., Sharma, A. P., McKay, A. K. A., Leckey, J. J., Welvaert, M., McCall, L. & Ackerman, K. E. (2019). A short-term ketogenic diet impairs markers of bone health in response to exercise. *Frontiers in Endocrinology, 10,* 880. https://doi.org/10.3389/fendo.2019.00880

Hew-Butler, T., Ayus, J. C., Kipps, C., Maughan, R. J., Mettler, S., Meeuwisse, W. H., Page, A. J., Reid, S. A., Rehrer, N. J., Roberts, W. O., Rogers, I. R., Rosner, M. H., Siegel, A. J., Speedy, D. B., Stuempfle, K. J., Verbalis, J. G., Weschler, L. B. & Wharam, P. (2008). Statement of the Second International Exercise-Associated Hyponatremia Consensus Development Conference, New Zealand, 2007. *Clinical Journal of Sport Medicine: Official Journal of the Canadian Academy of Sport Medicine, 18* (2), 111-121. https://doi.org/10.1097/JSM.0b013e318168ff31

Hew-Butler, T. D., Eskin, C., Bickham, J., Rusnak, M. & VanderMeulen, M. (2018). Dehydration is how you define it: Comparison of 318 blood and urine athlete spot checks. *BMJ Open Sport & Exercise Medicine, 4* (1), e000297. https://doi.org/10.1136/ bmjsem-2017-000297

Hill, D. W., Riojas, A. E., McFarlin, B. K. & Vingren, J. L. (2020). An alternative to oxygen deficit as a way to quantify anaerobic contributions in running. *Journal of Human Sport and Exercise, 15* (4). https://doi.org/10.14198/jhse.2020.154.11

Hodson-Tole, E. F., Blake, O. M. & Wakeling, J. M. (2020). During cycling what limits maximum mechanical power output at cadences above 120 rpm? *Medicine and Science in Sports and Exercise, 52* (1), 214-224. https://doi.org/10.1249/MSS.0000000000002096

Hoffman, M. D. & Stuempfle, K. J. (2016). Is sodium supplementation necessary to avoid dehydration during prolonged exercise in the heat? *Journal of Strength and Conditioning Research, 30* (3), 615-620. https://doi.org/10.1519/JSC.0000000000001138

Hoogkamer, W., Kipp, S., Frank, J. H., Farina, E. M., Luo, G. & Kram, R. (2018). A comparison of the energetic cost of running in marathon racing shoes. *Sports Medicine (Auckland, N.Z.), 48* (4), 1009-1019. https://doi.org/10.1007/s40279-017-0811-2

Hosokawa, Y., Johnson, E. N., Jardine, J. F., Stearns, R. L. & Casa, D. J. (2019). Knowledge and belief toward heat safety and hydration strategies among runners: A preliminary evaluation. *Journal of Athletic Training, 54* (5), 541-549. https://doi.org/10.4085/1062-6050-520-17

Hue, O., Le Gallais, D., Chollet, D., Boussana, A. & Préfaut, C. (1998). The influence of prior cycling on biomechanical and cardiorespiratory response profiles during running in triathletes. *European Journal of Applied Physiology and Occupational Physiology, 77* (1-2), 98-105. https://doi.org/10.1007/s004210050306

Hue, O., Chabert, C., Collado, A. & Hermand, E. (2019). Menthol as an adjuvant to help athletes cope with a tropical climate: Tracks from heat experiments with special focus on Guadeloupe Investigations. *Frontiers in Physiology, 10*, 1360. https://doi.org/10.3389/fphys.2019.01360

Hulme, A., Thompson, J., Nielsen, R. O., Read, G. J. M. & Salmon, P. M. (2019). Towards a complex systems approach in sports injury research: Simulating running-related injury development with agent-based modelling. *British Journal of Sports Medicine, 53* (9), 560. https://doi.org/10.1136/bjsports-2017-098871

Hulston, C. J. & Jeukendrup, A. E. (2008). Substrate metabolism and exercise performance with caffeine and carbohydrate intake. *Medicine and Science in Sports and Exercise, 40* (12), 2096-2104. https://doi.org/10.1249/MSS.0b013e318182a9c7

Hulston, C. J. & Jeukendrup, A. E. (2009). No placebo effect from carbohydrate intake during prolonged exercise. *International Journal of Sport Nutrition and Exercise Metabolism, 19* (3), 275-284. https://doi.org/10.1123/ijsnem.19.3.275

Hulston, C. J., Wallis, G. A. & Jeukendrup, A. E. (2009). Exogenous CHO oxidation with glucose plus fructose intake during exercise. *Medicine and Science in Sports and Exercise, 41* (2), 357-363. https://doi.org/10.1249/MSS.0b013e3181857ee6

Hunter, I. & Smith, G. A. (2007). Preferred and optimal stride frequency, stiffness and economy: Changes with fatigue during a 1-h high-intensity run. *European Journal of Applied Physiology, 100* (6), 653-661. https://doi.org/10.1007/s00421-007-0456-1

Hyldahl, R. D. & Peake, J. M. (2020). Combining cooling or heating applications with exercise training to enhance performance and muscle adaptations. *Journal of Applied Physiology (Bethesda, Md.: 1985), 129* (2), 353-365. https://doi.org/10.1152/japplphysiol.00322.2020.

Ichinose-Kuwahara, T., Inoue, Y., Iseki, Y., Hara, S., Ogura, Y. & Kondo, N. (2010). Sex differences in the effects of physical training on sweat gland responses during a graded exercise. *Experimental Physiology, 95* (10), 1026-1032. https://doi.org/10.1113/expphysiol.2010.053710

Jay, O. & Morris, N. B. (2018). Does cold water or ice slurry ingestion during exercise elicit a net body cooling effect in the heat? *Sports Medicine (Auckland, N.Z.), 48* (Suppl 1), 17-29. https://doi.org/10.1007/s40279-017-0842-8

Jeffries, O., Goldsmith, M. & Waldron, M. (2018). L-menthol mouth rinse or ice slurry ingestion during the latter stages of exercise in the heat provide a novel stimulus to enhance performance despite elevation in mean body temperature. *European Journal of Applied Physiology, 118* (11), 2435-2442. https://doi.org/10.1007/s00421-018-3970-4

Jeffries, O., Waldron, M., Patterson, S. D. & Galna, B. (2019). An analysis of variability in power output during indoor and outdoor cycling time trials. *International Journal of Sports Physiology and Performance*, 1273-1279. https://doi.org/10.1123/ijspp.2018-0539

Jentjens, R. L. P. G., Achten, J. & Jeukendrup, A. E. (2004). High oxidation rates from combined carbohydrates ingested during exercise. *Medicine & Science in Sports & Exercise, 36* (9), 1551-1558. https://doi.org/10.1249/01.mss.0000139796.07843.1d

Jentjens, R. L. P. G. & Jeukendrup, A. E. (2005). High rates of exogenous carbohydrate oxidation from a mixture of glucose and fructose ingested during prolonged cycling exercise. *The British Journal of Nutrition, 93* (4), 485-492. https://doi.org/10.1079/bjn20041368

Jentjens, R. L. P. G., Venables, M. C. & Jeukendrup, A. E. (2004). Oxidation of exogenous glucose, sucrose, and maltose during prolonged cycling exercise. *Journal of Applied Physiology (Bethesda, Md.: 1985), 96* (4), 1285-1291. https://doi.org/10.1152/japplphysiol.01023.2003

Jeukendrup, A. E. & Moseley, L. (2010). Multiple transportable carbohydrates enhance gastric emptying and fluid delivery. *Scandinavian Journal of Medicine & Science in Sports, 20* (1), 112-121. https://doi.org/10.1111/j.1600-0838.2008.00862.x

Jeukendrup, A. (2013). The new carbohydrate intake recommendations. *Nestle Nutrition Institute Workshop Series, 75*, 63-71. https://doi.org/10.1159/000345820

Jeukendrup, A., Rollo, I. & Carter, J. (2013). Carbohydrate mouth rinse: Performance effects and mechanisms. In W. M. Adams & J. F. Jardine (2020), *Exertional heat illness.* Springer International Publishing. https://doi.org/10.1007/978-3-030-27805-2

Jeukendrup, A. (2014). A step towards personalized sports nutrition: Carbohydrate intake during exercise. *Sports Medicine (Auckland, N.Z.), 44, Suppl 1*, S25-33. https://doi.org/10.1007/s40279-014-0148-z

Jeukendrup, A. E. (2010). Carbohydrate and exercise performance: The role of multiple transportable carbohydrates. *Current Opinion in Clinical Nutrition and Metabolic Care, 13* (4), 452-457. https://doi.org/10.1097/MCO.0b013e328339de9f

Jeukendrup, A. E. (2011). Nutrition for endurance sports: Marathon, triathlon, and road cycling. *Journal of Sports Sciences, 29 Suppl 1*, S91-9. https://doi.org/10.1080/02640414.2011.610348

Jeukendrup, A. E. (2013). Oral carbohydrate rinse: placebo or beneficial? *Current Sports Medicine Reports, 12* (4), 222-227. https://doi.org/10.1249/JSR.0b013e31829a6caa

Jeukendrup, A. E. (2017). Periodized nutrition for athletes. *Sports Medicine (Auckland, N.Z.), 47, (Suppl 1)*, 51-63. https://doi.org/10.1007/s40279-017-0694-2

Jeukendrup, A. E. (2017). Training the gut for athletes. *Sports Medicine (Auckland, N.Z.), 47, (Suppl 1)*, 101-110. https://doi.org/10.1007/s40279-017-0690-6

Jeukendrup, A. E., Currell, K., Clarke, J., Cole, J. & Blannin, A. K. (2009). Effect of beverage glucose and sodium content on fluid delivery. *Nutrition & Metabolism, 6*, 9. https://doi.org/10.1186/1743-7075-6-9

Julian, R., Hecksteden, A., Fullagar, H. H. K. & Meyer, T. (2017). The effects of menstrual cycle phase on physical performance in female soccer players. *PloS One, 12* (3), e0173951. https://doi.org/10.1371/journal.pone.0173951

Keller, S., Kohne, S., Bloch, W. & Schumann, M. (2021). Comparison of two different cooling systems in alleviating thermal and physiological strain during prolonged exercise in the heat. *Ergonomics, 64* (1), 129-138. https://doi.org/10.1080/00140139.2020.1818835

Kenefick, R. W. (2018). Drinking strategies: Planned drinking versus drinking to thirst. *Sports Medicine (Auckland, N.Z.), 48*, (Suppl 1), 31-37. https://doi.org/10.1007/s40279-017-0844-6

Kipp, S., Kram, R. & Hoogkamer, W. (2019). Extrapolating metabolic savings in running: Implications for performance predictions. *Frontiers in Physiology, 10*, 79. https://doi.org/10.3389/fphys.2019.00079

Knechtle, B., Nikolaidis, P. T., Rosemann, T. & Rüst, C. A. (2016). Der Ironman-Triathlon [Ironman Triathlon]. *Praxis, 105* (13), 761-773. https://doi.org/10.1024/1661-8157/a002369

Koehler, K. (2020). Energy deficiency and nutrition in endurance sports – focus on rowing. *Deutsche Zeitschrift für Sportmedizin, 71* (1), 5-10. https://doi.org/10.5960/dzsm.2019.409

Kopetschny, H., Rowlands, D., Popovich, D. & Thomson, J. (2018). Long-distance triathletes' intentions to manipulate energy and macronutrient intake over a training macrocycle. *International Journal of Sport Nutrition and Exercise Metabolism, 28* (5), 515-521. https://doi.org/10.1123/ijsnem.2017-0135

Kreider, R. B., Boone, T., Thompson, W. R., Burkes, S. & Cortes, C. W. (1988). Cardiovascular and thermal responses of triathlon performance. *Medicine & Science in Sports & Exercise, 20* (4), 385-390. https://doi.org/10.1249/00005768-198808000-00010

Krüger, R. L., Aboodarda, S. J., Jaimes, L. M., MacIntosh, B. R., Samozino, P. & Millet, G. Y. (2019). Fatigue and recovery measured with dynamic properties versus isometric force: Effects of exercise intensity. *The Journal of Experimental Biology, 222* (Pt 9). https://doi.org/10.1242/jeb.197483

Kumstát, M., Hlinský, T., Struhár, I. & Thomas, A. (2018). Does sodium citrate cause the same ergogenic effect as sodium bicarbonate on swimming performance? *Journal of Human Kinetics, 65*, 89-98. https://doi.org/10.2478/hukin-2018-0022

Kunz, D. (2016). Schlaf, circadiane Rhythmen und Olympische Spiele in Rio 2016. *Leistungssport, 46* (4), 5-8. https://www.iat.uni-leipzig.de/datenbanken/iks/open_archive/ls/lsp16_04_5_8.pdf

Lamberts, R. P. (2014). Predicting cycling performance in trained to elite male and female cyclists. *International Journal of Sports Physiology and Performance, 9* (4), 610614. https://doi.org/10.1123/ijspp.2013-0040a

Landers, G. J., Blanksby, B. A., Ackland, T. R. & Monson, R. (2008). Swim positioning and its influence on triathlon outcome. *International Journal of Exercise Science, 1* (3), 96-105.

Larsen, E. L., Poulsen, H. E., Michaelsen, C., Kjær, L. K., Lyngbæk, M., Andersen, E. S., Petersen-Bønding, C., Lemoine, C., Gillum, M., Jørgensen, N. R., Ploug, T., Vilsbøll, T., Knop, F. K. & Karstoft, K. (2020). Differential time responses in inflammatory and oxidative stress markers after a marathon: An observational study. *Journal of Sports Sciences, 38* (18), 2080-2091. https://doi.org/10.1080/02640414.2020.1770918

Laursen, P. B. (2016). From science to practice: Development of a thermally-insulated ice slushy dispensing bottle that helps athletes "keep their cool" in hot temperatures. *Temperature (Austin, Tex.), 3* (2), 187-190. https://doi.org/10.1080/23328940.2016.1165786

Laursen, P. B. & Jenkins, D. G. (2002). The scientific basis for high-intensity interval training: Optimising training programmes and maximising performance in highly trained endurance athletes. *Sports Medicine (Auckland, N.Z.), 32* (1), 53-73. https://doi.org/10.2165/00007256-200232010-00003

Lee, J. K. W., Koh, A. C. H., Koh, S. X. T., Liu, G. J. X., Nio, A. Q. X. & Fan, P. W. P. (2014). Neck cooling and cognitive performance following exercise-induced hyperthermia. *European Journal of Applied Physiology, 114* (2), 375-384. https://doi.org/10.1007/s00421-013-2774-9

Lee, J. F., Brown, S. R., Lange, A. P. & Brothers, R. M. (2013). Effect of an aerodynamic helmet on head temperature, core temperature, and cycling power compared with a traditional helmet. *Journal of Strength and Conditioning Research, 27* (12), 3402-3411. https://doi.org/10.1519/JSC.0b013e318291b29f

Legerlotz, K. & Hansen, M. (2020). Editorial: Female hormones: Effect on musculoskeletal adaptation and injury risk. *Frontiers in Physiology, 11,* 628. https://doi.org/10.3389/fphys.2020.00628

Leong, C. (2014). The influence of noncircular chainrings on maximal and submaximal cycling performance. In.

Levels, K., Koning, J. de, Broekhuijzen, I., Zwaan, T., Foster, C. & Daanen, H. (2014). Effects of radiant heat exposure on pacing pattern during a 15-km cycling time trial. *Journal of Sports Sciences, 32* (9), 845-852. https://doi.org/10.1080/02640414.2013.862843

Lieberman, D. E. & Bramble, D. M. (2007). The evolution of marathon running: Capabilities in humans. *Sports Medicine (Auckland, N.Z.), 37* (4-5), 288-290. https://doi.org/10.2165/00007256-200737040-00004

Lievens, E., Bellinger, P., van Vossel, K., Vancompernolle, J., Bex, T., Minahan, C. & Derave, W. (2020). Muscle typology of world-class cyclists across various disciplines and events. *Medicine and Science in Sports and Exercise.* Vorab-Onlinepublikation. https://doi.org/10.1249/MSS.0000000000002518

Lievens, E., Klass, M., Bex, T. & Derave, W. (2020). Muscle fiber typology substantially influences time to recover from high-intensity exercise. *Journal of Applied Physiology (Bethesda, Md.: 1985), 128* (3), 648-659. https://doi.org/10.1152/japplphysiol.00636.2019

Logan-Sprenger, H. M., Heigenhauser, G. J. F., Killian, K. J. & Spriet, L. L. (2012). Effects of dehydration during cycling on skeletal muscle metabolism in females. *Medicine and Science in Sports and Exercise, 44* (10), 1949-1957. https://doi.org/10.1249/MSS.0b013e31825abc7c

Lorenzo, S., Halliwill, J. R., Sawka, M. N. & Minson, C. T. (2010). Heat acclimation improves exercise performance. *Journal of Applied Physiology (Bethesda, Md.: 1985), 109* (4), 1140-1147. https://doi.org/10.1152/japplphysiol.00495.2010.

Lowdon, B. J., McKenzie, D. & Ridge, B. R. (1992). Effects of clothing and water temperature on swim performance [Auswirkungen der Bekleidung und der Wassertemperatur auf die Schwimmleistung]. *Australian Journal of Science & Medicine in Sport, 24* (2), 33-38.

Ludyga, S., Hottenrott, K. & Gronwald, T. (2017). Four weeks of high cadence training alter brain cortical activity in cyclists. *Journal of Sports Sciences, 35* (14), 1377-1382. https://doi.org/1 0.1080/02640414.2016.1198045

Luna, N. M., Alonso, A. C., Brech, G. C., Mochizuki, L., Nakano, E. Y. & Greve, J. M. (2012). Isokinetic analysis of ankle and ground reaction forces in runners and triathletes. *Clinics, 67* (9), 1023-1028. https://doi.org/10.6061/clinics/2012(09)07

MacInnis, M. J. & Gibala, M. J. (2017). Physiological adaptations to interval training and the role of exercise intensity. *The Journal of Physiology, 595* (9), 2915-2930. https://doi.org/10.1113/JP273196

Main, L. & Grove, J. R. (2009). A multi-component assessment model for monitoring training distress among athletes. *European Journal of Sport Science, 9* (4), 195-202. https://doi.org/10.1080/17461390902818260

Martin, K., Staiano, W., Menaspà, P., Hennessey, T., Marcora, S., Keegan, R., Thompson, K. G., Martin, D., Halson, S. & Rattray, B. (2016). Superior inhibitory control and resistance to mental fatigue in professional road cyclists. *PloS One, 11* (7), e0159907. https://doi.org/10.1371/journal.pone.0159907

Maughan, R. J., Shirreffs, S. M. & Watson, P. (2007). Exercise, heat, hydration and the brain. *Journal of the American College of Nutrition, 26*, (5 Suppl), 604S-612S. https://doi.org/10.1080/07315724.2007.10719666

Maughan, R. J., Merson, S. J., Broad, N. P. & Shirreffs, S. M. (2004). Fluid and electrolyte intake and loss in elite soccer players during training. International *Journal of Sport Nutrition and Exercise Metabolism, 14* (3), 333-346. https://doi.org/10.1123/ijsnem.14.3.333

Maughan, R. J. & Shirreffs, S. M. (2019). Muscle cramping during exercise: Causes, solutions, and questions remaining. *Sports Medicine (Auckland, N.Z.), 49*, (Suppl 2), 115-124. https://doi.org/10.1007/s40279-019-01162-1

Maughan, R. J., Shirreffs, S. M. & Leiper, J. B. (2007). Errors in the estimation of hydration status from changes in body mass. *Journal of Sports Sciences, 25* (7), 797-804. https://doi.org/10.1080/02640410600875143

Maunder, E., Plews, D. J., Merien, F. & Kilding, A. E. (2020). Exercise intensity regulates the effect of heat stress on substrate oxidation rates during exercise. *European Journal of Sport Science, 20* (7), 935-943. https://doi.org/10.1080/17461391.2019.1674928

Maunder, E., Laursen, P. B. & Kilding, A. E. (2017). Effect of ad libitum ice-slurry and cold-fluid ingestion on cycling time-trial performance in the heat. *International Journal of Sports Physiology and Performance, 12* (1), 99-105. https://doi.org/10.1123/ijspp.2015-0764

McBride, J. M., Davis, J. A., Alley, J. R., Knorr, D. P., Goodman, C. L., Snyder, J. G. & Battista, R. A. (2015). Index of mechanical efficiency in competitive and recreational long distance runners. *Journal of Sports Sciences, 33* (13), 1388-1395. https://doi.org/10.1080/02640414.2014.990487

McCartney, D., Desbrow, B. & Irwin, C. (2017). The effect of fluid intake following dehydration on subsequent athletic and cognitive performance: A systematic review and meta-analysis. *Sports Medicine – Open, 3* (1), 13. https://doi.org/10.1186/s40798-017-0079-y

McCubbin, A. J., Allanson, B. A., Caldwell Odgers, J. N., Cort, M. M., Costa, R. J. S., Cox, G. R., Crawshay, S. T., Desbrow, B., Freney, E. G., Gaskell, S. K., Hughes, D., Irwin, C., Jay, O., Lalor, B. J., Ross, M. L. R., Shaw, G., Périard, J. D. & Burke, L. M. (2020). Sports dietitians Australia position statement: Nutrition for exercise in hot environments. *International Journal of Sport Nutrition and Exercise Metabolism*, 1-16. https://doi.org/10.1123/ijsnem.2019-0300

McCubbin, A. J., Cox, G. R. & Costa, R. J. S. (2019). Sodium intake beliefs, information sources, and intended practices of endurance athletes before and during exercise. *International Journal of Sport Nutrition and Exercise Metabolism, 29* (4), 371-381. https://doi.org/10.1123/ijsnem.2018-0270

McCubbin, A. J., Zhu, A., Gaskell, S. K. & Costa, R. J. S. (2019). Hydrogel carbohydrate-electrolyte beverage does not improve glucose availability, substrate oxidation, gastrointestinal symptoms or exercise performance, compared with a concentration and nutrient-matched placebo. *International Journal of Sport Nutrition and Exercise Metabolism*, 1-9. https://doi.org/10.1123/ijsnem.2019-0090

McNulty, K. L., Elliott-Sale, K. J., Dolan, E., Swinton, P. A., Ansdell, P., Goodall, S., Thomas, K. & Hicks, K. M. (2020). The effects of menstrual cycle phase on exercise performance in eumenorrheic women: A systematic review and meta-analysis. *Sports Medicine (Auckland, N.Z.), 50* (10), 1813-1827. https://doi.org/10.1007/s40279-020-01319-3

McWhorter, J., Wallmann, H., Landers, M., Altenburger, B., LaPorta-Krum, L. & Altenburger, P. (2003). The effects of walking, running, and shoe size on foot volumetrics. *Physical Therapy in Sport, 4* (2), 87-92. https://doi.org/10.1016/S1466-853X(03)00031-2

Mears, S. A., Boxer, B., Sheldon, D., Wardley, H., Tarnowski, C. A., James, L. J. & Hulston, C. J. (2020). Sports drink intake pattern affects exogenous carbohydrate oxidation during running. *Medicine and Science in Sports and Exercise, 52* (9), 1976-1982. https://doi.org/10.1249/mss.0000000000002334

Michaelson, J., Brilla, L., Suprak, D., Mclaughlin, W. & Dahlquist, D. (2019). Effects of two different recovery postures during high-intensity interval training, *Translational Journal of the ACSM, 4* (4), 23-27. https://doi.org/10.1249/TJX.0000000000000079

Migliorini, S. (Ed.). (2020). *Triathlon medicine*. Springer International Publishing. https://doi.org/10.1007/978-3-030-22357-1

Millet, G. P., Chollet, D., Chalies, S. & Chatard, J. C. (2002). Coordination in front crawl in elite triathletes and elite swimmers. *International Journal of Sports Medicine, 23* (2), 99-104. https://doi.org/10.1055/s-2002-20126

Millet, G. P., Millet, G. Y., Hofmann, M. D. & Candau, R. B. (2000). Alterations in running economy and mechanics after maximal cycling in triathletes: Influence of performance level. *International Journal of Sports Medicine, 21* (2), 127-132. https://doi.org/10.1055/s-2000-8866

Montain, S. J. & Coyle, E. F. (1992). Influence of graded dehydration on hyperthermia and cardiovascular drift during exercise. *Journal of Applied Physiology (Bethesda, Md.: 1985), 73* (4), 1340-1350. https://doi.org/10.1152/jappl.1992.73.4.1340

Moore, I. S., Ashford, K. J., Cross, C., Hope, J., Jones, H. S. R. & McCarthy-Ryan, M. (2019). Humans optimize ground contact time and leg stiffness to minimize the metabolic cost of running. *Frontiers in Sports and Active Living, 1*, 53. https://doi.org/10.3389/fspor.2019.00053

Mora-Rodriguez, R. & Hamouti, N. (2012). Salt and fluid loading: Effects on blood volume and exercise performance. *Medicine and Sport Science, 59*, 113-119. https://doi.org/10.1159/000341945

Morgan, P. T., Black, M. I., Bailey, S. J., Jones, A. M. & Vanhatalo, A. (2019). Road cycle TT performance: Relationship to the power-duration model and association with FTP. *Journal of Sports Sciences, 37* (8), 902-910. https://doi.org/10.1080/02640414.2018.1535772

Morris, N. B., Coombs, G. & Jay, O. (2016). Ice slurry ingestion leads to a lower net heat loss during exercise in the heat. *Medicine and Science in Sports and Exercise, 48* (1), 114-122. https://doi.org/10.1249/MSS.0000000000000746

Moscicki, B., Burrus, B., Matthews, T. & Paolone, V. (2016). Triathlon cycling with shorter crank lengths at same VO_2 leads to increased power output. *Medicine & Science in Sports & Exercise, 48*, 703. https://doi.org/10.1249/01.mss.0000487113.47010.33

Mujika, I., Sharma, A. P. & Stellingwerff, T. (2019). Contemporary periodization of altitude training for elite endurance athletes: A narrative review. *Sports Medicine (Auckland, N.Z.), 49* (11), 1651-1669. https://doi.org/10.1007/s40279-019-01165-y

Müller, B., Wolf, S. I., Brueggemann, G. P., Deng, Z., McIntosh, A., Miller, F. & Selbie, W. S. (Eds.). (2017). *Handbook of human motion.* Springer International Publishing. https://doi.org/10.1007/978-3-319-30808-1

Mündel, T. & Jones, D. A. (2010). The effects of swilling an L(-)-menthol solution during exercise in the heat. *European Journal of Applied Physiology, 109* (1), 59-65. https://doi.org/10.1007/s00421-009-1180-9

Mündel, T., King, J., Collacott, E. & Jones, D. A. (2006). Drink temperature influences fluid intake and endurance capacity in men during exercise in a hot, dry environment. *Experimental Physiology, 91* (5), 925-933. https://doi.org/10.1113/expphysiol.2006.034223

Murakami, I., Sakuragi, T., Uemura, H., Menda, H., Shindo, M. & Tanaka, H. (2012). Significant effect of a pre-exercise high-fat meal after a 3-day high-carbohydrate diet on endurance performance. *Nutrients, 4* (7), 625-637. https://doi.org/10.3390/nu4070625

Naito, T. & Ogaki, T. (2017). Comparison of the effects of cold water and ice ingestion on endurance cycling capacity in the heat. *Journal of Sport and Health Science, 6* (1), 111-117. https://doi.org/10.1016/j.jshs.2015.12.002

Nakamura, M., Yoda, T., Crawshaw, L. I., Yasuhara, S., Saito, Y., Kasuga, M., Nagashima, K. & Kanosue, K. (2008). Regional differences in temperature sensation and thermal comfort in humans. *Journal of Applied Physiology (Bethesda, Md.: 1985), 105* (6), 1897-1906. https://doi.org/10.1152/japplphysiol.90466.2008

Neufer, P. D., Young, A. J. & Sawka, M. N. (1989). Gastric emptying during exercise: Effects of heat stress and hypohydration. *European Journal of Applied Physiology and Occupational Physiology, 58* (4), 433-439. https://doi.org/10.1007/BF00643521

Nieman, D. C. & Wentz, L. M. (2019). The compelling link between physical activity and the body's defense system. *Journal of Sport and Health Science, 8* (3), 201-217. https://doi.org/10.1016/j.jshs.2018.09.009

Nordin, A. D. & Dufek, J. S. (2020). Footwear and footstrike change loading patterns in running. *Journal of Sports Sciences, 38* (16), 1869-1876. https://doi.org/10.1080/02640414.2020.1761767

Nugent, F., Comyns, T., Kearney, P. & Warrington, G. (2019). Ultra-short race-pace training (USRPT) in swimming: Current perspectives. *Open Access Journal of Sports Medicine, 10*, 133-144. https://doi.org/10.2147/OAJSM.S180598

Nummela, A. T., Paavolainen, L. M., Sharwood, K. A., Lambert, M. I. [Mike I.], Noakes, T. D. [Timothy D.] & Rusko, H. K. (2006). Neuromuscular factors determining 5 km running performance and running economy in well-trained athletes. *European Journal of Applied Physiology, 97* (1), 1-8. https://doi.org/10.1007/s00421-006-0147-3

Nybo, L., Rasmussen, P. & Sawka, M. N. (2014). Performance in the heat-physiological factors of importance for hyperthermia-induced fatigue. *Comprehensive Physiology, 4* (2), 657-689. https://doi.org/10.1002/cphy.c130012

Nyein, H. Y. Y., Bariya, M., Kivimäki, L., Uusitalo, S., Liaw, T. S., Jansson, E., Ahn, C. H., Hangasky, J. A., Zhao, J., Lin, Y., Happonen, T., Chao, M., Liedert, C., Zhao, Y., Tai, L. C., Hiltunen, J. & Javey, A. (2019). Regional and correlative sweat analysis using high-throughput microfluidic sensing patches toward decoding sweat. *Science Advances, 5* (8), eaaw9906. https://doi.org/10.1126/sciadv.aaw9906

Olbrecht, J. (2011). Triathlon: Swimming for winning. *Journal of Human Sport and Exercise, 6*, (2 (Suppl.)), 233-246. https://doi.org/10.4100/jhse.2011.62.04

Oliveira, E. P. de & Burini, R. C. (2011). Food-dependent, exercise-induced gastrointestinal distress. *Journal of the International Society of Sports Nutrition, 8*, 12. https://doi.org/10.1186/1550-2783-8-12

Pacheco, A. G., Leite, G. D. S., Lucas, R. D. de & Guglielmo, L. G. A. (2012). A influência da natação no desempenho do triathlon: implicações para o treinamento e competição. DOI: 10.5007/1980-0037.2012v14n2p232. *Revista Brasileira de Cineantropometria e Desempenho Humano, 14* (2). https://doi.org/10.5007/1980-0037.2012v14n2p232

Paton, C. D. & Jardine, T. (2012). The effects of cycling cleat position on subsequent running performance in a simulated duathlon. *Journal of Science and Cycling, 1* (1), 15-20. http://www.jsc-journal.com/ojs/index.php?journal=JSC&page=article&op=view&path%5B%5D=14

Payton, C. J. & Lauder, M. A. (1995). The influence of hand paddles on the kinematics of front crawl swimming [Der Einfluss von Handpaddeln auf die Kinematik des Kraulschwimmens]. *Journal of Human Movement Studies, 28* (4), 175-192.

Peake, J. M., Neubauer, O., Walsh, N. P. & Simpson, R. J. (2017). Recovery of the immune system after exercise. *Journal of Applied Physiology (Bethesda, Md.: 1985), 122* (5), 1077-1087. https://doi.org/10.1152/japplphysiol.00622.2016

Pérez, S., Fernández-Sáez, J. & Cejuela, R. (2019). Pyramidal training intensity distribution: Relationship with a half-ironman distance triathlon competition. *Journal of Sports Science & Medicine, 18*, 708-715.

Périard, J. D., Racinais, S. & Sawka, M. N . (2015). Adaptations and mechanisms of human heat acclimation: Applications for competitive athletes and sports. *Scandinavian Journal of Medicine & Science in Sports, 25, Suppl 1*, 20-38. https://doi.org/10.1111/sms.12408

Périard, J. D., Eijsvogels, T., Daanen, H. A. M. & Racinais, S. (2020). Hydration for the Tokyo Olympics: To thirst or not to thirst? *British Journal of Sports Medicine.* Vorab-Onlinepublikation. https://doi.org/10.1136/bjsports-2020-102803

Pfeiffer, B., Stellingwerff, T., Hodgson, A. B., Randell, R., Pöttgen, K., Res, P. & Jeukendrup, A. E. (2012). Nutritional intake and gastrointestinal problems during competitive endurance events. *Medicine and Science in Sports and Exercise, 44* (2), 344-351. https://doi.org/10.1249/MSS.0b013e31822dc809

Pfeiffer, B., Stellingwerff, T., Zaltas, E. & Jeukendrup, A. E. (2010). CHO oxidation from a CHO gel compared with a drink during exercise. *Medicine and Science in Sports and Exercise, 42* (11), 2038-2045. https://doi.org/10.1249/MSS.0b013e3181e0efe6

Pfeiffer, B., Stellingwerff, T., Zaltas, E. & Jeukendrup, A. E. (2010). Oxidation of solid versus liquid CHO sources during exercise. *Medicine and Science in Sports and Exercise, 42* (11), 2030-2037. https://doi.org/10.1249/MSS.0b013e3181e0efc9

Piacentini, M. F., Vleck, V. & Lepers, R. (2019). Effect of age on the sex difference in Ironman triathlon performance. *Movement & Sport Sciences – Science & Motricité (104)*, 21-27. https://doi.org/10.1051/sm/2019030

PoffÉ, C., Ramaekers, M., Bogaerts, S. & Hespel, P. (2021). Bicarbonate unlocks the ergogenic action of ketone monoester intake in endurance exercise. *Medicine and Science in Sports and Exercise, 53* (2), 431-441. https://doi.org/10.1249/MSS.0000000000002467

Poole, D. C., Burnley, M., Vanhatalo, A., Rossiter, H. B. & Jones, A. M. (2016). Critical power: An important fatigue threshold in exercise physiology. *Medicine and Science in Sports and Exercise, 48* (11), 2320-2334. https://doi.org/10.1249/MSS.0000000000000939.

Poole, D. C., Rossiter, H. B., Brooks, G. A. & Gladden, L. B. (2021). The anaerobic threshold: 50+ years of controversy. *The Journal of Physiology, 599* (3), 737-767. https://doi.org/10.1113/ jp279963

Potdevin, F., Bril, B., Sidney, M. & Pelayo, P. (2006). Stroke frequency and arm coordination in front crawl swimming. *International Journal of Sports Medicine, 27* (3), 193-198. https://doi. org/10.1055/s-2005-837545

Racinais, S. [Sebastien], Moussay, S., Nichols, D., Travers, G., Belfekih, T., Schumacher, Y. O. & Periard, J. D. (2019). Core temperature up to 41.5°C during the UCI Road Cycling World Championships in the heat. *British Journal of Sports Medicine, 53* (7), 426-429. https://doi. org/10.1136/ bjsports-2018-099881

Racinais, S., Alonso, J. M., Coutts, A. J., Flouris, A. D., Girard, O., González-Alonso, J., Hausswirth, C., Jay, O., Lee, J. K. W., Mitchell, N., Nassis, G. P., Nybo, L., Pluim, B. M., Roelands, B., Sawka, M. N., Wingo, J. & Périard, J. D. (2015). Consensus recommendations on training and competing in the heat. *Sports Medicine (Auckland, N.Z.), 45* (7), 925-938. https://doi.org/10.1007/ s40279-015-0343-6

Ramos-Álvarez, J. J., Lorenzo-Capellá, I. & Calderón-Montero, F. J. (2020). Disadvantages of automated respiratory gas exchange analyzers. *Frontiers in Physiology, 11*, 19. https://doi. org/10.3389/fphys.2020.00019

Rapoport, B. I. (2010). Metabolic factors limiting performance in marathon runners. *PLoS Computational Biology, 6* (10), e1000960. https://doi.org/10.1371/journal.pcbi.1000960

Reeve, T., Gordon, R., Laursen, P. B., Lee, J. K. W. & Tyler, C. J. (2019). Impairment of cycling capacity in the heat in well-trained endurance athletes after high-intensity short-term heat acclimation. *International Journal of Sports Physiology and Performance, 14* (8), 1058-1065. https://doi.org/10.1123/ijspp.2018-0537

Rehrer, N. J., Beckers, E. J., Brouns, F., Hoor, F. ten & Saris, W. H. (1990). Effects of dehydration on gastric emptying and gastrointestinal distress while running. *Medicine & Science in Sports & Exercise, 22* (6), 790-795. https://doi.org/10.1249/00005768-199012000-00010

Rehrer, N. J., Brouns, F., Beckers, E. J., Frey, W. O., Villiger, B., Riddoch, C. J., Menheere, P. P. & Saris, W. H. (1992). Physiological changes and gastro-intestinal symptoms as a result of ultra-endurance running. *European Journal of Applied Physiology and Occupational Physiology, 64* (1), 1-8. https://doi.org/10.1007/BF00376431

Rehrer, N. J., Janssen, G. M., Brouns, F. & Saris, W. H. (1989). Fluid intake and gastrointestinal problems in runners competing in a 25-km race and a marathon. *International Journal of Sports Medicine, 10, Suppl 1*, S22-5. https://doi.org/10.1055/s-2007-1024950

Rehrer, N. J., van Kemenade, M., Meester, W., Brouns, F. & Saris, W. H. (1992). Gastrointestinal complaints in relation to dietary intake in triathletes. *International Journal of Sport Nutrition, 2* (1), 48-59. https://doi.org/10.1123/ijsn.2.1.48

Reilly, T. (2009). How can travelling athletes deal with jet-lag? *Kinesiology (kinesiology.office@kif. hr), Vol. 41, No. 2, 41.*

Richards, C. E., Magin, P. J. & Callister, R. (2009). Is your prescription of distance running shoes evidence-based? *British Journal of Sports Medicine, 43* (3), 159-162. https://doi.org/10.1136/bjsm.2008.046680

Roach, G. D. & Sargent, C. (2019). Interventions to minimize jet lag after westward and eastward flight. *Frontiers in Physiology, 10*, 927. https://doi.org/10.3389/fphys.2019.00927

Robbins, S., Waked, E., Allard, P., McClaran, J. & Krouglicof, N. (1997). Foot position awareness in younger and older men: The influence of footwear sole properties. *Journal of the American Geriatrics Society, 45* (1), 61-66. https://doi.org/10.1111/j.1532-5415.1997.tb00979.x

Robbins, S., Waked, E. & McClaran, J. (1995). Proprioception and stability: Foot position awareness as a function of age and footwear. *Age and Ageing, 24* (1), 67-72. https://doi.org/10.1093/ageing/24.1.67

Robinson, M. E., Plasschaert, J. & Kisaalita, N. R. (2011). Effects of high intensity training by heart rate or power in recreational cyclists. *Journal of Sports Science & Medicine, 10* (3), 498-501.

Rodríguez-Marroyo, J. A., Villa, J. G., Pernía, R. & Foster, C. (2017). Decrement in professional cyclists' performance after a grand tour. *International Journal of Sports Physiology and Performance, 12* (10), 1348-1355. https://doi.org/10.1123/ijspp.2016-0294

Romanov, N. & Fletcher, G. (2007). Runners do not push off the ground but fall forwards via a gravitational torque. *Sports Biomechanics, 6* (3), 434-452. https://doi.org/10.1080/14763140701491625

Romanov, N. S. & Robson, J. (2014). *The pose method of triathlon techniques: A new paradigm in triathlon. Dr. Romanov's sport education series.* Pose Tech Press.

Roos, L., Taube, W., Beeler, N. & Wyss, T. (2017). Validity of sports watches when estimating energy expenditure during running. *BMC Sports Science, Medicine and Rehabilitation, 9.* https://doi.org/10.1186/s13102-017-0089-6

Rosen, P. von, Frohm, A., Kottorp, A., Fridén, C. & Heijne, A. (2017). Too little sleep and an unhealthy diet could increase the risk of sustaining a new injury in adolescent elite athletes. *Scandinavian Journal of Medicine & Science in Sports, 27* (11), 1364-1371. https://doi.org/10.1111/sms.12735

Rothschild, J. A., Kilding, A. E. & Plews, D. J. (2020). Prevalence and determinants of fasted training in endurance athletes: A survey analysis. *International Journal of Sport Nutrition and Exercise Metabolism*, 1-12. https://doi.org/10.1123/ijsnem.2020-0109

Rowlands, D. S. & Houltham, S. D. (2017). Multiple-transportable carbohydrate effect on long-distance triathlon performance. *Medicine and Science in Sports and Exercise, 49* (8), 1734-1744. https://doi.org/10.1249/MSS.0000000000001278

Ryan, A. J., Lambert, G. P., Shi, X., Chang, R. T., Summers, R. W. & Gisolfi, C. V. (1998). Effect of hypohydration on gastric emptying and intestinal absorption during exercise. *Journal of Applied Physiology (Bethesda, Md.: 1985), 84* (5), 1581-1588. https://doi.org/10.1152/jappl.1998.84.5.1581

Samson, M., Bernard, A., Monnet, T., Lacouture, P. & David, L. (2017). Unsteady computational fluid dynamics in front crawl swimming. *Computer Methods in Biomechanics and Biomedical Engineering, 20* (7), 783-793. https://doi.org/10.1080/10255842.2017.1302434.

Sanders, R. H., Andersen, J. T. & Takagi, H. (2017). The segmental movements in front crawl swimming. In B. Müller, S. I. Wolf, G.-P. Brueggemann, Z. Deng, A. McIntosh, F. Miller & W. S. Selbie (Eds.), *Handbook of human motion* (pp. 1-15). Springer International Publishing. https://doi.org/10.1007/978-3-319-30808-1_132-1

Sandig, D. (2014). Menstruation und Ausdauer: Zyklusgesteuertes Training als Leistungsreserve für Frauen. *trainingsworld.* https://www.trainingsworld.com/sportexperten/menstruationszy klusgesteuertes-ausdauertraining-eine-leistungsreserve-frauen-3364415

Saunders, A. G., Dugas, J. P., Tucker, R., Lambert, M. I. & Noakes, T. D. (2005). The effects of different air velocities on heat storage and body temperature in humans cycling in a hot, humid environment. *Acta Physiologica Scandinavica, 183* (3), 241-255. https://doi.org/10.1111/j.1365-201X.2004.01400.x

Saunders, P. U., Garvican-Lewis, L. A., Chapman, R. F. & Périard, J. D. (2019). Special environments: Altitude and heat. *International Journal of Sport Nutrition and Exercise Metabolism, 29* (2), 210-219. https://doi.org/10.1123/ijsnem.2018-0256

Saunders, P. U., Pyne, D. B., Telford, R. D. & Hawley, J. A. (2004). Factors affecting running economy in trained distance runners. *Sports Medicine (Auckland, N.Z.), 34* (7), 465-485. https://doi.org/10.2165/00007256-200434070-00005

Saw, A. E., Main, L. C. & Gastin, P. B. (2016). Monitoring the athlete training response: Subjective self-reported measures trump commonly used objective measures: a systematic review. *British Journal of Sports Medicine, 50* (5), 281-291. https://doi.org/10.1136/bjsports-2015-094758

Sawka, M. N. (1992). Physiological consequences of hypohydration: exercise performance and thermoregulation. *Medicine & Science in Sports & Exercise, 24* (6), 657-670.

Sawka, M. N. & Greenleaf, J. E. (1992). Current concepts concerning thirst, dehydration, and fluid replacement: Overview. *Medicine & Science in Sports & Exercise, 24* (6), 643-644.

Schofield, K. L., Thorpe, H. & Sims, S. T. (2020). Where are all the men? Low energy availability in male cyclists: A review. *European Journal of Sport Science,* 1-12. https://doi.org/10.1080/17461391.2020.1842510

Schubert, A. G., Kempf, J. & Heiderscheit, B. C. (2014). Influence of stride frequency and length on running mechanics: A systematic review. *Sports Health, 6* (3), 210-217. https://doi.org/10.1177/1941738113508544

Schwellnus, M., Soligard, T., Alonso, J. M., Bahr, R., Clarsen, B., Dijkstra, H. P., Gabbett, T. J., Gleeson, M., Hägglund, M., Hutchinson, M. R., van Janse Rensburg, C., Meeusen, R., Orchard, J. W., Pluim, B. M., Raftery, M., Budgett, R. & Engebretsen, L. (2016). How much is too much? (Part 2) International Olympic Committee consensus statement on load in sport and risk of illness. *British Journal of Sports Medicine, 50* (17), 1043-1052. https://doi.org/10.1136/bjsports-2016-096572

Seifert, L., Chollet, D. & Allard, P. (2005). Arm coordination symmetry and breathing effect in front crawl. *Human Movement Science, 24* (2), 234-256. https://doi.org/10.1016/j.humov.2005.05.003

Seiler, S. & Hetlelid, K. J. (2005). The impact of rest duration on work intensity and RPE during interval training. *Medicine & Science in Sports & Exercise, 37* (9), 1601-1607. https://doi.org/10.1249/01.mss.0000177560.18014.d8

Sharma, A. P. & Périard, J. D. (2020). Physiological requirements of the different distances of triathlon. In S. Migliorini (Ed.), *Triathlon medicine* (pp. 5-17). Springer International Publishing. https://doi.org/10.1007/978-3-030-22357-1_2

Sharma, A. P., Saunders, P. U., Garvican – Lewis, L. A., Périard, J. D., Clark, B., Gore, C. J., Raysmith, B. P., Stanley, J., Robertson, E. Y. & Thompson, K. G. (2018). Training quantification and periodization during live high train high at 2100 M in elite runners: An observational cohort case study. *Journal of Sports Science & Medicine, 17* (4), 607-616.

Shirreffs, S. M., Armstrong, L. E. & Cheuvront, S. N. (2004). Fluid and electrolyte needs for preparation and recovery from training and competition. *Journal of Sports Sciences, 22* (1), 57-63. https://doi.org/10.1080/0264041031000140572

Simpson, N. S., Gibbs, E. L. & Matheson, G. O. (2017). Optimizing sleep to maximize performance: Implications and recommendations for elite athletes. *Scandinavian Journal of Medicine & Science in Sports, 27* (3), 266-274. https://doi.org/10.1111/sms.12703

Sims, S. T., Rehrer, N. J., Bell, M. L. & Cotter, J. D. (2007). Preexercise sodium loading aids fluid balance and endurance for women exercising in the heat. *Journal of Applied Physiology (Bethesda, Md.: 1985), 103* (2), 534-541. https://doi.org/10.1152/japplphysiol.01203.2006

Sims, S. T., Rehrer, N. J., Bell, M. L. & Cotter, J. D. (2008). Endogenous and exogenous female sex hormones and renal electrolyte handling: Effects of an acute sodium load on plasma volume at rest. *Journal of Applied Physiology (Bethesda, Md.: 1985), 105* (1), 121-127. https://doi.org/10.1152/japplphysiol.01331.2007

Soligard, T., Schwellnus, M., Alonso, J. M., Bahr, R., Clarsen, B., Dijkstra, H. P., Gabbett, T., Gleeson, M., Hägglund, M., Hutchinson, M. R., van Janse Rensburg, C., Khan, K. M., Meeusen, R., Orchard, J. W., Pluim, B. M., Raftery, M., Budgett, R. & Engebretsen, L. (2016). How much is too much? (Part 1) International Olympic Committee consensus statement on load in sport and risk of injury. *British Journal of Sports Medicine, 50* (17), 1030-1041. https://doi.org/10.1136/bjsports-2016-096581

Souza, M. J. de, Williams, N. I., Nattiv, A., Joy, E., Misra, M., Loucks, A. B., Matheson, G., Olmsted, M. P., Barrack, M., Mallinson, R. J., Gibbs, J. C., Goolsby, M., Nichols, J. F., Drinkwater, B., Sanborn, C., Agostini, R., Otis, C. L., Johnson, M. D., Hoch, A. Z., . . . McComb, J. (2014). Misunderstanding the female athlete triad: Refuting the IOC consensus statement on relative energy deficiency in sport (RED-S). *British Journal of Sports Medicine, 48* (20), 1461-1465. https://doi.org/10.1136/bjsports-2014-093958

Speedy, D. B., Noakes, T. D., Rogers, I. R., Thompson, J. M., Campbell, R. G., Kuttner, J. A., Boswell, D. R., Wright, S. & Hamlin, M. (1999). Hyponatremia in ultradistance triathletes. *Medicine & Science in Sports & Exercise, 31* (6), 809-815. https://doi.org/10.1097/00005768-199906000-00008

Speedy, D. B., Rogers, I. R., Noakes, T. D., Thompson, J. M., Guirey, J., Safih, S. & Boswell, D. R. (2000). Diagnosis and prevention of hyponatremia at an ultradistance triathlon. *Clinical Journal of Sport Medicine: Official Journal of the Canadian Academy of Sport Medicine, 10* (1), 52-58. https://doi.org/10.1097/00042752-200001000-00010

Sperlich, B., Aminian, K., Düking, P. & Holmberg, H.C. (2019). Editorial: Wearable sensor technology for monitoring training load and health in the athletic population. *Frontiers in Physiology, 10,* 1520. https://doi.org/10.3389/fphys.2019.01520

Stanley, J., Halliday, A., D'Auria, S., Buchheit, M. & Leicht, A. S. (2015). Effect of sauna-based heat acclimation on plasma volume and heart rate variability. *European Journal of Applied Physiology, 115* (4), 785-794. https://doi.org/10.1007/s00421-014-3060-1

Steege, R. W. F. ter, Geelkerken, R. H., Huisman, A. B. & Kolkman, J. J. (2012). Abdominal symptoms during physical exercise and the role of gastrointestinal ischaemia: A study in 12 symptomatic athletes. *British Journal of Sports Medicine, 46* (13), 931-935. https://doi.org/10.1136/bjsports-2011-090277

Stellingwerff, T., Bovim, I. M. & Whitfield, J. (2019). Contemporary nutrition interventions to optimize performance in middle-distance runners. *International Journal of Sport Nutrition and Exercise Metabolism, 29* (2), 106-116. https://doi.org/10.1123/ijsnem.2018-0241

Stellingwerff, T., Morton, J. P. & Burke, L. M. (2019). A framework for periodized nutrition for athletics. *International Journal of Sport Nutrition and Exercise Metabolism, 29* (2), 141-151. https://doi.org/10.1123/ijsnem.2018-0305

Stellingwerff, T., Peeling, P., Garvican-Lewis, L. A., Hall, R., Koivisto, A. E., Heikura, I. A. & Burke, L. M. (2019). Nutrition and altitude: Strategies to enhance adaptation, improve performance and maintain health: A narrative review. *Sports Medicine (Auckland, N.Z.), 49, (Suppl 2),* 169-184. https://doi.org/10.1007/s40279-019-01159-w

Stellingwerff, T., Spriet, L. L., Watt, M. J., Kimber, N. E., Hargreaves, M., Hawley, J. A. & Burke, L. M. (2006). Decreased PDH activation and glycogenolysis during exercise following fat adaptation with carbohydrate restoration. *American Journal of Physiology, Endocrinology and Metabolism, 290* (2), E380-8. https://doi.org/10.1152/ajpendo.00268.2005

Stevens, C. J., Thoseby, B., Sculley, D. V., Callister, R., Taylor, L. & Dascombe, B. J. (2016). Running performance and thermal sensation in the heat are improved with menthol mouth rinse but not ice slurry ingestion. *Scandinavian Journal of Medicine & Science in Sports, 26* (10), 1209-1216. https://doi.org/10.1111/sms.12555

Stevens, C. J. & Best, R. (2017). Menthol: A fresh ergogenic aid for athletic performance. *Sports Medicine (Auckland, N.Z.), 47* (6), 1035-1042. https://doi.org/10.1007/s40279-016-0652-4

Stevens, C. J., Kittel, A., Sculley, D. V., Callister, R., Taylor, L. & Dascombe, B. J. (2017). Running performance in the heat is improved by similar magnitude with pre-exercise cold-water immersion and mid-exercise facial water spray. *Journal of Sports Sciences, 35* (8), 798-805. https://doi.org/10.1080/02640414.2016.1192294

Stevens, C. J., Dascombe, B., Boyko, A., Sculley, D. & Callister, R. (2013). Ice slurry ingestion during cycling improves Olympic distance triathlon performance in the heat. *Journal of Sports Sciences, 31* (12), 1271-1279. https://doi.org/10.1080/02640414.2013.779740

Stevens, C. J., Ross, M. L., Périard, J. D., Vallance, B. S. & Burke, L. M. (2020). Core temperature responses to elite racewalking competition. *International Journal of Sports Physiology andPperformance, 15* (6), 892-895. https://doi.org/10.1123/ijspp.2019-0397

Suito, H., Nunome, H. & Ikegami, Y. (2017). A quantitative evaluation of the high elbow technique in front crawl. *Journal of Sports Sciences, 35* (13), 1264-1269. https://doi.org/10.1080/026 40414.2016.1221517

Suriano, R. & Bishop, D. (2010). Combined cycle and run performance is maximised when the cycle is completed at the highest sustainable intensity. *European Journal of applied Physiology, 110* (4), 753-760. https://doi.org/10.1007/s00421-010-1547-y

Sutehall, S., Galloway, S. D. R., Bosch, A. & Pitsiladis, Y. (2020). Addition of an alginate hydrogel to a carbohydrate beverage enhances gastric emptying. *Medicine and Science in Sports and Exercise, 52* (8), 1785-1792. https://doi.org/10.1249/mss.0000000000002301

Sylta, O., Tønnessen, E. & Seiler, S. (2014). From heart-rate data to training quantification: A comparison of 3 methods of training-intensity analysis. *International Journal of Sports Physiology and Performance, 9* (1), 100-107. https://doi.org/10.1123/IJSPP.2013-0298

Tartaruga, M. P., Brisswalter, J., Peyré-Tartaruga, L. A., Avila, A. O. V., Alberton, C. L., Coertjens, M., Cadore, E. L., Tiggemann, C. L., Silva, E. M. & Kruel, L. F. M. (2012). The relationship between running economy and biomechanical variables in distance runners. *Research Quarterly for Exercise and Sport, 83* (3), 367-375. https://doi.org/10.1080/02701367.2012.10599870

Terrados, N., Melichna, J., Sylvén, C., Jansson, E. & Kaijser, L. (1988). Effects of training at simulated altitude on performance and muscle metabolic capacity in competitive road cyclists. *European Journal of Applied Physiology and Occupational Physiology, 57* (2), 203-209. https://doi.org/10.1007/BF00640664

Toussaint, H. M. & Beek, P. J. (1992). Biomechanics of competitive front crawl swimming. *Sports Medicine (Auckland, N.Z.)*, *13* (1), 8-24. https://doi.org/10.2165/00007256-199213010-00002

Tran Trong, T., Riera, F., Rinaldi, K., Briki, W. & Hue, O. (2015). Ingestion of a cold temperature/menthol beverage increases outdoor exercise performance in a hot, humid environment. *PloS One, 10* (4), e0123815. https://doi.org/10.1371/journal.pone.0123815

Tucker, R., Marle, T., Lambert, E. V. & Noakes, T. D. (2006). The rate of heat storage mediates an anticipatory reduction in exercise intensity during cycling at a fixed rating of perceived exertion. *The Journal of Physiology, 574* (Pt 3), 905-915. https://doi.org/10.1113/jphysiol.2005.101733

Tyler, C. J. & Sunderland, C. (2011). Cooling the neck region during exercise in the heat. *Journal of Athletic Training, 46* (1), 61-68. https://doi.org/10.4085/1062-6050-46.1.61

Tyler, C. J. & Sunderland, C. (2011). Neck cooling and running performance in the heat: Single versus repeated application. *Medicine and Science in Sports and Exercise, 43* (12), 2388-2395. https://doi.org/10.1249/MSS.0b013e318222ef72

Tyler, C. J., Wild, P. & Sunderland, C. (2010). Practical neck cooling and time-trial running performance in a hot environment. *European Journal of Applied Physiology, 110* (5), 1063-1074. https://doi.org/10.1007/s00421-010-1567-7

Ueberschär, O., Fleckenstein, D., Warschun, F., Walter, N., Wüstenfeld, J. C., Wolfarth, B. & Hoppe, M. W. (2019). Energy cost of running under hypogravity in well-trained runners and triathletes: A biomechanical perspective. *International Journal of Computer Science in Sport, 18* (2), 60-80. https://doi.org/10.2478/ijcss-2019-0014

Ueberschär, O., Fleckenstein, D., Wüstenfeld, J. C., Warschun, F., Falz, R. & Wolfarth, B. (2019). Running on the hypogravity treadmill AlterG® does not reduce the magnitude of peak tibial impact accelerations. *Sports Orthopaedics and Traumatology, 35* (4), 423-434. https://doi.org/10.1016/j.orthtr.2019.10.001

van Gent, R. N., Siem, D., van Middelkoop, M., van Os, A. G., Bierma-Zeinstra, S. M. A. & Koes, B. W. (2007). Incidence and determinants of lower extremity running injuries in long distance runners: A systematic review. *British Journal of Sports Medicine, 41* (8), 469-80; discussion 480. https://doi.org/10.1136/bjsm.2006.033548

van Hooren, B., Fuller, J. T., Buckley, J. D., Miller, J. R., Sewell, K., Rao, G., Barton, C., Bishop, C. & Willy, R. W. (2020). Is motorized treadmill running biomechanically comparable to overground running? A systematic review and meta-analysis of cross-over studies. *Sports Medicine (Auckland, N.Z.), 50* (4), 785-813. https://doi.org/10.1007/s40279-019-01237-z

van Hooren, B., Goudsmit, J., Restrepo, J. & Vos, S. (2020). Real-time feedback by wearables in running: Current approaches, challenges and suggestions for improvements. *Journal of Sports Sciences, 38* (2), 214-230. https://doi.org/10.1080/02640414.2019.1690960

van Janse Rensburg, D. C. C., Fowler, P. & Racinais, S. (2020). Practical tips to manage travel fatigue and jet lag in athletes. *British Journal of Sports Medicine.* Vorab-Onlinepublikation. https://doi.org/10.1136/bjsports-2020-103163

van Nieuwenhoven, M. A., Brouns, F. & Kovacs, E. M. R. (2005). The effect of two sports drinks and water on GI complaints and performance during an 18-km run. *International Journal of Sports Medicine, 26* (4), 281-285. https://doi.org/10.1055/s-2004-820931

van Nieuwenhoven, M. A., Brummer, R. M. & Brouns, F. (2000). Gastrointestinal function during exercise: Comparison of water, sports drink, and sports drink with caffeine. *Journal of Applied Physiology (Bethesda, Md.: 1985), 89* (3), 1079-1085. https://doi.org/10.1152/jappl.2000.89.3.1079

Vialleron, T., Delafontaine, A., Ditcharles, S., Fourcade, P. & Yiou, E. (2020). Effects of stretching exercises on human gait: A systematic review and meta-analysis. *F1000Research, 9*, 984. https://doi.org/10.12688/f1000research.25570.1

Viker, T. & Richardson, M. X. (2013). Shoe cleat position during cycling and its effect on subsequent running performance in triathletes. *Journal of Sports Sciences, 31* (9), 1007-1014. https://doi.org/10.1080/02640414.2012.760748.

Wallis, G. A., Dawson, R., Achten, J., Webber, J. & Jeukendrup, A. E. (2006). Metabolic response to carbohydrate ingestion during exercise in males and females. *American Journal of Physiology, Endocrinology and Metabolism, 290* (4), E708-15. https://doi.org/10.1152/ajpendo.00357.2005

Wallis, G. A., Yeo, S. E., Blannin, A. K. & Jeukendrup, A. E. (2007). Dose-response effects of ingested carbohydrate on exercise metabolism in women. *Medicine & Science in Sports & Exercise, 39* (1), 131-138. https://doi.org/10.1249/01.mss.0000241645.28467.d3

Walsh, N. P. (2018). Recommendations to maintain immune health in athletes. *European Journal of Sport Science, 18* (6), 820-831. https://doi.org/10.1080/17461391.2018.1449895

Wanner, S. P., Prímola-Gomes, T. N., Pires, W., Guimarães, J. B., Hudson, A. S. R., Kunstetter, A. C., Fonseca, C. G., Drummond, L. R., Damasceno, W. C. & Teixeira-Coelho, F. (2015). Thermoregulatory responses in exercising rats: Methodological aspects and relevance to human physiology. *Temperature (Austin, Tex.), 2* (4), 457-475. https://doi.org/10.1080/23328940.2015.1119615

Webster, C. C., Swart, J., Noakes, T. D. & Smith, J. A. (2018). A carbohydrate ingestion intervention in an elite athlete who follows a low-carbohydrate high-fat diet. *International Journal of Sports Physiology and Performance, 13* (7), 957-960. https://doi.org/10.1123/ijspp.2017-0392

Wei, C., Yu, L., Duncan, B. & Renfree, A. (2020). A plyometric warm-up protocol improves running economy in recreational endurance athletes. *Frontiers in Physiology, 11*, 197. https://doi.org/10.3389/fphys.2020.00197

Wickwire, P. J., Buresh, R. J., Tis, L. L., Collins, M. A., Jacobs, R. D. & Bell, M. M. (2012). Comparison of an in-helmet temperature monitor system to rectal temperature during exercise. *Journal of Strength and Conditioning Research, 26* (1), 1-8. https://doi.org/10.1519/JSC.0b013e31823b0a5a

Wu, S. S. X., Peiffer, J. J., Brisswalter, J., Nosaka, K., Lau, W. Y. & Abbiss, C. R. (2015). Pacing strategies during the swim, cycle and run disciplines of sprint, Olympic and half-Ironman triathlons. *European Journal of Applied Physiology, 115* (5), 1147-1154. https://doi.org/10.1007/s00421-014-3096-2

Yamanaka, Y. & Waterhouse, J. (2016). Phase-adjustment of human circadian rhythms by light and physical exercise. *The Journal of Physical Fitness and Sports Medicine, 5* (4), 287-299. https://doi.org/10.7600/jpfsm.5.287

Yang, H., Cao, B., Ju, Y. & Zhu, Y. (2019). The effects of local cooling at different torso parts in improving body thermal comfort in hot indoor environments. *Energy and Buildings, 198*, 528-541. https://doi.org/10.1016/j.enbuild.2019.06.004

Zurawlew, M. J., Walsh, N. P., Fortes, M. B. & Potter, C. (2016). Post-exercise hot water immersion induces heat acclimation and improves endurance exercise performance in the heat. *Scandinavian Journal of Medicine & Science in Sports, 26* (7), 745-754. https://doi.org/10.1111/sms.12638

3   About the author

Mario Schmidt-Wendling majored in sports studies and holds a coaching license from the German Triathlon Union. He has been a professional triathlon coach since 2004, and since then has coached almost 1,300 long-distance races and 15 overall victories on long course. He is also the founder of sisu-training.de, which is considered one of the world's most successful triathlon-coaching services, and has coached multiple world, European, and national champions. Before starting to compete in triathlons in the early 1990s, his athletic roots were in mid-distance running. He competed as a cyclist, including as a professional road cyclist from 1999–2005, before fully transitioning to his passion of coaching. He now competes in triathlons for work–life balance. He lives in Frankfurt am Main, Germany with his wife and four daughters.

Credits

Cover design:	Claudia Klasing Pandolfi, www.thelimedrop.com; Anja Elsen
Interior design:	Anja Elsen, Katerina Georgieva
Layout:	DiTech Publishing Services, www.ditechpubs.com
Cover image:	Courtesy of Willy Hirsch
Interior images:	Claudia Klasing Pandolfi
Managing editor:	Elizabeth Evans
Copy editor:	Anne Rumery
Translation:	AAA Translation, www.aaatranslation.com